Canine Behaviour in Mind

Canine Behaviour in Mind

Applying Behavioural Science to Our Lives with Dogs

Edited by Suzanne Rogers

 Books

First published 2022

Copyright © 5m Books Ltd 2022

Published by
5M Books Ltd,
Lings, Great Easton,
Essex CM6 2HH, UK,
Tel: +44 (0)330 1333 580
www.5mbooks.com

A Catalogue record for this book is available from the British Library

ISBN 9781789181371
eISBN 9781789182064
DOI 10.52517/9781789182064

Book layout by Cheshire Typesetting Ltd, Cuddington, Cheshire
Printed by Replika Press Pvt Ltd, India
Photos and illustrations by the authors unless otherwise indicated
Cover photos: front top small picture – photo of Pebbles © Suzanne Rogers; front bottom small pic – photo of Gru, Fish and Mouse © Nat Light; front main – Dylan © Lara Maskell – LM Photography; back Dylan © Angela Doyle

Contents

Meet the authors

Elizabeth Ayrton – advanced practitioner, companion animal behaviour

I am a veterinary surgeon with a master's degree in clinical animal behaviour, advanced practitioner status in clinical animal behaviour and I am also a certified clinical animal behaviourist (CCAB). I work in a referral practice helping owners and vets with complex behavioural cases in dogs, often with underlying medical problems that contribute to their behaviour. I worked for many years in general veterinary practice initially with many species and then increasingly concentrating on small animals before specialising in behaviour. Outside of work I am breed health co-ordinator for the bearded collie, which involves looking at the health of the breed by carrying out annual health surveys, identifying areas in which to fund research to aid the breed and advising owners and breeders. This work has to allow for the fact that the bearded collie has been on the vulnerable breeds list in recent years and therefore has a limited gene pool. Outside work I enjoy walking and photographing my own bearded collie in the stunning scenery of the Lake District.

Amber Batson – Understand Animals

I qualified from the Royal Veterinary College, London, in 1999. Almost immediately, I was fascinated by how many consultations involved discussions about behaviour, whether that was the reason the owner's had noticed a problem/ illness, perhaps because the behaviour had injured the dog (maybe an injury required exercise or physical restriction for a period) or perhaps because the dog was so fearful at the vets that examinations were far from ideal. I went on to undertake a number of qualifications in behaviour and welfare and began offering behaviour consultations a few years later. Today, I mostly work offering an education service for owners and dog professionals in which I aim to bridge the gap between scientific published studies and making that information understandable and practical for everyone to help dogs. I also work part time in clinical practice with dogs, cats and horses, as well as offering vet-based behaviour consultations and offering my services as an expert witness. I strongly believe we can improve the lives of dogs by using science-based knowledge in a practical way involving the whole team of people who participate in the care of each individual dog.

Rosie Bescoby – clinical animal behaviourist

I am an Animal Behaviour and Training Council registered clinical animal behaviourist and animal training instructor based in Bristol and North Somerset. My business, Pet Sense, provides behavioural advice to owners, professionals and the media. I am passionate about imparting appropriate and accurate information to benefit the welfare of pets and the human–animal bond. My primary focus is helping caregivers understand their pets to reduce the chance of undesirable behaviours materialising, teaching students including vets, vet nurses, rescue staff and dog trainers, providing CPD for co-professionals, training veterinary staff in low-stress handling techniques and running puppy clinics and 'parties', and pet industry consultancy. I have made guest appearances on various television and radio shows, been featured in national press, write articles and answer reader's questions for consumer magazines as well as for veterinary journals and have been published in peer-reviewed publications. I am currently Press and Media Officer for the Association of Pet Behaviour Counsellors (APBC).

Nina Bondarenko

I am the author and illustrator of *Hearts, Minds and Paws* – a book on working dogs with unusual roles and my training work was featured in the BBC documentary series 'Doghouse' in 2007 and 'Pedigree Chums' in 1994. Australian-born, I bred and trained working Rottweilers in Australia; I trained and trialled in Schutzhund, obedience, agility, IPO, search and rescue, stock work and for film, TV and theatre, and judged Rottweilers internationally. As Development and Training Director for Canine Partners UK, I developed the unique training approach, techniques and theory of assistance dog training and development, utilising my Puppy Education System of component behaviours and errorless learning principles. I use TAG teach and T Touch with a behaviour analytic approach in my animal behaviour and training consultancy. I am a Delta Pet Partners Evaluator, and as a member of the Assistance Dogs International (ADI) committees for trainers and training standards, I helped develop accreditation practices and procedures for assistance dog organisations throughout the world. I have presented at the IAADP and the ADI annual conferences on my training approach and developments as well as at international conferences – IAHAIO, ISAZ, SCAS, IWDBA, CSF, IDDC and more.

Tamsin Durston – accredited dog training instructor, clinical animal behaviourist and registered veterinary nurse

I have worked as an animal welfare professional for over 20 years, predominately within the charity sector. Very quickly into my nursing career I realised that approaching veterinary care with behavioural understanding could enhance patient experience and treatment outcomes. This lightbulb moment led me into lifelong study of companion animal behaviour and training, with a special emphasis on dogs (because even though we should not have favourites … dogs really are the best!).

Having gained degrees in both Companion Animal Behaviour and Canine Behaviour and Training, I have undertaken behavioural consultations and facilitate evidenced, reward-based training for pet dog owners and instructors alike, in a variety of activities including agility, life-skills and scent work. I believe in building an empathetic relationship as the foundation for enriched lives together – a gift for which I am indebted to my own beloved teachers, Scruff, Lelki and Coconut.

Steve Goward – Head of the Professional Development in Canine Behaviour Department, Dogs Trust

I started as a volunteer at Dogs Trust in 1999 while studying animal welfare at a local college. Fast forward 22 years and several different periods of study and job roles, you now find me managing teams that develop and deliver training on all things behaviour and welfare related across our organisation, a team that supports our staff with their most complex behaviour cases in our 22 rehoming centres and one that delivers staff training to shelters in the USA. I sit on the Dogs Trust Ethical Review Board and have been fortunate to have travelled extensively, working with dog welfare organisations around the world. I have spoken at various conferences in the UK and abroad and am passionate about sharing information and improving what we do to support the dogs we share our lives with. This passion has come from the dogs and people who I have gained so much knowledge, inspiration and experience from. There are too many to mention but I thank them all.

Kirsty Grant – The Dog Nose

I am an Animal Behaviour and Training Council (ABTC) Animal Training Instructor (ATI) and run The Dog Nose in Wiltshire. While working as kennel staff I completed a 5-week intensive grooming course and then accidentally became a groomer for the next 15 years. Running my own salon from home gave me the opportunity to move to a free-to-roam model and to prioritise cooperative care. This led me to complete courses with some of the people at the forefront of ethical dog care. In 2018, I closed my grooming salon to concentrate full time on The Dog Nose and feel that getting to watch dogs being dogs is the best job in the world.

Sarah Heath – European veterinary specialist in behavioural medicine

I qualified as a veterinary surgeon from Bristol University in 1988 and set up Behavioural Referrals Veterinary Practice in 1992. I see clinical cases across north-west England and wider afield through video platform consultations and have a special interest in the interplay between emotional and physical illness in dogs and cats. In 2018, I was made a Fellow of the Royal College of Veterinary Surgeons (FRCVS) for meritorious contributions to the profession in recognition of my work in establishing behavioural medicine as a veterinary discipline. I am a Royal College of Veterinary Surgeons (RCVS) and EBVS® European veterinary specialist in behavioural medicine and an external lecturer in small animal behavioural medicine on the veterinary undergraduate course at Liverpool University. In 2019, I gained my Postgraduate Certificate in Veterinary Education.

Natalie Light – certificated clinical animal behaviourist

I am an Association for the Study of Animal Behaviour (ASAB) accredited certificated clinical animal behaviourist, an Animal Behaviour and Training Council (ABTC) registered clinical animal behaviourist and animal training instructor, a full member of the Association of Pet Behaviour Counsellors (APBC), and a member of the Fellowship of Animal Behaviour Clinicians (FABC). I am also Head of Behaviour at PACT, the Professional Association of Canine Trainers. I have been working professionally in the companion animal sector since 2006 having been awarded a Zoology BSc by the University of Southampton and an Applied Animal Behaviour and Welfare PGDip by Newcastle University. I am currently seeing private clients, writing my PhD and lecturing on the Animal Welfare & Society BA Hons course at the University of Winchester. My aim as a behaviourist and trainer is to help people understand their dogs by teaching them the subtle signals dogs use to communicate how they are feeling. I empower my clients with the understanding, knowledge and practical skills that allow them to provide for their dogs' needs. I believe that by focusing on the relationship that dogs and their humans have, and encouraging effective communication, we can live much happier and more successful lives together. I live in Hampshire with my lovely husband Jason and our menagerie of rescued non-human animals; five wonderful dogs: Jack, Gru, Mouse, Fish and Drax; seven adorable ducks known as 'the girlies' and Sir David Attenborough the tortoise.

Laura McAuliffe – clinical animal behaviourist

I am a clinical animal behaviourist living in Surrey, UK, where I run Dog Communication and specialise in helping dogs with anxiety and reactivity issues. I worked with Penel Malby for 15 years until her recent move away and we set up Doggoland at our venue at Dog Communication, a unique outdoor enrichment course designed to help anxious dogs. My real love in life is working with owners of reactive dogs, reducing stress in all their lives (human and canine), helping them to find joy in the new normal of life with a reactive dog and helping them overcome their anxiety issues. I have lived with, and loved, three reactive dogs over the past 20 years. I currently have an eclectic mix of dogs and have a Northern Inuit, a Dalmatian and a Yorkshire terrier puppy and I also foster puppies for rescue. I am a full member of the Association of Pet Behaviour Counsellors (APBC) and have a degree in behaviour, a PhD in something much less interesting and recently updated my ethology knowledge with a postgraduate course at Newcastle University.

Suzanne Rogers – Human Behaviour Change for Animals (HBCA)

 I am an animal welfare consultant, Co-Director of Human Behaviour Change for Animals CIC, and an IAABC (International Association of Animal Behaviour Consultants) certified horse behaviour consultant registered with the ABTC (Animal Behaviour & Training Council). After a ten-year career in scientific publishing, I re-qualified in animal behaviour and welfare, gained extensive practical experience with several animal welfare organisations, and founded Learning About Animals, running educational events with a focus on pet behaviour. In 2007, I became a Programmes Manager at WSPA (now World Animal Protection) first managing international dog population management and working equine programmes and later as the Technical Advisor for Human Behaviour Change Programmes across species and issues. Since 2011, I have worked as an animal welfare consultant, alongside my work as an equine behaviour consultant. I am also on the board of trustees for the World Cetacean Alliance (WCA). In 2016, I co-founded Human Behaviour Change for Animals CIC (HBCA) with Jo White. We recognize that insight into how and why people behave the way they do can provide solutions to challenging issues that affect animals. Dogs have a special place in my heart, especially Pebbles – a saluki x greyhound who features in some of the photographs in this book.

Caroline Warnes

 I qualified as a veterinary surgeon from the University of Bristol in 1985 and worked for 10 years in general veterinary practice, during which time I developed a special interest in companion animal behaviour. I gained an MSc in Companion Animal Behaviour Counselling from the University of Southampton and went on to become an ASAB accredited Certificated Clinical Animal Behaviourist and a Royal College of Veterinary Surgeons (RCVS) advanced practitioner in companion animal behaviour. I then ran a companion animal behaviour referral practice based near Swindon in Wiltshire for over 20 years, alongside various other activities including running a veterinary practice. I also enjoy teaching and have been very fortunate to have been invited to participate in several different speaking and teaching engagements over the years. I retired from my behaviour referral practice at the end of 2020, and am now enjoying exploring the coast of North Devon and Cornwall with my family and Jimmy the Border Terrier.

Jo White – Human Behaviour Change for Animals (HBCA)

 Throughout my career and personal life, the well-being of animals has been central. Fascinated by the behaviour of animals, canine, human or others since childhood, I have committed myself to a lifelong journey of development and learning in this area. My experience and knowledge have developed through practical work with animals but also through leading educational, advocacy and campaigning projects to improve the lives of animals in varying parts of

the world. In 2016, I became Co-Director of Human Behaviour Change for Animals, supporting organisations to apply human behavioural science to their work. I have an MSc in Behaviour Change, a degree in Equine Studies, among other equine qualifications, and a Certificate in Campaigning. My current area of study involves harnessing human habits to improve animal welfare, including the human animal's welfare. Over the years my love of dogs has seen me share my life with four rescue dogs, spending time re-building their confidence and supporting them to be the happy big personalities they should be.

Introduction

Why another book about dog behaviour?

Dog training and advice about how to care for pet dogs is changing; it has probably always been changing, and now more than ever before with such a vast range of 'methods' being promoted it can be difficult for dog owners (and anyone involved with dogs professionally or otherwise), to identify approaches that work and that have compassion at their heart. There are many fantastic resources already available about canine behaviour. However, there are also many resources that go against the modern understanding of behaviour and promote methods that are potentially harmful to dogs. Therefore, another book on canine behaviour will add to the number of available 'kind' resources. Also, sometimes it can be difficult to make the connection between the theory and practice and to apply what you have learned when you are standing next to your expectant dog, so the more resources to help, the merrier.

A few years ago, I edited (and wrote some of the chapters for) *Equine Behaviour in Mind*[1] and ever since I have been keen to publish a dog version. Although I have more experience professionally with horses, I have a deep love for dogs and my saluki cross greyhound Pebbles has been on the sofa next to me through every stage of putting this book together. If you have already read the horse version, then you will recognise some of the text in the introductions in both books and

in the human behaviour change chapter as so much is relevant across species.

Many books about dog behaviour approach the subject from a theoretical angle and then include practical examples. This book has a different approach – we investigate different elements of dog ownership. Through case studies that bring to life the ways different people have worked to meet their dog's needs, you will achieve a better understanding of what we can do to make a difference to the lives of dogs.

The field of dog training has become fragmented, with owners choosing between training methods and teachers, each of whom often has a particular 'brand' and training systems that they sell and promote. This division of the market has meant that books focused on training have an ever-decreasing audience as owners turn to one big name or system. By steering clear of promoting any single trainer and covering all aspects of living with dogs, not just training, this book hopes to be of interest to owners across chosen training approaches.

The authors of this book approach training and behaviour modification with methods confidently supported by robust science as changing behaviour and teaching in ethical ways which dogs and owners alike will find enjoyable and engaging, and which therefore enhance the owner–dog bond. Techniques that use force, fear or intimidation can be incredibly damaging for the dog–owner relationship, and might result in dogs who are frightened or worried about what might happen to them in response to their behaviour. The authors of this book only promote evidence-based methods which enrich the lives of all involved, and help dogs to thrive, living their best lives, as happily and healthily as possible.

The purpose of the book is to encourage you to consider how the way we care for dogs, train them, and the activities we do with them affect our canine companions, and how, if we understand canine behaviour, we can make changes that improve the lives of the animals we love. Where suggestions for alternative methods or changes are made, the aim is to motivate the reader to make positive changes for their dog or dogs they work with. Care has been taken to avoid the book seeming judgemental and overly critical – however, it is likely that the content will highlight for some readers that the way dogs are trained and cared for often impacts their behaviour and well-being in a negative way.

Focusing on the good

Throughout the book the content is illustrated by case studies, providing real-life examples and inspiration from professionals. We unashamedly do not support many of the things humans expect of dogs or the way they are treated as objects rather than as sentient individuals. However, we are all also strongly motivated to do what we can to promote change and to address issues so entrenched in human society that poor animal welfare is considered normal. We believe that change requires an approach that embraces good things, however small, and celebrates small changes.

The stories and case studies that we have chosen are not an indication that everything about the people featured and the way they manage and work their dogs is exemplary, we are merely including an example of one element of a person's relationship with their dog that we think shows a behaviourally minded approach. Some would say these should not be included for fear of promoting practices that compromise welfare by association but if we only included examples of where everything is perfect it would be a very short book.

Furthermore, when helping owners to support their dogs in solving 'behavioural problems', we take small steps towards the change. Highlighting and building on the good things we come across is very powerful in driving further change. Often the response to suggesting changes is that resources and time are too limited ('I can't afford to do that for my dog') but not all changes require resources or time, rather creative thinking. There is a case study in the human development world that illustrates this nicely.[3] In a low-income region of Vietnam many aid agencies had tried to address childhood malnutrition to no avail. All the typical actions were suggested with no resulting change. One person, however, noted that even though all the families had access to very similar restricted resources some children were healthier than others. Upon investigation it transpired that the mothers of the healthier children were managing their resources in a way that prevented the nutritional problems the others faced – even though they had access to the same resources as the other mothers, they were producing more balanced meals. The 'successful' mothers showed the other mothers how to manage their resources in this way and mentored them to ensure the new way of thinking was taken up. This was successful and finally malnutrition rates decreased. This is a great example of managing, rather than increasing, resources and there are parallels throughout the dog world whether the resource is financial, material or even compassion!

A note on terminology

Throughout this book we have been careful to not use 'it' when talking about dogs – we use 'he, she, they, their, the dog' and so on. Dogs are sentient individuals, and the use of language matters. As we move away from thinking about animals as commodities, objects and 'things', then as a society we might be more likely to treat them accordingly. We have also considered how to refer to the human–dog relationship and although we think of dogs as much *much* more than possessions, we have largely retained the term 'dog owner' and sometimes used the terms guardian or caregiver.

What do dogs need?

I have asked the question 'What do dogs need?' many times in many different situations in many different countries. The answers are never the same and always provide new insights into the complicated nature of the relationship between dogs and humans. At first, people answer with the obvious response – food and water – but further probing prompts discussions about training, grooming, veterinary care and much more. I often run this exercise as a framework for an introduction to welfare, so next, I ask the group to explore the criteria that should be met to fully meet that need. For example, under the need for 'food', criteria might be that food is nutritionally appropriate for the individual dog, provided in a clean bowl (or a portion scattered where possible), that food is good quality, perhaps a specific supplement is offered once a week and so on. The group themselves come up with the needs, the facilitator just uses the questions as a framework for discussion; without having a strict idea of what the answers should be, the result is very much owned by the group.

As each need is identified, the group creates and places drawings depicting each one on small pieces of paper arranged in a large circle. Next, for each need, the group places a mark between the middle and the edge of the circle to represent a score for how well each need is met for the average dog in that community (a community could be a geographical area, or a 'functional' community such as members of a dog training club, dogs in a rescue centre or dogs owned by families who all attend the same school). Alternatively, it could be done individually by participants in relation to their own dog(s). If the mark is placed close to the centre of the circle, the need is not met at all and if it is placed at the edge of the circle, it is well met. Once placed, the marks are connected forming one 'round' of a spider's web and hence this exercise is called a Cobweb analysis (Figure I.1). The resulting chart for a community where the dogs enjoy a good quality of life, therefore, would have all the marks very near the edge of the circle whereas a community where the dogs' needs are not met would have a round of the spider web very near the centre. Of course, usually the result is an irregular shape as some needs are met to a greater extent than others. The scores can be allocated considering the typical dog in a community or could be done for a specific individual dog.

The exercise is interesting for two reasons. First, it shows that people have very varied ideas about what a dog needs. If we consider the animal irrespective of where they live, what activities they might be involved with and what culture their owners are from, what do they really need? How much of what we think dogs need reflects the culture in which we have grown up? Second, the resulting diagram from the exercise described above, shows the whole life of a dog in a way that is easy to understand. By looking at where the scores lie we can, together with the criteria

Figure I.1: Cobweb of needs. Photo: © Suzanne Rogers.

given for each need, be gently guided towards how improvements can be made little by little. It is this big picture I am interested in and will keep coming back to. Many of the suggestions and ideas in this book will seem tiny and almost insignificant to you but when we consider the context, and imagine each improvement as chipping away to move those scores a little nearer to the ideal, we are reminded that everything is worthwhile when considering improvements to the quality of life of an animal in our care. Please do the exercise right now for your own dog, you can add needs, criteria and assessments as you read the book and by the end you will at least have a pretty picture if not an epiphany.

The chapters explore how we can have 'behaviour in mind' in the daily care of our dogs, in how we breed and train them, in the activities we choose to do with them, and in caring for them as they get older. The sections on

teaching, rehabilitation and rescue, and vets provide a framework to discuss other ways behaviour can be considered in our dogs' lives.

A few words about welfare

Perhaps far into the future humans will have come to the understanding that even though animals might not think and feel in exactly the same way as we do, their lives are valuable, they are capable of suffering mentally and physically and we should do everything we can to avoid this. We are not there yet. Although the term 'animal welfare' is used extensively in many countries and is included in policies and legislation, it is sometimes misunderstood and misapplied. For example, consider the phrase 'behaviour and welfare' – this is widespread and even used as the title of some qualifications. However, welfare includes behaviour,

Figure I.2: The 'alien' exercise. Photo: © Suzanne Rogers.

so the phrase 'behaviour and welfare' clearly shows that behaviour is still not seen as being an intrinsic part of welfare.

Let us take a moment to explore what welfare really means. Imagine that you run a rescue centre and one day, you found a little alien-like creature in a box that had been dumped by your gates (Figure I.2). There is a note that says, 'We can no longer care for this creature, there is only one person in the world who can tell you how to look after him/her but he only responds to direct questions, you can contact him at ...'. So, you phone the number provided and ask questions – what would you ask? Here are some examples:

- What does he/she eat? How much? How often? In a bowl? From the ground?

- What is the normal length of time he/she should sleep for?
- What does he/she like to do? Climb? Burrow? Dig? Jump? Hide?
- How can I tell if he/she is healthy?
- What does he/she do when she is frightened? Happy? Sad?
- Does he/she like to live in groups or alone?
- How far would he/she naturally roam in a day?

All these questions could be clustered into the Five Freedoms, a framework for considering welfare:[4]

1. freedom from hunger and thirst
2. freedom from discomfort

3. freedom from pain, injury and disease
4. freedom to express natural behaviours
5. freedom from fear and distress.

These freedoms are not hierarchical; they are all equally important for 'good' welfare. The freedoms from fear or to act out normal behaviour, are not added on luxuries but an intrinsic part of good welfare. Armed with the answers to our questions we would have a much better idea of how to look after the little creature than we did before – meeting his/her physical and mental needs. It is easy to think about the things the alien might need, and usually when I do this exercise in training situations, people come up with a huge range of questions we would need to ask to be sure we could take care of the little creature well. What if, instead of the alien, we consider the domestic dog? Are we so quick to consider all the things they need? I have found that owners often consider canine welfare as mostly about health – but welfare is more than just a shiny coat. Welfare is the mental, as well as the physical well-being of an animal, and it is the mental and behaviour elements that many owners do not consider as fully as we should. Although it is easy to get carried away looking at things you can buy for your dog online or in a shop, if a dog could choose what you were to buy them the items would probably be different from what we would choose. Rather than a lovely new food bowl, they might prefer to have some of their food scattered in your garden, for example or have a raised comfy place to sleep.

The Five Freedoms have been superseded by the Five Needs to frame welfare as elements animals need, rather than what they need to avoid. More recently, welfare science has moved to consider quality of life: what makes a life worth living? This more modern framework, the Five Domains, places more emphasis on the mental state of the animal and

can be used as a welfare assessment tool.[5] This model sets out four predominantly physical/functional domains: nutrition, environment, health and behaviour; and a fifth 'mental' domain, including positive and negative emotions. A balance of outcomes across the Five Domains expresses the dog's overall 'bank account balance' in terms of their physical, mental and emotional states. To enable our animals to thrive, not just survive, we must minimise negative experiences and maximise positive experiences. The challenge is that the ability to recognise the mental states of dogs is not widespread, behaviour is often misinterpreted, and some behaviours are often anthropomorphically labelled as positive when they are in fact negative (for example, some obsessive compulsive behaviours). However, there is an increasing body of work addressing these gaps and the mental suffering of dogs is increasingly difficult to ignore.

A behaviourally minded future

My vision for the future, is that the sometimes empty words about welfare translate into actual welfare improvements, that rules and regulations in existence to protect welfare are enforced and that 'welfare' is not a buzzword that needs to be included to meet requirements but is valued in its own right. We will get there by building on glimpses of good practice, actions that show consideration for the animals' needs, and by promoting them so that those glimpses become less transient and increasingly part of culture. Never before has the world had the infrastructure to disseminate ideas as we have now in the age of social media and web-based communication. In writing this book, the authors have searched for and found glimpses of behaviourally minded aspects of dog ownership and by putting them all together in the same place we hope that the reader will find changes they want to introduce to their lives with dogs and find their place in promoting the positive changes they do and see.

We will receive criticism from promoting good things that many believe do not go far enough in changing the lives of dogs but all-or-nothing arguments are not helpful for driving mainstream change. The ideas in this book will not give dogs a perfect life, not even close, but if ideas are acted on, seen and spread, then we are edging towards real change, making positive changes in the lives of individual animals along the way.

References

1. Rogers, S. (ed.) (2018) *Equine Behaviour in Mind: Applying Behavioural Science to the Way We Keep, Work and Care for Horses.* Sheffield: 5m Publishing.
2. Lindsay, S. (2001) *Handbook of Applied Dog Behavior and Training.* Vol. 3. Wiley, Hoboken, NJ.
3. Tuhus-Dubrow, R. (2009) The power of positive deviants: a promising new tactic for changing communities from the inside. *Boston Globe*, 29 November 2009.
4. Brambell, R. (1965) Report of the technical committee to enquire into the welfare of animals kept under intensive livestock husbandry systems. Brambell Report, December. London: HMSO London.
5. Mellor, D.J. and Beausoleil, N. (2015) Extending the 'five domains' model for animal welfare assessment to incorporate positive welfare states. *Animal Welfare* 24, 241–253.

Chapter 1

Daily care

Natalie Light

This chapter sets the scene for what our dogs need from their daily routine and how we can adjust our lifestyle to ensure they have the opportunity to feel safe, get enough sleep, and have enjoyable interactions with people, animals and the wider environment.

The canine ethogram

In order to cater for our dog's natural, biological and social needs, we need to first understand what those needs are. The canine ethogram can help us to do this as an ethogram is simply a catalogue of 'normal' behavioural repertoires for a particular species – the word ethology is the study of natural behaviour.

Dogs are considered to be one of the oldest domesticated species, that have a decorated history of fulfilling significant roles within human society relating to companionship, pest control, farming and hunting. The earliest fossils of domesticated dogs have been dated at originating between 13,000 and 45,000 years ago and while the origin of the domestic dog is a complex story, it is generally agreed that dogs as we know them now have evolved from a common ancestor – the grey wolf. The field and study of animal cognition has increased hugely in the past 100 years or so and although there are still some disagreements among scientists as to how our dogs may perceive us and the world around them, Coren[1] neatly summarises the key elements that are generally accepted as scientific fact.

- Dogs sense the world and take in information from it.
- Dogs learn and modify their behaviour to fit circumstances.
- Dogs have memories and can solve certain problems.
- Early experiences as a puppy can shape the behaviours of the adult.
- Dogs have emotions.
- Individual dogs seem to have distinct personalities and different breeds seem to have different temperaments.
- Social interactions, including play, are very important to dogs.
- Dogs communicate with each other and with humans.

What do dogs need?

Canine behavioural needs are essential elements of natural behaviour that all dogs should be given the opportunity to engage in on a daily basis. Table 1.1 summarises the core elements of natural canine behaviour and needs, along with depicting the related hierarchical importance of each of the needs. This concept

Table 1.1 The behavioural needs of dogs.

Need	Description	Actions
Eating and drinking	Canine obesity is a growing concern among veterinary professionals so consider weighing your dog's meals and learn how to adequately assess your dog's body condition to establish if they need to lose or put on weight. Chewing is a natural behaviour for dogs that they would normally engage in for long periods of the day. The volume dogs drink varies widely depending on many factors including diet, activity levels, temperature and exercise.	• Unlimited access to water. Do not withhold water overnight during toilet training your puppy or if your older dog sleeps in a crate. • Consider how food and water is provided (multiple bowls on non-slip surfaces) and the bowl material (metal bowls can create noise and glare).
Housing	Most of our companion dogs sleep in our houses so are afforded the warm shelter that they require. As a social species, dogs need regular company and their home environment should provide that.	• Provide clean, warm, comfortable and ample sleeping areas in a quiet place. • Ensure your dog has their own space and adequate resources – food, water, toys. • Teach your dog to cope being home alone to avoid future separation-related behaviour issues later in life. Use family members or dog sitters to provide company if your dog is worried about your absence.
Safety	Dogs need to feel safe in the confines of their home and in the wider environment. Failure to feel safe can result in behavioural problems based on fear or frustration and may lead to aggressive responses. All owners are required to keep members of the public and visitors to their home safe under the Dangerous Dogs Act 1991. All dogs are now required to be microchipped by law and must wear a collar and ID tag in public.	• Secure gardens and use adequate and appropriate measures to ensure your dog cannot stray or get injured in nearby traffic. • When in public, use appropriate lead/collar/harness equipment to restrain your dog without causing pain or discomfort. • Use a muzzle if your dog is worried by people or dogs and do not expose your dog to triggers they find fear-eliciting. Walk in quieter areas, shut them away in a safe place in the house when you have visitors or consider hiring a private, secure field to exercise them safely in. • Make sure your details are kept up to date on your dog's microchip.

Table 1.1 (continued)

Need	Description	Actions
Rest & sleep	Dogs are crepuscular (most active at dawn and dusk) with polyphasic sleep patterns (sleeping, idling, dozing or resting for short periods of time throughout a 24-hour period). Sleep can be disrupted by social isolation, busy households, lack of appropriate and comfortable resting places, inconsiderate training or exercise routines, medical conditions and numerous other environmental factors.	• Adequate space and comfort to facilitate preferred sleeping position. • Safe space to rest and relax away from or close to companions. • Management and training to support appropriate sleeping habits and ability to relax and rest despite potentially disruptive environments.
Body care and health	Dogs require regular grooming, nail and teeth care and weight management to prevent health issues. Appropriate parasite control should also be used along with annual vet checks and vaccinations. Dogs will need a separate latrine area from where they sleep and rest. If dogs are confined in a crate or pen, they should have adequate space to stretch out and lie flat.	• Introduce grooming equipment from an early age. Keep grooming sessions short and use food to create positive associations. • Maintain a good routine of preventative healthcare including flea, tick and worming treatments. • Regular health checks and body condition monitoring will help to prevent development of illness or obesity. • Provide enough space to stretch out. • Provide an appropriate toilet area or access to the outdoors regularly if you don't have a garden.
Physical exercise and freedom of movement	Dogs should have sufficient space to choose to perform essential movement behaviours that keep them fit and healthy, including walking, running and playing with people or other animals.	• Provide regular, daily opportunities for safe, off-lead exercise in the outdoors.
Consistency and emotional support	For optimum emotional development, dogs need a wealth of experiences in their vital socialisation period (between 3 and 14 weeks). Continuation of experiences with positive associations should occur throughout puppyhood, adolescence and adulthood.	• Choose a responsible breeder that provides appropriate socialisation during the puppy's sensitive periods. • Use food and toys to create positive associations with people. • Provide a regular routine and consistency. • Avoiding training methods that cause fear or pain.

Play	Dogs should have space and opportunity through movement and object play to explore different environments. Species-specific games and activities should be encouraged to allow sniffing, chasing and biting.	• Provide appropriate toys and activities for your dog to engage with/in. • Enable opportunities to play with other dogs that are well matched to the personality and preferences of your dog.
Relationships	Dogs have a basic need to form bonds with people and other dogs. In order for these relationships and social experiences to be pleasurable, dogs will need to feel sufficiently safe to interact.	• Allow the opportunity to interact with or avoid people and other animals. • Provide companionship and relationships that are tailored to suit the individual preferences of your dog.
Choice, novelty & problem solving	Freedom to approach and avoid as they investigate new environments, people, animals or objects will build trust and confidence. Appropriate toys or puzzle feeders should be provided to encourage problem solving without creating frustration.	• Provide the opportunity for investigation and exploration. • Allow choice and freedom of movement in social situations or when your dog is exploring a new environment. • Provide age and skill appropriate challenges in the form of activities and puzzles.

of a hierarchy of needs has been popular and well-respected in human psychology since it was published in 1943 by Maslow[2] and canine behaviour experts have adapted and modified this model to create the 'hierarchy of dog needs'[3] (Figure 1.1). The pyramid structure neatly illustrates the importance for physiological health and safety, with the ability to achieve the needs higher up the pyramid being distinctly unlikely if the simple foundations are not met. The behaviour modification and management work undertaken by clinical animal behaviour professionals often uses this hierarchy to assess and address any welfare concerns where meeting particular needs may be lacking. Most behavioural concerns arise from the absence of feeling safe or secure and so this must be addressed and alleviated before any more proactive training

such as recall or walking nicely on a lead can be tackled. Without considering the lower-level needs, training and behaviour modification can be almost impossible. The apparent 'failure' or lack of progress in a training programme can often be attributed to the dog feeling unwell or unsafe.

Striving for optimum canine welfare

To be an ethical dog owner involves having an understanding of your responsibilities from both a legal and welfare point of view. The Animal Welfare Act 2006 sets out the requirements that all animals must be provided with in a list commonly referred to as the Five Freedoms:

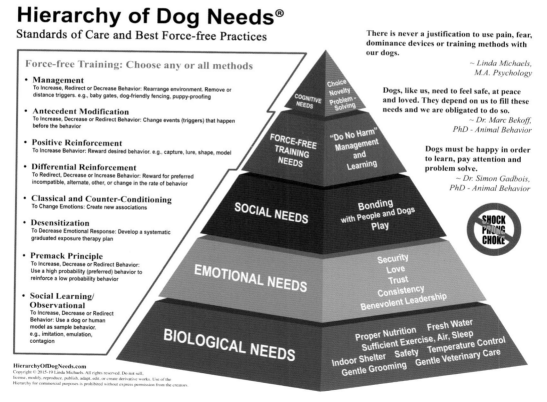

Hierarchy of Dog Needs®
Standards of Care and Best Force-free Practices

Force-free Training: Choose any or all methods

- **Management**
  To Increase, Redirect or Decrease Behavior: Rearrange environment. Remove or distance triggers. e.g., baby gates, dog-friendly fencing, puppy-proofing

- **Antecedent Modification**
  To Increase, Decrease or Redirect Behavior: Change events (triggers) that happen before the behavior

- **Positive Reinforcement**
  To Increase Behavior: Reward desired behavior. e.g., capture, lure, shape, model

- **Differential Reinforcement**
  To Redirect, Decrease or Increase Behavior: Reward for preferred incompatible, alternate, other, or change in the rate of behavior

- **Classical and Counter-Conditioning**
  To Change Emotions: Create new associations

- **Desensitization**
  To Decrease Emotional Response: Develop a systematic graduated exposure therapy plan

- **Premack Principle**
  To Increase, Decrease or Redirect Behavior: Use a high probability (preferred) behavior to reinforce a low probability behavior

- **Social Learning/Observational**
  To Increase, Decrease or Redirect Behavior: Use a dog or human model as sample behavior. e.g., imitation, emulation, contagion

COGNITIVE NEEDS — Choice, Novelty, Problem-Solving

FORCE-FREE TRAINING NEEDS — "Do No Harm" Management and Learning

SOCIAL NEEDS — Bonding with People and Dogs, Play

EMOTIONAL NEEDS — Security, Love, Trust, Consistency, Benevolent Leadership

BIOLOGICAL NEEDS — Proper Nutrition, Fresh Water, Sufficient Exercise, Air, Sleep, Indoor Shelter, Safety, Temperature Control, Gentle Grooming, Gentle Veterinary Care

There is never a justification to use pain, fear, dominance devices or training methods with our dogs.
~ Linda Michaels, M.A. Psychology

Dogs, like us, need to feel safe, at peace and loved. They depend on us to fill these needs and we are obligated to do so.
~ Dr. Marc Bekoff, PhD - Animal Behavior

Dogs must be happy in order to learn, pay attention and problem solve.
~ Dr. Simon Gadbois, PhD - Animal Behavior

NO SHOCK PRONG CHOKE

Figure 1.1: Hierarchy of Dog Needs.[3]

- freedom from hunger and thirst
- freedom from discomfort
- freedom from pain, injury or disease
- freedom to express normal behaviour
- freedom from fear and distress.

The Code of Practice for the Welfare of Dogs is a useful document that provides some further guidance about the species-specific needs of dogs, along with advice about how you can meet these needs with appropriate housing, diet, social interactions, healthcare and behavioural understanding.

When we consider the welfare of our dogs, the focus is commonly on the relief of suffering by preventing/treating physical illness and providing a suitable environment with appropriate resources. However, good mental health involves much more than the absence of suffering. Animal welfare advocates are now advising that in order to address welfare concerns, we need to facilitate good mental health for our dogs by helping them to attain positive emotional states such as happiness and contentment.[4] Welfare assessments often include the concept of 'quality of life' in which the physiological and behavioural indicators relating to pain and suffering are judged and evaluated to establish whether the individual is experiencing a good or poor quality of life. The concept of 'a life worth living' is an additional measure that is an ethical consideration rather than the purely scientific welfare assessment model. Establishing whether an animal has a life worth living can be useful in evaluating housing or continuation of medical care but is quite subjective and relies on a human judgement as we cannot ask the animal whether they would prefer to live or die.[5] Companion animal ethics suggest that in order to ensure an animal's best possible welfare, we need to do more than simply use animal welfare science to work out whether an animal is experiencing positive or negative welfare. We should be making an ethical judgement by weighing up the positives and negatives.[6]

Appreciating your dog as an individual

While a dog's day-to-day lifestyle may vary throughout their lifetime, and should be tailored to cater for the individual, there are fundamental needs that must be taken seriously by all owners and provided to all dogs. It is generally reported that there is more variation within breeds than there is between them. When we are considering the needs of individual breeds and the potential for genetic predisposition of particular behaviours, we must not assume that this will be the case and apply to all members of that particular breed. However, doing some research into your dog's breed, their genetic lineage and their early experiences can help you better understand the likely motivations that your dog will have, and will ultimately help you to cater for them as an individual by providing opportunities to perform those behaviours in a safe way. Setting up regular activities that allow your dog to fulfil these needs is likely to provide them with the outlet they need and will minimise the potential for unwanted or nuisance behaviour such as chasing wildlife, digging up the lawn or disappearing after a sniff.

Does the average pet dog have their needs met?

Dogs can be highly adaptable and resilient to a varying routine provided that their early experiences have given them the skills to cope with change and that their fundamental needs are being met. Although dogs might be able to deal with a change in the length of the walk, the

Figure 1.2: Fish (left) and Mouse (right) Jack Russell Terriers. Dogs of the same breed are likely to have different motivations and personalities. Fish loves to roll in bird poo and Mouse prefers to dig mole hills! Photo: © Natalie Light.

timing of their breakfast or dinner mealtimes, or the amount of time that they have to interact with their human or doggy friends; if sleep, rest, safety and trust are disrupted, then you are likely to see undesirable changes in behaviour resulting in compromised welfare.

Let us consider what a normal weekday for a dog living with a single owner that works in an office might involve. This case study involves a Labrador called Leo.

Leo's day

Leo is a 3-year-old male Labrador who lives with his owner Sam in a relatively quiet suburban town. Sam works as an office manager at the local school, so he relies on a network of people to help him care for Leo during the day. Here is a standard 24 hours for Sam and Leo.

At 6 am Leo wakes up downstairs in the utility room where he sleeps and pads around, feeling hungry and needing a pee. After 30 minutes he hears Sam's alarm clock and movement from upstairs and begins to whine and bark at the impending arrival of his owner. Sam finds this annoying! The morning routine involves a 20 minute on-lead walk around the local streets. Sam is always in a bit of a hurry and does not want to be late for work, so Leo does not get a chance to sniff every lamppost or greet any of the dogs and people they meet. As soon as they get home, Sam gives Leo his breakfast of supermarket-bought dry kibble and leaves him to eat alone in the kitchen while he goes to get ready for work. Leo watches Sam leave and stands by the door whining for a few minutes before remembering he is a Labrador and there's food available! He eats his breakfast and returns to the door to wait for Sam to come back down. Sam is running late (again!) so has a quick coffee and some toast while Leo goes out in the garden for a quick toilet break. Sam gives Leo a quick pat on the head and one of his toast crusts as he leaves the house at 8 am. Leo settles down on the sofa for a snooze but is woken at 9 am by the postman trying to deliver a parcel. At 10.30 am, Leo's dog walker Justine arrives to pick him up for a group walk. They head to the local park in her van and there are two new dogs to the group today that seem to take a dislike to Leo. Leo spends the whole walk next to Justine to feel safe, which she thinks is lovely as usually Leo is off jumping in puddles and ignoring her attempts to call him back, 'Perhaps the training is finally paying off.' she thinks to herself. Leo is dropped back off at home at 1 pm and after a brief chew on one of Sam's shoes, he drifts off to sleep. At 3.30 pm the local school children start to walk home and Leo watches them through the window, barking occasionally and wagging his tail. Sam usually arrives home not long after the school kids have gone past so Leo remains at the window, waiting, listening and watching for the familiar sound and sight of Sam's car. Sam had a late meeting and then went to the gym after work so does not arrive home until 6.30 pm by which time Leo is SUPER excited to see him. Sam takes Leo into the garden for a toilet break and 10 minutes of play time with a tug toy before preparing both of their dinners – a microwave meal for Sam and a bowl of supermarket kibble for Leo. At 7.30 pm Sam sits in the lounge with Leo to watch his favourite TV show – Leo snuggles up to Sam and falls into a deep, contented sleep. It does not last long though as it is the pub quiz at 8.30 pm so Sam leaves Leo home alone in the kitchen, getting home just after last orders. A quick pee in the garden and a dog biscuit for Leo and then he is tucked back up in the utility room where his bed is.

This is a normal weekday for Leo and probably not an uncommon daily routine for many of our companion dogs. If we consider Leo's experiences in that 24-hour period, do you feel his needs were being met? Did he get enough sleep? Did he engage in many natural behaviours such as chewing, digging or sniffing? Did he have ample opportunities to interact socially with people and dogs? Did Leo have access to activities that provided physical, mental and emotional enrichment?

This chapter aims to explore these questions in more detail to empower you with the knowledge and understanding of the needs of dogs so that you can provide the optimum home environment for your dog to have a happy, healthy and fulfilled life.

Canine activity budgets

In order to provide for the needs of your dog on a daily basis, it is important to understand what the research and observations of their natural behaviours can tell us about how they would choose to spend their time. The concept of an activity budget is a way of illustrating how much time is spent on a particular behaviour within a particular timeframe. For the benefit of dog owners, it is useful to think about how much time your dogs would spend doing particular behaviours within a 24-hour period if they were given free choice to do so. Much of the data collated and analysed comes from observations of free-ranging dog populations who have more autonomy over how they spend their time than their house-dwelling cousins. While there will be differences in the preferences of individual dogs, aiming for some of the general activity budgets will provide your dog with the experiences and environments that they need for optimum welfare.

The topics that follow suggest how much time your dog might naturally engage in particular activities and the key components of an appropriate environment for dogs. Of course, there is no one-size-fits-all approach and there will be variations depending on your dog's age, size, health, fitness, activity level, personality, preferences, motivations and sociability with people and other animals. However, the following sections aim to provide a useful comparison for your daily routine and environmental set-up at home – how well do the recommendations match your dog's current lifestyle and fundamentally, are you doing all you can within your capability to meet your dog's needs?

The home environment

Desirable features of the home environment include:

- non-slip flooring
- chew toys
- adequate resources in multi-dog households
- a range of options for resting and sleeping
- secure garden
- ability to avoid and safety from stressors such as noise.

Interpreting behaviour

Social behaviours

Canine communication and natural/normal behaviours are complex repertoires that all dog owners should strive to have at least a moderate appreciation and understanding of. Dogs use their body language, vocalisation and scent

Figure 1.3: Allowing a range of options for resting and sleeping places will provide your dog(s) with the choice to use the one they feel most relaxed in. Some might prefer to rest close to you, some on the floor, and some on a raised bed away from others. Photo: © Natalie Light.

to communicate with one another and with humans. Put simply, canine communication can be categorised into distance-increasing behaviours (designed to manage and avoid social interactions) and distance-reducing behaviours (designed to invite and facilitate social interactions).

Natural and normal behaviours

Behaviours that are considered to be natural and normal by canine experts and research (such as the canine ethogram) can often be considered a nuisance, destructive or problem behaviours for owners. Providing appropriate outlets for your dog to engage in these activities not only provides them with a safe, species-specific enriching activity but also your dog is less likely to perform these behaviours in less favoured areas. If your dog has plenty of

Figure 1.4: Regular opportunities to interact socially with other well-matched dogs from an early age will help your dog to develop effective canine communication skills and the ability to read and react to their body language. Photo: © Natalie Light.

Table 1.2 Summary of the simple components of canine body language that either invite or avoid social interactions.[7,8]

Distance-reducing behaviours	Distance-increasing behaviours
Affiliative greeting behaviour involves soft body language, an open mouth and fleeting eye contact. More sensitive dogs may show low, wiggly body language designed to appease. Dogs will avoid direct eye contact and pass each other to sniff the face and groin of the other dog before moving on or inviting play.	Behaviour designed to avoid an interaction involves more erect and rigid body language and in the initial stages, confident dogs may simply avert their body and gaze to turn away from an approaching dog. Dogs will avoid direct eye contact initially and may engage in a displacement activity such as sniffing the ground or move away if they are free to in order to display their disinterest in an interaction.
A play bow is an invitation to engage in a game that mimics the predatory sequence but is clearly signalled with a bow to indicate 'this is play, not real'. A play bow involves direct eye contact, an open mouth, lowered shoulders and a waggly bottom in the air. It is often followed by a sideways pounce and run to elicit chase.	More overt behaviour to avoid an interaction will occur if the dog that does not want the greeting is less confident or if the approaching dog has ignored or misinterpreted the more subtle signs that an interaction is unwanted. Defensive behaviour involves direct eye contact, a close, tense mouth, stiff body language and slow, deliberate movements. It may escalate to lip curling, air snaps, growling or barking depending on the reaction of the approaching dog and whether the dog is restrained by a lead.

access to chews such as Kongs™, Nylabones™, stag and antler bars, Yak chews and so on they are less likely to chew your furniture or other items. If your dog has plenty of opportunity to engage in scent work activities with you such as scatter feeding their meals or hiding titbits around the house for them to find, they are less likely to go scavenging or disappear on walks after a scent. If your dog has their own dig pit (a child's sand pit filled with woodchip or similar) that you routinely hide toys or food in and encourage them to dig to their heart's content, they are less likely to dig up your flower beds or lawn. Accepting that dogs are highly motivated to perform particular behaviours and providing them with a safe, appropriate opportunity to engage in them will not only ensure they are fulfilled, but it will also lead to far less conflict and frustration, and hopefully result in an improved relationship and understanding of your dog.

Sleep

It is well accepted in human medicine and well-being that getting ample rest and good quality sleep is vital for maintaining a healthy body and mind. There is nothing in the literature to suggest that this does not also apply to our dogs. Research into the lives of feral populations of dogs has shown that their activity patterns differ from ours, and that they lead a mostly crepuscular existence – being active at dawn and dusk.[9] Further studies have shown that peak activity within a 24-hour period occurs during the hours of 5–8 am and 7–10 pm and often involves a lot of physical activity,[10] which questions the 'lunchtime walk' that many dogs are taken on. Sleep-wake cycles in dogs are much shorter and more frequent than humans, with each sleep cycle varying from 15–45 minutes and as many as 23 cycles in an 8-hour period. This polyphasic sleep pattern consists of wake periods in between sleep cycles, which last an average of 5 minutes – this is usually when the dog may switch positions, move to another area of the room, rearrange their bed by scratching, digging, circling or snuggle up to their human

Figure 1.5: Individual dogs will have their own preferred sleeping positions, places and routines. If you can identify these, you can provide sleeping and resting areas that are appropriate for your dog. Photo: © Natalie Light.

Figure 1.6: Companionship and company is important for some dogs to be able to fully rest and relax, so provide opportunities for them to be close to you. Photo: © Natalie Light.

for warmth or comfort.[11] It has been reported that 86% of dogs that were given access to sleep on the bed with or close to their owners chose to,[12] suggesting that preventing your dog from being able to sleep near you could be a major cause of sleep deprivation and potentially detrimental to their health and welfare.[12]

Exercise

Conflict can arise between owner expectations and the needs of an individual dog when it comes to the daily dog walk. Of course, all dogs should be given the opportunity to explore their environment free from the confines of their harness and lead, but it is not always safe or appropriate to do this. Factors such as your dog's social skills and how much training you have put in to having an effective recall, will dictate whether they should be afforded off-lead privileges in busy, public areas. Bradshaw writes 'In the future I predict that dogs will need all the help they can get from scientists and enthusiasts alike. Dogs in the West will never return to the freedoms they were once afforded where they could roam the streets meeting (or avoiding) dogs as and when they chose before returning home to their owners in the evening. Society requires much more of dogs and dog owners that it did then.'[13] As dog lovers and owners, we must embrace this change in societal expectations and adapt our previously carefree attitude to exercising our dogs to ensure that our dogs are still welcome in public spaces in the years to come. Dogs with a sensitive temperament that may be worried about other dogs or people, or those that are undergoing training or have a strong prey drive need not miss out on off-lead exercise as there is a growing trend for secure fields (or 'freedom fields') that can be hired by the hour for sole use. We can also re-frame the 'on-lead' walk in

Figure 1.7: Regular off-lead opportunities are an important requirement for dogs and need to be done safely so that your dog has a positive experience and they do not create a nuisance for other people or dogs in public areas. Photo: © Natalie Light.

our minds and accept that walking on a lead can still be a hugely enriching experience for our dogs if we allow them to sniff, explore and even guide us in the direction they wish to travel (if it is safe to do so).

Research conducted in 2017 by Westgarth et al. found that owners described walking as being principally done 'for the dog'.[14] Exercise was universally expressed as a fundamental need of the dog and walking a 'responsibility' of dog ownership, with the owner deriving pleasure from the pleasure they interpret from their dog's behaviour. This need was largely based anthropomorphically on the relationship between physical and mental health and exercise in human beings. Figure 1.8 shows the relationship between the dog and owner needs, possible actions taken by the owner and perceived outcomes. Note, however, that all walks are not necessarily a pleasurable experience for dogs if they are exposed to things they find frightening such as noisy traffic or busy streets. We must therefore strive to adapt our plans for what constitutes an enjoyable walk and aim to incorporate the canine needs in our daily outings into the wider environment.

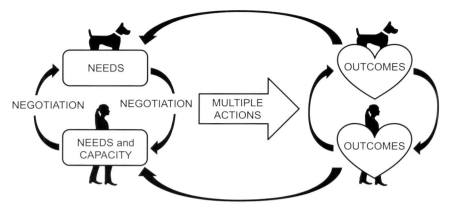

Figure 1.8: Reproduced, with permission, from Westgarth et al.,[14] this model shows the relationship between the dog and owner needs (which include internal and external influences), multiple possible actions taken by the owner, and perceived outcomes for dog and owner (internally and externally; for example, connectedness).

Figure 1.9: Lead walks can provide masses of enrichment in the form of social interaction (or avoidance if your dog is worried by people or other animals) and exploration of the sights and smells of the wider environment. Photo: © Natalie Light.

Play

Play is a hugely important and valuable part of the canine behaviour repertoire and helps to build and maintain the relationships dogs have with their humans and other animals. Some dogs are particularly playful and will seek out another dog to play with at every opportunity whereas some may be more reserved and only play with chosen friends or familiar dogs that have similar play styles to them. Get to know the types of play that your dog enjoys and find appropriate play mates or move them away to safety if they are overwhelmed by another dog's attempt to make friends. Dog–human play is much easier to provide your dog with if you struggle to find dogs that your dog wants to interact with. Most owners will engage in a game on a walk, but we could be offering so much more within the confines of our home and garden and mixing up the games we play to provide our dogs with physical and mental enrichment. One study reported that a survey of Swiss pet owners said they spent 17.5 hours a week interacting and playing with their pet dogs, and another found that 36% of the dog walkers observed at a particular park played a chase game with a ball or similar toy.[15] Although 'fetch' may be a favoured and traditional game for humans and dogs to play together, there is actually a long list of more appropriate games that do not have the associated risks of physical injury and high arousal that chasing a ball at top speed does. Many owners also get hung up on the action of throwing the ball repetitively, which can become frustrating for dogs that simply want to retain and hold their treasure (particularly in retrieving gundog breeds).

Some suggestions for games to try with your dog

- **'Go find'** – Hide a toy or treat in some longer undergrowth (being careful not to disturb wildlife!) and ask your dog to 'go find'. You can either drop them secretly as you walk past a particular point and send your dog back, or if you have a good 'wait' command or someone else to hold your dog's lead, you can set up the game, and then return to your dog to release them.

- **'Treat tree'** – Exploring different surfaces and vertical tree trunks or fallen logs (if safe and secure) is a fantastic way to engage your dog's nose and build their confidence at independent problem solving. Simply squish several soft treats into the bark of a log or tree, stand back and watch your dog go to work – it is a moment of calm for both of you.

- **'Tug and thank you'** – This is a high-octane game that not only teaches impulse control, it allows your dog to have fun right next to you, which will certainly help with your recall and general attentiveness when you're out on walks. You need two identical toys that are quite long and soft – I like fleece tugs from Tug-E-Nuff or the hoops from Puller. Stick one out of sight and out of reach but close to hand. Offer one to your dog with a 'READY' (this will become your 'we're gonna play!'

Figure 1.10: Physical and mental enrichment in the form of a 'treat tree' scent work activity. Photo: © Natalie Light.

cue) 'GET IT!' (this will become your 'take' cue). Move the toy around slowly, keeping it low to the ground to prevent any jumping up. Let go of the toy and grab the second one, holding it out of reach of your dog initially. Repeat 'READY' and wait for your dog to drop the first toy. As soon as they do say 'THANK YOU' (this will become your 'drop' cue) and offer them the second toy with a 'GET IT'. Repeat for a few times, allowing your dog to parade around with the toy in between bouts of tug. If your dog runs off with the toy, you might need to do some work with your dog or the toy on a long line initially. After a high-arousal game like this, calm things down gradually and scatter some food for your dog to sniff out to help them relax before you head back inside. Games like this are much better played in the garden or a separate room to the lounge, and the toys should be inaccessible to your dog when you are not playing so that they retain their novelty and value. Otherwise, you will be creating expectations of play when you want to relax, and your dog may lose interest in the toys if they see them all the time (or they may pester you to play continually).

Social interaction

Dogs are a highly adaptable and social species that are uniquely able to build special relationships with humans due to the methods and modes of domestication and selective breeding of particular, juvenile characteristics.[16] The adaptations to social behaviours that dogs have undergone during domestication seem to counteract their social communication with other conspecifics, meaning that dogs now depend on humans and have become more well-adapted to communication with humans than other dogs.[17] These findings suggest that the common belief of getting another dog for company may not provide for your dog's social needs and is not an adequate substitute for spending quality time with their human. Adapting your lifestyle to be able to spend time at home or at work with your dog is one of the simple ways to prevent separation distress and potential behaviour issues related to stress and anxiety. If you are unable to provide a network of dog sitters or regular company for your dog, it may be worth considering ensuring that they are happy when they are home alone by installing some dog-cams, and even, whether your current lifestyle is appropriate for a dog.

Enrichment

'Variety is the spice of life' and this is also true for our dogs. Providing them with new and exciting experiences on a regular basis has a range of physical, mental and emotional benefits that should not be considered as optional extras but should instead be embedded into your daily routine and lifestyle. We take a lot of choice away from our dogs – we choose what they eat, where they sleep, when they go outside, how much time they get to spend with us or other dogs – and so providing novel and interesting enrichment activities should be the very least we can offer them to brighten up their world. Remember, the whole concept of enrichment is that it is actually enriching. Here are some suggestions to try with your dog but be aware that not all dogs will enjoy all of these activities so observe their behaviour when you offer them something to establish whether they are having fun or not.

Figure 1.11: Chew toys and Lickimats™ can help your dog to settle in public areas or at home in the lounge. Photo: © Natalie Light.

- **Boredom busters and activity feeders –** These could be toys that you place food in or a more complex puzzle that your dog has to solve to release the treat. Be careful that you do not make it too difficult to start with as you could create frustration or your dog might simply give up.

- **Rotating a toy box –** Often we place our dog's toys in a box in the corner of the room and wonder why they lose interest in a previously favourite toy. Toys can lose their novelty if they are always available and smell like the rest of the house. You can create novelty by having a box with a lid (to keep the smells in) in an area of the house that your dog does not have access to. Leave a few toys out but place the rest in the box with some kibble. Rotate the toys on a daily or weekly basis to maintain interest.

- **Novel objects and smells –** Have you ever noticed how interested your dog is in you when you return home from a friend's house that also has a pet? The scent is carried on your clothes and you can create the same effect by setting up a toy swap with friends or asking them to

have a couple of your dog's toys at their house for a while before offering them back to your dog.

- **Recycling phase 1 –** There is no need to spend lots of money on chews and toys designed for dogs as they may be just as happy with a cardboard box, a plastic bottle or a yoghurt pot. Simply put dog-safe items to one side and let your dog have an hour or so with them before you pop them in your recycling bin. Empty toilet roll tubes are a favoured chew toy in my household!

- **The rucksack (or backpack) walk –** This concept was first demonstrated by Steve Mann of the Institute of Modern Dog Trainers and encapsulates a lot of the wellness concepts of meditation. It involves being in the moment on a dog walk and taking time to explore sniffs with your dog. Simply pack a rucksack with some yummy treats and novel sniffs and head off into the countryside for a mindfulness-focused bimble with your dog. This is described in more detail in the 'Activities' chapter of this book.

Nutrition and behaviour

There is a wealth of evidence that nutrition and behaviour have a close relationship. A healthy, balanced diet, regular feeding routine and opportunity to engage in natural sniffing, chewing and hunting activities are the minimum that all dog owners should strive to provide. All of the canid species (which domestic dogs belong to) are generalist in their eating habits and unlike obligate carnivores (such as cats) they consume plant matter in addition to the flesh of their prey. Dogs are very flexible and can adapt to different feeding schedules, although it is suggested that a minimum of two meals per day will help to maintain gastrointestinal health and reduce the risk of hunger-related issues.[18] When deciding how, when, what and how much you feed your dog, considerations must be made relating to your dog's age, size, activity level, general health and preference. A successful balanced diet that maintains a healthy weight also involves regular monitoring and body scoring to ensure your dog does not become over or underweight.

Training and behavioural considerations

Thankfully, interest in the previously popular dominance theory and related 'alpha' methods of training dogs is beginning to wane and being replaced by more ethologically minded training that accepts that dogs are not in a dominance–submissive relationship and instead simply do what is most advantageous to them and provides them with access to resources they want.[19] Positive reinforcement is not only an effective way to train a dog but also it has the added benefit of not carrying the risks of a punishment-based approach. The science of dog training methods and how they affect welfare is an ever-expanding discipline of research that all dog owners should follow with interest to ensure the trainer or behaviourist they are working with or following is advising and applying reward-based methods that have not only been shown to be better for dog welfare, they also seem to be more effective.[20] However, there is still work to do regarding educating owners and professionals about the importance of assessing the underlying emotion and motivation of behaviours before moving forward with a training plan that aims to 'stop' an unwanted behaviour. A combination of canine ethology, canine needs, classical and operant conditioning along with environmental management and client education is the key to a successful outcome in most behaviour cases.

How can we change our lifestyles or daily routines to better cater for our dogs' needs?

Having read through the suggestions this chapter has given to help our dogs live happy, fulfilled lives, you may now have some ideas about how you can adapt certain aspects of your routine to benefit you and your dog's quality of life. Change can seem daunting and a bit of a challenge, but it need not be. Here are some inspiring, real-life suggestions from my wonderful clients, which highlight the steps they take every day to make their dogs as happy as could possibly be. These fantastic owners were not canine professionals when they decided to share their home with a dog but are now experts in their own dog having learned what their dogs need and how they can provide it simply and effectively while working through a behaviour treatment plan. The quotes below are excellent examples of responsible, educated, ethical, compassionate, considerate and empathetic dog ownership in action. Thanks to all of my wonderful clients in the Natdogs Gang Facebook page for providing their dogs with such fantastic lives and adjusting their lifestyle to meet their dogs' needs.

- Mabel is a sniff-loving spaniel and loves nothing more than following a scent, so we make sure we have enough hot dog cut up in the fridge for a scenting/sniffing/go find game every day.
- I live with Fidget, a 7-year-old kelpie mix with lots of fear issues due to his early experiences. I try every day to make sure he feels safe, for example walking him late at night when it's quieter. Because he doesn't leave the house often, we play lots of brain games, scent games and I let him dig up my flowerbeds to satisfy as many natural instincts as possible!
- Toby Scottie dog came to us when he was just 5-years old from a non-pet first home. A very scared, reactive but sweet boy. Now an 11-year-old gentleman, he has taught us to enjoy the 'terrier' things of life … daily marathon 'sniffaris' with exemplary social distancing, digging of holes for critters in a safe/secure field where nothing can sneak up and surprise him. The odd squirrel/cat/fox chase an absolute CV delight when it happens … but non-live toys and playing are still a mystery to him – so we use brain games with 'high-end' titbits … and skill training … and scent tracking sessions. We all appreciate the life we now share together … although I will pass on the hole-digging!
- Lucas is a wonderful rescue lurcher who has taught me so much. Most notably that your dog is who he/she is just as we are who we are … don't try and change them, learn how to work with them.

- Rosa is my 3-year-old rescue (possibly collie cross) and she is highly anxious so I provide her with lots of opportunities to be calm and relax and encourage a routine that is predictable and where she can sleep well.
- Two of my dogs, Pete and Ru, aren't keen on unknown dogs so I travel out of the busy local area to quiet areas where they can be themselves with no pressure. My other dog, Maple, is very sociable so I tend to walk her places where she can meet other sociable dogs and people. And as my oldest has got older we do less walking and he does more sniffing, we don't get far but he's happy!
- My Ziggy is a beagle collie cross who I adopted when he was 4-months old. He is frustrated on-lead and a chaser. Of everything! We tour car parks to try and desensitise him to cars and other traffic including people. Play ball and find it on a long line in public, open, not too busy areas. And I hide treats (food and toys) for him in all of my recycling to keep his brain busy when we are at home.
- My 6-year-old rehomed husky/GSD called Chief is reactive to strangers and some new dogs so all new introductions are made very slowly in controlled environments to increase his circle of trust and build his confidence to new friendships. We ensure he has a simple name for each that he can relate to and get rewarded with each time he hears the name.
- Bosco is a 6-year-old Labrador mix with separation anxiety. Every day I ensure he is never left on his own, so he's not scared or frightened, so he cannot hurt himself by trying to eat his way out of the front door and so he knows he's loved, protected and safe forever.
- My terrier Evie tends to get overexcited about most things and barks at noises. So

I provide her with healthy chews and her meals in puzzle toys (Kongs™/'snuffle mats' and so on) throughout the day if I'm home (evening on workdays) and also help her practice calm behaviours. She can also be mildly reactive when we are on walks so I always try to give her as much space as possible when avoiding or saying hello to dogs, we also play 'go find' on her walks so she gets lots of opportunities to sniff every blade of grass possible (sniffing is a favourite pastime of hers!).

- We have a 8-year-old ex-racing greyhound called Billy who came to us 2 years ago with a fear of pretty much everything. We take him out for a daily early morning walk on a route he is comfortable with. We do lots of games with his 'magic' treat bowl and lots of other treat finding games to encourage him to explore and be happier in the outside world.

- Carly is a 7-year-old staffie who is glued to my side. She loves exploring in the woods and as an extra adventure, we hide food in high and low places in the woodland.

- I've looked after Chewee (9-year-old rescue Saluki mix/lurcher) for over 6 years and he's had separation anxiety from me since day 1 so he is rarely without me and never alone, if I go to the office he comes too and when he can't be with me he's with close friends/family. He's also reactive to other dogs and while he's now much better we tend to drive to walks in the countryside that mean not only is there lots of wildlife to sniff but we don't see many other people, I always have treats with me and if any dogs are too close, I treat/scatter feed if we can't get enough distance.

- Logan is a 12-year-old rescue Siberian husky, we have 3 second meets with other dogs on our walk, which has helped him overcome his nervousness. We provide him with mental stimulation via puzzle feeders in addition to his exercise needs met by walks and hiring a secure offload field for runs.

- I rescued a wonderful Staffy cross named Billy when he was 5-years old. Like some dogs he would suffer great anxiety hearing fireworks. I eliminated the sounds of them as much as possible. Knowing that New Year's Eve was just around the corner, I found a suitable dog-friendly hotel to retreat to where we were highly unlikely to hear any fireworks. It was perfect and completely stress free as he did not hear a thing.

- I have a 3-year-old Dalmatian, he is a rescue who is anxious, frustrated and overexcited about everything. I do whatever I can to make home as safe, quiet and relaxing as possible to help him cope with everyday life. He loves to learn so I pay for private dog sport sessions so we can learn new things together in safety. He gets all the chews he wants and I try to make his life as enriching as possible.

- I have a 10-year-old rescue Siberian husky called Kayla with the desire to run free but she can't safely go off-lead due to a high prey drive and unreliable recall. I provide her opportunities to run in a secure off-lead field and through sled dog sports with her husky team.

- I have a 5-year-old rescue lurcher called Harvey who has a high prey drive. We hire a secure field for safe off-lead exercise and give him lots of soft, squeaky toys to tug, chase, shake and shred so he can act out his natural behaviours without causing harm to real furries.

- I have an 8-year-old lurcher called Taylor. He has complex medical and behavioural issues, so I strive to improve my knowledge in these areas to help support and understand him. We manage his environment to help him to feel safe by avoiding unnecessary interactions and using food to create positive associations. We also use a lot of puzzles and games to help with frustration and anxiety.

- I have a 14-year-old collie who loves to sleep so I try to encourage his old bones into his raised bed. He is much slower on walks now and we let him spend the majority of his time sniffing.
- I have a 7-year-old beagle called Scooter. She loves sniffing so we go for sniffy walks where she guides the pace and direction (within reason ... not into the local butchers, although she's tried!). We play sniffy games in the house with treats in a bag filled with cardboard bits and bobs.
- My working cocker spaniel Milo is very anxious and needy for strokes and attention. I sit on the floor with him in the lounge and give him lots of attention and touch.

I hope these examples of how simple changes can dramatically affect your relationship with your dog and their happiness and well-being have given you some ideas about what your dog might need or enjoy. These owners have taken the time to get to know their dogs and what their likes/dislikes are and most importantly have put activities or environmental changes in place to cater for what their dogs love.

With this in mind, let us return to Leo the Labrador and think about how his daily routine may benefit from some change. As a clinical animal behaviourist, I work with the client to fit a plan around the existing lifestyle so that we can implement simple changes that are easy to embed into their routines and ultimately improve the welfare of their dog. Often there are cases where the welfare of the dog and/or human are being severely compromised, and it is my professional responsibility to discuss whether rehoming or even euthanasia of their dog may be the most appropriate course of action. However, most of the time, clients have contacted me because they love their dog and they want to make sure they are giving them the best life they possibly can or there are a few behaviours that they find annoying or troublesome. So what would I advise if Sam came to me as a client and what would I feel was the priority for Leo?

1. Social isolation – Simply put, Leo is spending too much time alone during the week. Obviously Sam still has to work (someone's got to pay for Leo's food!) but I would work with him to explore options about how we could break up the week. Are there any nearby friends or family that could come and sit with him or take them to their house for a few hours twice a week? Could Sam work from home a couple of afternoons a week? Is Leo happy and settled at the pub as he could have been an extra quiz team member rather than leaving him home alone?
2. Sleep – Leo is hardly getting any rest during the daytime due to all of the interruptions. He also sleeps alone downstairs and while I follow a 'your house, your rules' approach to my client work, I would want to establish why Leo sleeps where he does and whether Sam would mind him sleeping on the landing or even in his room.
3. Justine – I would want Justine to be involved in the process to establish whether Leo is finding the walks with

her fun and enjoyable or whether the large group and travel in her van could be overwhelming for him. We could look at doing some 1:1 walks or simply ask Justine to check in on Leo either side of her group walk to do some scent work in the garden or simply sit with him and offer him some companionship.

4. Enrichment to provide natural behaviour outlets – The day that we looked at did not involve very much sniffing, chewing or play at all and this is something that I would address in the treatment plan. Leo's breakfast could be scattered around the house or garden to get him sniffing, some tasty chews or boredom busters would be a good activity to leave him with when Sam heads off to work, and the morning walk could be more 'dog-friendly' allowing Leo to sniff, watch, listen and explore rather than having a set route around the block.

5. Exercise – Most dog owners are so concerned about walking their dog two or three times a day that they forget it is all about quality, not quantity! 5 minutes of scent work in the garden with your undivided attention can easily provide a more positive experience for you and your dog than a 30-minute pavement pounding route march around the streets. Imagine being taken to a beautiful scenic nature reserve by a loved one but you are not allowed to stop, look or take in the surroundings. Instead, your hand is held, and you are whisked around at full speed to get back to the car. That is what some of our dogs' walks have become and I urge all of my clients to slow down, enjoy the moment and most importantly be present in the walk rather than feeling it is something you need to tick off your 'to do' list.

6. Health and nutrition – Leo is a young dog so part of my consultation assessment would involve ensuring he has had a recent vet check and observing his body condition. If there were any concerns, we would address them with medical and nutritional interventions from the referring vet.

Providing an ethologically sensitive approach to living with dogs

It is often felt that our pet dogs have an 'easy' life without any responsibilities but living in a captive environment without freedom, choice, predictability and enjoyable challenges can be a barren and distressing existence. The concept of 'agency' is ever-increasingly appearing in animal welfare literature and concerns 'the propensity of an animal to actively engage in the environment with the main purpose of gathering knowledge and enhancing their skills for future use'.[21] If we are to provide for and engage a companion dog's agency, their environments need to be rich and complex while also providing opportunities for natural behaviour, exploration, play and problem solving.[21]

Final thoughts

This chapter has set out the welfare considerations and canine needs that those of us lucky enough to share our homes with dogs should be striving to provide on a regular basis. By following the simple yet effective ethologically sensitive and species-specific advice in this and the following chapters, you can be assured that you are providing an optimum environment and experiences for your dog. Our modern lives are busy and our dogs have been expected to

Figure 1.12: Being aware of and striving to fulfill your canine companion's ethological needs is likely to lead to a happy, healthy, enriched life for your dog. Photo: © Natalie Light.

adapt and change to the fast-paced lifestyle that many of us lead. Responsibly breeding dogs that will be successful companions, preparing puppies to cope with the world around them from an early age and ensuring that dogs can still 'be dogs' by having their dog-specific needs met in their homelife is key for dogs to remain a well-loved, highly valued and hugely respected member of our human families. It is a massive privilege to be able to share our lives with dogs and the least we can do is understand their ethology, meet their needs and provide the best possible environment for them to thrive in. As Wynne writes, 'If dogs' ability to love is what makes them unique, it also stands to reason that it gives them unique needs. And if there is a simple conclusion to be drawn from my research, it is that we humans need to be doing much more to honour and return our dogs' affections'.[22]

References

1. Coren, S. (2005) *How Dogs Think: Understanding the Canine Mind.* Simon and Schuster, London.
2. Maslow, A.H. (1943) A theory of human motivation. *Psychological Review* 50(4), 370.
3. Michaels, L.J. (2015) *Hierarchy of Dog Needs* [Pyramid Graphic]. Washington, DC. Patent and Trademark Office. https://hierarchyofdogneeds.com.
4. Estep, D.Q. and Hetts, S. (2019) Fostering mental and behavioural wellness during upbringing and throughout life. In: McMillan, F.D. (ed.) *Mental Health and Well-being in Animals.* CABI, Wallingford, p. 1235.
5. Broom, D.M. (2014) *Sentience and Animal Welfare.* CABI, Wallingford.
6. Sandøe, P., Corr, S. and Palmer, C. (2015) *Companion Animal Ethics.* John Wiley & Sons, Chichester.
7. Case, L.P. (2010) *Canine and Feline Behavior and Training: A Complete Guide to Understanding our Two Best Friends.* Delmar Cengage Learning, Clifton Park, NY.
8. Overall, K.L. (1997) *Clinical Behavioral Medicine for Small Animals.* Mosby, Maryland Heights, MS.
9. Beck, A.M. (1973) *The Ecology of Stray Dogs: A Study of Free-ranging Urban Animals.* York Press, Baltimore, MD.
10. Boitani, L., Francisci, F., Ciucci, P., Andreoli, G. and Serpell, J. (2017) The ecology and behavior of feral dogs: a case study from central Italy. In: Serpell, J. (ed.) *The Domestic Dog: Its Evolution, Behaviour and Interactions with People,* Cambridge University Press, Cambridge, pp. 342–356.
11. Adams, G.J. and Johnson, K.G. (1993) Sleep-wake cycles and other night-time behaviours of the domestic dog *Canis familiaris. Applied Animal Behaviour Science* 36(2–3), 33–248.
12. Kinsman, R., Owczarczak-Garstecka, S., Casey, R., et al. (2020) Sleep duration and behaviours: a descriptive analysis of a cohort of dogs up to 12 months of age. *Animals (Basel)* 0(7), 1172. Doi:10.3390/ani10071172.
13. Bradshaw, J. (2011) *In Defence of Dogs.* Penguin, London.
14. Westgarth, C., Christley, R.M., Marvin, G. and Perkins, E. (2017) I walk my dog because it makes me happy: a qualitative study to understand why dogs motivate walking and improved health. *International Journal of Environmental Research and Public Health* 14(8), 936.

15. Hart, L.A. and Yamamoto, M. (2017) Dogs as helping partners and companions for humans. In: Serpell, J. (ed.) *The Domestic Dog: Its Evolution, Behavior, and Interactions with People*, 2nd edn. Cambridge University Press, Cambridge, pp. 247–270.

16. Virányi, Z. and Range, F. (2014) On the way to a better understanding of dog domestication: aggression and cooperativeness in dogs and wolves. In: Kaminski, J. and Marshall-Pescini, S. (eds) *The Social Dog*. Academic Press, New York, pp. 35–62.

17. Feddersen-Petersen, D.U. (2007) Social behaviour of dogs and related canids. In: Jensen, P. (ed.) *The Behavioural Biology of Dogs*. CABI, Wallingford, pp. 105–119.

18. Case, L.P. (2014) *Dog Food Logic: Making Smart Decisions for Your Dog in an Age of Too Many Choices*. Dogwise Publishing, Wenatchee, WA.

19. Ryan, D. (2018) *Dominant Dogs: Handling myths and Training Insights*. Dog Secrets Publishing.

20. Todd, Z. (2020) *Wag: The Science of Making Your Dog Happy*. Greystone Books, Vancouver.

21. Pierce, J. (2016) *Run, Spot, Run: The Ethics of Keeping Pets*. University of Chicago Press, Chicago, IL.

22. Wynne, C.D. (2019) *Dog Is Love: Why and How Your Dog Loves You*. Houghton Mifflin Harcourt, Boston, MA.

Chapter 2

Breeding

Sarah Heath and Elizabeth Ayrton

Ideally the breeding and raising of puppies should focus not only on potential physical health considerations but also on the emotional health of the bitch and her offspring. To optimise emotional health and breed well-balanced puppies it is necessary to take into account the physical and emotional development of the puppy from the point of conception right through to the relatively independent puppy that leaves the breeder. The duty of a good breeder, however, does not finish when the puppy is handed over to the new caregiver at 8 weeks of age. Animals who display unwanted behaviours are at increased risk of surrender to rescue with all the inherent welfare implications[1] and a good breeder will provide ongoing support and advice to maximise the potential for the development of a lifelong relationship between the puppy and their caregiver.

Buster

The Clark family were a busy young family with parents, Neil and Carol, and three children, Sophie who was 12, William who was 8 and young Ava who was 4-years old. Neil and Carol had always had a dog since they were married and their last dog was a 13-year-old Border Terrier called Maya, who fitted really well into their family, was loved by everyone and great with the children. When Maya became ill the family followed the advice from their vet and took the heartbreaking decision to have her put to sleep. Their house felt very empty after this. The following spring Neil and Carol started researching breeders to find a new family dog and eventually located a breeder not too far away who had a litter of Border Terriers. It was with great excitement that the parents went, initially alone, to view the puppies and when they decided that one particular puppy was the right one for them, they also took the children to meet their new puppy who they named Buster.

Buster came home with them at 8-weeks old. He settled in well and proved to learn really fast. He slept in his crate in the kitchen and, with close attention from Carol, he was house trained within a few weeks, so his crate was very quickly able to be replaced with a bed. Buster was taken to puppy classes to socialise him with other dogs and the children all took part in training him. Everything seemed to be going really well until Buster was about 4.5-months old, when he became increasingly very mouthy and started biting at hands and feet especially in the evenings when all the family were at home. He was also jumping up and grabbing at the children's sleeves when they were playing ball with him. This escalated over a period of a few weeks culminating in Buster making a grab at William's hand and puncturing the skin. Although it was not a serious injury, the family realised that this behaviour could not continue or there was a risk that one of the children was going to have a more serious bite so they sat down as a family to discuss what they should do about it.

Neil and Carol decided that as Buster was a family dog, they should discuss the problem with the children to try to arrive at a solution. Carol also read as many books as possible and discussed it with the trainer at puppy classes. Carol first asked the family why they thought Buster was mouthing and was surprised at how perceptive they all were.

- Neil said he felt it was because Buster was teething and therefore felt more of a need to mouth.
- Carol said that she felt that Buster got overexcited when all the children were playing especially when they had lots of friends around.
- Sophie said that she had seen Ava getting Buster to play chase games by moving her feet or hands quickly across the floor. When Carol thought about this she realised that these games combined with Buster's instinct as a terrier to chase and catch things was a bad combination.
- William said that Buster was worse when they played lots of ball games as he got really excited and started grabbing at sleeves and hands and therefore there was a risk in this situation that someone was going to get bitten.
- Even young Ava said she thought that Buster was worse before they went to bed so maybe he was tired.

When Carol and Neil thought about all these suggestions, they realised that they were all very sensible so they asked each family member to come up with a solution to the problem they had raised.

Neil suggested that they should get lots of suitable things for Buster to chew on while he was teething such as chew toys and edible chews and they also should get Buster a bigger Kong™ in which they started to put some of his food and freeze it to make it last longer. They also remembered that when Buster was younger, he loved chewing on things like frozen carrots.

Carol suggested that sometimes when friends came round one of them could take Buster out for a calm walk in the woods, where he loved to sniff in the undergrowth, or he could spend some time in with her mum who enjoyed his company but had a relatively quiet house.

Sophie suggested that she and William should help to watch Ava when she was playing with him but that they should have a family rule that they should not play games getting him to chase hands and feet. She also suggested getting him to play with some long rope tugs that kept his distance from hands.

William suggested that they should stop playing ball with him but felt sad as Buster did enjoy his ball games. Carol suggested that maybe they could give Buster something else to do instead of his ball so they came up with the idea of giving Buster an old sandpit they had and hiding treats and toys in it that he could dig up.

Ava said he needed to go to bed for a sleep. Neil then suggested putting Buster's crate back up in the office, which was a quiet room. They combined putting him in his crate for a regular sleep with a frozen Kong™ when the house was quiet after the children had gone to school in the morning and even continued this routine in the holidays.

The family wrote up all the new rules on a piece of paper, which they put up on their noticeboard to remind them all – they also agreed to nag each other if they saw anyone breaking the rules. It took time for Buster to settle down, but as he grew older the new management they had put in place along with his teething finishing meant that over the next few months Buster became a much nicer dog to live with. Carol also realised that because everyone in the family had contributed to the new way of managing Buster, they all were much more invested in implementing it. This led her to realise that this was also a useful tool for dealing with other family problems that needed a solution. In time Buster developed into the nice family dog that they wanted but they appreciated him all the more because they had all learned from trying to solve his problems.

Prospective parents

Selection of suitable parents is the first important stage in breeding physically healthy and emotionally stable puppies. A large proportion of the selection process is related to physical factors such as good conformation and movement and, for a working dog, the ability to work well. Ideally parents who are healthy and free from physical disease themselves should be selected but it is also important to consider their emotional and cognitive health.

Pedigree dogs in the UK are registered with the Kennel Club (KC). The KC has an Assured Breeders Scheme (ABS), which can be helpful in respect of the physical health consideration of potential parents as it advises on health tests that are either compulsory or advisable for a variety of breeds. These tests include the British Veterinary Association/Kennel Club (BVA/KC) hip and elbow dysplasia scheme, BVA/KC, the International Sheepdog Society (ISDS) eye examination and an increasing number of DNA tests for various diseases, which can be

Case study – working together

Breed clubs and interested parties have worked together to raise money for further research into diseases that are recognised as having a hereditary basis but where the mode of inheritance is unclear. The aim is to improve understanding so that tests to predict dogs at risk of developing these diseases can be developed in the future. One example is Addison's disease in the Bearded Collie – Addison's disease is an autoimmune condition that has the potential to cause death in young dogs and, even if diagnosed and treated, has potential for life-threatening episodes and needs lifelong veterinary care. It is seen in dogs from a young age and is considered to be highly heritable, although the precise mode of inheritance has not been determined,[2] Addison's disease, along with other autoimmune diseases, is a cause for concern within an otherwise long lived and relatively healthy breed. The Joint Breed Liaison Committee (JBLC) formed from all the different Bearded Collie clubs raised money through crowdfunding to work with the Animal Health Trust and KC to sequence the genome of a healthy Bearded Collie and one affected with Addison's and have also funded work by research scientists at the Royal Veterinary College aimed at developing a screening test in the future. There are many examples of this process of working together between breeders, breed clubs and other interested parties to improve the health of pedigree dogs and indeed the KC have been working in recent years to produce a breed health and conservation plan for each breed. This is a document that shows the evidence base for the health of the breed, prioritises the concerns, gives guidance for breeders and looks to areas where further research and funding are required.

carried out using either a cheek swab or a blood sample from the dog. Anyone wishing to breed can look up the appropriate health tests for a breed on the KC web site.

There are some diseases that occur within breeds that are recognised as having a hereditary basis but the mode of inheritance is unclear, and no test is available. The best that can be done in this situation is to avoid breeding from affected parents or repeating any mating that has produced affected puppies.

Line breeding is often carried out in pedigree animals – this breeding practice breeds animals with similar ancestry in order to consolidate certain physical characteristics and produce a 'type'. While this is a well-recognised method of breeding, it can result in dogs that are very closely related being bred together. This can be detrimental in terms of physical health as many diseases with a genetic basis have an autosomal recessive mode of inheritance and therefore the more closely related two parents are the greater the chance of them having duplicates of the same gene, which could lead to disease. Recently, calculators for the Coefficient of Inbreeding (COI) have become available on pedigree software and the KC website, which enable breeders to calculate the COI of any potential mating. The higher the COI of any mating the greater the relatedness of the parents and the more chance of duplicate genes leading to problems. Advice is generally to produce a mating with a COI lower than the breed average.

In recent years, one particular problem affecting pedigree dogs has been a reduction, in many breeds, of the number of puppies being bred. This has reduced the size of the gene pool and led to loss of genetic diversity. One way in which this has been addressed has been by the importation of dogs from other countries to use in breeding programmes or by the importation of frozen semen.

Epigenetics is the process by which the expression of a gene can be affected by environmental factors so that the phenotype (what the animal looks like) may be different to the genotype. It has become an increasingly researched field in recent years and the variation caused by epigenetics can affect several generations. It applies not only to maternal lines but also to paternal lines and is described in humans as well as non-human animals. For example, it has been shown in humans that paternal diet can affect sperm quality and offspring health.[3]

Finally, it cannot be emphasised strongly enough that selection of parents should take into account emotional and cognitive health. Ideally both parents, but especially the mother, should be emotionally stable and exhibit a predominance of positive or engaging emotional motivations, which influence their cognitive processes and result in optimistic approach traits. Temperament is highly heritable and when offspring of a mating are likely to be used for future breeding stock, the potential to influence future generations should be considered. Temperament of the dam in particular not only has a genetic influence on the puppies but also could affect the impact of stressors that she experiences in pregnancy on the development of her unborn offspring. The quality of her maternal care may also be affected and go on to impact on the emotional development of the puppies in the litter. All of this has implications for the emotional stability of the puppies and the selection of breeding stock from perspectives other than that of physical health concerns is therefore very important.

The perfect dog does not exist so the final selection of potential parents will be based on a balance of all these factors and the two parents should be selected to complement each other. The aim is to produce puppies that are fit for function and can lead long, healthy and happy

Figure 2.1: Fit German Shorthaired Pointer bitch.
Photo: © Elizabeth Ayrton.

lives whether that be as pet dogs, breeding dogs or working dogs. Some key recommendations regarding the parents when breeding are the following.

- Ensure that sires and dams have reached maturity in terms of their physical and emotional health before breeding.
- Ensure that sires and dams are physically fit and healthy before mating and have been screened where possible for physical health issues.
- Ensure that both parents selected for breeding are emotionally and cognitively healthy. In bitches this is particularly important in order to reduce the risk of chronic physiological stress related to life events during pregnancy.

Mating

Mating can be natural or by artificial insemination (AI) using either frozen or fresh semen. In the UK, only non-surgical AI is used because surgical AI has been banned by the Royal College of Veterinary Surgeons. Non-surgical AI can be either transcervical or vaginal. However, transcervical is considered an act of veterinary surgery and therefore may only be carried out by a veterinary surgeon whereas vaginal insemination may be carried out by a suitably competent lay person. Transcervical AI is often used for frozen and chilled semen. Generally, natural mating has been considered to be the most successful method but increasingly AI, especially with fresh semen, can be a useful alternative. AI success depends on having good quality semen used at the correct time in the bitch's cycle and a good operator carrying out the insemination. The use of AI with frozen semen can limit the amount of travelling needed to achieve a mating with the dog of choice and also allows semen to be stored and brought in from different countries, which can increase the gene pool.

To achieve a successful mating, the bitch needs to be mated at the correct time in her oestrus cycle. The timing of this can vary widely with different bitches as the length of the oestrus cycle is variable, as is the timing of ovulation. Various methods are used to determine the optimal timing of mating for bitches, such as vaginal smears, use of a dog to indicate when she is ready, semiquantitative progesterone test kits and quantitative progesterone evaluation. Quantitative progesterone evaluation when done on more than one occasion gives the most accurate prediction of time of ovulation and based on this also gives the predicted date of whelping, which can be very useful to enable breeders to make necessary logistical arrangements. It does require blood samples to be taken and is the most expensive way to evaluate ovulation. However, knowing when the bitch is ready to be mated can reduce time and costs relating to making repeated journeys to the stud dog, make it more likely that the bitch and dog will mate and also maximise the number of puppies produced from that mating. This is because bitches produce multiple eggs normally and mating at the right time maximises the number of eggs fertilised and therefore the number of puppies produced. Occasionally there is only one puppy but this is the exception rather than the rule.

Another consideration in relation to the mating process is the emotional impact of the experience for the stud and the bitch. Lust motivation needs to be significant for both parties in order for successful mating to occur and ensuring that they each have a predominance of positive emotional motivation will improve the chances of a better experience for the dogs and a more successful outcome for the breeder. Minimising protective emotions of fear-anxiety, pain or frustration will also help to optimise the experience.

Mating is usually done at the home of the stud dog to give him the added confidence of being in familiar surroundings and optimising his emotional health at the point of mating. It is important to spend time introducing the stud and the bitch to optimise the emotional balance for both of them. Bitches can sometimes react confrontationally towards stud dogs when the dog attempts to mount them and this has implications for the stud in terms of reducing their confidence or even leading to injuries. Confrontational responses from the bitch can be indicative of problems from her perspective. This may be related to poor timing of the mating and her not being at her most receptive, but it may also occur if she has a protective emotional bias for other reasons, such as fear-anxiety related to the novel surroundings. Selecting bitches with good emotional health will also be a factor as those with fear-anxiety motivation, which is triggered by a range of different stimuli, may be more prone to being in a protective emotional bias when mating is attempted. A bitch is also more likely to accept

Case study – natural matings

Liz Jay is an experienced breeder of Bearded Collies and has owned and handled several stud dogs. In recent years, she imported a dog from France, Leroy, to use at stud. His first mating was with a bitch whose caregivers had previously tried to mate to other stud dogs but had not been successful. Liz tried to introduce the dogs to each other but the bitch was not keen and bared her teeth and growled at him and he ran away. At this point Liz decided to give up.

I asked Liz how he then managed to go on and become a very successful stud dog after this experience. Liz explained that the next time she mated him she did so to one of her own bitches. This meant she could allow them lots of time to flirt together in the initial stages of her season. She then separated them until the bitch was ready to mate, at which time they were given plenty of time to flirt again until he was ready to mate her. Once he had mated her, he was more confident, so she allowed him to mate the bitch several times during that season while the bitch was willing and after that he was keen to work.

Liz believes the key to successful stud work is having time to allow the dogs to become introduced on long leads so they can be controlled if the bitch reacts aggressively, and the dog can also be managed if he is very keen. She also believes that some dog–bitch combinations just do not work; the animals just do not like each other and you need to accept this. She suggests it is a good idea for caregivers of bitches to have a second dog in mind in case the dog they have chosen is not keen to mate the bitch. Also having enough people to handle the dog and bitch without lots of extra people standing round watching them is important. Liz feels that if an inexperienced dog does the wrong thing, such as try to mount the bitch from in front, it is best just to encourage the dog to move away and try again rather than tell him off, which can upset sensitive dogs and make them less likely to want to 'work' in the future.

delivery might be successful but if this is not possible or if the bitch has uterine inertia then a caesarean section under general anaesthetic may be necessary.

After a caesarean, most veterinary practices will discharge the bitch as soon as possible to allow her to bond with her puppies in her familiar surroundings. This is important from an emotional perspective both for the bitch and for her puppies. The breeder will ensure they have available transport, help to manage the bitch and puppies while being transported, a suitable box and bedding to put the puppies in and a source of heat to keep the puppies warm during the journey. The bitch needs to be closely monitored as she will be sleepy after having a general anaesthetic and so may inadvertently lie on puppies and squash them. It is important for the bonding process that the puppies are allowed to suckle the bitch as soon as possible so that they pick up her scent, which will aid in bonding, and this can sometimes be more problematical after a caesarean section. Ideally the puppies should be put on the bitch while she is recovering from her anaesthetic but the bitch will need to be monitored carefully as she will be physically uncoordinated as she recovers and may be overwhelmed by the presence of the puppies as she regains consciousness. If there is a delay in physically placing the puppies with the bitch it is better if they are dried but not excessively cleaned so that they retain necessary scent. The smoother the anaesthetic recovery for the bitch and the less physiological stress she experiences the more likely she is to go on and mother her puppies successfully.

The breeder will need to be on hand at home to watch both the bitch and the puppies closely especially in the 24 hours following a caesarean. Food and water for the bitch needs to be readily accessible so that she does not need to move too far away from puppies and the breeder needs to be present to intervene if for any reason the bitch shows signs of rejecting her offspring.

Rejection is more likely following surgery as the bitch has not had the natural process of licking her puppies and bonding with them slowly as they were born. They may also smell of the veterinary surgery rather than her if they have been excessively 'cleaned off'. This bonding process is likely to be even harder following caesarean for a first pregnancy. A caesarean section is major abdominal surgery and the wound is very close to the mammary tissue where the puppies will suckle. Excellent postoperative care including successful pain management is therefore crucial. A painful wound is one of the reasons that a bitch is unlikely to want the puppies suckling and can contribute to rejection. Puppies will have a far better chance of survival and of developing optimally in relation to their emotional and cognitive health if they are raised by the bitch. For this reason, it is worth persevering with the introduction of the puppies to the dam and careful supervision to ensure she bonds with them in the early days is a valuable investment of the breeder's time. Even the most attentive hand rearing is a poor substitute for natural mothering but in some circumstances it may be necessary.

The bitch might need additional care in the first few weeks following a caesarean section. She may be physically tired while recovering from major surgery but she may also struggle to eat as gastric reflux is a common complication when a heavily pregnant bitch is anaesthetised. She may need additional nursing care particularly in relation to encouraging her to eat in order to encourage milk production.

Care of the puppies

Once whelping has occurred, the role of the breeder in optimising the physical, emotional and cognitive health of the puppies becomes the priority. Physical healthcare requirements should be discussed with the veterinary practice and involve providing appropriate preventative health care in the form of parasitic control, suitable nutrition after weaning, and vaccinations.

When considering the emotional and cognitive health of the puppies there are several things to consider dependent on the developmental stage that the puppy is at. Preventative emotional and cognitive healthcare is as important as physical healthcare and has implications for the rest of the puppies' lives.

Jakk Panksepp describes seven different emotional systems associated in the brain.[5] Four of these are present from birth.

- **Seeking (DESIRE) system** – This emotional system is involved in the seeking out of resources. For the newborn puppy these will be food and heat along with the safe protection of their mother. Later in life this system is a positive emotional system involved in general exploration and learning.
- **Frustration system** – This emotional system is activated when an animal is thwarted from achieving an expectation (for example, in a newborn puppy this could be triggered if access to the teat is unsuccessful). Note that the term 'rage' is used by Panksepp but can lead to confusion, due to some of the ways in which that word has been misused in the past in a veterinary context, and it is therefore less commonly used in the context of non-human animals. Frustration is a negative emotional system that protects the individual from failure and it is associated with more rapid and intense behavioural responses, often associated with confrontation. It also leads to problem-solving behaviours, which enable the individual to overcome barriers

to success. Learning to manage frustration is an important part of emotional development and is associated with developing realistic expectations in a variety of contexts. When expectations are unrealistic and frustration is readily triggered it can be detrimental to the individual and lead to problematic behavioural responses.

- **Fear (ANXIETY) system** – This is a negative emotional system that protects an animal from personal threat or threat to the resources that it needs to survive. In a newborn puppy this system would be activated when straying too far from the nest and starting to feel cold. In this situation the fear-anxiety leading to avoidance of the cold location combined with the desire-seeking motivation for warmth will bring the puppy back to the nest.
- **Panic (GRIEF) system** – This is a negative emotional system, which is activated in order to regain interaction with a nurturing source. In newborn puppies panic-grief motivated behaviours will solicit attention from the mother and reunite them. This system can also be activated later in life when animals lose a close and nurturing companion.

All four emotional circuits are essential to behavioural development and puppies need both positive and negative emotions to be activated at appropriate times in order for their behaviour to be balanced and their survival to be assured. In the sink analogy of emotional health developed by Dr Sarah Heath FRCVS (co-author of this chapter), Panksepp's negative emotional systems are referred to as protective emotions and the positive ones as engaging emotions. When the engaging emotional systems are predominant, such as desire-seeking, the behavioural responses of approach, engagement and interaction will be seen. When the protective emotions are predominant, such as fear-anxiety, frustration or panic-grief, there are four types of behavioural responses that can be displayed and these are referred to in the sink model as repulsion, avoidance, inhibition and appeasement. Within each of these responses there are a spectrum of behaviours varying from low to high intensity and individuals can display behaviours from more than one category at the same time as well as change between categories depending on their success.

- Repulsion – The aim of this response is to increase distance from and decrease interaction with the stimulus by causing it to take some form of action. Repulsion may be in the form of low intensity responses, such as grumbling or growling, or higher intensity behaviours, such as barking or biting.
- Avoidance – The aim of this response is to increase distance from and decrease interaction with the stimulus by the individual taking some form of action. Avoidance may be displayed in a low intensity form such as turning the head or may be more intense and involve hiding or running away.
- Appeasement – The aim of this response is to obtain more information about the situation or stimulus through any of the senses (visual, olfactory, auditory or tactile). It achieves this by exchanging information through gathering it from the stimulus and offering information to signal lack of threat in return. It can involve dogs engaging in behaviours such as licking and sniffing to gather pheromone information about another dog and rolling over or urinating to give information about themselves.
- Inhibition – The aim of this response is to obtain more information about the situation or stimulus through any of the senses (visual, olfactory, auditory or tactile). It

achieves this by gathering the information without offering anything in return. For example, when a puppy sees something for the first time, they may just stop and stare initially and wait until they have more information before selecting how to respond.

The emotions experienced by puppies and the behavioural responses that they display as a result will vary depending on their stage of development as well as their physical and social environment.

Care of the puppies up to 2-weeks old (neonatal period)

Puppies are born altricial – that is they are unable to sustain their own survival and have underdeveloped neurological systems. They are deaf and blind, and in the early stages of their life are reliant on parental care.

Puppies are motivated by desire-seeking to engage with their mother and will orientate towards her by gravitating towards heat and responding to touch. They can also respond to protective emotions and painful or threating stimuli. Although they are unable to hear, they do vocalise and make crying noises, which once the mother has finished whelping, she

Figure 2.3: Two-day-old puppy, note closed eyes, and nose as yet unpigmented. Photo: © Elizabeth Ayrton.

Figure 2.4: Two-day-old puppy showing lack of canalisation of external ear canal meaning the puppy is deaf at this stage. Photo: © Elizabeth Ayrton.

maternal care has led to differences in adult behaviour in response to physical and social engagement and 'aggression' in work carried out to assess military working dogs.[7]

During the neonatal period, human interaction with the puppies is valuable and research has shown that handling is important for puppies from an early age. Handling has been shown to increase calmness and to increase the length of time before vocalisation when the puppies are left on their own. The puppies receiving handling also show more exploratory activity compared with puppies that are handled less.[8]

Transitional period (2–3-weeks old)

During this period there is a wealth of physical development, which will impact not only on the physical health of the puppy but also on their emotional and cognitive health as they are able to learn more about their environment and display a wider range of behavioural responses to their emotional motivations. One of the major physical developments is the opening of the eyes and ears, which increases the puppies' abilities to gather information from the world around them. Their locomotory abilities also change at this stage of development and the puppies start to support weight on their limbs and display behaviours such as sitting, standing and starting to walk. Towards the end of this period, they also start to eliminate spontaneously.

At this stage, a fifth emotional system influences their development. This is the social play system, which is a positive, or engaging, emotional system and motivates behavioural interactions, which are crucial for learning appropriate social skills with other dogs within a safe and secure context. When both parties are motivated by social play the rehearsal of threatening

responds to by showing care motivated behaviour towards them.

In this early stage of development, the breeder's prime responsibility is to care for the bitch so that her physical, emotional and cognitive health is optimal and she can provide the best care possible for her puppies. She is responsible for providing their nutrition and taking care of them physically through providing warmth and licking to clean them and to stimulate them to eliminate. As she starts to lactate, she will need increasing nutrition. Her physical health should be monitored carefully to ensure early onset of treatment for common problems that may arise post whelping such as mastitis, which will make suckling painful, and uterine discharges, which can be associated with noticeable deterioration in the bitch's demeanour.

It has been shown in rats that maternal care involving more licking and grooming of the young in the first 10 days of life affects the developing HPA axis leading to reduced detrimental responses to physiological stress, which persists throughout life.[6] In dogs increased

Figure 2.5: Social play between two 4-week-old litter mates.
Photo: © Elizabeth Ayrton.

interactions is possible and each individual can learn how to threaten and be threatened without the triggering of fear-anxiety.

Driven by social play motivation litter mates will play intense physical games involving behaviours such as growling, biting and wrestling, and will do so with significant intensity. In the early stages, the bitch may also engage in social play with her puppies but as they develop it becomes more likely to involve the puppies playing with one another. Through this form of interaction puppies learn how to control behavioural responses and the term bite inhibition is often used to describe the way in which puppies learn when bite interactions are appropriate and when not. They also learn the appropriate amount of pressure to use with their mouths when engaging in social interaction. Litter mates will make a lot of noise when hurt in play, which teaches others to control their interactions and the dam will also respond to inappropriate interactions at this age thereby helping the puppies to develop appropriate social skills.

Social play is not only important for puppies to learn about appropriate use of threat and successful response to it but also to learn appropriate

engaging behaviours and to start to recognise the signalling and body language of other dogs. Orphaned pups who do not have maternal care can struggle to learn these skills and single puppies who do not have the benefit of interaction with litter mates may also be at a disadvantage. These individuals will need social interactions as soon as it is possible with an appropriate canine companion in order to learn to have successful relationships with other dogs and to know when it is inappropriate to approach another dog.

Socialisation or sensitive period (3–18 weeks, approximately)

During this period, the puppies continue their physical development with increasing capability in terms of locomotion and use of their sensory systems. Catering for their physical needs is essential in terms of providing the opportunity for interactions with different surfaces and textures and making the physical environment increasingly complex and challenging in terms of their neurological development. At the same time consideration needs to be given to their emotional and cognitive development and it is important to remember that all three aspects of their health triad (physical, emotional and cognitive) are interlinked and cannot be thought about in isolation. During this period of development puppies are building up a bank of new experiences and it is critical that their exposure to many different stimuli and situations occurs when they are in a predominantly positive, or engaging, emotional bias. If a puppy is overwhelmed by an experience (for example, exposure to a loud noise or to too much activity or interaction) and enters into a negative or protective emotional state there is a risk that they will become sensitised to that stimulus and react with protective emotions in the future when they encounter it again. While it can be very tempting to want to introduce the puppies to as many sights, sounds and experiences as possible it is crucial to remember that more is not always better. Controlled introduction with a 'little and often' approach can enable the breeder to ensure that all of the puppies are driven by engaging emotions and can benefit from interacting with novelty in ways that set them up for success in later life.

In order to ensure that development during the socialisation period is successful the breeder needs to recognise when the puppy is struggling with a stimulus and becoming overwhelmed. It can be entirely appropriate for a puppy to display protective emotion in the form of fear-anxiety when they meet someone or something for the first time and it is important to allow them to take time to gather information, through inhibition or appeasement responses, and wait for the emotional motivation to change to an engaging system, such as desire-seeking, and the behavioural response to change to one of approach and engagement. This change is seen when puppies stop what they are doing briefly and watch or listen to something novel before cautiously approaching. The breeder should pay careful attention to the puppies' behaviour during these introductions. If they show intense behaviours associated with protective emotion, such as avoidance behaviours, trying to move away, or intense inhibition, standing and staring for a prolonged period, it is important to reduce the impact or intensity of the stimulus. Once the puppy has recovered, the stimulus can be re-introduced in a way that is less intense. The process of introduction to new stimuli and experiences at this early age is going to form the basis of the puppies' responses to the social and physical environment as adults. If negative, protective, emotions are generated in association with experiences at this young age it is

likely that low intensity behavioural responses of avoidance, inhibition and appeasement will be seen. While these responses may not be viewed as being significantly problematic at this age it is important to remember that they may intensify or alter as the puppy matures. More intense responses and 'repulsion' behaviour at a later age can lead to significant difficulties for the puppy and their new caregiver. If the earlier behaviours have been overlooked or misinterpreted, then the puppy can become labelled as difficult, so early recognition of the low intensity and more passive behavioural responses to protective emotions is essential so that later problems can be avoided.

The aim is to appropriately introduce puppies to a wide range of stimuli and experiences and some to be considered include the following.

◆ **Noises** – It is important to ensure that the sounds are not overwhelming. For example, getting a puppy exposed to the noise of a vacuum cleaner should start with hearing it at reduced intensity either via a recording or with someone vacuuming at a distance and for a short space of time. As the puppies become familiar with the noise, they can be exposed to it for longer and at closer proximity. The human domestic environment is a very noisy one and there are a wide range of noises that puppies should ideally be exposed to early in life. While experiencing a home environment and a garden can supply many of the common noises, such as appliances, people, other pets, birds, distant traffic and so on, it is advisable to expand the range by using recordings of more unusual noises, or those that do not exist in the breeding environment. The Dogs Trust provides free access to a compilation of soundtracks, including the 'Sounds Sociable' collection, which comes with a comprehensive manual and guidance as to how to introduce the sounds to ensure that the puppies form positive emotional associations (https://soundcloud.com/dogstrust/sets/sound-therapy-sounds-sociable).

- **People** – Puppies need careful exposure to a variety of people from an early age while adhering to the same important principle of ensuring that they are in a positive, engaging, emotional bias. Gradual introduction to the sight, sound and scent of people can be followed by gradual exposure to handling. When puppies are very young it can be so tempting to rush in to pick them up but it is important to consider their emotional responses and ensure that introductions are gradual and respectful. Variety is also key – it is useful for puppies to meet and be handled by men, women, gentle children and older people, to be exposed to people wearing different things like headscarves and hats, and to see people who may walk 'differently' or use sticks or mobility aids. Handling gently all over the body including lifting ear flaps, looking at eyes, handling paws and running hands over the body is important preparation for veterinary examination but also for the delivery of first aid if that should be necessary in the future. For long coated dogs it is good to introduce them to the concept of being groomed – this could include putting them on a grooming table with a snuffle mat or a scatter of treats once they are able to eat solid food. Grooming can start with something gentle, such as a grooming mitt or a plastic type of brush, and progressed to using a soft brush.
- **Other dogs and other domestic pets** – Exposure to older safe dogs can be beneficial provided it is done with careful monitoring to ensure that neither the puppy nor the older dog are overwhelmed. Similarly, introduction to other domestic species within the household can be beneficial and help to prepare puppies for life in multi-species households with their new caregivers.
- **Movement** – The domestic world is full of movement, sometimes silent and sometimes in combination with noise. Introducing young puppies to moving objects, such as brushes, mops, bikes, prams and skateboards, can be beneficial in the early weeks of life and this can be expanded to introduction to traffic from a safe distance. Exposure to differing objects in the environment not only assists with emotional development but also helps physical development through stimulating and developing the nervous system. Walking on different surfaces, such as a smooth tile, a piece of carpet, a rubber mat, a piece of tarpaulin, can be beneficial and specifically designed sensory mats can also be used. The provision of safe toys for the puppies to explore is another part of this process and it does not have to be expensive, puppies love exploring cardboard boxes that have little windows and doors cut in them and a cut down cardboard box can also be filled with balls to make a ball pool to explore.
- **Isolation** – In addition to considering the various stimuli that puppies need to be introduced to in a domestic environment it is also important to remember that the majority of domestic dogs will be expected to spend some time alone. Puppies should therefore also be introduced to very short periods of solitude and as they develop it can be helpful if the breeder gives them very brief spells away from their litter mates. It is important that the puppy is given some positive perception of this time alone, through provision of a toy or some

Figure 2.6: Pen set-up for puppies – note the objects to play with both on the floor and suspended and also the different surfaces. Photo: © Elizabeth Ayrton.

food, and it is better to do this exercise when they have eaten and are tired as they are more likely to settle and sleep.

- **Car travel** – The majority of puppies will travel to their new home by car and introduction to cars is therefore an important part of the rearing process. Getting puppies used to the stationary car, the stationary car with the engine running and the moving car with their litter mates in a crate will help them on the day when they finally leave the breeder.

The amount of introduction to novelty that can be done at the breeder's premises during the socialisation period will not only be limited by the environment but also by the time available. It is essential to remember that gradual controlled exposure at this age is crucial. Trying

Figure 2.7: Puppy engaging in object play at 3-weeks old. Photo: © Elizabeth Ayrton.

Anne Taylor has had dogs for many years and has shown, bred and judged Labradors and worked her dogs. She has a reputation in south Cumbria for breeding calm well-adjusted Labrador Retrievers. Anne lived in a lovely house down a very quiet road, which was a dead end and so there was little passing traffic. The house itself was surrounded by quite large gardens so the dogs would see little from the house. She was asked how she managed to breed and rear such well-adjusted puppies given that things were so quiet at home.

Her answer was as follows. From about 4 weeks old the pups come into the living room, one or two at a time, to play and watch the television. They have a radio on in their room next to the kitchen, and hear the washing machine, hoover, pans, dishes and so on in the kitchen. Anyone who comes to the house is encouraged to see the pups and talk to them, but not touch. My pups first go out in the car when they are about 6-weeks old. I take them to a supermarket car park and open the back of the car so they can watch people and cars coming and going from their cage. Normally people stop to talk to them but they are not allowed to touch the pups at this stage because they have not been vaccinated yet. We take runs out in the car to get them used to the movement and sound of it before they go to their new homes. Once vaccinated they start walking on leads, short distances, anywhere there are people and things going on. They are free to talk to people now and can learn about bikes, prams, children and much more.

I generally take two pups and leave one in the car, with an older dog, while walking the other one, to teach them to think for themselves. They also go to puppy classes a few times, if possible, to get them used to other dogs and breeds. I am a believer that pups should experience as much as possible before they go to their new homes. Time consuming but well worth it if it enables them to adjust to their future lives with no problems.

to do too much and overwhelming the puppies can be detrimental so it is important to think in terms of preparing the puppies for the next stage of their development in the new home, rather than completing the task.

Weaning

The process of weaning is about much more than just starting the puppies on solid food. It is about the slow withdrawal of the mother's milk and her interaction. As the dam starts to move away without allowing the puppies to suckle to satiation, they will experience a degree of frustration. This is to be expected as they have a high expectation of their mother and her milk

being freely available to them. In order to reduce the impact of this frustration, the process of weaning has been very gradually prepared for over the preceding weeks. In the initial stages, the dam spends much time with the puppies licking them to clean them and stimulate elimination. She also keeps them warm and feeds them. Puppies suckle very frequently to start with as they take in colostrum and stimulate the dam's milk supply. Once the milk comes through after 2–3 days the puppies start to settle between episodes of feeding – it is at this stage that the bitch is often happy to leave them while they are asleep. These inter-suckling intervals are short at first but gradually extend as the puppies get older. At around 3–4 weeks of age solid food is introduced and this has numerous

Figure 2.8: Puppies spaced out around a feeder with individual bowls. Photo: © Elizabeth Ayrton.

benefits; it gets the puppies used to eating a solid diet before they go to their new home and also helps to supplement the bitch's milk as the puppies get increasingly large and take their toll on her. Introducing solid food is not only beneficial for the puppies' physical health but also prevents the bitch getting a potentially life-threatening condition called eclampsia, which happens when her serum calcium levels get low. Eclampsia is more common in bitches on a poor diet or those nursing a large litter of big puppies.

As puppies get their deciduous teeth around 4–6 weeks the bitch is less keen to allow them to suckle although she does not withdraw maternal attention and she will still be attentive to them and clean and lick them. With the breeder increasing the number of solid food meals being fed, the bitch can gradually withdraw the milk feeding and the weaning process naturally occurs. In addition to the physical benefits, weaning helps in setting realistic expectations for puppies over the availability of food and thereby improves their frustration tolerance.

When puppies are suckling from their mother there can be incidents of competition for teats and this can continue over solid food during the weaning process. Although the need to wait for access to food can be a helpful part of the process of developing frustration tolerance it is important to remember that food is an essential resource and restriction of access to it can lead to complications not only in terms of suboptimal nutrition but also emotionally. The process of eating should be associated with a predominantly parasympathetic state and it is therefore important for puppies to be given the opportunity to eat slowly and calmly. If this is not possible there may be health implications in relation to digestion and those puppies who are struggling to gain access to the food may also learn to value it more highly and to anticipate threat more readily in a feeding context. For these reasons it is advisable to give puppies individual bowls of solid food rather than one large communal bowl.

When puppies are orphaned, the human will supply all the care in terms of keeping them warm, stimulating them to eliminate and feeding them. It is important to remember that these puppies also need to experience a slow withdrawal of care so that they can be successfully weaned and learn to be behaviourally independent. This can be accomplished by giving them more time alone with a heat pad and a radio on for comfort, and by withdrawing the feeding of milk slowly as they start to take solid food. It is very easy for the human caregiver to enjoy the level of dependence that hand rearing brings but in order to provide these puppies with the best chance of a normal life in the future it is important that they learn to be independent and to be a dog, so ideally these orphaned puppies should also be given suitable interaction with calm dogs.

The new caregiver

Communication between the breeder and the new caregiver is key. Ideally, the puppy will have got to know the new caregiver in the breeder's house through a series of visits before being transferred to the new home. The puppy should therefore be used to the smell and voice of the new caregiver and have been handled by them. It is important for the new caregiver to know how the puppy has been cared for so far. Information about the physical health of the puppy, the worming and vaccination records and what and when the puppy is being fed is commonly provided in documentation that the breeder gives to the caregiver on collection of the puppy. In addition, the breeder should talk to the new caregiver about the puppy's emotional and cognitive development and explain what has been done in terms of habituation, socialisation and non-social environmental learning already and how the new caregiver can successfully continue these processes in the new home.

Continuity between the breeder's home and that of the new caregiver is beneficial for the puppy and it is important to have some food to take from the breeders so there is no sudden change in diet as well as a blanket and some toys that have been in the pen for a couple of days so carry the scent of the dam and litter mates. Ensuring familiarity for the puppy on arrival in the new home can help to ensure a positive emotional bias and the new caregiver should provide the puppy with a secure and safe resting place. The use of scent signals through commercial pheromone products can be beneficial as they provide a link between the maternal scent signals and the new environment. The diffuser style products should be switched on at least 24 hours before the puppy comes to their new home as it takes this time for the oil to heat up, become volatile and thereby release the pheromone analogue into the atmosphere. There is now a legal requirement in the UK for puppies to be microchipped at 8 weeks and the only exceptions to this are if a vet certifies that microchipping could adversely affect the dog's health or for some working dogs for whom it can be delayed to 12 weeks of age. For most pet dogs, microchipping will therefore have been done before they leave the breeder and the necessary certification should be provided. The new caregiver will also need to complete the transfer of ownership paperwork and ensure that the chip is registered to them at the new address.

Once the puppy leaves the breeder's premises their job is largely complete but reputable breeders are keen to maintain ongoing communication with new caregiver and this support can be very beneficial. The aim is for the puppy to go on to have a long and happy life in a safe secure home with a good bond between them and their caregiver. Sadly, this is not always the case and research suggests that behavioural problems are the number one reason for euthanasia in dogs under 1 year of age.[9] Ensuring a breeding approach that acknowledges the equal importance of physical, emotional and cognitive health at every step of the journey from parental selection to delivery of the puppy to his/her new home will be an important factor in changing this statistic.

Final words

Throughout the breeding process from planning the mating, through pregnancy, whelping and the stages of puppyhood before they move to their new homes, a behaviourally minded approach can be taken. By having behaviour in mind at each stage, responsible breeders are setting the puppies up for success and a happy life.

Further reading

England, G. and Von Heimendahl, A. (eds) (2010) *BSAVA Manual of Canine and Feline Reproduction and Neonatology*, 2nd edition. BSAVA, Gloucester.

References

1. Patronek, G.J., Glickman, L.T., Back, A.M., McCabe, G.P. and Ecker, C. (1996) Risk factors for relinquishment of dogs to an animal shelter. *Journal of the American Veterinary Medical Association* 209(3), 572–581.
2. Oberbauer, A.M. et al. (2002) Inheritance of hypoadrenocorticism in Bearded Collies. *American Journal of Veterinary Research* 63(5), 643–647.
3. Schagdarsurengin, U. and Steger, K. (2016) Epigenetics in male reproduction: effect of paternal diet on sperm quality and offspring health. *Nature Reviews Urology* 13, 584–595.
4. Huizink, A.C. et al., (2003) Stress during pregnancy is associated with developmental outcome in infancy. *Journal of Child Psychology and Psychiatry* 44(6), 810–818.
5. Panksepp, J. (2004) *Affective Neuroscience: The Foundations of Human and Animal Emotions*. Oxford University Press, Oxford.
6. Liu, D. et al. (1997) Maternal care, hippocampal glucocorticoid receptors, and hypothalamic-pituitary-adrenal responses to stress. *Science* 277(5332), 1659–1662.
7. Foyer, P. et al. (2016) Levels of maternal care in dogs affect adult offspring temperament. *Science Reports* 6, 19253.
8. Gazzano, A. et al. (2008) Effects of early gentling and early environment on emotional development of puppies. *Applied Animal Behaviour Science* 110(3–4), 294–304.
9. O'Neill, D.G., Church, D.B., McGreevy, P.D., Thomson, P.C. and Brodbelt, D.C. (2013) Longevity and mortality of owned dogs in England. *The Veterinary Journal* 198, 638–643.

Chapter 3

Training

Tamsin Durston

'She's your heart-dog', my instructor told me during a training session, 'You both understand how the other feels, and that connection makes your training successful.' She is so right, the quality of our relationship creates the foundation for everything we teach our dogs; how they feel about us, and the world around them, really matters.

In this chapter I aim to provide an overview of the basic concepts involved in dog training, while demonstrating the benefits of doing so with insight into dogs' normal behaviour, compassion for their perspective on life, and knowing how to make them feel like absolute superstars.

Dogs learn best when they feel safe, happy, and connected to the person training them

Training can generally be defined as 'the process of learning the knowledge and skills required for a particular job or activity',[1] and it is helpful because life is not always intuitive. I can safely

Cat the dog

'Cat the dog' is a stunning Staffordshire Bull Terrier puppy, belonging to my friends Neil and Louisa. They sensibly thought ahead to the kind of lifestyle they wanted to lead with Cat, which included visiting local dog-friendly restaurants and pubs – after walkies of course! They could have just taken the chance that Cat would comfortably relax in busy places, with the additional temptation of food being served. But that is a risky strategy, and Neil and Louisa did not want to gamble on Cat struggling and having a difficult time. They decided to train her to settle on a blanket, calmly and quietly. This would avoid any inconvenience for people

Figure 3.1: Cat as a proper wee pup. Photo: © Tamsin Durston.

Figure 3.2: Cat practising 'settle'. Photo: © Tamsin Durston.

Figure 3.3: Cat settle practice in a crate at dog-friendly cafe in street. Photo: © Tamsin Durston.

eating or drinking nearby, with Cat less likely to become excited, frustrated or worried by the hustle and bustle.

Interestingly, the challenging part of this training was politely preventing people from unsettling Cat by saying hello to her. Considerately managing well-meaning folks, who just want to meet your beautiful puppy, is an important element of training out in the real world. Inadvertently, people with the best intentions can quickly and easily 'undo' all your hard work. That is because, even with plenty of training, dogs are learning all the time. Dogs can find it very confusing when their owner is encouraging them to do one thing, such as settle down calmly, while someone else is encouraging them to come and say hello.

Neil and Louisa discovered that training certainly pays off. They can now visit any dog-friendly establishment knowing Cat will feel relaxed, settling comfortably without disturbing anyone. Thanks to a lot of training practice, if Cat does get taken by surprise by someone who just cannot resist rushing over – whether she wants to meet them or not, it is a hard life being irresistible – she quickly recovers and settles down again.

say there was absolutely no way I would have made sense of Excel spreadsheets without someone training me. Training a dog to behave just as we wish might feel imposing, but needn't be forceful or compulsive, and it certainly does not mean quashing their personality. It is a vital component of responsible, considerate dog ownership; enabling us, our dogs and communities to live happily together.

The importance of understanding how dogs learn

A general definition of learning is the 'acquisition of knowledge or skills through study, experience or being taught'.[2] This enables individuals, whether dogs or humans, to adapt their behaviour in order to survive, reaping the benefits of interactions and experiences.[3] Understanding how dogs learn helps explain why they might sometimes behave in ways we do not like, allowing us to be less frustrated and more forgiving when they do.

Learning by connecting separate events that always happen simultaneously or extremely closely together in time

Through experiencing repeated patterns of events reliably happening in *exactly the same way each time*, dogs learn that certain things *always* lead directly to others.[4] Scientist Ivan Pavlov's name might ring a bell? He accidentally discovered this in the 1890s, while investigating digestion in dogs. Pavlov noticed the dogs in his laboratory begin to salivate as soon as researchers arrived carrying food, and assumed salivation was associated with immediately being fed.

Pavlov introduced a unique sound just before feeding the dogs to see if they learned to associate this with imminently receiving food. He used a metronome, as its neutral, monotonous tone was unlikely to disturb the dogs. Just as predicted, it was not long before they began to salivate immediately upon hearing it, having learned it always led to food being delivered.[5]

This type of learning, where a profound association forms between something neutral (the metronome) and something meaningful (the food), is termed Pavlovian or classical conditioning. Once learned, the association is so strong that the neutral event produces the same response as the meaningful event. A rather scary example is 1920s 'Little Albert' experiment, involving a nine-month-old child.[6] Psychologist John. B. Watson wondered whether children could learn to feel frightened of something completely neutral, if this became associated with a scary sound. Watson used a rat, which Little Albert was not at all scared of. He was, however, terrified of loud noises. Watson placed the rat in front of Little Albert, then panicked him by suddenly striking a steel bar just behind him. Watson repeated this several times until Little Albert grew frightened as soon as the rat appeared.

What is truly fascinating is that Little Albert then became frightened of other furry animals, including a rabbit and a dog. Although Watson did not intend it, Little Albert's brain abstractly extended the 'rat and scary noise' association to 'furry animal and scary noise'. This makes sense given that learning helps protect us from what we perceive as dangerous, to help us thrive. Needless to say, this experiment would not be permitted today.

Neil and Louisa introduced 6.30 am walkies before breakfast. After just a few days, whenever either of them began to slip on their shoes, Cat would race to the front door, spin around on the spot then bounce up and down barking – every time! Cat had *learned* that someone putting on their shoes invariably led to her getting to experience the amazing outdoor world.

Without any training at all, Cat had learned when she was about to go for a walk. However, barking at 6.30 am is not generally considered socially acceptable, so Neil and Louisa were worried about upsetting their neighbours. They decided to *train* Cat to behave differently when they were preparing to go out together. Now, a puppy can just as easily learn to sit and wait quietly on a doormat before going out for walks, and Cat quickly did, but without training why on earth would they ever want to do that? Especially when their emotional and physiological response to going out for a walk gets their heart pumping and their body ready for action, not sitting still and being quiet.

Learning through the consequences of behaviour, and how these make you feel

In 1927, psychologist Edward Thorndike published his 'Law of effect'.[7] This stated that a behaviour resulting in an unpleasant consequence is *much less* likely to be repeated than a behaviour that has an enjoyable outcome. Simply put, dogs are more likely to behave in ways that make them feel good.

Thorndike studied cats learning how to escape from boxes to enjoy tasty pieces of fish placed just outside. Eventually, they chanced upon pressing a lever, which immediately opened an escape hatch. After enjoying their fish, the cats were placed back inside the box to see how quickly they escaped again. Escaping became quicker, then instantaneous, as the cats learned to press the lever straight away and release themselves. Through trial and error, the cats learned that scratching or pouncing behaviours were never successful, but lever-pressing *always* worked out well for them.[8]

Behaviourist B.F. Skinner investigated this further, naming this way of learning 'operant conditioning'. This describes an individual *operating* on their environment to bring about a desired consequence.[9] Skinner placed rats inside boxes containing levers, which would release food when pressed. However, the boxes could also administer an electric shock.

Reinforcement

Just like Thorndike's cats, Skinner's rats soon learned that lever-pressing always resulted in food. Because this was a welcome outcome, 'lever-pressing behaviour' was reinforced and indeed, the rats would press the lever again and again.[10] Skinner termed this *positive reinforcement*, using the mathematical term positive, meaning 'added', because food was *added* to the rat's world in response to them pressing the lever.

Next, Skinner ran electricity through the box, shocking the rats. Now, pressing the lever immediately turned the current off, stopping the shock. Unsurprisingly, the rats quickly learned to press the lever. Again, this initially happened accidentally, but because it *always* resulted in the same good consequence the rats quickly learned how to stop being shocked whenever Skinner turned the electricity on.

'Lever-pressing behaviour' was repeated and strengthened as before, but this time Skinner termed it *negative reinforcement*. He used the mathematical term negative, meaning 'subtracted', because the consequence of lever-pressing behaviour was the electric shock being *removed*.

Thanks to Skinner, we can see that: behaviours that have *beneficial consequences* become more likely, because they make the dog feel good, in two ways.[11]

- **Positively** – by introducing something the dog finds valuable to them or their environment.
- **Negatively** – by removing something the dog finds unpleasant, from them or their environment.

A simple mantra to remember this, shared by many an instructor, is 'a behaviour that is rewarded will be repeated'.

Punishment (in the scientific sense of the word)

The opposite of reinforcement, punishment weakens behaviour, making it less likely to happen again. This happens when a dog finds the consequence of their behaviour unpleasant and would likely make an effort to avoid.

Behaviours that have *detrimental consequences* become less likely, because they make the dog feel bad in two ways.[12]

- **Positively** – *introducing something a dog finds unpleasant*, to them or their environment.
- **Negatively** – *removing something a dog values*, from them or their environment.

Distinguishing between punishment and reinforcement can sometimes be difficult, as we might be doing both at the same time. Strengthening one behaviour might naturally weaken, or punish, another.

Neil and Louisa wanted to make sure Cat would always be welcomed by friends and family, however, Cat naturally wanted to jump up at anyone meeting her. Unfortunately, several people responded to this by leaning down and giving her a fuss. Because Cat really enjoys this type of interaction, 'jumping up behaviour' was positively reinforced by the pleasant consequence of receiving a fuss. This often happens with puppies who are so small that jumping up does not risk knocking anyone over but can be a real problem when they are bigger.

Louisa realised she needed to train Cat not to jump up. At the same time, she would need help from people, especially friends and family, not to encourage and reinforce it. Technically, Louisa wanted to punish jumping up behaviour and make it less likely to ever happen again, however, she set about reinforcing a different 'greeting other people' behaviour instead.

Louisa and Neil always had treats ready whenever they were about to meet friends and family. They encouraged Cat to remain on all fours by feeding her treats while she remained on the floor. Now, as much as

Cat loves treats, she actually prefers a fuss when meeting people. So, Neil and Louisa asked whoever was present to *only* give Cat a fuss if she kept her paws on the ground. The combination of 'fuss and treats' made Cat feel good about keeping her paws on the floor, positively reinforcing 'standing while greeting' behaviour. If Cat suddenly jumped up, the greeter would be asked to immediately withdraw their attention and stop interacting with Cat completely. This negatively punished jumping up by removing the interaction Cat valued and enjoyed.

Through a combination of positive reinforcement and negative punishment, jumping up behaviour eventually disappeared altogether. 'Standing while greeting' behaviour is now much more likely, always resulting in the outcome Cat wants and making her feel good. She gets a fuss – fabulous – and treats too – bonus.

Reinforcement played a vital role in training Cat how to behave, with punishment only happening if she jumped up. More times than not, quickly encouraging her to stand and eat a treat *before* getting a fuss was generally sufficient to avoid any jumping up at all – dogs do what works out well for them after all.

Dogs do not understand these terms, what really matters is how they *feel* about the consequence of their behaviour. Training with rewards a dog values creates anticipation for them, and we can all identify with the exhilarating feeling of something good about to happen. This expectancy releases the body's natural 'feel-good' chemistry, which can be so influential that a dog might actively seek out further opportunities to experience it.[13] Furthermore, scientific evaluation supports reward-based methods over punishment as the most beneficial training techniques, for both dog and owner.[14,15] I would much rather my dog feel good about doing something, looking forward to her reward, than do it just because she is worried about what might happen if she does not.

Reinforcement feels rewarding … but how does punishment feel?

Punishment makes it uncomfortable for a dog to behave in a particular way, but does not stop them from *wanting* to, which could create emotional conflict.[16] For example, a dog might suppress their desire to bark at another dog in the street if they have been yanked on-lead for doing so in the past. Inhibiting desired behaviour through fear of the consequences is likely to feel scary, frustrating or overwhelming – feelings that could affect overall happiness.

There might be times in our dogs' lives where we cannot avoid negative punishment, for example, safety reasons when we might need to remove items they value. It is always worth thinking about how to turn what might be negatively punishing experiences, such as tidying away our dogs' toys or leaving them alone for short periods, into feel-good experiences. However, people commonly think of punishment as consequences such as smacking, water-sprays, choke collars and electric shocks. We have no way of communicating 'If you lunge at another dog, you will be yanked by the neck,' hoping this prospect alone deters them from lunging. For dogs to associate lunging behaviour with the consequence of being yanked, they have to experience it.

Some people might find such methods acceptable within everyday life, some perhaps only in specific situations where dangerous behaviour could result in a disastrous outcome for the dog or someone else; for example, using an electric shock collar to stop a dog chasing livestock. Others might find positive punishment completely unacceptable. Management strategies preventing a dog from performing the

dangerous behaviour, rather than deliberately causing potential pain or distress, offer an effective alternative. For example, completely avoiding livestock or, if impossible, keeping the dog on a short lead when livestock are present and positively reinforcing them for walking nicely.

Skinner warned punishment should be used cautiously, with consideration, due to potentially negative effects.[17,18]

- Punishment could result in a dog behaving aggressively as a means of self-protection, wanting to drive away the threatening or painful punisher.
- Pain, fear or perceived threat arising through punishment could be associated with other things nearby. For example, a dog running towards a group of children in the park, who experiences an electric shock as a punishment for ignoring their owner, might consequentially associate the pain of the shock with children. They might then feel threatened and frightened by children in future, potentially behaving aggressively towards them as a means of self-protection.
- Punishment risks damaging the dog–owner bond, if a dog becomes anxious about their owner sometimes being relaxed and comforting, but other times angry and frightening.

The trouble with positive punishment is that it appears to work well, and quickly too, so it is naturally rewarding for the owner – they wanted to stop their dog behaving in a certain way, and now they have. Because rewarded behaviour will be repeated they might well be likely to use punishment again, and it could easily become a habit.

Additionally, the undesirable behaviour might simply be suppressed until such a time when the dog is so motivated to behave in the way they really want to, *that they do*, ignoring the risk of experiencing the unpleasant punishment. This could make an owner feel the level of positive punishment they were using is not working, so needs to be increased – but where does that stop?

Punishment does not offer any information about *how* to behave, it only informs *how not* to behave. If I asked my dog, I reckon she would much prefer me to help her behave in 'the right way' then reward her over being told off for 'getting it wrong', especially when she has no concept of what is right and wrong in the first place. Given what we know about the power of feeling good about being rewarded, would any dog choose differently?

Learning by observing the way others behave

Observational or 'social' learning is where a dog mimics behaviour they have seen other dogs or people doing.[19] This an area of growing interest among the scientific community, discovering more about the complexities of dogs' mental ability. However, when training our dogs, we can use their desire 'to be included' advantageously by being either calm and relaxed, or energetic and active, when we want them to be too.

Learning through play

Dogs play throughout their whole lives, with objects, and other dogs, animals or people with whom they have a trusting relationship.[20] Play can help dogs learn whether a new situation or object is dangerous or not, and how different items may be interacted with. Playing with littermates, then other dogs as they grow older, might help dogs learn how to avoid hazardous social situations. It also offers an opportunity to practice enjoyable social interaction in a safe setting.[21]

If playing with toys and their owner is something a dog really enjoys, this can be used to reinforce desired behaviour.

The better we get to know and understand not only our own dogs but also the entire species, the stronger our connection with them. We will get the most out of training if we understand what it means to be a pet dog and how they view the world.

When Cat first met Labrador Coconut, she paused, stood on tiptoes, held her ears slightly backwards and tail straight behind her, then ran up to the larger dog's side, jumping up to try and grab Coconut's ear. Coconut stood still, became very tense, tucked her tail beneath her and turned her head away from Cat.

Cat did not appear to notice Coconut's attempts to politely decline any sort of interaction and continued to jump up at her ears. Recognising Coconut was uncomfortable, and that Cat was now trying even harder to get Coconut to respond to her, Louisa immediately produced a fluffy toy from her pocket and called Cat's name.

Thanks to Neil and Louisa training Cat to respond to her name, by rewarding her many times in many different situations, Cat looked at Louisa now and saw the treasured toy – associated with great fun and excitement. Cat had a dilemma, continue trying to get Coconut to play or take up Louisa's offer of an exhilarating game. Louisa helped influence Cat's decision by animating the toy, encouraging her to pounce on it. Cat chose to leave Coconut in favour of playing with Louisa. Louisa positively reinforced this excellent decision with an exciting game of 'chase and tuggy', while Coconut happily trotted off to enjoy the smells of the park.

Using play to reward Cat for coming back enabled Louisa to give her exactly the type of exciting, physical activity she was expecting to engage in with Coconut. This type of experience makes Cat feel really good – how lovely that she got to associate this feeling with Louisa, deepening their bond.

Figures 3.4 and 3.5: Cat practising focusing on her owner rather than other dogs in the park. Photos: © Tamsin Durston.

Understanding dogs

Dogs live in groups, forming strong bonds while communicating, compromising and collaborating effectively.[22] They see well at dawn and dusk, can focus on fast movement, and hear high-pitched sounds across great distances, so they are good hunters.[23] They will also scavenge – why waste an opportunity to eat? However, their renowned sense of smell is perhaps what most consider dogs' 'superpower', even though there's still much to learn about it.[24]

Dogs are emotional, feeling what we experience as grief, panic, fear, anger and frustration, a desire to socially connect, lust and pleasure-seeking.[25] Just like us, they can experience more than one emotion at the same time, for example be frightened by something but also frustrated because they cannot avoid it.[26] However, they do not have a 'moral code' like us humans do. Dogs do not understand right or wrong, they just know what works out well for them, or not.[27]

When you live in a group, the better able you are to communicate, the more likely you are to thrive.[28] Dogs communicate with body language.[29] Postures, facial expressions and body movements range from the obvious, such as lunging and baring teeth, to the very subtle indeed. For example, a quick flick of the tongue or blink of the eyes can carry a great deal of meaning, and yet might be easily missed. The context in which behaviour happens is key, so when interpreting a dog's communication, observe their body and consider the circumstances.

Dogs also communicate through a range of vocalisations.[30] For example, a low growl might suggest unease or discomfort, while successive high-pitched, short, yaps could indicate frustration. Dogs also communicate with pheromones, and through shedding scent into the environment from various glands, urine, faeces and their fur.[31] This leaves a chemical 'message' for others about them as an individual. This type of social communication is vital for dogs, but as it is so different to our own, we might not pay it enough attention.

When we first started breeding dogs specifically for hunting and land management, we chose them for their skills and abilities.[32] As they became our pets, we began to choose dogs for their appearance, creating the huge variety of breeds we love today.[33] We might view particular breeds as having natural talents, for

How can we tell our dogs they are getting it right?

A *marker* is a way of telling your dog, *exactly at the time they are doing the behaviour you want*, that you are immediately going to begin delivering, or allow them access to, their reward.[40] Most people use a word like 'yes', but you can also use a handheld, mechanical device that makes a clicking sound, or a physical signal like a 'thumbs up' – useful if your dog is deaf.

Your dog needs to learn the marker means 'your reward is now on its way'. To teach this, sound the marker then immediately give them a reward – using treats is quick and easy. Repeat this several times so they associate the marker with receiving their reward. Once they have, you can mark a behaviour that you want, such as 'sit'. Mark exactly when your dog takes up a sitting position, then immediately follow this with a treat. Through successive repetition, your dog learns that sitting produces the marker which produces their reward. Because the consequence of sitting is the delivery of their reward, they will be more likely to sit again.

Consistency is key, so everyone training your dog should use the same marker, giving it precisely as the desired behaviour occurs.

Okay, realistically, we are not machines and no one is perfect, yet dogs are still trained, so do not worry if your timing is a teeny bit out, you will still be able to train your dog. But, if you mistime your marker so much that your dog cannot associate it with one particular behaviour, they might well become confused. Because they learn through association, the better your timing is the more helpful you are being.

Forgive yourself for mistakes and try your best not to make them again. Remember, you are learning at the same time as your dog, which is not necessarily straightforward.

Different training methods

Training is like giving dogs a puzzle to solve; our responsibility being to provide the information that helps them be correct first time. We want them to be relaxed, confident and enjoy training, so they will keep trying without feeling demotivated or anxious if they do not get it right straight away. One helpful 'clue' is the marker. You do not necessarily have to use a marker, as a reward being presented following the desired behaviour will still be reinforcing, however, a well-timed marker gives the dog much clearer information about *exactly* which behaviour to repeat.

With training we need to reinforce our chosen behaviour, but we need our dog to *do* that behaviour in the first place so we can.

Truth is, there are many ways to get a dog to behave in a particular way. Each will have pros and cons, depending on several factors including the behaviour itself, your collective previous experiences, your location and how motivated your dog is to gain the reward on offer in that moment, or how tempted they are by other activities.

Methods are also often combined – what matters is that you and your dog are enjoying yourselves, as that helps learning become a rewarding, meaningful experience.

Luring

Luring guides the dog into a specific behaviour, which is then marked and rewarded.[41] Move the lure, for example a treat or toy, for your dog to follow into your chosen movement or position. You could also carefully position it somewhere like your dog's bed, to lure them to that specific place. If the dog wants the reward enough, luring provides very clear information about how to behave to get it.

Luring might not be a suitable approach for complex behaviours, such as crossing paws over one another, because it can be difficult to lure a dog into moving individual body parts distinctly. But it can be a useful way for owners to begin training and practice consistently marking and rewarding behaviour as it happens. Luring is typically used to train dogs to sit and lie down, because they can gain a quick, easy reward for relatively simple, natural behaviours.

However, if a dog desperately wants the reward on offer, they might feel compelled to follow a lure, doing something they would actually prefer not to, and become emotionally conflicted – their desire for the reward outweighing their reluctance to do the behaviour. A dog might also become frustrated, upset or lose confidence about what to do if their owner suddenly tries to get them to do the

behaviour *without* the reward in their hand. Once the dog learns the desired behaviour, they are likely to do it as soon as the lure begins to move, especially if the owner gestures in the same way each time. At this point, the lure itself should gradually be removed, or 'faded', by being incrementally reduced until it is no longer present. The dog should now follow the owner's empty hand movement instead, still marked and rewarded.

Fading the lure completely means a dog will not rely on it, only performing the desired behaviour when they can see the reward beforehand. Very often, the owner's hand or arm movement continues to guide the dog, however, a verbal 'cue' can be introduced, triggering the desired behaviour without the need for any hand or arm movement.

Shaping

Shaping is where you break the behaviour you want to train into small steps, rewarding your dog for gradually progressing through these until reaching the end goal.[42]

Neil and Louisa's vet offers appointments to get dogs used to the clinic. Cat was initially worried about stepping onto the scales, so Louisa marked her for just looking at them. Louisa repeated this several times to help Cat associate looking at the scales with a good outcome.

Louisa then calmly waited for Cat to take a step towards the scales, then marked and rewarded her. Louisa took a step towards the scales to show Cat she had no concerns about approaching them herself, but did not drag or even encourage Cat over, just calmly waited for her to try moving closer herself, when she felt safe enough to do so.

Letting Cat go at her own pace made the scales 'a good place to go to but you can always choose to retreat from'. Encouraged by her choices being rewarded with good outcomes, Cat then took another step towards the scales. Louisa marked and rewarded. And so on, until Louisa had progressively shaped Cat to hop happily onto the scales, empowered through her own confidence and choices. No pushing or pulling, which might have made Cat associate the scales, or Louisa, with feeling uncomfortable.

Now when Cat visits the vet she jumps straight onto the scales, showing just how positively she has learned to feel about them.

With shaping, dogs learn and progress at their own pace, trying out different behaviours to see what their consequences are and what works out best. This can help them feel confident to try things out. If things are going well you can progress, marking and rewarding them for gradual steps closer and closer to your desired goal. Whenever they are struggling, always go back to a stage at which they appeared confident and comfortable. Reinforce this for a little while longer, before trying to progress again.

Effective shaping requires owner confidence too, and a structured plan of all the steps

Figure 3.6: Louisa taught Cat to stay building up distance very gradually. Photo: © Tamsin Durston.

involved; including which behaviours you will initially mark and exactly how each step will progress, so you can give very clear information to your dog about what they are doing. Some dogs appear naturally creative and confident to try different behaviours. However, others might need more guidance before feeling safe to try something out. Others might be reluctant to try anything, perhaps worried about not receiving any reinforcement, withdrawing emotionally or even physically from the training session.

Think carefully when setting up your training environment, ensuring your dog has as much information as possible to help them behave as you wish. To build confidence, reward your dog for making absolutely any teeny movement at all. This gives them a real boost as they really cannot go wrong. As their confidence grows you can then gradually start to wait for a glimmer of the behaviour you want, and if possible, reward them in a way that encourages them to do it again.

Some dogs might find shaping frustrating, especially where marking and rewarding timing is not consistent, and they are not rewarded as they expect. Some dogs might withdraw when this happens. Some might bark or need to take hold of something to shake in their mouths. Others might try so desperately to gain their reward, perhaps by offering a succession of behaviours they have been rewarded for in the past. They are unlikely to be learning anything in this kind of condition, so you will need to help them out by rewarding even teenier steps towards the desired behaviour and making sure rewards come frequently and quickly so they have more consistent information about exactly what to do. You could also consider luring elements of the desired behaviour too, to start them off successfully.

Working with an accredited instructor is invaluable. Despite instructing classes myself, I still have weekly lessons with my incredibly intuitive instructor Jodie Nazimi. Jodie is instrumental in helping me improve my communication and reflect on my dog's feelings. Jodie can observe me *and* my dog, so she will see things I cannot. I remember feeling overawed at such insightful guidance when she said, 'Your right arm movements are much more fluid and consistent than your left, practice more with your left arm to get better at it' – such good advice, which really helped.

Videoing sessions, once you get over what you look like, is another beneficial way to observe your technique, timing and how your dog responds to you.

Capturing

Capturing is a way of reinforcing behaviours you find difficult to lure or incrementally shape your dog into doing, when they happen naturally outside of a training session.[43] With capturing, *whenever* your dog displays a desired behaviour, simply mark and immediately reward. With capturing, your dog has freedom to behave as they like while you await the opportunity to mark and reward behaviours you like. However, they may never perform the behaviour you are waiting for in your presence, so the opportunity to reinforce it might never arise.

You can use capturing to strengthen behaviours you are training with other methods if you are quick to mark and reinforce these as they spontaneously happen. For example, if you are training your dog to lie down using a lure, you can still *capture* those moments when they naturally lie down of their own accord at any point in time, by marking and rewarding them.

Premack

The 'Premack Principle' suggests that least-probable behaviours can be reinforced by most probable behaviours.[44] Psychologist David Premack was a pioneering primatologist in the 1950s–1960s. He observed that monkeys could be motivated to behave in ways they would not normally, if they understood that doing so resulted in being able to do something they really wanted.[45] A simplified version for humans is 'finishing your greens' (least-probable behaviour) means you can 'eat pudding' (more-probable behaviour).

My dog would not necessarily ever choose to sit before crossing over a road, her most probable behaviour would be to continue walking. I have trained 'sitting at the pavement edge' because I believe this helps to keep us, and other road-users, safe. The consequence of sitting at the roadside until I say, 'c'mon let's go', is getting to 'carry on walking', which my dog really wants to do.

If we understand which behaviours our dogs are most likely to engage in, we might be able to use these to reinforce behaviours we would like them to do – as long as these activities are safe for our dogs, the environment and our communities. If you listed all the things your dog really enjoys doing, how many could you potentially use to reinforce behaviours during training sessions?

Cat really loves running to the pond in her local park. Louisa could soon tell, by the way Cat fixated on the pond as soon as they entered the park, that this was the 'most probable behaviour' at that moment in time. Louisa decided to use this to help reinforce the 'sit and wait' training she had been practising at home.

Louisa began to ask Cat to 'sit' before letting her off-lead to do as she pleased. Cat struggled to begin with, enticed by the prospect of dashing off to the pond. However, she soon realised getting to do so was contingent on her sitting and waiting patiently. Very quickly, sitting became much more reliable and Cat will now routinely – unless there's something extra unusual and distracting happening, which is kind of fair enough – automatically sit when Louisa goes into the park and stops to unclip the lead.

Being permitted to run off-lead and make her own choices about what to do reinforced sitting behaviour upon entering the park so strongly that Louisa no longer even needs to ask Cat to do it. 'Walking through the park gates' and 'Louisa standing still' have become an 'environmental' signal for Cat to sit.

How do we train our dogs to start, or stop, doing certain behaviours exactly when we want?

A 'cue' is anything that triggers the start of a behavioural response. For example, many owners train their dogs to lie down when they say 'down', pointing to the floor. We do not train dogs to lie down, they are born able to do that, what we are training is lying down immediately when owners say 'down' and point floor-wards.

We might tend to think of cues as signals *we* give our dogs, but it is important to remember cues can also happen naturally within the environment or body. A rabbit running might trigger chase behaviour, for example, whereas hunger might trigger food-stealing or attention-seeking behaviour. Dogs might not always follow the cue we are giving them, especially where another cue offers a shortcut to getting a more desired reward as quickly and as easily as possible.

We can introduce environmental cues, for example, laying a blanket down could trigger 'lie on this' behaviour. However, we commonly introduce verbal cues, a word or short phrase such as 'come', or gestures, such as spreading our arms to signal 'come to me'. Initially, our dogs will have no idea what these mean and we might easily confuse them, or become stressed ourselves, if they do not respond as we would hoped. Because dogs learn through association, we need them to be doing a behaviour consistently before we can then pair it with our chosen cue.

For example, when training a dog to sit using a lure, there's no point saying 'sit' at the start because they will not know what that means. Imagine someone holding a treat at their dog's nose, saying 'sit … sit … sit … SIT', their voice growing louder in exasperation while their dog mouths the treat, barks, spins on the spot, walks backwards, and only then slowly lifts up their head and tilts backwards into a sitting position, and is given the treat. They are not learning 'sit', they are learning 'sit … sit … sit … SIT'. Now imagine the owner quietly repeatedly luring their dog into a sit, marking and rewarding them. Once their dog begins to sit as soon as they start to move the lure, they *now* say 'sit' just once. Their dog is much more likely

to associate the single, verbal cue of 'sit' with sitting behaviour.

Because dogs are so clever at working out what we mean, we often get away with poor timing, repeated cueing or introducing cues before they really understand what to do. However, waiting until your dog consistently offers the behaviour you desire *before* adding in a cue avoids miscommunication or creating additional frustration for either of you. The clearer and more consistent your communication, the more effective your training is likely to be.

Training tip

For easy reference, make a note of all your cues and what they mean, so you do not forget or confuse your dog. For verbal cues, choose short, snappy words that do not sound like any other cues you use, and think about *how* you say them. I remember inspirational behaviourist Julie Bedford, also my treasured mentor, teaching me to think of verbal cues as gently whispered secrets to my dog, no need to raise your voice or shout, which might worry them. I love that!

Repetition is crucial

Because dogs learn by association, they can be excellent at recognising patterns, linking cues with their consequences. For this to happen, a dog must experience the same cue and consequence enough times for their brain to form the connection. For example, if something happens once it is simply random, twice could be a coincidence, but three times in exactly the same way and a pattern could be emerging. Repetition strengthens these connections, constructing robust networks within the brain and nervous system, while building muscle and mental memory.

Training should therefore involve repetition, but this needn't be boring for owners or require lengthy sessions, which could be off-putting for everyone. Training also uses such brainpower it can be mentally tiring, so shorter sessions can really pay off, optimising enthusiasm, motivation and energy. How much to do at any one time will depend on factors including your dog's view of the complexity of the skill being trained, and their attitude towards learning at that moment.

It can be helpful to record the number of repetitions you do during training sessions, and how your dog responded, to help you plan future sessions. For example, my dog prefers tricky problems to solve so if she is finding something very easy, I will use ten rewards for ten repetitions then have a short game. I might repeat that once more before training something different, avoiding her becoming bored or finding simplicity unnerving. This keeps my dog enthused without overdoing it; but remember every dog will engage differently, sometimes even from session to session. If training is not working, it is a sign the plan is not quite right. There's no point carrying on, as you will risk putting your dog off. Be prepared to adapt training sessions to get the best from them, and/or consult an accredited instructor for guidance.

It might feel as though things are getting worse to begin with, but there's a good reason for this

Because dogs do what works out well for them, and learn through their experiences, they might try even harder to bring about the result they are expecting should it no longer happen. For example, when we suddenly stop interacting with a dog who enjoys jumping up for a fuss, they might jump up with greater intensity, perhaps even try to grab hold of us so we cannot ignore them. It is almost as though they are saying, 'C'mon, what is wrong with you, where's my fuss?'

Many owners might give up at this point, feeling as though their training is not working, but understanding this natural part of the learning process means we can be prepared to keep going. The number of repetitions needed for the new behaviour to be associated with the reward will be different for every dog, but with patience and consistency they will learn that a different behaviour now works out well for them, and that the old behaviour is not worth bothering with at all. This is also why it is always important to reward them for the behaviour we *do* want at the same time, so they quickly learn how to get the reward they are expecting, reducing the risk of them becoming frustrated.

How long does training take?

Just like us, how quickly each dog learns any skill will be individual, related to many factors including their genes, upbringing and experiences, and the environment they are in at the time; as well as how they feel about doing the desired behaviour and the rewards available.

Training tip

There's no point ever comparing you and your dog to anyone else and their dog. Even if your sibling has your dog's littermate and you are in the same training class, there are many reasons why they might learn at different rates or behave in different ways. Your dog will learn some things quickly whereas others seem to take ages – just as you will find training some behaviours easier than others. There is only one of 'you and your dog', so concentrate on your unique relationship.

Your dog's concentration levels also depend on several things, including their age, previous experiences and health. Although dogs can develop training 'stamina', they might generally enjoy short training sessions with breaks in between. Because breaks give the brain vital processing time, many owners find that, next training session, their dogs have magically 'got it', when they would perhaps have struggled the day before.

When first training something, we generally reward dogs every single time to keep them engaged, enthusiastic and feeling good. But is it realistic for us to always carry rewards like treats or toys everywhere we go forever? For some dogs, getting rewarded every time could become boring, or demotivating as they learn they needn't make much of an effort. This also risks a dog *only* performing the desired behaviour when the reward is present, becoming reliant on it.

To avoid this, once your dog confidently and consistently repeats the desired behaviour you can start to reward intermittently,[46] or with a different 'value' of reward each time, so they never know when they are getting their favourite. Just like a seaside arcade slot machine, they keep 'putting pennies in' because they believe this'll eventually pay off and they will get the jackpot. This random-reward pattern mirrors real life in the way it can seesaw between whether things turn out beneficially for us or not. We keep going because it is thoroughly worthwhile when things do work out well. Just be careful you are not expecting too much effort from your dog, resulting in demotivation, frustration or anxiety, before rewarding them.

Coming when called is vital for Cat, especially after a 'disappearing down the street' adventure! Neil and Louisa reward Cat *every single time* but keep her motivated by mixing up types of reward. Sometimes Cat gets a treat, sometimes a game with her toy, and other times a 'you are the best dog ever', smiles and a gentle fuss – which she does like, but not so much outside the home, and never as much as a game or a treat.

Sometimes the treat will be a piece of cheese, or even better from Cat's perspective, leftover chicken or steak. This 'pic'n'mix' approach means that although she is continually rewarded for this potentially life-saving behaviour, Cat remains eager to return to Louisa and Neil whenever called. She is always excited about what her reward will be – because it *could* be steak!

Neil and Louisa are careful to always call Cat with a positive tone in their voices. Remember being in your bedroom and hearing your mum calling you downstairs? You would go no matter what, but you would go much quicker if she called your nickname in a positive tone, than your full name with a firm voice. Because Louisa and Neil always call Cat in an upbeat, excited way, she runs to them happily and confidently – just how we want our dogs to feel about coming to us.

When training lengthier behaviours, such as settling on a bed or staying in one place, you will need to trickle rewards quickly in succession to keep your dog on the spot, before gently eking out this time. This helps build the time your dog keeps doing the behaviour for, before being rewarded. Gradually increase the time between rewards, then start to switch things up, sometimes wait three seconds before rewarding, then seven, then two, then nine, so they cannot guess the pattern – as the anticipation of their reward might encourage them to move. This requires skill, understanding when to hold out a little longer between rewards without your dog becoming anxious or frustrated – another reason why learning with an accredited instructor is invaluable.

Is training 100% effective?

The behaviours we have trained *are more likely to happen* but that does not mean they will *always* happen. Your dog's health, including the ageing process, will affect their ability to concentrate, learn and remember, as well as do certain things you ask them to.[47] If you notice changes in your dog's behaviour *always* consult your vet. Pain and underlying medical conditions, even in the earliest stages when you might not realise there's anything wrong at all, can affect behaviour.[48] It is always worth ruling these out, and/or treating them if necessary, before asking your dog to do anything they are struggling with. If your vet feels the problem is purely behavioural, they can refer you to an accredited behaviourist for assistance.

Is training failsafe? Okay, I will admit it – I took my dog camping with a group of pals and after she very quickly snaffled a couple of sausages from the BBQ, I overheard one of the kids say, 'If she is supposed to be such a good dog trainer, how come the dog stole our dinner?' – woops!

Despite training, there could always be times in life when, of all the choices they could possibly make at that moment in time, opportunistic dogs will naturally choose what they perceive to be most rewarding. In the instant my dog pilfered those delicious sausages, she was simply doing what worked out best for her right then, regardless of whatever alternative behaviours I would have been careful to reinforce, *including* ignoring food positioned in front of her. Completely my responsibility, I *should* have managed things by keeping her lead shorter – yes, she was on-lead – moving away, or giving her a long-lasting treat instead. Managing things helps our dogs out when temptation might be too much – and that is the same for all of us.

One of the worst moments in Louisa's life was seeing Cat bolt straight out of the park and disappear along the pavement, without a glance behind. Terrified, Louisa caught up with Cat at the local mechanic's garage just along the street. If he saw them going past, the mechanic would give Cat a treat on her way to the park.

We will never know why Cat behaved as she did, so can only infer that at the exact moment she decided to run to the garage, of all the choices available to her once she was let off-lead, she felt this was the most rewarding – better than running to the pond even on this occasion.

That explanation did not remove Louisa's panic, or her anxiety about letting Cat off-lead now. How could she be sure it wouldn't happen again? Truth is, Louisa could never be sure, but she used training to help reinforce the behaviour 'follow me around the park', to make this alternative much more likely to happen. She also spoke to the kind-hearted mechanic, explaining they would take a different route to the park for a while to reduce Cat's expectation of seeing him, and possibly getting a treat, every day.

For her own confidence, and to manage Cat's behaviour while training 'follow me around the park', Louisa exercised Cat on a long line, instead of letting her completely off-lead. Louisa and Neil worked hard training Cat that remaining close to them throughout the park was *always* her best choice, using a mixture of exciting games with chase-catch-and-tuggy toys, 'hide and seek' where one of them would pop behind a tree for Cat to chase and find, scatter feeding, laying treat trails and exploring different areas of the park together. They also practised calling Cat to them several times during each walk, reminding Cat that this was *always* a good choice to make.

Cat now sees her mechanic friend again, just not so often and generally on the way home. Neil and Louisa have asked him to help with Cat's training, waiting for them to ask her to sit calmly, saying 'okay go say hi' before she greets him. Cat's self-control is rewarded with the interaction and treat she wants from him. They have also practised walking right past without saying hello and making that thoroughly rewarding too. Sometimes, as a reward for walking past, they let Cat go back and greet her pal.

Train everywhere!

It is not enough to train a dog at home then expect them to follow cues no matter what the situation. Training them in as many different situations as possible helps the behaviour become 'generalised'[49]. Humans can generalise pretty well, for example I learned to drive in a Ford but could drive any type of car without more lessons, just some time to acclimatise. Dogs can find generalising trickier, so benefit from practising within many different circumstances before training becomes reliable.

Proofing involves gradually introducing distractions while your dog is doing what you have asked and rewarding them for remaining focused,[50] which can be very challenging. Always begin training somewhere quiet and calm, and only start introducing distractions once your dog confidently, consistently responds to your cue.

Training tip

Whenever increasing the difficulty of your training, set your dog up for success by changing just one thing at a time so they are not overwhelmed. It is always tempting to try to progress quickly, but solid foundations, created through successful repetitions, will hold your training up under pressure.

Proofing and generalising also avoid us becoming frustrated or disappointed when our dogs do not behave as we expect. Rather than respond in ways that might cause our dog to feel upset, understanding why it is hard for them helps us calmly consider what else might be affecting their ability to behave as we would like.

Louisa trained Cat 'Sit, and when I say "stay" no matter what I am doing, do not move until I say "Okay then"' at home. Standing right beside Cat to begin with, Louisa began by rewarding her for sitting still with a steady stream of treats. She slowly progressed to being able to take one step away, then two, then three and so on, before returning to Cat's side.

Once Cat confidently sat still while Louisa walked across the room, paused,

Figure 3.7: Cat learning to sit and stay at home. Photo: © Tamsin Durston.

then returned, Louisa began to introduce movement by dancing about a little. Knowing this would distract Cat, she started right next to her so she could feed Cat treats while she boogied beside her, rewarding her for sitting still. Slowly, she built up the distance she could dance away, before returning to reward Cat.

Louisa then added further distractions in the same, gradual way, rewarding Cat more frequently whenever making things more difficult. After successive sessions and many repetitions, Cat would sit still no matter what Louisa did – dance across the room, pick up Cat's toys and juggle them or lie on the sofa.

Louisa wanted Cat to do the same in the park. She went right back to basics, rewarding Cat for sitting still while she stayed right beside her, then taking one step away, then two and so on. Louisa progressed through all stages fairly quickly, as Cat was now confident sitting still because this had been so heavily reinforced at home. She just needed to experience this would be the same outside too.

Because Louisa rewarded Cat very heavily again to start with outside, and did not try to move on too quickly, Cat was able to cope with the distractions of the outside world, learning 'Ah, so sitting still when my human has said "stay" is just as valuable a thing to do out here as it is at home.' Nicely done Louisa.

What to train?

It is vital to remember dogs get better and better at the behaviours they are naturally practising, so we need to decide whether these are, or could become, problematic for us. For some owners, pulling on-lead or jumping up can present huge issues, but for others – teeny Chihuahua owners maybe? – these really do not matter at all.

Every owner–dog partnership's needs are different, however, training classes commonly include:[51]

- walking nicely on-lead
- being handled all over, as though for a veterinary examination
- coming when called regardless of whatever else is happening
- paying attention to their name
- leaving something they want
- meeting people politely
- settling down when needed.

Training aims to make these behaviours 'self-reinforcing', so that eventually doing them feels good without any reward being given. That way, life itself provides the reinforcement so we do not always need to, and any reward we do give feels like an awesome bonus. Think of basic 'life-skill' training like high school education, a platform from which you could, if you wished, progress to 'higher education', such as trick-training or undertaking a dog sport. Dogs, and people, continually benefit from the opportunity to solve problems. Training offers a fantastic way of meeting this need for you both, helping you reach your full potential as a partnership.

Training can be so enriching, however, we are much more likely to train behaviours we find easy and enjoyable, than those we find challenging. Our dogs' education should not ever feel like a chore, but an opportunity to bond and enhance our relationship. My dog and I were gratefully instructed by exceptional trainer Allyson Tohme, who taught 'training should not involve tribulation – dogs should only be tested during a competition'. I love that! I do not want my dog to live her life 'under exam conditions' imposed by me.

Life is naturally stressful for everyone, dogs included, through the incredible variety of things we are exposed to which we might not have experienced before. Training can help our dogs learn to cope with minor stresses, under our care and guidance, but certainly should not add to them.

Training aids

Many products are advertised, and many owners naturally want to use gadgets that help train their dogs. If you are considering using any, it is worth considering *how* they will influence your dog's behaviour, and how your dog might feel in response, to help you decide whether you feel comfortable using them.

Training aids are designed to make a specific behaviour more or less likely to happen again, through making the outcome of that behaviour feel either good or bad for the dog. For example, some enable you to deliver rewards to your dog in helpful ways, encouraging behaviours you

want, such as food-releasing toys, which dogs enjoy interacting with. However, they often tackle unwanted behaviours, such as barking or pulling on-lead, commonly by making these unpleasant for the dog, so they will stop. Remember positive punishment does not feel good, could risk a dog becoming frustrated or dejected, and could damage your relationship.

If you are tempted to use aids that make the unwanted behaviour unpleasant for your dog, it is important to remember that they are intended to be temporary. The idea is to train your dog to feel and behave differently, so you no longer need to stop them doing things. Your dog needs to know what to do instead, so rewarding desired behaviour should mean you can soon remove training aids altogether; and remember, challenging situations like … ahem … BBQs, can be managed with foresight and planning.

For me, the greatest aid to training is my relationship with my dog. The quality of our connection, including how I present the opportunity for her to access rewards she wants, enhances her self-confidence, her trust and willingness to engage with me.

Training might sound straightforward but can sometimes feel incredibly difficult. We are engaging with an emotional animal, whose personal needs and desires might compete with how *we* want them to behave. Although it involves brainpower, training is a practical skill requiring development and refining. It is not enough to *know* what to do, we also need to *be able* to do it, and *believe* that we can. When you are training a dog for the first time, you are learning how to orient yourself, handle your dog, deliver rewards effectively – how best to hold the lead even.

But as with any skill, the more you practice the better you can become, and suddenly it will feel like second nature when you mark and reward your dog without even thinking about

Jennie and Charlie

Jennie and her siblings had grown up with dogs in her family home where they had a great outdoors life. The family had a large garden, horses and a busy, active household. Jennie was ready for her first dog as an adult and chose Charlie from a large rescue centre. Charlie had been found roaming in London, ended up in pound and after 7 days of not being claimed he was transferred to kennels and put up for rehoming. Jennie had no further history on Charlie but he was thought to be about 2-years old. Charlie reminded Jennie of her childhood dogs – he was a Collie cross, perhaps with some Springer and Staffy in his breeding. Jennie spent endless hours discussing with friends what breeds made up Charlie (it would have ruined the fun if she would just have done a DNA test!).

Jennie had enjoyed agility with the family dogs growing up and thought it would be a good idea to take it up with Charlie as he was so fit and active. She felt bad about leaving him alone for a few hours when she went to work and thought it would be a nice thing to do together in the evenings and weekends. Jennie found a local reward-based agility trainer who was happy for Jennie and Charlie to join a beginner class.

Charlie learned quickly how to move around the equipment. He really enjoyed the A-frame and after a few sessions he was brave enough to go through the tunnel. Jennie's trainer was very understanding of Charlie's needs and gave him space and time to get used to things that worried him and they were careful not to lure him towards things that he found scary (like the tunnel), rather they let him approach and interact with the equipment in his own time.

Although Charlie was doing well with the equipment and learning the cues, he found the presence of the other dogs quite stressful. He had started to growl if the other dogs were running in his direction when he was waiting for his turn and had started to stare at one particular dog in the class. He was not always able to eat the treats that Jennie offered him to try to distract him when the other dogs were running. Jennie was starting to worry when it was Charlie's turn to run and was finding the class quite stressful as she felt she needed to manage Charlie all the time. On his runs, Charlie had also started to jump up and mouth Jennie's sleeve at times and she felt worried by this as he had always been so gentle with her before.

Jennie had wanted to do agility so that they could have a nice pastime to do together and she was also looking forward to the social aspect, standing around with a coffee and chatting to agility friends. The social aspect was not working out well either as Charlie found standing around the hardest bit, he would lunge at the dogs if they edged towards him and found it really hard to settle.

Jennie's agility trainer gently suggested to Jennie that classes may not be working out for him. She discussed with Jennie that Charlie might have missed out on socialisation around other dogs or may perhaps have had bad experiences in the past and this was causing him to be anxious and therefore reactive (growling and lunging) when he saw the other dogs running in his direction. Charlie's inability to eat the treats he normally loved was another sign that he was finding things too stressful and his mouthing of Jennie's sleeve was another sign of stress – Charlie was showing this out of character behaviour as he was not coping well. Jennie's trainer had some alternative suggestions of what Jennie could do with Charlie. We will catch up on Jennie and Charlie later.

to run but who find it hard to find appropriate outlets in their daily life.

Agility is a highly arousing environment and dogs are likely to be barking with excitement in anticipation of their run. Although some dogs will thrive in this environment, it is not a suitable environment for dogs who are not at ease around other dogs or people or who do not cope well with high arousal. Agility is not the place to try to socialise a dog to other dogs, they need to have been well socialised as puppies in order to cope well in this environment. For dogs who are not comfortable in a highly arousing context, a calmer, less arousing activity would be more suitable. In order for a dog to cope well and enjoy agility, not only must they have been well socialised but also time and care must be taken to introduce them to the agility equipment to habituate them to it without stress. Incorrect or rushed introductions to contacts (markers they have to touch to be considered as successfully completing the obstacle, included on the seesaw, dog walk and other elements) could cause fear or result in physical injury.

Although agility is an exciting activity, enjoyed by many dogs, the high levels of arousal experienced by most dogs during agility could contribute to stress. Even if your own dog copes well in the agility environment and does not show signs of excessive arousal and is not barking or lunging, being exposed to other dogs who are stressed may in itself be stressful for them.

Studies have looked at the physical and behavioural measures of stress in agility dogs during competition. By measuring salivary cortisol, it was shown that cortisol levels rose during competition but that the levels reached may not be outside the normal range and that behavioural indicators of stress were seen both before and after competitions (restlessness, trembling, panting and body shaking). They concluded that agility could potentially be stressful for the dog.[18] Studies have looked at the impact of agility on arousal and whether this is linked to the physical activity of agility or to the environment of a competition and it seems the competition environment is a greater cause of stress than the activity itself.[19,20]

As with most activities, the environment can have an impact on how the dog copes behaviourally with the activity, and how the dog copes will depend on the individual dog. Stress can be minimised by our choice of environment in which we participate in the activity. Some dogs would never cope with the environment of a competition but may enjoy an agility class with a few familiar dogs and people. Some dogs would only cope in agility 1-2-1s with no other dogs present. Knowing what best meets our dogs' needs and being able to judge their emotional response to situations is a key part of being behaviourally aware.

Most stress can be avoided if owners have behaviour in mind and can ensure that their dog is not stressed and know what action to take if they are not coping well. Much can be done by owners to mitigate the impact of arousal – ensuring your dog has sufficient sleep, scheduling breaks from the activity and being mindful of your dog's behaviour and emotional state. Small changes can have a big impact on minimising stress and consequently on behaviour, such as asking a friend to queue for you at events so that your dog does not have to line up in close proximity to other excited dogs who may be barking and lunging, giving dogs space from other dogs after their run and letting them rest in a place they feel safe (for example, the car) rather than standing and talking to friends can also help to minimise stress.

Although agility dogs are generally at the peak of physical fitness and the activity provides a means to maintain this high level of fitness, there are physical risks associated with the activity that must be considered. A study of 1627 agility dogs found that around a third were currently injured and 58% of these injuries had occurred in competition.[21] Jumps, A-frame and dog walk were most commonly associated with injuries and the most common injuries in agility dogs are to the digits, shoulder and back.[22]

As Jacqui outlined above, the issue of how other peoples' dogs are feeling is a consideration in all activities but particularly in ones that are exciting or cause a high level of arousal.

Although our own dog may be completely at ease in their given activity and cope well with the level of excitement, other dogs may not cope so well and may be reactive and may bark and lunge or show other stress-related behaviours. High levels of arousal are linked to increased risk of aggression, poor motor skills and reduced cognitive processing.[23,24] Highly aroused dogs may make poor decisions, so it is key to give our dogs space and to think about the emotional impact of being in close proximity to other dogs who may not be coping so well.

Lyra

Jacqui, an experienced trainer and owner, adopted Lyra, a Bedlington whippet cross, from a local branch of a national rescue. Lyra was clearly an ex-working dog who had hunted in the past and who showed a keenness around all things she could chase. Jacqui had competed in agility in the past with her previous dogs and took Lyra to her agility club. Despite her poor start and lack of previous training, Lyra was a supremely confident and well-adjusted dog who was completely comfortable around people and dogs. Lyra took to agility with ease and showed a real talent and great speed given her sighthound genes. Lyra clearly showed a positive emotional response to agility, it gave her an appropriate outlet for her drive to run. Over 4 years, Jacqui and Lyra progressed through the ranks and in 2019 she competed at the agility final at Crufts with the remarkable achievement of runner up.

Figure 4.1: Lyra at Crufts in 2019. Photo: © Jacqui Ballantyne.

Key to Jacqui and Lyra's success has been Lyra's confident nature and Jacqui's behavioural awareness, which ensured that Lyra enjoyed the benefits of agility without exposure to stress. Jacqui describes that Lyra was clearly well socialised and at ease around everything she experienced, even at the challenging busy and noisy environment of Crufts, but that Jacqui still took steps to ensure that Lyra was not exposed to stress and in particular that she was given space from other dogs who may be highly aroused.

Hoopers

Hoopers is a relatively new sport that has its basis in agility. Hoopers is all at ground level with no jumps or contacts, instead Hoopers consists of a series of hoops (hence the name), barrels and tunnels. Hoopers does not have tight turns and is not high impact making it suitable for dogs who can no longer cope physically with agility or who are too young (or too old). Hoopers is generally less arousing than agility for dogs as it is a calmer activity, meaning it can be suitable for dogs who may struggle with the arousal. Dogs are guided by their handlers from a greater distance than with agility, meaning that it is also suitable for humans who may not cope as well with the athletic aspects of keeping up with an agility dog. The emphasis is on free-flowing movement in the dogs rather than speed. The equipment is also cheap and easy to make, meaning that it is accessible to many owners. As with most activities, it is possible to have 1-2-1s with a trainer if a class environment is not suitable. As with agility, care must be taken to habituate the dog to the equipment but this is generally an easy process as the equipment is all at floor level and is open and easy to move around.

Figure 4.2: A dog participating in Hoopers. Photo: © Celia Felstead.

Flyball

Flyball is a highly arousing sport in which teams of dogs and handlers compete side by side. Dogs traverse hurdles, retrieve a ball from a box and return back over their hurdles in a relay. The fastest team to complete the task with all dogs wins. Flyball involves high levels of arousal and dogs are potentially frustrated while waiting for their turn in the relay. As the sport involves two teams competing against each other, dogs are in close proximity to another team of dogs that they may not know, who are also likely to be highly aroused. The nature of the activity means that dogs return back over the hurdles towards the waiting dogs, so highly aroused dogs are running directly towards other dogs at speed. This type of head-to-head approach is likely to be a source of stress and is generally avoided by dogs if they have a choice. The Dog Pulse Project[25] measured the impact of dogs being approached directly head-on or being approached in a curved manner, as they would likely greet another dog if they were off-lead. The dogs who were approached directly head-on showed an elevated hear trate, likely a sign of stress.[25] A recent study looked at hair measurements of cortisol and found levels were higher in dogs who participated in flyball than dogs who participated in agility or who went to dog shows.[26] Owing to the highly aroused atmosphere, proximity of other aroused dogs and the nature of the movement, flyball is a difficult activity to participate in without causing stress for the dogs involved. Flyball is also a physically demanding sport, and the risk of injury is high with 39% of dogs surveyed acquiring an injury during flyball, mainly limb injuries.[27]

Heelwork to music

Heelwork to music (HTM) is an activity in which routines are choreographed to music and performed by a human and a dog together. HTM is divided into two categories – heelwork to music and freestyle. HTM originated in obedience and it requires that the dog walks/trots in any of the eight prescribed heelwork positions. The heelwork positions must comprise two-thirds of the routine and the remaining third can be freestyle. In freestyle the handler is not restricted to having the dog at heel and at least two-thirds of the routine should consist of a series of moves in free positions that reflects the timing and rhythm of the music. The routine should have a theme, tell a story or interpret the music in some way. The remaining third should be heelwork.

Dogs must be well socialised, be comfortable around props and costumes and be physically capable of performing the routine. In order to compete, they must be comfortable around the noises and sights they would experience at a busy show and also be comfortable around other dogs and people.

HTM as a physical activity does not fit naturally within the ethogram, there is no analogous natural behaviour, but travelling to new places and experiencing new sights may be rewarding as a form of exploratory behaviour as long as the dog does not find these experiences stressful. From a behavioural perspective, interacting with their guardian and the reward-based training that HTM entails is likely to be rewarding. However, the activity could become repetitive and care should be taken to ensure the dogs have as much free choice as possible.

HTM requires precise training using operant conditioning to teach the various dance moves and heelwork positions. This should, of course, be taught using positive reinforcement to avoid stress and negative welfare issues caused by punishment-based training. HTM can also be taught successfully using observational learning. The use of observational learning where the guardian demonstrates the behaviour and the dog copies it has been described in the 'Do As I Do' method of Claudia Fugazza where they reported that using this method was more effective than shaping/clicker training for teaching a dog to interact with an object.[28]

Joanna Mayston, dog trainer and owner of the Tricky Collies teaches HTM and obedience and competed at Crufts with her rescue Collie Swift. Jo obtained Swift when she was just 6 months old from Battersea and she competed at Crufts when almost 3 and again at aged 6. Swift achieved the amazing feat of achieving eighth in the Crufts HTM final in 2016, in the main arena.

Jo describes how she was hugely committed to helping Swift to become comfortable with the show environment, so that it would not be stressful for her and so that she would be able to perform at her best. Over a long period, Jo took Swift on lots of outings to anything that replicated a show as well as taking her to real ones. She started with small fun shows and also went to car boot fairs and country fairs locally to habituate Swift to the sights and sounds that she would experience at a busy show. It takes a lot of thinking outside the box to try to replicate the show environment and Jo also visited football matches to get Swift used to busy environments with lots of competing stimuli. Key to all of this was that Jo ensured that Swift was relaxed and able to learn in these environments and that it was a positive experience for her. Jo described that in the competition environment, being hyper-aware of your dog's needs is essential to ensure they have space if they need it. She also stressed the importance of being honest about your dog's ability to cope as it is difficult to prepare for an environment like Crufts, no matter how hard you work at it.

Jo describes that Swift thrived on working in partnership with her in HTM and that the undivided attention from her and also the social contact with other people was hugely rewarding for her. HTM gave Swift appropriate outlets for her 'collie drive' and in some way replicated part of her drive to herd, as part of her joy in HTM seemed to be anticipating and trying to pre-empt what Jo would request her to do. This close working relationship with her guardian seemed to be rewarding in its own right.

Jo says about Swift, 'I never had any expectations of Swift winning, I considered it a massive achievement to be there and for Swift to perform with such confidence. The cheer she got when it was announced that she was an ex-Battersea dog was worth much more than that first place for us, part of why I wanted to compete with her was to show rescues can be just as capable in the competitive arena and needn't be considered as limited, if you ensure you listen to their needs and gradually prepare them for competition.'

Positive gundog training

Positive gundog training, which is taught using reward-based methods, is becoming increasingly popular in the UK and several trainers now run workshops and 1-2-1s to introduce pet dogs to the activity. Although many people who take up gundog training do not intend to work on a shoot or have their dogs work with game, the training can be applied to dummies or toys. This type of training can be an asset not only to the gundog breeds but also to any breed and in particular to the large number of spaniel crosses – cockapoos and the like who are currently extremely popular in the UK and may have strong working heritage. Gundog training allows guardians to understand their

dog's drive better and to harness it in a more appropriate way.

Gundog training utilises the dogs' innate desire to hunt and retrieve and harnesses those skills in a controlled and appropriate way, it also enables the guardian to become part of the 'game', which can be a bonding experience. This activity enables dogs to meet some of their fundamental needs in terms of exploratory behaviour and also provides social contact around people and dogs. It is a physically demanding activity that provides mental stimulation too. Food is used to reinforce behaviours in the early stages of training but functional rewards are used later – this means that the dog is rewarded by being able to hunt and retrieve, inherently rewarding activities for a gundog. Premack's principle is used to reinforce desired behaviours, the dog is rewarded for doing a less desirable behaviour by a highly desired behaviour – the dog is asked to sit and wait while the dummy is thrown (less desirable behaviour) and is then rewarded by being released to go and retrieve the dummy (highly desirable behaviour).

There are some reported behavioural benefits from gundog work, a study of Labradors showed that dogs who participated in gundog work showed less excitability, abnormal behaviour, barking tendencies and a higher level of trainability than pet dogs or dogs who participated in dog shows.[29] As with most activities, dogs need careful introduction to the sights and sounds they will experience during the activity to ensure that it is not stressful for them. This is easier with puppies as they can be habituated from an early age. It may be possible to get an adult dog used to the stimuli, but loud noises are an inherent part of gundog work and so this activity would not be suitable for dogs with sound sensitivity issues. This activity would also not be suitable for dogs who are anxious around people or other dogs as it generally takes place in a group environment but there may be an option to participate in 1-2-1s.

Collette May of Lead and Listen is a leading gundog trainer in the UK. In contrast to traditional gundog training methods, Collette is a reward-based trainer – dogs are introduced to the various parts of gundog work gradually and punishment is not used. Collette recommends that anyone considering gundog work would need to get (with the help of a trainer) their dog used to:

- the noises they will experience – this is done by starting at a large distance away from the noise, muffling the noise and pairing the noise with food

- jumping fences and other obstacles – this is done by starting off with a really low obstacle and rewarding the jump with their favourite toy
- heavy cover (going through hedges, undergrowth and similar) and water – this is done by starting with light cover or a small stream and pairing with food/toys and building up to heavier cover/larger or faster moving bodies of water.

All of the elements listed above, are worked on using a combination of systematic desensitisation (getting the dog used to a 'less scary' version in the real thing) and counter conditioning (pairing with something the dog likes such as food or toys).

Collette and Loki

Collette describes the benefit that her method of training and gundog work had on her rescue Loki:

> I rescued an 18-month-old Springer Spaniel called Loki last year. His owners were at the end of their tether with his antics on walks especially as they had young children and did not have the time to commit to the training that he needed. He would run long distances away and not recall, he would chase anything that moved and had started to kill wildlife. Loki was therefore usually exercised on a lead, which he pulled on, and was not a happy boy because of it. I decided to give him a chance and see if I could harness the strong hunting instinct and his willingness to please. I spent months just bonding with him and keeping him on a long line to prevent him practising the problem behaviour. I then taught him the basic behaviours needed such as the retrieve, stop whistle, heelwork and basic whistle recall – all inside. I then progressed that training gradually to the yard and finally the fields. We are on the edge of a shoot, there are lots of pheasants in the fields, so I was careful not to rush this stage. After 3 months we are now at the stage that he can be walked off-lead in the fields and he has generalised the training he learned inside to the fields. This training included quartering with me (where a dog thoroughly and effectively searches an area of ground from side-to-side, in a zigzag pattern, rather than moving ahead with the handler In a straight line), hunting for hidden balls, long retrieves – all to keep him stimulated, focused and close to me. I hope he can work in future with me as a picking-up dog. He has gone from a dog kept on-lead and under-stimulated to a dog that has off-lead freedom and enjoys doing what he was bred for, with me and my team of Labradors.

Pulling activities

In recent years, pulling activities where the dog pulls their human partner either while running (canicross), on a bike (bikejor) or on a specially designed scooter/rig (scootering) have increased in popularity. These activities originated in Europe as an off-season activity for the mushing (sled-pulling) community to maintain fitness in their dogs. These activities are particularly popular with owners of northern breeds (Huskies, Malamutes, wolf-like dogs such as Northern Inuits and Tamaskan), hunt, point, retrieve gundog breeds and sighthounds, although the activities are open to all breeds. There have been increasing imports of dogs bred specifically for these activities such as Eurohounds (Husky/Pointer cross breed). The season runs from September to May, avoiding the hotter summer months. Specialised equipment is required and in all of the pulling sports the dog wears a pulling harness and is attached

Figure 4.3: Canicross requires specialist equipment.
Photo: © Claire Howard.

to the human (or bike/rig) using a bungee cord or elasticated line. Directional controls are based on mushing terms and must be taught to the dog prior to taking up pulling activities. As with most sports, it is essential that dogs are habituated to the equipment so that they are at ease around it. If dogs are not habituated to the equipment, then being 'chased' by a bike or scooter attached to them would potentially be a scary experience!

Canicross is the most popular of the sports, distances run are generally 5 or 10 km but longer endurance races of half marathon and marathon length are also popular. As with most sports there is quite a distinction between training to do the sports, either alone or in a small group of known dogs at a club or with a group of friends, and with competing at an event with unknown dogs. Training runs with known dogs can be a source of positive social contact if the dogs are all well socialised and would choose to spend time together. There are potential behaviour concerns if dogs are exposed to other dogs who may be reactive and the highly aroused atmosphere at the beginning of races may be stressful for the dogs involved as the dogs are often very vocal at the beginning, for example, barking in anticipation of the start of the run. There may also be potential sources of stress as dogs are approached from behind and passed by other dogs during races but this can be reduced if adequate space can be given between the passing dogs. Running in a large group of non-familiar dogs as is typical during a race is more likely to be stressful than running with familiar dogs or running alone.

The action of running with familiar dogs could fulfil part of the natural ethogram of travelling in a group of known dogs but it is likely that this would only occur over reactively short distances. Studies of free-living dogs in Peru and Chile showed that the mean distance travelled from the home territory was 0.5 to 6 km so a lot shorter than the distances covered in these sports.[30,31] We have selected for the ability to run long distances at speed in certain breeds (northern breeds in particular) but it is not a particularly natural behaviour and there may be health implications of prolonged running at speed as would be seen over the longer canicross distances (in excess of 10 km) as it is such a physically demanding activity.

Studies of canicross races in the UK showed that, even at relatively cool ambient conditions, at every race studied at least one dog developed a post-race body temperature that would be considered at risk for developing heat stroke although no clinical signs were seen.[32] The dense double coat of northern breeds means they are more prone to overheating and darker coloured dogs were also found to be at higher risk of heat stroke. Around 22% of dogs in a study were found to have been injured during canicross activities, a significant result although a lower injury rate than agility, with cuts and abrasions the most common injuries.[33] Although not directly comparable to canicross, studies of sled dogs running endurance races found that 48.5% of dogs had gastric disease[34] and another study found aspiration pneumonia, gastric disease and rhabdomyolysis were associated with long distance racing.[35] These health issues may only be associated with the endurance type races and shorter races of 5–10 km seem unlikely to be associated with the same issues.

Sue and Draco

Sue bought Draco, her Husky puppy, home at 8-weeks old. Sue had researched the breed and wanted an active dog that could accompany her on long walks. Sue worked part time and had found a day care who would take Draco during the days Sue worked. Draco was well socialised and Sue went to great lengths to ensure he met lots of other dogs during his socialisation period. Draco started at day care from 14-weeks old and initially Sue received glowing reports about his behaviour but quite quickly, Draco became 'too much' for the dogs in his age range with his boisterous play and he was moved up to the larger breed adolescent group when he was only 18-weeks old.

By the time he was 6 months old Draco was having difficulties in the adolescent group, other dogs did not take well to his play style and he was persistent in trying to make dogs play and did not know when to stop. Dogs also found him hard to read and interpreted his curled tail and upright stance as confrontational even when Draco was trying to be friendly. Draco got into a couple of full-on scraps with other dogs and had started to pin them down and it was no surprise when Draco was a year old and day care told Sue they could no longer take him.

Sue found a solo dog walker for Draco who would lead walk him in the middle of the day, a 30-minute lead walk with lots of slow sniffing enabled Draco to meet his behavioural needs for exploration as he gained so much information about the other dogs in the neighbourhood by smelling their scent. Sue also took Draco for long lead walks before and after work but he never seemed even in the slightest bit physically satiated. Draco was struggling without the stimulation he was used to in the day though and he became destructive – he chewed and shredded Sue's soft furnishings and dug huge holes in her formerly lovely garden. He was attention seeking from the moment Sue came home and would bark and paw at her unless she paid him attention. Sue felt exhausted and had started to dread coming home. Sue enlisted my help and we looked holistically at all aspects of Draco's life. Following my advice, Sue introduced lots more mental stimulation and enrichment into Draco's day, including scent work with him in the garden. Sue also worked on Draco's need for social contact as he had gone from spending all day playing at day care to barely seeing dogs on walks. Sue started walking several times a week with dogs that Draco knew as a puppy and he remembered his old friends and interacted nicely with them as Sue was careful to not let Draco get too over the top and she kept play sessions brief.

Despite all of the positive changes Sue had made in Draco's life he was still struggling with his need for physical exercise, Sue's garden had become a racetrack in between the cavernous tunnels that he had dug. His lead walks did not seem to meet his needs for physical exercise. As much as she loved him, Draco had become a handful and Sue was losing enjoyment in their time together. I talked to Sue about the sport of canicross and introduced to her a trainer who specialised in it. Sue had always been a keen runner and ran 5 km several times a week but had never taken Draco as she was worried about the impact on his joints and worried whether she would be able to hold him if he started really running! Sue was fitted with a waist belt, Draco was fitted for a canicross harness, and Sue worked on the directional cues that Draco would need. Within weeks, Sue and Draco had followed a canine couch to 5 km with their trainer and Sue was running 3–5 km with Draco a few times a week. Their runs were all on grass or woodland paths to prevent damage to Draco's joints (and Sue's too).

Sue took confidence in running with her trainer and Draco quickly became friends with the trainer's Malamute bitch. Sue was careful to carry on following all the other advice she had received about using enrichment and scent work to help Draco meet his needs and she found the addition of canicross runs together was the final piece of the puzzle for them both, Draco was much nicer to live with and their relationship was positive again. Sue had no interest in competing with Draco as she felt the atmosphere may be too much for him. She was also wary as he had been attacked so many times by other dogs but running with her trainer and a couple of other friends and their dogs was a really enjoyable experience for Draco and Sue.

Racing activities – lure coursing and straight racing

Amateur racing activities are popular with some sighthound owners and clubs exist for various breeds of purebred sighthounds and for lurchers too. Racing events are also held at country shows and game fairs; terrier racing, high jump and long jump may also feature and the events may be open to other breeds.

In straight racing, dogs are raced in a group (generally three to six) and chase a mechanical lure (a plastic bag or piece of fur) that resembles a prey animal moving at speed. The dogs are held by their owners and released when instructed by the race official. Dogs chase the lure over a set distance and then return to their owners. Dogs are muzzled, wear brightly coloured collars to identify them and they may be disqualified for barging other dogs or any aggressive behaviour. Dogs are raced according to size and race distances may vary but meetings often consist of a mix of shorter distances (250 yards [230 m]) and a long 'marathon' race (600–800 yards [545–730 m]). Lure coursing is increasingly popular, as with straight racing, the dog chases a mechanical lure but the lure follows a zig-zag course and the dogs have to follow the course as closely as possible through a series of 'gates' (often bales of straw). Just two dogs run together and, in competitions, rather than being handled and released by their owners they are held and then released by a professional race assistant – the 'slipper'. Distances for lure coursing vary but some courses are in excess of 1000 yards (910 m).

Beama

My first two dogs as an adult were two Saluki lurcher siblings, Luka and Beama, who I adopted from their working homes when the hare coursing ban was introduced in 2004. My dogs were hare coursing and sleeping outside in a kennel one day and the next they were in my home with me with the (unrealistic) expectation they would behave like pet dogs – a culture shock for all of us and the start of a long period of learning about each other. Predatory chase was hardwired in my dogs, they had been trained to chase hares and hunt rabbits from an early age. They were very proficient at their job, a skill that put them at odds with the way I hoped they would behave at home. I was aware that their predatory chase pathways were well practised and ingrained and would not be easy to change as they were also so rewarding to the dogs. Hunting and catching wildlife gave them a huge buzz of dopamine, you could see their emotional response when hunting and the 'joy' it appeared to give them. I had heard about the sport of lurcher racing and lure coursing from friends who also had lurchers and hoped this would give my dogs a more appropriate outlet for their drive. We found a club an hour away and quickly discovered that Beama was incredibly fast and capable of winning against the other dogs at the club and that Luka was the opposite and that instead of chasing the lure he was chasing the other dogs, a behaviour that soon got him

Figure 4.4: The author's dog Beama lure coursing. Photo: © Penelope Malby Photography.

disqualified. Beama started to win every week and a part of me became quite competitive about it all. This should have been a warning sign, as soon as you become competitive, you start to put your own needs first and your dog's behavioural needs second.

Beama won regularly over the shorter distances but started to fail to finish the longest race, the jewel in the crown of 800 m. She was physically more than capable of finishing this and beating most of the competition. We could not see what was happening in the race as the longest race went up and over a hill so we lost sight of her as she went over the brow. The race organiser called us over and told us we had a good dog who was always in the lead but she was stopping dead as she went over the hill and was turning round to come back to us. All we saw was her running back just as fast as she went out. We can surmise that Beama was becoming anxious when she went out of sight of us and she felt worried by being in a group of dogs she did not know. For her, although she had seemed to enjoy the shorter racing, she started to find the whole event stressful, rather than pulling towards the start as soon as we arrived, she hung back and seemed reluctant. We stopped straight racing after that as Beama no longer had a positive emotional response to activity, she was not enjoying it anymore.

I also competed at lure coursing with Beama and this was an activity she thrived in, it seems likely the movement of the lure and the zigzag course mirrored chasing a hare for her, an activity she had spent her early life doing before she came to me. I never saw the same level of excitement for anything else she did in life. Lure coursing seemed to be a positive experience for her as we were in sight of her at all times (as the course was flat) and as just two dogs raced together, she was not crowded by dogs she did not know. We also managed to set things up so that she could race with dogs she knew, which would also remove any stressful aspect of running with unknown dogs. Beama was very successful at lure coursing and won many races, her highlight was coming second in a knockout competition of 64 dogs at a race meeting in Peterborough, which I still remember as a highlight of our 14 years together.

There are aspects of racing that are potentially stressful, the same as there are with any sports that involve high levels of arousal. The stressful aspects were being in close proximity to other dogs who were all highly aroused, barking and lunging in anticipation of racing. Even well socialised dogs may find being around other aroused dogs stressful, even if they are not showing signs of arousal themselves. Being held by the collar in pairs and released by the slipper at lure coursing competitions is the part that many dogs found the most stressful; both being handled by an unknown person and being held by the collar, something they may not have been habituated to and that may have negative connotations for rescue dogs who might have been handled in this way in the past. Dogs are muzzled for racing and need to be habituated to this well beforehand so that it is not an added stressor on the day. Stress could be minimised, or completely avoided, by only participating with friends, releasing your dog to chase instead of the race assistant and by not exposing them to other aroused dogs before racing.

From a behavioural perspective, although these racing activities clearly enable dogs to perform predatory chase behaviours, there are some differences compared with natural predatory chase (chasing a prey animal), which may have behavioural implications. In true predatory chase, the dog will chase the animal and it will either end with the prey animal escaping (going into a burrow/hole/area the dog cannot access or running away) or the dog will catch the prey animal and will then perhaps follow through with other aspects of the predatory chase pathway such as killing and possibly consuming the animal. Either way in this scenario, there is a certain end to it. If the animal escapes, then the dog would normally investigate where the animal went by sniffing or perhaps digging or pawing, quite low arousal activities, and sniffing in particular is known to lower arousal (see below). The sudden cessation of chasing is thus followed by other natural behaviours if the animal escapes. If the dog catches the prey animal, then arousal also decreases as when dogs start to dissect and consume, their nervous system switches to calm, low arousal 'rest and digest' parasympathetic state. The problem with an activity such as racing or lure coursing is that the highly arousing chase aspect ends suddenly at the end of the race and is not followed by anything innately rewarding – typically the dog is briefly walked to cool down and then they are put back in the car. The dog may feel frustrated as they never get to catch the 'prey' (the lure). Frustration is a negative emotion that can lead to more reactive behaviours and means that the dog will never be satisfied following the activity.

Studies of racing greyhounds in Australia looked at their emotional response to the end of the race. They saw high levels of arousal and frustration-based behaviours at the end of the race when the dogs suddenly stopped running and they found they could improve this by allowing the dogs to have access to a bungee toy attached to a catching pen at the end of the race when the lure disappeared out of sight.[36] Allowing dogs participating in 'fun' racing activities to catch a lure or dummy at the end could perhaps help to alleviate some

aspects of frustration although this can be hard in muzzled dogs and being unable to grasp something due to being muzzled could also lead to frustration. As an alternative, setting up some scent work or allowing a calm chewing activity after a race may enable the dog to lower arousal and boost reward brain chemistry so that the dog would feel satiated.

A slower pace of life

The activities described so far are all physically demanding, and many can be quite arousing. These activities are popular as they are exciting for the dog and physically tire the dog but from a behavioural perspective, it is not ideal to only participate in these types of fast-paced activities as we need to try to achieve balance. Ideally, to achieve homeostasis and to maintain equilibrium both in terms of brain and body, we would try to balance any fast-paced activities with low arousal, calm activities. Many dogs may benefit from minimising arousing activities and heavily focusing on low arousal activities. When we think of the ethogram of a free-living dog, a study showed that over half of their time is spent sleeping; of their active time, only a small proportion of time is spent in active food searching, half is spent interacting with others (mainly other dogs) and half is spent as an individual – moving around and investigating. Majumder described free-living dogs as generally lazy and who survive by scavenging and very rarely hunting.[37]

There is increasing interest in adopting a slower pace of life with our dogs and being more mindful in our interactions and behaviour, this has been pioneered by Turid Rugaas and also by Amber Batson and inspired by their work, there is now a website dedicated to the Slow Dog Movement.[38] The Slow Dog Movement describes not only focusing on

Figure 4.5: The Slow Dog Movement encourages slow-paced sensory activities and free choice, such as freely investigating scents. Photo: © Laura McAuliffe.

slower paced activities but ensuring that any faster-paced pursuits are interspersed between longer periods of calm activity and low arousal. Independently, many dog professionals have also described activities that fit well within this slower pace of life and these are outlined below. These slow activities may include sensory-based activities and activities that give the dog free choice.

The backpack walk

Steve Mann developed the 'backpack walk' after he visited Peru and observed the village dogs there.[39] He noted their slow pace of life and how they actively sought out interaction with people. The backpack walk is easy to follow, it is accessible as you need no specialist equipment and you can do it anywhere; in a friend's garden, a freedom field or on a short walk to a quiet place, for example. It also only takes 15 minutes of your time but those entire 15 minutes are devoted to meaningful interaction with your dog, with no pressure or agenda, just 'being' together. This is beneficial for our dog and the mindfulness of this activity is relaxing for the human too.

For this activity you need a quiet, outdoor place where you will not be disturbed and where your dog feels comfortable, a long line (or long lead), a treat bag and a backpack. In the backpack you need a couple of small plastic containers – in one if these you place a novel food item, ideally one you can both share. In the other container you put a novel scent – for example, a catnip scented cat toy, a lavender bag, a sprig of rosemary in a sock, a fruit tea bag, a scent cloth that has been rubbed on your friend's dogs (as long as your dog likes them), you are only limited by your imagination. You also need a novel item in the bag – this can literally be anything that is safe and portable such as a hairbrush, a charity shop item, a piece of plastic hose or a piece of fabric. You could include a dog toy but the idea is to keep arousal low and to make this a calm sensory event so a toy that your dog finds arousing would not be ideal. You also need a chew – I prefer to use edible chews that the dog can eat entirely like a tripe stick, dried sweet potato chew or fish skin, rather than something like a plastic bone.

The backpack walk starts by arriving at a quiet outdoor space (garden/tennis court/ corner of a field even a car park) and giving the dog time to sniff the environment and eliminate should they need to. You should then ideally spend a few minutes doing some slow and calm recalls with a quiet calm voice, jogging slowly backwards away from the dog and calling them and rewarding with food from the treat bag. It helps to keep voices low, quiet and calm in this activity. After a few minutes of recalls and with the dog actively engaging with you, sit down together and start to investigate the backpack. Slowly take the items out one at a time and open them and let the dog investigate them – opening the pot with the scented item and quietly exclaiming wonder (acting skills are helpful) to encourage the dog to join in investigating the scent. After the dog has investigated each item, they are put away, back in the backpack and another item is taken out for the dog to explore. When you get to the pot with food to be shared, you can slowly eat a piece and give a piece to the dog. The novel item should be taken and carefully placed in your hands as if to emphasise how special it is (even if it is a hairbrush or piece of pipe) and the dog will normally carefully sniff and investigate the item if it is put on the floor. If the dog is interested in toys, you can bring one and participate in some slow calm toy play with the dog and they can then finish with the chew as a nice note to end on. The activity is designed to be taken slowly and not rushed and you must actively engage in the dog, giving them your full focus for the 15 minutes of the activity.

The backpack walk is one of few structured activities that enables multiple parts of the ethogram to be met. Not only does the backpack walk allow for exploration of the environment and good quality social contact, but also it enables social eating with the sharing of a novel food, sensory stimulation by the scent activity, object play with a toy and calm, relaxed chewing in a social context.

Using the natural environment as an enrichment activity

One of the most cited benefits of dog ownership is the enjoyment gained by walking them in the natural environment. The importance of the natural environment has also been shown in humans where exposure to the natural environment impacts on cognitive functioning, emotional well-being and emotional health.[40] Participating in physical activities in a natural environment rather than an urban environment has also been shown to increase positive emotional and cognitive outcomes.[41,42] The Japanese concept of 'forest bathing' is based around the principle that exposure to trees and the natural environment is good for physical and emotional health. Forest bathing includes physical contact with trees, slow breathing, observation and appreciation of the natural environment, unplugged from our phones and devices. In people, forest bathing has physiological benefits including reducing blood pressure, improvement of immune function and positive psychological effects.[43]

We can use these principles with our dogs too, they get exposure to the natural environment on their walks if we are lucky enough to walk in a rural environment or forest. We can also enjoy the benefits of the natural environment by just sitting with our dogs and sharing experience together rather than just focusing on a walk. Sitting together in the natural environment without distraction can be a fabulous source of social contact for our dogs as well as giving them the benefits of the natural environment. Our spending time with them in the natural environment without using screens is likely to be significant as they receive our full attention and we are fully present rather than being an 'absent presence', where we are physically present but have our minds elsewhere, typically on our phones or laptops.[44]

We can also go a step further by using elements of the natural environment to provide natural enrichment for our dogs. It has been shown how beneficial naturally enriched environments are to animals. Studies of rodents compared the use of natural and artificial enrichment. For example, using a plastic ladder in an artificially enriched environment and a wooden structure for climbing in a naturally enriched environment. It was shown that naturally enriched environments resulted in greater emotional resilience, more social behaviour and neurobiological changes that resulted in lower anxiety in certain tests.[45] Natural enrichment is an easy activity to engage our dogs in, whether it is using fallen down trees or stumps to climb on a walk, doing scent work in leaves or collecting natural items such as shells, feathers and pinecones for our dogs to explore and interact with in the home or garden. Natural enrichment can also work perfectly as part of balance and proprioception exercises.

Proprioception and sensory experience activities

Proprioception exercises include a range of body movements that focus on balance and bodily awareness. Problems with proprioception are linked to sensory seeking or sensory avoidant behaviour in children – sensory seekers may engage in rough play, crash into things or bite or chew excessively and sensory avoidant children may sit still instead of engaging in running, may lean into things or slump on them or may appear clumsy. Children with poor proprioception were shown to be more likely to have emotional difficulties and poor social skills.[46] Problems with the vestibular (balance) system are linked to anxiety in humans and animals.[47] Group proprioception activities were shown to reduce aggression in a study of children with sensory processing issues[48] and also reduced symptoms of anxiety and depression in adults.[49] On a physical level, anxiety is thought to cause patients to increase tension in anti-gravity muscles and impacts on proprioception and vestibular systems and these can be improved by proprioceptive therapy.[50] Although the benefits of proprioceptive work in dogs have not been well documented, it seems feasible that they would gain similar benefits as people and anecdotal evidence of the benefits abounds.

Proprioception and balance exercises generally involve climbing on and off, stepping over, crawling under, walking over and balancing on objects in a slow and controlled way. Exposure to different textures and sounds may add to the sensory experience and is described as part of a 'sensory diet', which can help improve behaviour in children.[51] The use of the natural environment as part of this sensory experience has shown to be beneficial in children who were provided with a therapeutic garden for a full sensory experience.[52] It seems likely that similar

Doggoland, a playground of natural enrichment and proprioception

An activity that combines natural enrichment for proprioception has been developed by Penel Malby when she designed 'Doggoland' – an outdoor activity area modelled on a natural children's playground and partly consisting of a natural wooden structure, on woodchip and grass with wild plants between the equipment. Penel says:

> The intention when designing Doggoland was to build a structure that could be used calmly, as a form of natural enrichment and could help with proprioception. Many dogs have poor proprioception – poor awareness of their own bodies – usually stemming from chronic tension and stress. And of course, the more anxious they become, the worse it gets. We'd been aware for many years that confidence building via natural enrichment has an effect on the rest of a dog's life too. We explain it to clients that it's like us doing something like Pilates, becoming more aware of your body, using slow careful body movements, making us breathe slower, relaxing us. So, we wanted to include different textures, different materials and all sorts of uses for the equipment we had built.

> The main elements are from aged tree trunks but there are also wooden platforms of different widths, slatted wooden ramps and slices of tree to climb on. This activity is multipurpose – it can be used for proprioception exercises by slowly stepping and climbing on the structure, it can be used as part of scent activities by hiding or smearing treats in

Figure 4.6: Natural enrichment using a purpose built wooden structure for balance and proprioceptive exercises (Doggoland). Photo: © Laura McAuliffe.

the groves of the tree trunks and it can be used totally freely – allowing the dog to use it as they choose, whether that be lying under the platforms or standing on them to get a high vantage point or sleeping in the sun on them.

Natural enrichment can also be added to the activity by collecting boxes of leaves from different places (feathers, herbs and sheep wool and so on) that can be placed around the wooden structure to add extra enrichment and the dog can explore and interact with them at will, having a sensory experience.

Key to the use of these areas is speed. We do not want them to become a form of 'natural agility' and be used at speed as a form of exercise, the emphasis is on a slow and relaxing experience for all.

Penel describes the impact using Doggoland and focusing on proprioception had on her dog, Morris, 'Really we try to encourage as many different body movements as possible – increasing mobility increases confidence too. I have a Pointer x Setter, Morris, who has always been a very anxious dog. After we had Doggoland built, I started taking him up there several times a week, and after a couple of months he became so much more confident, even to the point he would walk up the ramp into the car – which was unheard of!'

Other natural enrichment areas that provide a sensory experience and can be used for proprioceptive exercises have been created at freedom fields in the UK (including Dogs and Dandelions, Surrey, UK) and across Europe. As the benefit of these areas is more widely recognised, hopefully, they will become more widespread in freedom fields and dog walking areas.

types of outdoor sensory garden could also be beneficial to dogs.

Animal centred education– giving animals a choice and a voice

Proprioceptive exercises and sensory experience are a key feature of animal centred education (ACE). ACE was established in 2018 by Sarah Fisher, inspired by her work with the dogs in the care of Battersea. The ethos is that animals are at the heart of all interactions and all learning is introduced at a pace to suit each individual dog. This emphasis on letting the dog lead the activities and complete lack of pressure or coercion means that ACE appeals to behaviourally minded dog owners. There is no direct hand contact in free work, the dog

leads the activities and has complete freedom to explore them at will.

In ACE, owners are guided to develop quiet observation skills of their dog as they move around the free work. The free work consists of various objects that the dog can step on, walk over, investigate and walk over or through, such as tiles of different textures, 'snuffle mats', platforms, poles and ball pits. The focus on observation helps owners to develop a better understanding of canine body language and to recognise postural and behaviour patterns that enable them to modify their own interactions or seek help from other professionals such as vets as mobility issues are more easily identified when a dog is moving slowly around a free work setup. ACE also enables owners to get a much clearer picture of their dog's choices – which activities do they seek out first and which do they avoid? Sarah states that through ACE

Figure 4.7: Henry exploring ACE Free work. Photo: © Sarah Fisher.

Free Work, 'the smaller threads that weave together to create the more obvious behaviour and movement patterns become clear. In short, ACE Free Work can give you answers to questions you didn't know you'd asked'.

ACE uses principles of environmental enrichment but it goes further than that. ACE Free Work is rewarding for the dog as they choose to move around and interact with the equipment but there are also additional benefits as the activities are designed to be a sensory experience for the dog and to focus on proprioception and vestibular balance.

Cookie Dough Dynamo, Henry and Sarah

Sarah describes her experiences with Cookie Dough and Henry and their role in the development of ACE.

When a young bull breed blend called Cookie Dough Dynamo came to Tilley Farm on foster over a decade ago, it was evident that she struggled with many aspects of the human world. She was tense in the body and in a constant state of arousal. Body contact triggered more arousal, as did movement and noise. Cookie Dough mouthed hard and grabbed clothing, hands and hair. When a dog is in a constant state of arousal they cannot learn; their behaviours are automatic and can quickly become a habit. While there is always a reason for all behaviour, those behaviours are not conducive to harmonious relationships with humans and other animals, and these behaviours are signs that a dog is struggling on both a physical and emotional level.

A climbing frame to meet the needs of her developing vestibular system, and a variety of sensory items made of different textures and shapes, some of which made a noise when touched, were made available to Cookie Dough so she could explore and expand her experiences at her own pace. It was Cookie Dough who inspired the ball pit over thirteen years ago. This gave her the opportunity to search for treats among the plastic balls, which she could touch with her paws and nose, and gave her an outlet for her innate desire to dig. It also helped to pair positive experiences with sound.

Henry, another youngster with similar struggles, bounced his way through the gates of Tilley Farm in May 2018 following a referral from another behaviourist. Like Cookie Dough, Henry mouthed and grabbed when touched, when he heard any noise, and when walking on the lead. Anyone sitting down or talking also triggered the mouthing and grabbing. Henry helped to establish ACE Free Work as a rewarding foundation on which all further learning can be built. In just three and a half weeks Henry's life completely changed, and although I didn't know it at the time, mine changed too. Henry is now a permanent member of my family.

ACE gives animals choice and a voice, and recognises the value of building calm foundations on which further learning can be built using reward-based, kind and gentle techniques. Meeting the individual needs of animals and acknowledging the inextricable link between mental, emotional and physical well-being is an integral part of ACE.

Scent work

Scent work (or nose work) is becoming a popular pastime for dogs and their guardians, and it has an array of positive benefits in terms of behaviour and emotional health. Scent work includes everything from structured scent work to find specific scents, less formal scent work to find hidden food (even simple 'scatter feeding'), enrichment work where dogs investigate different scents at will and tracking to follow a trail to an endpoint. Scent work is an activity that is accessible to all dogs – from puppies to senior dogs; all breeds and types are capable of participating. Its suitability for all breeds is shown by the finding that the brachycephalic pug may outperform German Shepherds and greyhounds in some scent tests.[53] Dogs with mobility issues or physical disabilities are also capable of participating.

Scent work is an activity that works well for dogs who have anxiety or reactivity issues and do not cope well with high arousal or in a normal class environment. Scent classes are an option for many dogs who would be excluded from other types of classes as the nature of scent work tends to mean that dogs can be worked individually and that other dogs are out of sight/in their cars until it is their turn. Scent work has great appeal for behaviourally aware owners and reward-based, considerate and gentle handing of dogs is a requirement of the main scent work organisations in the UK. Scent work is also versatile as it can be performed at home or in 1-2-1s with a trainer and the coronavirus pandemic has shown it works very well via virtual 1-2-1s where you can be coached by a trainer online.

Our dog as our leader

Dogs live in an olfactory world and their sensory experience is very different from ours. Dogs have a far better sense of smell than us, perhaps 10,000 or 100,000 times better and the area of their brain devoted to scent analysis is 40 times bigger than ours.[54] Participating in scent work with our dogs can enable us to enter their sensory world and allows our dogs to become the leaders and our guides as we explore their hidden world with them. In terms of our relationship with dogs, engaging in an activity where they have the skills and we are the lesser-skilled co-partner can be enlightening and can enable guardians to see their dogs in a new light. From an ethological perspective, scent work enables dogs to display the natural behaviour of gathering information via their primary sense – their olfactory sense.

Simon Gadbois conducted a field study of using a tracking dog to locate coyotes who were feasting on a moose carcass.[55] He was struck that early humans would have relied on scavengers and predators to locate food and would quickly have realised that the keen sense of smell of wolves was an asset. The complementary, mutualistic relationship of visual humans and olfactory canids may have gone back millennia.

Studies have shown the benefits of scent work and its impact on dogs' emotional states by looking at the impact of scent work on a dog's cognitive bias.[56] Cognitive bias refers to whether a dog anticipates an ambiguous event will have a good or bad outcome, it is a measure of optimism, put simply. If a dog responds positively, they have an optimistic emotional state and if they react negatively, they have a pessimistic emotional state. We can tell if they are a glass half full or a glass half empty kind of dog at the time. In this study, they used a simple scent work task of treats hidden in boxes and compared this with dogs who were trained to walk on a loose lead using reward-based methods – this means that both groups of dogs had a positive interaction with people. Dogs who had two weeks of scent training were found to be more optimistic than the heelwork group, they anticipated that an empty bowl was likely to have treats in more

often – they had a more positive emotional state than the heelwork trained dogs. Although this is a small study, it is significant as it shows the changes that can occur, after just two weeks of simple scent work.

Scent work is an ideal activity for dogs who have high hunt and prey drive and they may be more adept at scent work than other dogs.[57] It can provide an appropriate outlet for dogs with high prey drive as it activates both anticipatory and reward systems in the brain. Searching for the scent is part of exploratory, foraging type behaviours and actually finding the scent is associated with 'feel-good' behaviours.[55] On a neurotransmitter level, the search is linked to dopamine and the find is linked to endorphins (feel-good 'high'). We can see from this why scent work is so rewarding for dogs as both the search and the actual find is linked to positive emotional states and feel-good brain chemistry.

Studies using fMRI imaging showed the caudate area of the brain was activated in response to all scents but particularly to familiar human scents, this area is associated with positive expectations and 'reward process' and it could be assumed that dogs are experiencing a positive emotional response to scent.[58]

Scent work for specific scent

Scent work classes and workshops have become hugely popular in the last 10 years as owners and professionals recognise the benefits offered by scent activities. Scent activities generally rely on the dog finding a specific scent item but food is often used in the initial stages as the 'find'. Popular scents for dogs to find are clove, gun oil, truffle oil, anise, catnip and small pieces of Kong™ rubber. Care must be taken to ensure that the scents used are safe, as a popular scent oil, birch, has been shown to be toxic to dogs.[59]

Dogs are taught to either 'passively indicate' by a sit/down/freeze or bark when they have found the scent or to 'actively indicate', which means they pick up the item or interact with it in some way.

Scent work is generally a fun and low-stress activity for dogs. The only potential source of negative emotion could be if too much focus is placed on achieving a perfect passive indication as this can become frustrating. It is also important to be careful what you choose as an indication as behaviours such as barking to indicate are driven by frustration and can also expand into more negative behaviours such as pawing or biting[60] and so may not help encourage a positive emotional response.

Tracking

Tracking refers to a dog's ability to detect and follow a specific scent. Tracking has been pioneered in a behaviourally minded way by Pat Tagg at DogTaggs in Dorset, UK. Pat runs a tracking programme alongside her 'shepherd school'. Tracking is an integral part of herding behaviour that has been used by shepherds long before the military and other services sought to use that aspect of olfactory behaviour. Shepherds were reliant on the tracking ability of all animals in their care for various tasks including the recovery of lost flock family members. Pat describes, 'the tracking programme sits firmly in the exploratory behavioural range and brings with it all the health, welfare, emotional and behavioural benefits we associate with exploratory behaviour. A two-way learning process is utilised in teaching tracking, where social learning approaches are used to invite the animals to join us and by acting mindfully and reflectively, we can become a predictable pivot point within the environment in which animals choose to attach themselves. A study in mindful self-control enables humans to become effective partners to the tracking dog rather than an added load that causes impairment to the natural easy manner in which dogs will track if the conditions are right.' Participant animals are referred to as coaches to emphasise the importance of allowing the dog to lead and for us to appreciate the dog's far superior abilities in this field. The use of mindfulness allows humans to change their outward behaviour to become calmer and more self-controlled, which in turn, then gives their dog a space in which to 'speak' and to be heard. This is a role reversal of who is learner and who is coach.

Pat's overarching ethos across her programmes is that humans learn appropriate control over their own bodies and minds enabling them to become the best behavioural fit with the skills that the dogs already have. The beauty of this program is that it is transferable to urban life, with practice and support, and many participants go on to become 'urban trackers', setting up trails in urban parks and landscapes and taking away the skills to allow their dogs to thrive in their tracking ability. Pat sees tremendous changes in relationship between dogs and their humans using this approach and the skills of quiet observation and listening to what the dogs are trying to communicate translates to other aspects of life together too outside of tracking.

Man-trailing

Man-trailing is a form of scent activity that is becoming increasingly popular and offered at workshops and classes. Dogs are rewarded for successfully finding 'missing people' with food and/or toys and lots of positive attention. This activity is quite distinct from the tracking described above as it relies on a controlled, 'starting ritual'. This ritual becomes a specific cue to the dog so that they know they are about to start trailing and so that they can anticipate what will happen next. The ritual involves putting on a specific harness (or other piece of equipment, such as a bandana if the dog is not comfortable in a harness) and introducing the dog to the scent of the missing person (on an item/object that the person has been in contact with). The starting ritual ensures that there is a discriminatory stimulus, the dog only performs the trailing behaviour when they are wearing the harness, it also makes the activity predictable for the dog, they know what will happen next. The dog sets off to find the missing person (on a long 10 m line) with their human following and carefully handling the lead. When the dog finds the missing person, they are rewarded with high-value food (and a toy if desired) and praised.

This activity, like many scent activities, can be tailored for anxious or reactive dogs, dogs are generally worked individually with no other dogs present (as they would act as a distraction) and so it can be suitable for dogs who are not comfortable around other dogs. Dogs with anxiety issues around people can be accommodated if they would be comfortable in the environment – it would be safe to do so, as they can find a person they are familiar with and comfortable with and not a stranger. This activity also does not require any hands-on handling from the instructor which means that stress can be minimised for all dogs as all handling is by their familiar caregiver.

Emma Golding-Bosworth is a dog trainer who became a man-trailing instructor after she discovered a love of man-trailing with her Staffy mix Sookie. Emma says about man-trailing:

I love it as no dog is left out, anyone can take part. I found it most beneficial when

I wasn't able to exercise Sookie for long periods as she was having issues with her legs. So, I adapted each trail to what she was able to do. I also love the element of team. Your dog is a major part of your team, your team leader and if you don't learn to listen and observe each movement they make, then you won't be successful. Most sports teach dogs what to do in order for you to succeed as a team, this one teaches the human how to listen to their dog more in order to succeed. It's all about the dog.

Back to Jennie and Charlie

We left Jennie feeling quite disheartened as agility classes had not been a good fit for Charlie and he had become stressed and reactive. Jennie was still keen to find a fun activity that would suit Charlie and her trainer put her in touch with a local scent class. Jennie went for a 1-2-1 and found that Charlie had an amazing nose, within the first session he was finding a small tin that had clove scent inside it. Charlie was a natural and within a few 1-2-1s he was showing a beautiful passive indication – holding his nose just above where he had detected the scent, his tail wagging widely the whole time. Jennie felt she had unlocked Charlie's hidden talent, of course his talent had always been there, he just needed Jennie to enter his world and see it. Charlie was able to join a class as all the dogs were worked separately initially and then dogs were worked together but at opposite ends of the hall, Charlie never stared or lunged and seemed relaxed, he could cope so much better as the other dogs were not barking and aroused and the scent work was inherently so calming for him. Charlie did so well that Jennie was encouraged by her trainer to enter him into some trials. He competed in timed trials to find hidden items at different locations including a stadium and a disused railway station. Charlie excelled, and the rosettes he won meant so much to Jennie. Jennie also enjoyed the social aspect of classes and both Jennie and Charlie had found the perfect activity that suited them as a team.

References

1. Kobelt, A., Hemsworth, P., Barnett, J. and Coleman, G. (2003) A survey of dog ownership in suburban Australia – Conditions and behaviour problems. *Applied Animal Behaviour Science* 82, 137–148.
2. Bennett, P. and Rohlf, V. (2007) Owner-companion dog interactions: Relationship between demographic variables, potentially problematic behaviours, training engagement and shared activities. *Applied Animal Behaviour Science* 102, 65–84.
3. Zilocchi, M., Tagliavini, Z., Cianni, E. and Gazzano, A. (2016) Effects of physical activity on dog behavior. *Dog Behavior* 2, 9–14.
4. Tiira, K. and Lohi, H. (2015) Early life experiences and exercise associate with canine anxieties. *Public Library of Science ONE* 10, e0141907.
5. Heijnen, S., Hommel, B., Kibele, A. and Colzato, L. (2016) Neuromodulation of aerobic exercise – a review. *Frontiers in Psychology* 6, 1890.
6. Bjørnebekk, A., Mathé, A. and Brené, S. (2005) The antidepressant effect of running is associated with increased hippocampal cell proliferation. *International Journal of Neuropsychopharmacology* 8, 357–68.
7. Raichlen, D., Foster, A., Seillier, A., Giuffrida, A. and Gerdeman, G. (2013) Exercise-induced endocannabinoid signaling is modulated by intensity. *European Journal of Applied Physiology* 113, 869–875.
8. Zilocchi, M. and Carlone, B. (2016) Problem-solving games as a tool to reduce fear of strangers in dogs. *Dog Behavior*, 2, 3–12.
9. Zilocchi, M. (2018) Problem-solving games as a tool to increase the well-being in boarding kennel dogs. *Dog Behavior* 4, 9–19.
10. Hiby, E., Rooney, N. and Bradshaw, J. (2004) Dog training methods: their use, effectiveness and interaction with behaviour and welfare. *Animal Welfare* 13, 63–70.

11. Cooper, J., Cracknell, N., Hardiman, J., Wright, H. and Mills, D. (2014) The welfare consequences and efficacy of training pet dogs with remote electronic training collars in comparison to reward based training. *Public Library of Science ONE* 9, e102722.

12. Vieira de Castro, A., Fuchs, D., Morello, G., Pastur, S., de Sousa, L. and Olsson, A. (2020) Does training method matter? Evidence for the negative impact of aversive-based methods on companion dog welfare. *Public Library of Science ONE* 15, e0225023.

13. Marshall-Pescini, S., Valsecchi, P., Petak, I., Accorsi, P. and Previde, E. (2008) Does training make you smarter? The effects of training on dogs' performance (*Canis familiaris*) in a problem-solving task. *Behavioural Processes* 78, 449–454.

14. Handlin, L., Nilsson, A., Ejdebäck, M., Hydbring-Sandberg, E. and Uvnäs-Moberg, K. (2012) Associations between the psychological characteristics of the human–dog relationship and oxytocin and cortisol levels. *Anthrozoös* 25, 215–228.

15. Miller, S. C., Kennedy, C. C., DeVoe, D. C., Hickey, M., Nelson, T. and Kogan, L. (2009) An examination of changes in oxytocin levels in men and women before and after interaction with a bonded dog. *Anthrozoös* 22, 31–42.

16. Meyer, I. and Forkman, B. (2014) Dog and owner characteristics affecting the dog–owner relationship. *Journal of Veterinary Behavior* 9, 143–150.

17. Payne, E., Bennett, P. and McGreevy, P. (2015) Current perspectives on attachment and bonding in the dog–human dyad. *Psychology Research and Behavior Management* 8, 71.

18. Pastore, C., Pirrone, F., Balzarotti, F., Faustini, M., Pierantoni, L. and Albertini, M. (2011) Evaluation of physiological and behavioral stress-dependent parameters in agility dogs. *Journal of Veterinary Behavior* 6, 188–194.

19. Carpenter, A., Guy, J. and Leach, M. (2020) Influence of the Competition Context on Arousal in Agility Dogs. *Journal of Applied Animal Welfare Science* 23, 410–423.

20. Roth, L., Faresjö, Å., Theodorsson, E. and Jensen, P. (2016) Hair cortisol varies with season and lifestyle and relates to human interactions in German shepherd dogs. *Scientific Reports* 6, 1–7.

21. Levy, I., Hall, C., Trentacosta, N. and Percival, M. (2009) A preliminary retrospective survey of injuries occurring in dogs participating in canine agility. *Veterinary and Comparative Orthopaedics and Traumatology*, 22, 321.

22. Cullen, K., Dickey, J., Bent, R., Thomason, J. and Moëns, N. (2013) Internet-based survey of the nature and perceived causes of injury to dogs participating in agility training and competition events. *Journal of the American Veterinary Medical Association* 243, 1010–1018.

23. Noteboom, J., Fleshner, M. and Enoka, R. (2001) Activation of the arousal response can impair performance on a simple motor task. *Journal of Applied Physiology* 92, 821–831.

24. Roets, A. and Van Hiel, A. (2011) An Integrative Process Approach on Judgment and Decision Making: The Impact of Arousal, Affect, Motivation, and Cognitive Ability. *The Psychological Record* 61, 497–520.

25. The Dog Pulse Project (n.d.) http://www.dogpulse.org (accessed 30 May 2021).

26. Packer, R., Davies, A., Volk, A., Puckett, H., Hobbs, S. and Fowkes, R. (2019) What can we learn from the hair of the dog? Complex effects of endogenous and exogenous stressors on canine hair cortisol. *Public Library of Science ONE* 14, e0216000.

27. Montalbano, C., Gamble, L., Walden, K., Rouse, J., Mann, S., Sack, D., Wakshlag, L., Shmalberg, J. and Wakshlag, J. (2019) Internet survey of participant demographics and risk factors for injury in flyball dogs. *Frontiers in Veterinary Science*, 6, 391.

28. Fugazza, C. and Miklósi, Á. (2015) Social learning in dog training: the effectiveness of the Do as I do method compared to shaping/clicker training. *Applied Animal Behaviour Science* 171, 146–151.

29. Lofgren, S., Wiener, P., Blott, S., Sanchez-Molano, E., Woolliams, J., Clements, D. and Haskell, M. (2014) Management and personality in Labrador Retriever dogs. *Applied Animal Behaviour Science* 156, 44–53.

30. Raynor, B., De la Puente, M., Johnson, A., Díaz-Espinoza, E., Levy, M. and Castillo-Neyra, R. (2019) Movement patterns of urban free-roaming dogs: implications for rabies control in Arequipa, Peru. *BioRxiv* 68438131.

31. Sepúlveda, M., Pelican, K., Cross, P., Eguren, A. and Singer, R. (2015) Fine-scale movements of rural free-ranging dogs in conservation areas in the temperate rainforest of the coastal range of southern Chile. *Mammalian Biology* 80, 290–297.

32. Carter, A. and Hall, E. (2018) Investigating factors affecting the body temperature of dogs competing in cross country (canicross) races in the UK. *Journal of Thermal Biology* 72, 33–38.

33. Lafuente, P. and Whyle, C. (2018) A retrospective survey of injuries occurring in dogs and handlers participating in canicross. *Veterinary and Comparative Orthopaedics and Traumatology* 31, 332–338.

34. Davis, M., Willard, M., Nelson, S., Mandsager, R., McKiernan, B., Mansell, J. and Lehenbauer, T. (2003) Prevalence of gastric lesions in racing Alaskan sled dogs. *Journal of Veterinary Internal Medicine* 17, 311–314.

35. Dennis, M., Nelson, S., Cantor, G., Mosier, D., Blake, J. and Basaraba, R. (2008) Assessment of necropsy findings in sled dogs that died during Iditarod Trail sled dog races: 23 cases (1994–2006). *Journal of the American Veterinary Medical Association* 232, 564–573.

36. Starling, M., Spurrett, A. and McGreevy, P. (2020) A pilot study of methods for evaluating the effects of arousal and emotional valence on performance of racing greyhounds. *Animals* 10, 1037.

37. Majumder, S., Chatterjee, A. and Bhadra, A. (2014) A dog's day with humans–time activity budget of free-ranging dogs in India. *Current Science* 874–878.

38. The Slow Dog Movement (n.d.) www.slowdog movement.org (accessed 30 May 2021).

39. Mann, S. (2020) *Easy Peasy Puppy Squeezey: The Ultimate Puppy Training Handbook*. Bonnier Books, London.

40. Bratman, G., Anderson, C., Berman, M., Cochran, B., De Vries, S., Flanders, J. and Daily, G. (2019) Nature and mental health: An ecosystem service perspective. *Science Advances* 5, eaax0903.

41. Mayer, F., Frantz, C., Bruehlman-Senecal, E. and Dolliver, K. (2009) Why is nature beneficial? The role of connectedness to nature. *Environment and Behavior* 41, 607–643.

42. Araújo, D., Brymer, E., Brito, H., Withagen, R. and Davids, K. (2019) The empowering variability of affordances of nature: why do exercisers feel better after performing the same exercise in natural environments than in indoor environments? *Psychology of Sport and Exercise 42*, 138–145.

43. Furuyashiki, A., Tabuchi, K., Norikoshi, K., Kobayashi, T. and Oriyama, S. (2019) A comparative study of the physiological and psychological effects of forest bathing (Shinrin-yoku) on working age people with and without depressive tendencies. *Environmental Health and Preventive Medicine* 24, 1–11.

44. Gergen, K. (2002) The challenge of absent presence. In J.E. Katz and M. Aakhus (eds) *Perpetual Contact: Mobile Communication, Private Talk, Public Performance*. Cambridge University Press, Cambridge, pp. 227–241.

45. Bardi, M., Kaufman, C., Franssen, C., Hyer, M., Rzucidlo, A., Brown, M., Tschirhart, M. and Lambert, K. (2016) Paper or plastic? Exploring the effects of natural enrichment on behavioural and neuroendocrine responses in long-evans rats. *Journal of Neuroendocrinology*, 28, doi: 10.1111/jne.12383.

46. Cummins, A., Piek, J. and Dyck, M. (2005) Motor coordination, empathy, and social behaviour in school-aged children. *Developmental Medicine and Child Neurology* 47. 437–442.

47. Viaud-Delmon, I., Venault, P. and Chapouthier, G. (2011) Behavioral models for anxiety and multisensory integration in animals and humans. *Progress in Neuro-Psychopharmacology and Biological Psychiatry* 35, 1391–1399.

48. Lopez, M. and Swinth, Y. (2008) A group proprioceptive program's effect on physical aggression in children. *Journal of Occupational Therapy, Schools, and Early Intervention* 1, 147–166.

49. Abdelbasset, W., Alrawaili, S., Nambi, G., Yassen, E., Moawd, S. and Ahmed, A. (2020) Therapeutic effects of proprioceptive exercise on functional capacity, anxiety, and depression in patients with diabetic neuropathy: a 2-month prospective study. *Clinical Rheumatology* 39, 3091–3097.

50. Bratberg, G., Leira, K., Granan, L., Jonsbu, E., Fadnes, B., Thuland, S. and Myklebust, T. (2020) Learning oriented physiotherapy (LOP) in anxiety and depression: an 18 months multicentre randomised controlled trial (RCT). *European Journal of Physiotherapy*, 23, 295–304.

51. Pingale, V., Fletcher, T. and Candler, C. (2019) The effects of sensory diets on children's classroom behaviors. *Journal of Occupational Therapy, Schools, and Early Intervention* 12, 225–238.

52. Hussein, H. (2012) The influence of sensory gardens on the behaviour of children with special educational needs. *Procedia-Social and Behavioral Sciences* 38, 343–354.

53. Hall, N., Glenn, K., Smith, D. and Wynne, C. (2015) Performance of Pugs, German Shepherds, and Greyhounds (Canis lupus familiaris) on an odor-discrimination task. *Journal of Comparative Psychology* 129, 237.

54. Walker, D., Walker, J., Cavnar, P., Taylor, J., Pickel, D., Hall, S. and Suarez, J. (2006) Naturalistic quantification of canine olfactory sensitivity. *Applied Animal Behaviour Science* 97, 241–254.

55. Gadbois, S. and Reeve, C. (2014) Canine olfaction: scent, sign, and situation. In A. Horowitz (ed.)

Domestic Dog Cognition and Behavior, Springer, Berlin, pp. 3–29.

56. Duranton, C. and Horowitz, A. (2019) Let me sniff! Nosework induces positive judgment bias in pet dogs. *Applied Animal Behaviour Science*, 211, 61–66.
57. Beebe, S., Howell, T. and Bennett, P. (2016) Using scent detection dogs in conservation settings: a review of scientific literature regarding their selection. *Frontiers in Veterinary Science*, 3, 96.
58. Berns, G., Brooks, A. and Spivak, M. (2015) Scent of the familiar: An fMRI study of canine brain responses to familiar and unfamiliar human and dog odors. *Behavioural Processes* 110, 37–46.
59. Swenson, C. (2014) Veterinary toxicology alert: Oils used in 'scent training' can harm dogs. DVM360 (https://www.dvm360.com/view/veterinary-toxicology-alert-oils-used-scent-training-can-harm-dogs).
60. Hurt, A. and Smith, D.A. (2009) *Conservation Dogs. Canine Ergonomics: the Science of Working Dogs*. CRC Press, Boca Raton, FL.

Chapter 5

Teaching

Rosie Bescoby

The majority of the time when we are working with dogs, there are people involved too – we have two learners (the dog and the human). Human partnerships with dogs can be traced back more than 20,000 years.[1] We live and work with dogs, and they depend on us. Sometimes we need to teach people about dogs without a dog being present, or sometimes in cases where the person themselves does not own one. It is estimated that there are approximately 12 million dogs in the UK,[2] representing a significant increase since the coronavirus pandemic, and dog behaviour inevitably affects anyone who is exposed to (or interacts with) dogs – for example, when visiting dog owner's homes, or in public spaces. Ultimately, we are unable to produce long-lasting change without the understanding and cooperation of all people who interact with dogs. Teaching *how* to train a dog and increasing understanding of dog behaviour all need to be done with human behaviour in mind too. Many of the same principles and methods used in dog training and behaviour modification can be applied to human students, although inevitably there are also some important differences.

The most obvious benefits of teaching with behaviour in mind are the following.

- Animal welfare – improving both emotional and physical welfare by ensuring the dog feels safe and comfortable. The Animal Welfare Act 2006 states that animals need to be able to exhibit normal behaviour patterns and need to be protected from pain and suffering.[3]
- Safety – reducing incidents of conflict behaviours such as biting, by considering the dog's emotional state.
- Human welfare – protecting/enhancing mental health and ability to concentrate and learn.

This chapter will explore the importance of teaching with human behaviour in mind, look at the ways different formats for teaching can consider human and canine behaviour, and discuss what elements of dog behaviour are essential to teach.

The importance of teaching with human behaviour in mind

In 1943, psychologist Abraham Maslow proposed an idea in his paper 'A theory of human motivation' comprising a five-tier hierarchical model of human needs illustrated as a pyramid.[4] He suggested that the needs at the bottom of the pyramid should be satisfied before individuals can be expected to attend to needs higher up.

Physiological requirements for survival such as food, water, warmth and rest, and feeling

Jimmy the Chihuahua

Over the past six months, Jimmy (a 1-year-old unneutered male Chihuahua) had snapped at both familiar and unfamiliar people who had tried to pick him up. He had also been incessantly barking at activity outside the home while looking out of the lounge window. Maggie, a busy single working mum to 6-year-old Reuben, sent Jimmy to a residential trainer for a fortnight. After his 2-week stay, Jimmy was passed back to Maggie and Reuben with the trainer stating that the problems were resolved – no handover was conducted. Within a week after returning home, Jimmy was expressing all the same behaviours he was initially sent away to resolve.

safe and secure are classed as 'basic human needs'. These should be addressed before attending to 'psychological needs', such as feeling a sense of belonging, trust and acceptance, followed by 'esteem needs', which include achievement and feeling respected. At the top of the pyramid are 'self-fulfilment needs' such as achieving one's full potential and personal growth. Although academically Maslow's ideas are contested due to individual and cultural differences, the model provides a useful framework to consider how to create an optimum environment for human learners to achieve their full potential.

Considerations for fulfilling *basic human needs* when teaching people about dog training or behaviour might include the following.

- Providing or ensuring there is access to refreshments and a toilet.
- Ensuring the environment is a comfortable temperature or has adequate shelter (or providing prior guidance about appropriate clothing).
- Providing food (and confirming dietary requirements in advance) or instructions for bringing food if teaching might be over a long period of time.
- Making sure there is appropriate space between unfamiliar people (both teacher and learner, and different learners within

a group), so that all humans and dogs involved feel safe.
- Ensuring no individual is put into a situation or asked to do something that they do not feel safe or comfortable with.
- Implementing essential management strategies if safety is jeopardised by a dog's behaviour.
- Conducting risk assessments in advance of any teaching.

Attending to *psychological needs* could involve the following.

- Providing information prior to meeting the owner outlining (in detail) what they might need to prepare or bring to the session, where they might need to go/park (use clearly visible signs on the premises if relevant too), and what to expect from the session. At the end of the session, verbally outlining what the next stages are (reiterate in writing if required). Effectively removing all the 'unknowns' that can induce anxiety.
- Structuring the environment appropriately so that all individuals feel included (regardless of age, ability, space requirements and so on).
- Emphasising collaboration between learner and teacher (the language used can aid this,

for example, use of 'we', as well as providing support outside of in person contact sessions, and asking the learner about their thoughts and ideas).

- Using genuine and appropriate humour and finding familiar ground to enhance the relationship between teacher and learner.
- 'Receive-listening'[5] – dialogue is more efficient if we avoid interrupting and formulate our response after the learner has finished speaking. The pause this creates communicates with the caregiver that you are processing their words.
- Considering the emotional state of all learners (aiming for a learning environment where everyone is in a positive emotional state).
- Providing the learner with a sense of control.
- Building trust and rapport using open-ended questions, paraphrasing what the caregiver has said to ensure you understood them correctly, using lay language and expressing empathy and authentic kindness.
- Creating a non-critical environment by using positive reinforcement liberally. Social reinforcers such as smiling, genuine praise, head nods and quiet encouragement provided during tasks can help reduce anxiety that can interfere with learning. Further positive feedback can then be given at the end of the activity.
- Staying within one's own professional remit.
- Being mindful of language used and body language that might be translated as judgemental.
- Explicitly stating protocols regarding client confidentiality and GDPR compliance on websites or within confirmation details.

Esteem needs should be considered.

- Setting goals for individual learners to achieve.
- Respecting all individuals and ensuring other learners who might be in the same environment respect one another.
- Focusing on teaching alternative human behaviours rather than responding to incorrect or undesirable behaviours (to avoid damaging self-esteem or causing defensiveness).

Some human beliefs about and attitudes towards dogs are incompatible with the aim of teaching with canine behaviour in mind.

- Anthropomorphism – thinking dogs are capable of spite, guilt and other terms that imply that the dog is at fault or flawed in character.
- Objectification – degrading dogs to the status of an insentient object.
- Confrontational attitudes – often stemming from the theory that the human has to assert dominance.

Addressing these beliefs requires a level of tact and patience synonymous with meeting 'psychological and esteem needs'. If new ideas are not presented carefully, they may either be rejected or cause the owner to feel inadequate, guilty and experience 'cognitive dissonance', which produces a feeling of mental discomfort when presented with conflicting attitudes, beliefs or behaviours. Teaching people about dogs should aim to help them consider *why* dogs might exhibit certain behaviours: Is the dog in physical pain? Are they frightened? Do they understand the cue? Is the dog relaxed enough to be able to pay attention? If learners can be encouraged to see that a dog might need help rather than be at fault, they can start to consider what *they* can do in order to help the dog (and, consequently, themselves). Helping owners to develop an awareness of how their dog is feeling engages interest and prevents the teacher needing to actively address any incompatible beliefs head-on. Indeed, a powerful tool in changing human perspective is our use of language. If a teacher's language and attitude towards the dog and/or human reflects the belief that both are thinking, feeling beings with underlying reasons for behaviour, the learner will usually be motivated to share the same views, especially when they see the effect this has on their dog. If, in our great enthusiasm and desire to change views, the learner is flooded with information, we run the risk of appearing dictatorial, and if our information conflicts with the owner's current beliefs and habits, they might not be able to accept these new ideas.

Enquiring about an owner's aims and expectations enables the teacher to provide guidance on goals, timescales and further information on requirements to meet those aims (or to reduce expectations tactfully if required). Drifting on without any structure will not be productive for either learner but setting goals too early on can also lead to disappointment and a sense of failure. *Self-fulfilment* should always be a teacher's aim, so that the learner feels the experience has produced personal growth and achieved their full potential as a dog–human team (even if the teacher knows that the dog has not achieved their full potential).

Risë Van Fleet, a psychologist, play therapist, certified dog behaviour consultant and author of the book *The Human Half of Dog Training*[6] outlines five steps to apply when teaching humans a new skill.

1. Provide an explanation including a rationale for its use. (What is it? How do we do it? Why are we doing it, and why in this way? Give an example.)

2. Demonstrate the skill (use video footage, a live demo with your own dog and/or a live demonstration with the client's dog – if the dog will be relaxed and happy to work with you or it is essential for you to handle the dog, for example, veterinary treatment).

3. Observe the client practising the skill (if necessary, break it down into smaller sections to set the client up for success and include several repetitions at each step).

4. Provide positive individualised feedback (praise effort as well as outcomes and be specific. If necessary, provide just one or two suggestions for improvement to avoid feelings of frustration or failure).

5. Suggest next steps to work on and set goals (focus on just one or two behaviours that entail practising similar skills just covered).

Generally, when working with humans, we have the advantage of using language and conversation that we do not have when working directly with dogs. This enables us to provide corrective feedback or suggestions (when unwanted behaviours are repeated despite a teacher's best efforts to redirect the person to alternative behaviour), but it ideally needs to be delivered only occasionally, tactfully, embedded within positive feedback and once a decent relationship has been formed between teacher and learner.

Alongside potentially helping owners alter their attitudes, beliefs and emotional responses, and to develop more awareness of their dog's emotions, teachers also need to help learners become aware of their own behaviour and develop their physical dog handling skills. This includes lead handling (as well as other equipment that might be recommended), timing of reward markers, timing and placement of reward delivery, toy play, even how they touch their dog (taking consent into account) and their observational skills.

One tool that can be particularly useful for helping people to learn new skills is TAGteach[7] (Teaching with Acoustical Guidance) – an instructional protocol for humans that shares the same underlying principles of marker-based animal training (see Chapter 3, Training). Specific learning goals are marked with a previously defined signal when they are reached by the student/learner. TAGteach works on the premise that clear communication and positive reinforcement increase effectiveness of teaching, while minimising the potential for frustration. It involves simplifying the instructions to learners by breaking the skills down, presenting instructions in a logical and organised manner, and providing instant, meaningful and positive feedback, which leads to fast results and self-correction when necessary. If incorrect behaviour is offered, the learner is not interrupted while they are working. After their learning trial, the teacher goes back a step and breaks the exercise down into even smaller components. This method enables the teacher to talk less (use fewer words) but communicate more effectively by separating 'lecture time' and hands-on practical time. Practical teaching initially does not involve the dog so that the owner can practice their mechanical skills – for example, throwing food accurately or lead handling skills. Then the same exercise is repeated with the dog so the teacher can observe and refine the instructions and marker points as necessary. It can be common for canine professionals to want to share all their knowledge, but sometimes this can result in information overload, especially if an owner is trying to focus on their dog or puppy – TAGteach helps to avoid this situation from occurring.

A lack of any human teaching following Jimmy's residential stay meant that neither Maggie nor Reuben understood the motivations behind Jimmy's behaviour nor what was maintaining the problem – they received no guidance on appropriate environmental modification, or on changing their own behaviour. (In addition, no veterinary referral had been requested so pain or other medical differentials contributing to or causing the behaviour had not been ruled out or addressed.) Unfortunately, upon Jimmy's return and the continued expression of his undesirable behaviour, Maggie became overwhelmed and started squirting Jimmy with water whenever he started barking or growling. In this case, the lack of any teaching directed at the owners resulted in failure for both the dog and the humans involved. Looking back at Maggie and Jimmy's case, it is clear that teaching the client is an integral part of a behaviour modification programme. It would not matter how brilliant the residential trainer was – the ability to train a dog is a wasted skill in this context if the client is not taught the skills needed to maintain the changes made. More importantly, if the clients do not receive any explanations to enable them to understand the reasons for the dog's behaviour and the approach that was taken to address it, they will not understand how to manage and interact with the dog so that the unwanted behaviour does not return. If people are not given the opportunity to explore how their attitudes, beliefs, behaviour and environment are affecting their dog it is likely that the problem will recur, as was sadly the case for Jimmy. Regardless of how a trainer or behaviourist chooses to work, the practitioner is not going to be available at all times to implement the training or behaviour modification programme – only the owners can do that. In Jimmy's case, a complete change in environment at the residential setting and the trainer interacting with him in a different way (while it remained unclear exactly how the trainer interacted with Jimmy) led to the changes observed in Jimmy's behaviour.

Different teaching formats

Any situation in which we liaise with a dog owner, handler or anyone who has anything to do with dogs provides an opportunity to educate people about dog behaviour. As already outlined, it is important that in order to do this effectively we need to also consider human behaviour. Let us take a look at some of the different teaching formats.

Group classes

Application of a reasonable depth of knowledge of canine behaviour should not be seen as an additional benefit in dog training classes, but as an essential part of improving human–animal interactions and canine welfare. When teaching a group of people, general goals can be set for a lesson but with awareness that every individual (dog and person) will be starting from a different point and have different requirements, so the exercises and potential achievements will not be the same for everyone. The individuals involved may need this to be carefully explained to them so that they do not have unrealistic expectations or are left feeling inadequate.

Traditionally, a group training class was set up with puppies and dogs of various ages, usually in a hall environment. The format was fairly regimented, based solely upon obedience training, rather than focusing on the emotional state of the dogs. Today there are various different setups for group training classes, which are run with both human and dog behaviour in mind.

Puppy classes

Nowadays it is popular for new puppy owners to attend classes designed specifically for puppies from when they receive their first vaccination to around 16 weeks of age. Some are run as a rolling programme, so caregivers can join any week (because exercises are not conducted in any order that requires prior knowledge or understanding), while others are run as a block of sessions, with each session leading on from the previous week. Generally, these are run weekly, although it may benefit some slightly older puppies to have more frequent sessions (for example, twice weekly).

Clinical animal behaviourist and author Gwen Bailey founded Puppy School[8] in 2003 after working as Head of Animal Behaviour for a rescue charity for 13 years. During this time, many of the dogs being relinquished had behaviour problems, which made it harder for them to find new homes, and it became clear to Gwen that focus needed to be on the education of new owners, particularly during the early stages of puppyhood when owners are keen to learn and puppies are very impressionable. Gwen already knew the beneficial impact of running a 'behaviourally aware' puppy class at a local level so wanted to roll that out to more places. Puppy School has since grown into a UK network of professional tutors who are taught how to coach people and who receive significant behavioural training.

Roz Pooley of The Mutty Professor[9] based in Bristol runs puppy classes specifically with behaviour in mind, focusing on 'everyday life' – namely, teaching owners to be able to walk safely and live harmoniously with their canine companions. Just four puppies are booked on each course to allow everyone individual coaching from two staff members. The class is set up to adapt to each puppy as an individual and not rush them with a generic approach. Puppies are protected from negative experiences while giving them the opportunity to flourish when they are ready. In addition, owners are given a level of coaching that sets them up to confidently grasp and apply positive reinforcement training principles. The first week consists of meeting the owners without their puppies present. This enables the instructors to explain the set-up of the classes, what can be expected and allows the opportunity for caregivers to ask questions – all without the distractions of the puppies being present at the same time. Owners, to prepare them for bringing their puppies with them to the next session, are advised to wait in their cars or are shown where to take their puppies while waiting for the puppy class to start – this prevents a group of on-lead puppies all meeting in an uncontrolled manner. Each puppy is then brought into the training room one at a time with a teacher, allowing individuals to acclimatise to the novel environment at their own pace. The owners and puppies left outside are introduced to street walk related behaviours and loose lead walking in this time, with the second teacher. These classes are run in a suburb of a city so street walks include getting the puppies used to traffic, not picking things up in their mouths (litter and so on), staying on the pavement not straying into the road, letting them work it all out in their own time and so on.

Like Puppy School classes, the training room is setup with each puppy and family member(s) having their own area with barriers between each puppy so that initial greetings between the puppies can be done carefully to ensure it is a positive experience for all involved (see Figure 5.1). The barriers are low enough so that the owners can talk over the top and feel social cohesion. The barriers are removed as the course progresses if the puppies are sufficiently confident. Owners are asked to bring their dog's own bed (so that the puppies can be comfortable and have something that smells like home) and are taught how to encourage their puppies to settle in their bed. Gwen explains that on week one of the Puppy School course, each puppy is allowed to sniff every bed to help introduce them to the other puppies but without the potential stress of being sniffed themselves. Other exercises both courses cover include food and toy manners and handling and grooming, so owners learn how to manage and interact with their puppies in non-confrontational ways. The final week is an 'in the wild' outdoor session,

Figure 5.1: Mutty Professor puppy class setup. Photo: © Roz Pooley.

which enables owners to be coached on recall and lead walking in the real-life setting. In addition, owners receive a 40-page book written by Roz (a clinical animal behaviourist) with 16 accompanying video tutorials to support learning. Owners also have access to an online support group where they can upload videos and ask further questions. 'We try to cover all the different learning styles in the support and guidance we provide', explains Roz.

Maggie and Jimmy had attended a puppy class that was described as 'noisy and chaotic' – it was in a small hall with eight dogs in total, ranging from 10-week-old puppies up to 6-month-old adolescent dogs. The dogs were all straining to get to each other and there was a lot of barking. Maggie admitted herself she felt stressed and could not really concentrate. She remembered one exercise where they were asked to 'pass their puppy' to the person next to them and continue around the group with the intention of getting their puppies used to unfamiliar people and being 'handled' by someone unfamiliar to them. However, Maggie realised in hindsight that Jimmy was scrabbling to get away from each new person he was passed to and at one point almost somersaulted off someone's lap in an attempt to get back to her. Unfortunately, it is likely that Jimmy was actually 'sensitised' to handling by this experience, as well as learning that attempts to get away from something he found unpleasant were not effective.

Online classes

The emergence of COVID-19 and the related social restrictions led to many classes moving to an online format and both owners and professionals have recognised there have been some advantages to this.

- No travel is required – this might be beneficial to puppies/dogs (or humans) who do not travel well, or have no ability to access in person training classes (live rurally, no private vehicle, no access to public transport or inconvenience of travel).
- Online classes are appropriate for any dog regardless of specific needs – there are no distractions of other dogs, no unfamiliar people and the environment is familiar.
- Online classes are accessible to all – removes geographical/physical limitations as well as social anxiety restrictions (video and microphone can be turned off during live classes if individuals prefer).
- Online classes allow owners to learn new skills at home and gain a better understanding of applying what they learn to the real world, rather than assuming that the class environment is the only place where learning occurs.
- Improved safety – training a dog at home has arguably reduced risks to both dogs and humans.
- Physiological and basic needs more likely to be met – the familiar environment is more conducive to learning.

Some courses are run with pre-recorded content that owners can access when it is convenient to them, while others are conducted as live scheduled sessions – and many as a hybrid of the two. Jane Ardern, owner of WaggaWuffins Canine College in Manchester,[10] has been running online training courses since 2016 alongside in person classes. All of Jane's training, from puppies and adolescents through to advanced obedience and gundog courses, involves relating each training exercise with canine behaviour in terms of why it is being taught (that is, how it applies to the real world) and how it is being taught (and the relevance to the emotions induced in the dog during training). Over each course, the behavioural content that is covered includes information on drive and motivation, developmental stages and instincts, frustration and impulse control, and emotions, stress and body language. Initially the content was pre-recorded with people signing up either to a course or a monthly membership option. From this grew a whole online community and support group, consisting of both owners and professionals, video tutorials, written content, weekly live sessions or webinars, training challenges and a safe place for confidential discussion. March 2020 saw all face-to-face classes move to an online format that consisted of weekly live scheduled sessions with access to literature, support and video tutorials. Jane found that puppy owners were originally reluctant to join an online course for a number of reasons.

- They wanted to be able to socialise their puppy. This suggested a potential lack of understanding of the purpose of the training classes, an expectation of what would be involved during an in person class, and that the desire to socialise was more important than the information or training being taught.
- They spent all day working via video calling and could not face remote training after-hours on a computer. This outlook tended to change once people became accustomed to other aspects of their lives also moving online as the pandemic continued.
- They did not want their home environment being seen by other people. Options were discussed such as turning their own camera off and sharing training videos in real-life scenarios for feedback, using a virtual background or finding an area of the home with a neutral backdrop.

For most people, live online training has been a steep learning curve. To minimise human stress levels, Jane asks everyone to log in 10 minutes before their class is due to start to allow for any technical issues to be addressed and has a member of staff available on the phone to help if needed. She provides information in advance about where to place the screen and instructors demonstrate exercises in their own homes (with similar space restrictions to owners). Whereas the environment of an in person class inevitably creates arousal, puppies taught at home were initially fast asleep in the evening when classes were scheduled – 'the puppies went from one extreme to the other in terms of nervous system arousal levels!' This was resolved by advising owners to change their routines so that training for 10–15 minutes every evening at a similar time to the training class became a habit. Jane has decided to keep running the first session of each course virtually because it allows the teacher to assess the human learner's skills, and to teach some foundation exercises while the dogs are relaxed in their own home, and then progress to in person teaching for the rest of the course to enable the dogs to work in a new environment around the distractions of unfamiliar people and dogs.

Puppy parties at the vets
Typically, these involve a set number of puppies in the reception area or waiting room of the veterinary practice and a member of staff providing information to owners about preventative healthcare together with some training and/or behaviour topics. Generally, the puppies are allowed off-lead time in order to 'learn social skills' and the owners are sent home with an information pack covering what was discussed in more detail. These sessions are advantageous in terms of human and dog behaviour for various reasons.

- They aim to create a positive association with the veterinary practice.
- Staff can teach owners about basic dog behaviour – many owners will choose not to proceed with any further professional guidance, such as from trainers or behaviourists, and so this is an important opportunity to influence the way they interact with their dogs moving forward.
- A relationship is formed between the veterinary practice/staff and new owners.
- The veterinary practice becomes a source of information about behaviour, which means owners are more likely to turn to veterinary staff for behavioural advice in future if required.

It is vital that staff members conducting puppy parties have some behavioural training in order to ensure that they are actually of benefit to the current and future behavioural health of puppies. The benefits and risks regarding off-lead play between puppies are widely debated among behavioural professionals. Some firmly believe that off-lead social interactions between evenly matched puppies (in terms of boldness, size and age) is an imperative part of learning social skills. Others are of the view that puppies are not ideal candidates to teach one another appropriate social skills and there is a risk of puppies forming a high expectation of getting to play with other dogs (which can have implications on walks). Some professionals therefore suggest that these environments can be used to teach the puppies to enjoy interacting with their owner while surrounded by the distractions of other puppies – owners should then be encouraged to introduce their puppies to appropriate adult dogs. What *is* universally agreed, however, is that if off-lead play is going to be part of these sessions, they must be overseen by someone experienced in dog behaviour so that it is not only a positive experience for all

the puppies involved but also that no puppy is rehearsing inappropriate behaviour. This also enables the owners to be taught about appropriate dog interactions. The setups outlined above in 'puppy classes' can be considered for an ideal environment for humans and puppies to learn effectively. Vet staff running puppy parties might want to consider changing the name of the service that is being offered, to adjust expectations about what puppy social interactions might look like – puppy pre-school has been used with good effect. It is also worth reflecting on the amount of information that is attempted to be relayed in these sessions, particularly when puppies are present.

Adolescent or adult classes

In person classes for older dogs may be more logistically challenging to ensure they are run with both canine and human behaviour in mind. The dogs may not have previously attended classes (and are therefore unfamiliar with a class setup), may not have any basic level of training, have a longer learning history than puppies (for example, will already have expectations about interactions with people and dogs), will come from a variety of backgrounds (including rescue) and owners are likely to have different aims and potentially some undesirable behaviours that they are seeking help for (as opposed to focusing more on problem prevention in puppy classes).

Assessing each individual dog during a 1-2-1 training session prior to signing them up for a course is a sensible prerequisite for all, to ensure that a group session is appropriate for the dog and to establish any particular difficulties the owner might be experiencing. Further 1-2-1 sessions or recommendation of a consultation with a clinical or veterinary behaviourist may be more appropriate. Equipment may need to be discussed at this session, to ensure that owners have adequate physical control (due to strength and size of older dogs). Additional space will be required between each learner–dog combination (due to the size of the dog) to ensure that no individual dog can gain unsolicited access to another dog in the group.

Outdoor classes

The outdoor environment provides its own advantages and challenges in terms of both dog and human behaviour. The additional stimulation the environment itself provides can lead to dogs exhibiting arousal issues, and subsequent restriction from gaining free access to the environment can lead to frustration-related behaviour. In addition, people and dogs are less likely to be as static as in an indoor environment. While this can be beneficial to an individual dog who is able to move around and engage with the environment, the increased movement and activity of other dogs in the group (particularly as more arousing activities, such as sports, may be taught outdoors) can lead to increased arousal and stress due to anxiety and/or frustration. However, outdoor classes also provide a more real-life setup and the ability for owners to train their dogs in a more distracting environment (if the dog is ready for that level of distraction). There may also be the benefit of additional space, so dogs who require a greater distance from unfamiliar people or dogs can often be accommodated. In order for basic needs to be met, weather conditions do need to be taken into account and classes may need to be cancelled if conditions are extreme and not suitable for dogs or humans to learn.

Training workshops/CPD for professionals

Teaching professionals encompasses both theory-based conferences and practical workshops where dogs are being trained. Human behaviour needs to be considered for optimal learning conditions at conferences. In particular, sitting down for long periods of time and the length of the day may lead to discomfort and over-tiredness (basic needs no longer being met). It can be advantageous for sessions to be interactive, for delegates to have to change rooms between each session or for the format of each session to be different and for an informal atmosphere so delegates can stand and move around or leave the room if required for their own comfort.

When dogs are used either as demonstration dogs by the teacher and/or where participants bring their dogs to train, dog welfare (in terms of both physical and emotional states) should always be priority for every dog involved, even if that restricts the human teaching element of the course. For example, if there is inadequate space or too many people for an individual dog to be able to remain relaxed, the demonstration or training of that dog in that environment may need to be abandoned.

At the veterinary practice

All veterinary staff, from receptionists to nurses, care assistants and vets could teach owners about canine behaviour. It might be as simple as a receptionist asking an owner whether they would like to wait outside with their dog if the dog is becoming increasingly stressed in the waiting area, or perhaps moving a chair for the owner so that the dog has more space or is not sitting directly opposite or next to another dog in reception. Perhaps a nurse could teach an owner how to put eye drops in while highlighting some body language signs that indicate when to stop and give the dog some space. Or indeed a vet might be able to explain to a client why they are letting the dog sniff around the consult room while they take the dog's history and why they are examining the dog on the floor instead of the table. Vets also have the opportunity to explain to owners the potential links between physical and behavioural issues and why it is important to address both, because the emotional welfare of the dog is equally as important as the physical welfare.

Of course, vet staff will also receive clients specifically asking for behavioural advice and it is important that there is a member of staff available to provide appropriate management advice to prevent the undesirable behaviour from escalating and to ensure everyone is kept safe. If an owner seeks further advice, it is important that information is not given beyond a staff member's knowledge or experience because inappropriate advice may be more detrimental to the dog's behaviour than providing management advice only. Contacting a local behaviourist (lists available at the Animal Behaviour and Training website[11]) to discuss further options would be advised.

There may be a member of the vet team who has additional qualifications in dog behaviour who might be able to teach colleagues 'on the job'. This is ideal and should be embraced because the whole veterinary team can become effective in reduced-stress handling procedures, dog body language and behaviour, and make visits as stress free as possible. If owners know that a veterinary practice works in this way, their own anxiety about their dog's vet visit will also be significantly reduced.

On return from Jimmy's residential trip, once it became apparent that there was no significant change in his behaviour at home, Maggie asked her vet for advice during a routine vaccination appointment. Her vet discussed how Jimmy may be responding defensively to handling due to underlying pain but recognised that (due to his history) it would be stressful for Jimmy if he were to attempt a full clinical examination to determine this and pointed out some body language signs such as lip licking, staring and freezing during his brief physical examination prior to vaccination. Instead, Jimmy's movement was observed, and no obvious concerns were noted as well as there being no other indicators of underlying medical issues. At this stage, the vet recommended referral to me – a clinical animal behaviourist. 'First aid' advice was also provided to ensure everyone was kept safe and to avoid rehearsal of the undesirable behaviours, which included avoiding picking Jimmy up, blocking visual access through the windows to activity outside the house and muzzle training. The option of a pain relief trial was discussed with the owner but it was agreed that the vet would liaise with me about this.

Puppy pre-purchase consultations

Expectant first-time puppy owners are similar to expectant parents in many respects and providing forthcoming owners with behavioural advice prior to choosing a breed, finding their breeder, picking the puppy from the litter or bringing the puppy home is hugely effective in reducing the chances of undesirable behaviour materialising later on. Pre-purchase consultations also provide the opportunity to discuss expectations in terms of 'normal' puppy behaviour, preventing undesirable behaviour developing, settling the puppy into its new environment and building relationships with its new family. Perhaps most importantly, questions can be asked in advance of obtaining or bringing a puppy home. In fact, the information provided can sometimes be sufficient for an interested party to realise that dog ownership is not for them, not at this particular time or perhaps at all. Prospective owners may seek advice at this stage from various professionals including vet staff, dog trainers, behaviourists, breeders or rescue centres. It is important that whoever provides the advice has sufficient behavioural knowledge to help at arguably the most crucial part of the relationship that is about to develop. The teacher also has the responsibility of pointing the almost-owner in the direction of further assistance once the puppy is brought home (continuing the theme of providing realistic expectations as to how much support might be needed to work through puppyhood and into adolescence collaboratively).

There is potential for successful pre-purchase group courses to be run to allow enthusiastic future puppy caregivers to share questions and potentially continue supporting each other (much like human antenatal classes). Indeed, some behaviour-aware breeders make attendance of such classes a compulsory condition of taking one of their puppies. The idea could also extend to group courses for potential new rescue dog owners.

Behaviourists and 1-2-1 training

When people have issues with their dog or puppy, the first step for any behaviourist or trainer is to help the owner develop a management strategy to contain the problem. This is important both for the dog(s) (to prevent the dog or dogs involved rehearsing undesirable behaviour), but also for the humans who usually will have exhausted their own repertoire of interventions by the time help has been sought.

A behaviourist's job is to then gain information about a dog through their medical history, verbally questioning the owner or handler, observing the dog (including his/her body language), assessing the dog's response to certain situations or stimuli (while not purposefully putting the dog into a situation that will induce a stress response) and/or any other

history that is available to them. Using this information, the behaviourist determines the potential motivations underlying any undesirable behaviour, identifies what is maintaining the behaviour, and explains this in simplified form to the owners (and, if necessary, other relevant people involved in the dog's care). A behaviour modification programme can then be devised, that aims to continue controlling the dog's exposure to antecedents for the undesirable behaviour, and address altering the dog's emotional responses using classical conditioning and behavioural responses using operant conditioning. The owner is then coached through practical handling and training skills required to implement the behaviour modification programme. A collaborative model enables the owner to be an active participant in the learning process and together the practitioner and client share thoughts and ideas to ensure successful implementation of skills and strategies in everyday life. The teacher is an expert in the knowledge and skills being taught and the student is an expert in their own family and lifestyle.

A trainer typically instructs owners how to train their dog using operant conditioning. However, as Bob Bailey once said: 'While Pavlov is on one shoulder, Skinner is on the other.'[12] This means that when we are training operantly, there are still classical associations occurring. Equally, when we are training using classical conditioning, there are operant behaviours being reinforced. Therefore, it is vital that trainers are always aware of the dog's emotional state, can read dog body language and know how to respond appropriately when a dog is exhibiting signs of anxiety, fear or frustration – in particular when it might be the training or environment that is inducing these emotional responses. Trainers also need to appreciate their limitations and refer on to a behaviourist when relevant.

An initial consultation with me was conducted at Maggie's home with Reuben also present. A full medical history was obtained from the vet along with referral beforehand. There had been no further events of growling, snapping or barking at external activity since implementing the vet's management advice. I was able to create a timeline of relevant events that had occurred in Jimmy's life that may have initiated and contributed to Jimmy's current behaviour. Maggie reported when she was reflecting that when Jimmy was a puppy, Reuben had once dropped him from standing height. Observations were continuously made about Jimmy's behaviour during the consultation and open questions asked about Jimmy's behavioural responses and body language in different scenarios. The underlying motivations for Jimmy's behaviour were explained to the owners, so they had a better understanding that Jimmy was barking out of the window due to anxiety and frustration associated with unfamiliar people near his territory, and represented attempts to repel the unfamiliar people from the home. It was also rationalised that Jimmy may have been hurt when Reuben dropped him, and that incident along with being passed around during puppy class meant that Jimmy was now fearful of being picked up. Factors maintaining Jimmy's behaviour were also outlined – the reinforcement of barking at potential intruders and observing them retreating from his territory and a person attempting to handle him withdrawing when snapped at were relayed. A discussion was then had with both Maggie and Reuben about how Jimmy was likely to feel safer both at home and around familiar and unfamiliar people since no attempts to pick him up had been made.

Human behaviour change takes time and everyone has different learning styles. After the consultation, a written report was provided so that Maggie could refer back to what had been discussed. Video clips were also sent showing a consent-based protocol to handling so that the owners understood the end goal. Follow-up support was then provided in the form of both practical training sessions and remote contact sessions. Desensitisation and counter conditioning to being handled were implemented using a mixture of explanation, demonstration, implementation and feedback. Muzzle training had already commenced on advice from the vet, and an improved-fitting muzzle for a Chihuahua nose was recommended for better comfort. This was advised as a precautionary measure for any essential handling, examination or treatment of Jimmy before he might be comfortable to accept such procedures through training.

Residential training and rehabilitation

Residential training can have significant benefits to both dog and owner. It provides the owner with a break from their dog's potentially difficult behaviour and allows the dog to learn new behaviour in a different context and novel environment with no previous learning history. However, if this service is offered it is vital that sufficient handover and client teaching is provided. It is also important that the environment the dog is entering is suitable for the individual and will not cause a level of stress that will impact their welfare. An initial consultation will need to be conducted to take the dog's history (see above) and an explanation provided to the owner outlining reasons why the dog is exhibiting the undesirable (or indeed not exhibiting the desirable) behaviour. The owners will then require regular updates from the trainer or behaviourist in between weekly or fortnightly coaching sessions. A final handover session should be conducted and if undesirable behaviour is being exhibited in the home environment, it is also likely to be beneficial for the behaviourist to visit the home. Further follow-up support in the form of remote sessions is vital, and further face-to-face sessions may be necessary.

Children and parents

The education and community officers at Dogs Trust teach children aged between 7–11 how to behave safely around dogs. The team runs workshops in primary schools with class-sized groups of children and life-sized fake dogs (real dogs are not used within the workshops for welfare reasons) (see Figure 5.2). The canine welfare priority for these workshops is 'safe behaviour around dogs'. Maria Kyle, family engagement manager at Dogs Trust, explains that research shows that it is well-meaning, often 'benign' behaviours performed by children that can lead to an unsafe response from dogs.[13,14] The aim of the workshops is to educate children in a way that will lead to a change in the behaviours of children that impair dog welfare. This is done by teaching that dogs are capable of experiencing emotions, that emotions drive behaviour, and discussing how dogs express emotion in their body language. The emphasis is on helping children understand that dogs respond to the way we behave around them and that in any scenario involving a dog, the dog must be free to move away without being followed. Specific information is given about how it is safest to behave in these situations to ensure both the child's safety as well as the dog's well-being (that is, when a dog is sleeping, resting or eating they should be left alone, avoid hugging and kissing dogs, no poking or pulling, never tease a dog and avoid loud noises and

chasing). The aim is to provide safe, alternative ways for children to interact with dogs in order to facilitate and nurture the canine-human bond.

Dogs Trust also have a range of online resources aimed both at parents who are dog owners and those who do not own a dog, to help educate families about how to behave around dogs – this includes dogs that the child might want to interact with, as well as children who are not confident around dogs and may not appreciate a dog advancing towards them. (see Figure 5.3).

> Maggie was provided with the Dogs Trust website as an information resource and the Be Dog Smart poster provided to help prevent Jimmy from feeling threatened in the first place. I discussed with Reuben how he could call Jimmy to him if he wanted to interact with Jimmy, and to avoid approaching Jimmy when he was resting, sleeping, eating or chewing. Reuben was shown how to 'ask' Jimmy if he wanted to receive interaction and then Reuben was given the opportunity to practice 'asking'. A step for Jimmy to get up onto the sofa was also discussed, as Jimmy liked to sit next to Reuben but sometimes being picked up to put on the sofa was a trigger for Jimmy to growl and air snap.

Antenatal parenting advice

Dogs Trust also provide information for prospective parents about preparing their dog for the impending arrival of their baby. Their guidance (also aimed at midwives) incorporates how a dog might feel about the different elements of babyhood – for example, frustration when the parent's attention is not available as much as it used to be, or anxiety associated with the change in routine or unfamiliar baby items being brought into the house, or fear of the baby

Figure 5.2: Dogs Trust education team workshops.

Be Dog Smart

Hey kids! Let's learn how to be safe around dogs.

When you are at home or at a friend's or relative's house...

Be calm

No loud noises, running or chasing games, which can worry a dog.

Give a dog space

Dogs don't like hugs and kisses, try cuddling a teddy bear instead.

Play fairly

Never ever tease a dog with toys, games or food.

Leave a dog alone

Don't disturb a dog when resting or eating. Being disturbed can worry them.

Keep your hands away

Don't put your hands near a dog's eyes, mouth or ears. No pulling or poking – it can hurt them.

Remember...

Dogs have feelings and needs and it's important that we respect them and behave kindly and safely around them.

 DogsTrust

Figure 5.3: Dogs Trust online resources.

noises or the baby itself. The advice explains how to prevent problems from arising in relation to having a new baby and existing dog living in the same house, and teaches owners (and maternity services) to be aware of dog body language and behaviour.

Dog shows and events

Although these events are not necessarily attended by people specifically seeking advice about dog behaviour, they nevertheless provide an opportunity to educate. The physical set-up of the event can be considered to help the dogs who attend – for example:

- having distributed areas for people to rest with their dogs
- carefully considering prospective stalls that might attend and the products they are selling
- contacting a local trainer and behaviourist to offer them the opportunity of a free stall in exchange for being on hand for people to ask questions
- asking local trainers and behaviourists to put on a display with the dog's body language and behaviour being explained to the audience as it is performed
- providing competition prizes for the 'most relaxed dog' or 'happiest dog' as part of the show
- having an organiser going around the showground and presenting awards to anyone they notice who is doing something with their dog's behaviour in mind.

'In the wild' walks

Accompanying owners on walks with their dogs might be provided as part of a training or behaviour modification programme but is also hugely beneficial as a service in itself. Such walks might be offered either with one dog at a time or as a group. They allow the professional to help teach owners in the environment and with scenarios they experience with their dogs every day. As you walk, conversation can be more casual and less intense than it might otherwise be and the teacher can coach the learners through real-life situations.

Social media

Interactive online platforms such as Facebook and Instagram involve much discussion about dog behaviour. Public pages and groups can be a challenging environment in terms of human behaviour (basic needs in terms of feelings of safety are often not met, as well as other aspects in the hierarchy of needs) but the basic principles of using positive reinforcement in humans should be maintained for any possibility of human behaviour change.

Essential dog behaviour to teach

An understanding of *Canis familiaris* as a species (and the breed – or mix of breeds) is important in terms of general dog behaviour (what is 'normal') and the potential underlying motivations for some behaviours, including what 'drives' a dog. Learning how dogs communicate and understanding emotional states are arguably the most important parts of forming a solid dog–owner relationship. Observing a dog's body language enables us to understand their emotional state, what their intentions might be, what they are communicating with other animals (including humans) and allows us to respond appropriately.

What is a dog?

Canis familiaris was the first species to be domesticated and this has led them to be uniquely attuned to human behaviour. The dog has been selectively bred for various behaviours, sensory capabilities and physical attributes, and modern dog breeds show more behavioural and morphological variation than any other land mammal. Highlighting behavioural traits of the species in general can help prevent human misunderstandings.

*   Dogs are predators – they have powerful muscles, large and sharp claws and teeth, and they hunt and chase things that move (different breeds have enhanced parts of the predatory action sequence:
    Eye → Orient → Stalk → Chase → Grab bite → Kill bite → Dissect → Consume).
*   Dogs are scavengers – as the majority of dogs in the world are unowned, this is how the majority survive.
*   Dogs are group-living – they are a social species.
*   Dogs bark and produce other vocalisation patterns (for a variety of reasons).
*   Dogs are territorial – they urine mark and alert to potential territory invasion.
*   Dogs have around 300 million olfactory receptors in their nose.
*   A dog's communication system is designed to diffuse tension.
*   Dogs reach sexual maturity between around 6 to 12 months of age – hormones influence the nervous system, which in turn affects behaviour.

An understanding of Jimmy's behaviour at a species level helped Maggie appreciate that his behaviour was (while undesirable from a human perspective) completely normal.

Through discussion, it was ensured that all of Jimmy's innate behaviours and requirements were fulfilled.

Developmental stages

Knowing what to expect at each stage of canine development helps create realistic expectations and a thorough understanding of why a dog might be behaving in a certain way, and allows owners to make informed choices throughout their dog's development.

*   **Socialisation period** – there appears to be significant individual and breed differences in the precise timing of the upper boundary of the socialisation period, which has implications in terms of lack of vaccination status versus socialisation opportunities. While there is likely to be some fluidity, this sensitive period of development could end as early as 12 weeks of age. Evidence suggests that dogs who are well socialised at three months can still regress and become fearful in the absence of periodic social reinforcement until the age of around six to eight months of age.[15]
*   **Fear impact stage** – a single fear-inducing situation that occurs between 8 and 11 weeks of age tends to leave a fairly permanent impression on a puppy,[15] which has implications for those running face-to-face puppy classes of any kind.
*   **Puberty** – sexual development occurs between 6 and 9 months of age in males and 6 and 16 months of age in females. Hormonal changes lead to an increased interest in other dogs, increased scent marking behaviour (from both males and females) and may lead to phantom pregnancies in bitches (which includes behavioural symptoms such as restlessness,

nesting behaviour, mothering inanimate objects, and possibility of aggression).[16]

- **Secondary fear stage** – some evidence suggests that a second, sudden onset phase of heightened sensitivity to threatening stimuli can occur at around 4 to 6 months of age.[15] Owners may notice their dog showing a fear response to things they have previously appeared to quite happily accept or interact with.

- **Adolescence** – this is the period of development when a juvenile becomes an adult, both behaviourally and reproductively. During adolescence, intense neurological and hormonal changes occur that lead to increased risk-taking behaviour, reduced regulatory control of behaviour and emotions, reduced levels of obedience towards the owner[17] and increased sensitivity to stressors (which can have long-term implications).

How emotions influence behaviour

Despite the fact that dogs are legally seen as property in the UK, research shows that non-human animals are sentient and capable of experiencing pain and a range of positive (engaging) and negative (protective) emotions. Consequently, there has been a shift away from using dominance-based training methods. It is clear that using forceful methods in an attempt to gain higher status often increase dogs' anxiety and fear,[18] that the domestic dog's social system is dyadic rather than a linear hierarchy, that dominance is not a personality type (it is a fluid relationship between two familiar individuals based on a series of interactions and outcomes determined by the context and individual motivations), and that emotions can drive behaviour. However, because dominance-reduction theory and owners believing they had to be the 'alpha' has been the widely accepted method of training and modifying behaviour (and is unfortunately still regularly referred to in media and on television shows), the belief is still popular among the general public. Lack of regulation in the dog behaviour and training industry also means the public is exposed to conflicting, and often outdated, advice on dog behaviour.

In 1992, Jaak Panksepp coined the term 'affective neuroscience' as the name for the field that studies the neural mechanisms of emotion.[19] He proposed seven primal emotions of 'PLAY/Social Joy', 'SEEKING/Expectancy', 'LUST' and 'CARE/Nurturing' (pleasant, positive affects) and 'PANIC/Sadness, 'FEAR/Anxiety' and 'RAGE/Anger' (aversive, negative affects). These emotions all promote survival and reproduction, drive behaviour and serve as internal reinforcers and punishers for behaviours that activate them. What triggers these emotions can improve human interactions with dogs and their subsequent welfare.

Linda Michaels adapted Maslow's Hierarchy of Needs to produce a 'Hierarchy of Dog Needs'.[20] Dogs, like humans, need to feel safe and relaxed in order to learn behaviours outside of survival mode. The same concepts apply as to Maslow's Hierarchy of Needs – we must first meet our dog's biological needs, followed by emotional and social needs, before addressing training needs and finally, cognitive needs can be met (see Chapter 1).

Jimmy had begun barking at activity outside the window at around the same time he had started cocking his leg. The growling and snapping when being picked up was described as a 'gradual change'. Understanding that Jimmy's growling and snapping behaviour was due to underlying fear of being picked up, and his barking behaviour due to anxiety about territory invasion (as well as the reinforcing aspects when the desired outcomes occurred), helped Maggie and Reuben empathise with Jimmy's behaviour. This alone caused Maggie to comment on her use of a water pistol when Jimmy was already in a negative emotional state, and I made no judgement about this. The Hierarchy of Dogs Needs was then worked through, primarily ensuring that Jimmy felt safe, secure and could trust both his owners and any unfamiliar people not to attempt to pick him up.

Fear can be defined as perception of danger, pain or harm, whereas anxiety is experienced when an individual anticipates a negative event. Kendal Shepherd's Ladder of Aggression (see Figures 5.4 and 5.5) is an excellent place to start in terms of recognising signs of fear or stress.[21] Escalation of a dog's communication signals up the ladder is driven by frustration (when an attempted response to a threat is ineffective in protecting the individual) or the level/intensity of the perceived threat – this can occur very quickly (within one social interaction, if the perceived threat occurs nearby and quickly) or over a period of time (when appeasement behaviour is chronically misunderstood and not effective in obtaining the socially expected outcome). The domestic dog is a social species and successful appeasing and threat-averting behaviour is highly adaptive and essential to avoid the need for potentially injurious behaviours. This concept allows owners (and non-owners) to understand that reducing the intensity of the perceived threat (for example, by giving space) will prevent the dog from having to escalate their defensive body language. It also helps compliance in terms of understanding the importance of managing the environment and/or human behaviour towards the dog to prevent rehearsal of behaviours higher up the 'ladder' that are more undesirable from a human perspective. Communication signals being displayed at the time the level of

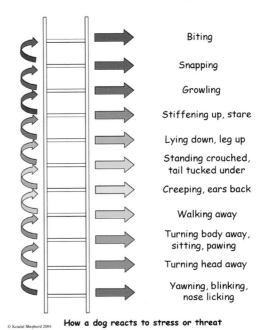

The Canine 'Ladder of Aggression'

Biting

Snapping

Growling

Stiffening up, stare

Lying down, leg up

Standing crouched, tail tucked under

Creeping, ears back

Walking away

Turning body away, sitting, pawing

Turning head away

Yawning, blinking, nose licking

© Kendal Shepherd 2004   **How a dog reacts to stress or threat**

Figure 5.4: The Ladder of Aggression, BSAVA Manual of Canine and Feline Behavioural Medicine. Reproduced with permission.

Figure 5.5: Nose licking is an early step on the Ladder of Aggression. Photo: © Natalie Light.

perceived threat is reduced are reinforced by the apparent success of the strategy. If a dog has learned that growling (for example) is effective in reducing the feeling of being threatened, the individual may become more proactive in using this behaviour (rather than relying on its use defensively) and may learn to dispense with more subtle body language signs over time (if repeated measures to appease are responded to inappropriately). The ladder also identifies how suppressing behaviours (rather than addressing the underlying emotions for the expression of the behaviour) can lead to escalation.

'Trigger stacking' is stress accumulation due to exposure of chronic and/or acute triggers either simultaneously or closely in time so that the animal does not have a chance to reach emotional homeostasis in between. Every dog differs in terms of how many triggers (or stressors) they might be able to cope with – this will depend on genetics, stress in utero, early life experiences, breed and individual temperament among other predisposing factors. It is important to recognise that 'stressors' include any stimuli that put either physical demands on a body or mental demands, including activities a dog may enjoy (generally high-arousal activities).

Using the Ladder of Aggression diagram, Maggie and Reuben were able to develop a greater understanding of Jimmy's emotional states, anticipate situations that might be stressful for him and watch carefully for his communication signals. If he exhibited signs of perceiving a threat, they could withdraw until he relaxed or remove him (or the unfamiliar person) from the situation. Jimmy had learned through extinction and operant conditioning that attempts to request space using more subtle communication had not been successful in achieving emotional homeostasis but growling and snapping made people withdraw from him (in other words, it was an appropriate protective strategy for him to use). Through classical conditioning, he also learned that being picked up made further unpleasant things happen such as being verbally scolded or squirted with a water pistol, therefore engraining Jimmy's negative association with being picked up. The visual representation of the ladder enabled Maggie and Reuben to understand the importance of altering their behaviour, as well as managing the environment when visitors came to the house (and, if relevant, on walks), as well as ensuring Jimmy remained relaxed during desensitisation and counter conditioning sessions to handling. In addition, comprehension of trigger stacking meant they could implement advice in terms of managing or altering his exposure to other potential stressors so that Jimmy was better able to cope with uncontrollable stressors.

Frustration (RAGE/Anger) is an emotional state that can arise when a dog is thwarted from obtaining something he/she is motivated to gain or retaining something under their control. Frustration can occur where previously learned expectations are not met (absent, reduced or delayed reward) as well as in situations where there are actual or potential barriers to autonomous control (for example, restraint, intrusion into personal space including territory).[22] Frustration invigorates behaviour and from an evolutionary perspective is very important for survival. It is the emotional response when a dog experiences failure of engaging emotional systems to succeed or failure to resolve distress, and frustration plays a significant role in dog behavioural responses. Unfortunately, it is often misdiagnosed and not considered as a likely motivation for behaviour. It is important that owners understand the potential for frustration-related behaviours due to creating high expectations of the dog being able to gain access to things they are motivated to engage with, and/or failing to protect a dog from unpleasant situations. In addition, individuals differ in their ability to tolerate frustration (due to predisposing factors, early life experiences and learned expectations).

If professionals can be aware of a dog's emotional states and cater the learning environment to set them up for success, for positive emotional states and teaching frustration tolerance, this concept can then be transferred to owners while we teach the importance of recognising emotional states. Once we have considered the environment and training methods, we can implement teaching techniques to ensure we are communicating with our clients in the most effective ways.

Finally, it is worth considering our responsibilities. All professionals work as part of a team who look after a dog's physical and emotional well-being. This team will include vet staff, behaviourists, trainers, groomers, physiotherapists, nutritionists, dog walkers and day care providers. It is essential to stay within our area of expertise for the welfare of the dog. If, as a behaviourist, it is suspected there is a physical problem with a dog, the referring vet is liaised with, rather than giving an opinion on what might be wrong. Likewise, behavioural problems require diagnosis and treatment based on that diagnosis and working with a behaviourist can be very beneficial for all concerned. Recognising your area of expertise, sticking to it and referring to other professionals as appropriate keeps everyone safer, happier and is a great way of learning more – because we are all still learning.

Frustration occurred when Jimmy's desired outcome did not occur (the person picking him up did not withdraw or the person outside the property did not move away) leading to escalation of his behaviour. I liaised with Jimmy's groomer and a veterinary nurse at the referring practice to help ensure that Jimmy felt safe also in these environments (where picking up would be common practice). Alternative methods of Jimmy being placed on a table were discussed including keeping him in his carrier, placing this on the table and opening it, and providing Jimmy with kennel space at ground level if relevant. The veterinary nurse expressed enthusiasm for Maggie to bring Jimmy into the veterinary practice to rehearse desensitisation and counter conditioning sessions in that environment and wrote substantial notes on Jimmy's medical records so that any staff member treating Jimmy at any time would be aware of the need to avoid picking him up and if essential to use his muzzle.

References

1. Perri, A.R., Feuerborn, T.R., Frantz, L.A.F., Larson, G., Malhi, R.S., Meltzer, D.J. and Witt, K.E. (2021) Dog domestication and the dual dispersal of people and dogs into the Americas. *Proceedings of the National Academy of Sciences* 118, 6.
2. Pet Food Manufacturers Association (PFMA) (2020) www.pfma.org.uk (accessed 9 April 2021).
3. Animal Welfare Act 2006 (2006) www.legislation.gov.uk/ukpga/2006/45/contents (accessed 9 April 2021).
4. Maslow, A.H. (1943) A theory of human motivation. *Psychological Review* 50, 370–396.
5. Sawyer, H. (2021) Critical techniques for effective client communication. DVM360 https://www.dvm360.com/view/critical-techniques-for-effective-client-communication (accessed 30 May 2021).
6. Van Fleet, R. (2013) *The Human Half of Dog Training: Collaborating with Clients to Get Results*. Dogwise Publishing, Wenatchee, WA.
7. TAGteach (n.d.) www.tagteach.com (accessed 9 April 2021).
8. Puppy School (n.d.) www.puppyschool.co.uk (accessed 9 April 2021).
9. The Mutty Professor (n.d.) www.themuttyprofessor.co.uk (accessed 9 April 2021).
10. WaggaWuffins (n.d.) www.waggawuffins.com (accessed 9 April 2021).
11. Animal Behaviour and Training Council (ABTC) (n.d.) www.abtc.org.uk (accessed 9 April 2021).
12. Bailey, B. (2006) *The Fundamentals of Animal Training*. Dog Sports Video.

13. Kyle, M. (n.d.) Dogs Trust education and community manager, personal communication.

14. Arhant, C., Beetz, A.M. and Troxler, J. (2017) Caregiver reports of interactions between children up to 6 years and their family dog – implications for dog bite prevention. *Frontiers of Veterinary Science* 4, 130.

15. Serpell, J., Duffy, D.L. and Jagoe, J.A. (2017) Becoming a dog: early experience and the development of behaviour. In: Serpell, J. (ed.) *The Domestic Dog: Its Evolution, Behaviour and Interactions with People*. Cambridge University Press, Cambridge.

16. Singh, G., Dutt, R., Kumar, S., Kumari, S. and Chandolia, R.K. (2019) Gynaecological problems in she dogs. *Haryana Vet* 58, 8–15.

17. Asher, L., England, G.C.W., Somerville, R. and Harvey, N.D. (2020) Teenage dogs? Evidence for adolescent-phase conflict behaviour and an association between attachment to humans and pubertal timing in the domestic dog. The Royal Society Publishing. https://doi.org/10.1098/rsbl.2020.0097.

18. Herron, M.E., Schofer, F.S. and Reisner, I.R. (2009) Survey of the use and outcome of confrontational and non-confrontational training methods in client-owned dogs showing undesired behaviours. *Applied Animal Behaviour Science* 117, 47–54.

19. Panksepp, J. (1992) A critical role for 'affective neuroscience' in resolving what is basic about basic emotions. *Psychological Review* 99, 554–560.

20. Bekoff, M. (2017) A hierarchy of dog needs: Abraham Maslow meets the mutts *Psychology Today*. https://www.psychologytoday.com/gb/blog/animal-emotions/201705/hierarchy-dog-needs-abraham-maslow-meets-the-mutts (accessed 20 December 2021).

21. Shepherd, K. (2019) The ladder of aggression. *BSAVA Manual of Canine and Feline Behavioural Medicine*. BSAVA, Quedgeley.

22. McPeake, K., Collins, L.M., Zulch, H. and Mills, D.S. (2019) The canine frustration questionnaire – development of a new psychometric tool for measuring frustration in domestic dogs *(Canis familiaris). Frontiers of Veterinary Science* 6, 152.

Chapter 6

The older dog

Caroline Warnes

While it is important for anyone who lives with dogs to keep behaviour in mind, this becomes particularly important with older dogs. A dog's behavioural and physical needs will change as they get older. It is important that we recognise and act to meet these changing needs to ensure the well-being of our elderly dogs is maintained throughout their old age. In addition, changes in an older dog's behaviour can be an indication of more serious physical or psychological problems developing. Recognising this can speed up identification of the underlying problem and potentially improve the likelihood of treating it successfully, or if not, help the dog to live with it as comfortably as possible.

I have written this chapter partly from the perspective of being a vet and behaviourist. Throughout my career I have tried to help owners of older dogs manage both physical and behavioural problems in order to improve their dogs' well-being in the last years of their life. In some cases, I have also had the privilege of helping to end their lives, with as much dignity and compassion as possible. I have also seen several dogs of my own through old age over the years, and my current dog, a Border Terrier called Jimmy, is now 11-years old and starting to show some age-related physical and behavioural changes. However, I am also aware that the process and effects of ageing in dogs can be very variable, both for individual dogs and for their people. I have therefore asked some of my friends and colleagues for their thoughts and experiences of living with older dogs and these are included below. I am deeply indebted to Julie Bedford, Tamsin Durston, Stephanie Hedges, Tanya Jeffery and Pat Tagg for their wisdom and insights into their own experiences of living with elderly dogs, how we can help dogs to continue to live their best lives throughout their old age and also how best to make the difficult end-of-life decisions about when and how to say goodbye.

When do dogs become elderly?

Many vets and pet food manufacturers tend to take the pragmatic view that dogs can be regarded as elderly or 'senior' once they reach 7 years of age. However, in reality, dogs age at different rates, just as people do. In dogs this is strongly influenced by size, as smaller dogs tend to age more slowly and generally live longer than larger dogs. The rate of ageing is also influenced by many other factors, some genetic and some related to the animal's health and present and past environmental influences (see Wallis et al.[1] for a more detailed look at the factors that can influence ageing in dogs).

Causes of behavioural changes in older dogs

Just as in people, ageing in dogs is associated with changes in their physical and mental abilities and these can result in changes in their behaviour. In addition, older dogs have an increased risk of developing a whole range of medical problems that can also affect their physical and/or mental health and therefore their behaviour. As dogs get older their behaviour is increasingly likely to be impacted by both normal ageing-related changes and chronic medical conditions, often in combination.[2] Some conditions that are classed as medical problems, such as canine cognitive dysfunction (CCD), are probably advanced stages of normal ageing processes.

Ageing-related changes affecting physical and mental health

Ageing is associated with a gradual deterioration in the ability of cells throughout the body to function normally. This can result in several detrimental effects that tend to reduce resilience and increase the risk of both physical and mental health problems. Physical effects include deterioration in the function of individual organs, such as the kidneys, liver, heart and skin. This may also include sense organs, resulting in reductions in vision, hearing, balance and potentially also olfactory ability. Changes in the tissues of the musculoskeletal system tend to reduce strength and flexibility and increase the risk of joint and ligament problems.

Cells in the brain are particularly susceptible to the adverse effects of ageing. There may be detrimental effects on important regulatory processes such as energy metabolism, the stress response and other hormone cycles, control of temperature and the sleep–wake cycle and also on cognitive function, which is important for information processing, including learning, memory formation and retrieval. Cognitive decline is associated with a gradual reduction in an individual's ability to perceive, process and respond appropriately to social and environmental information. When cognitive decline becomes severe enough to impact significantly on an individual's daily life, in people this is classed as dementia, and in dogs as CCD.

The effects of ageing on both the stress response and cognitive function mean that elderly animals may find it harder to adapt to changes in their routine and environment. They may be quite anxious generally and they also have an increased risk of developing more specific fear and anxiety-related behaviour problems, such as separation related distress and noise fears.[2]

Many of these ageing-related effects in dogs are very similar to those that occur in people, and in some cases, including cognitive decline and sleep disturbances, the dog has been used as a model to study age-related changes in humans.[3–5] There is great individual variation, both in dogs and in humans, in the rate at which ageing occurs and the type and severity of the detrimental effects it causes. This appears to be influenced by several different factors including genetics, disease, chronic stress, diet and exposure to environmental pollutants.[1,4,6]

CCD, also known as cognitive dysfunction syndrome, is classed as a neurogenerative disease, and is associated with several different types of behavioural changes, traditionally categorised using the mnemonic DISHA:

- Disorientation
- altered Interactions with humans and other animals
- changes in the Sleep–wake cycle

- **H**ouse-soiling
- changes in **A**ctivity levels.

More recently a couple of additional categories have been added to reflect more accurately the potentially broad range of changes in behavioural and emotional responses seen in dogs with CCD:[6]

- anxiety
- learning and memory deficits.

These are explored further below in relation to specific types of behaviour changes seen in older dogs.

In the early stages of cognitive decline, behaviour changes are often very subtle. Owners may not notice them until they start to become associated with more obvious and potentially problematic changes in their dog's behaviour and personality. The age at which this happens, and when a dog can be classed as having CCD, is extremely variable. In one study, signs suggestive of cognitive dysfunction were shown by 5% of dogs aged 10 to 12 years, 23.3% of dogs aged 12 to 14 years and 41% of dogs older than 14 years.[7]

Chronic medical conditions affecting physical and mental health in older dogs

In addition to, or in many cases because of, the normal ageing-related changes outlined above, older dogs are more susceptible to a range of different medical conditions that can also affect their behaviour.[2] Although it is beyond the scope of this chapter to discuss these in detail, I have outlined examples of some of the more common types of medical conditions that can potentially affect behaviour in older dogs.

Conditions causing pain and discomfort

Older dogs are particularly prone to developing a range of medical conditions that are associated with discomfort including osteoarthritis, dental disease and some forms of neoplasia (cancer). Painful animals will tend to try to avoid the situations that cause them discomfort, which can result in changes in their behaviour, such as avoiding certain locations or reluctance to perform certain behaviours or activities. However, it is important to be aware that some animals may continue to do activities that cause them discomfort, such as chasing a ball, presumably because the enjoyment they get from performing that behaviour outweighs the discomfort, at least in the short term. Pain can also be associated with changes in emotional responses, particularly increased anxiety and frustration, and painful animals are more likely to show behaviour problems associated with anxiety or irritability. Pain will also affect the dog's ability to rest and sleep (see below).

Conditions affecting mobility

In addition to painful conditions affecting the joints and the rest of the musculoskeletal system, conditions that cause weakness, such as muscle wasting or neurological problems, can also affect an individual's ability to move around freely and access important resources such as food, water, resting places and toileting locations.

Conditions that alter appetite, thirst, urination and defecation

Age-related conditions can result in changes in toileting behaviour and an increased risk of a dog toileting indoors or waking their owners at night asking to be let out to toilet. Conditions that are more common in older dogs include chronic renal failure, prostate disease in male dogs, digestive problems including inflammatory bowel disease and endocrine problems including diabetes mellitus or hyperadrenocorticism (Cushing's Disease). In addition, some conditions including diabetes mellitus and hyperadrenocorticism can increase a dog's appetite and can potentially increase the risk of the dog showing aggressive behaviours to people or other dogs that approach while they are eating.

Conditions associated with sensory decline/sensory impairment

Vision loss as a result of dense cataracts or medical conditions affecting the retina at the back of the eyes, or age-related hearing loss can both potentially affect social behaviour. They make it harder for a dog to recognise and respond appropriately to social signals from other dogs and people. Animals with poor vision or hearing loss may also be more easily startled, for example, by someone touching them when they were not aware of them approaching. This can result in anxiety and potentially to them snapping. Sensory decline can also affect play behaviour, making it harder for the dog to see moving toys, or reducing interest in squeaky toys for example.

Conditions affecting brain function

There are a several medical conditions that can directly affect brain function in older dogs such as brain tumours, hypothyroidism, kidney and liver failure. These can potentially exacerbate cognitive dysfunction as well as having other effects on the brain and behaviour.

Medications used to treat other medical conditions

Some medications prescribed to treat other medical conditions can themselves also affect a dog's behaviour. For example, corticosteroids, widely prescribed to treat various allergic and inflammatory conditions, can increase thirst and the risk of toileting accidents, increase appetite with resulting increased risk of food-related aggressive behaviour, and increase fearfulness. They can also increase irritability resulting in an increased risk of a dog responding aggressively in other situations.[8] Phenylpropanolamine (Propalin™), sometimes used to treat urinary incontinence in bitches can sometimes cause restlessness and increased irritability, especially at higher doses.

Common behaviour changes seen in older dogs

Some of the most common types of behavioural changes that may be seen in older dogs and their potential underlying causes are outlined here and summarised in Table 6.1.

Changes in activity levels and mobility

Like Ben's owners (we will meet Ben on the next page), we tend to expect that dogs will become less active and playful as they get older. Ageing is associated with gradual changes in several things that can affect activity levels and mobility including energy metabolism, reduced ability to maintain and repair body tissues,[9] and a deterioration in proprioceptive abilities, which can affect both agility and balance. All of these are likely to negatively impact an older dog's mobility and activity levels. However, while it is true that an older dog will generally

Ben the not-so-bouncy Golden Retriever

Ben was a lovely, friendly but rather overweight 8-year-old Golden Retriever. Like most Retrievers he had been a very lively, active dog when he was younger. He enjoyed chasing his ball, riding in the car and long walks in the countryside with his owners. He loved to meet people and would greet visitors by jumping up and planting his paws on their chest, while wagging his tail and with a big grin on his face.

Ben's owners had noticed that he had gradually become less active over the previous year or so. He did not seem to want to walk as far or chase his ball for as long as before. They put this down to him becoming older and did not think too much about it. He had also stopped jumping up to greet visitors, which the owners and most visitors regarded as a good thing. However, his owners started to become concerned when Ben began to refuse to jump up into the back of their car, because he had always appeared to love car outings. Ben's size meant that his owners struggled to lift him into the back of the car, and it was becoming more difficult to persuade him to get into the car by himself, even using his favourite treats.

Around the same time, Ben's owners also started to notice some other changes in his behaviour. He sometimes seemed slow to get to his feet after laying down, particularly after a long rest, and he had also started to hesitate before walking across the kitchen floor, which was covered in smooth vinyl floor tiles. Ben needed to cross the kitchen regularly, to get to his food and water bowls and to access the back garden. Ben would sometimes stand by the door leading into the kitchen from the hallway and look worried. If his owners tried to persuade him to enter the kitchen, he would sometimes creep around the edge of the floor, staying close to the edges, and sometimes he would rush across the middle of the floor, paws scrabbling, apparently trying to cross it as quickly as possible. At first Ben's owners thought that he was just being silly but they gradually became more concerned about him, and eventually decided to take him to his vet for a check-up. We will come back to Ben a bit later in the chapter, to find out the outcome of the vet's appointment, and to see what happened next.

be less energetic than a much younger dog, it is important to be aware that there are also many health problems that can reduce both the activity levels and mobility of an older dog.

Mobility can be adversely affected by conditions affecting the musculoskeletal system, such as joint disease, spinal disease or muscle wasting that can occur secondary to various metabolic or endocrine diseases.

Changes in mobility can present in various ways. For example, like Ben, owners may notice their dog struggling or being slow to stand up from lying down. They may also show signs of reluctance to jump up onto or off things such as getting onto or off furniture or jumping into or out of a car. Or they may become hesitant to go up or down stairs, or to walk across a slippery floor for example (Figure 6.1). The pattern of the altered behaviours may give some indication of the source of discomfort or weakness as reluctance to jump up onto things or to climb stairs is often associated with problems affecting the dog's hind end while reluctance to jump down from things or go downstairs can be associated with problems at the front end. These changes may occur suddenly, if an animal has an acute injury for example, but they often occur quite gradually, and at first owners may not notice them or realise their significance.

Figure 6.1: Rusty – reluctant to go downstairs. Photo: © Stephanie Hedges.

A dog's general activity levels will be influenced by the same conditions that can reduce mobility, but they can also be affected by other conditions that affect energy metabolism such as obesity, diabetes mellitus and hypothyroidism. Obesity will also exacerbate joint disease and the effect this has on a dog's mobility.

Changes in sensory perception as a result of vision, hearing and potentially olfactory loss can also impact adversely on an older dog's desire and/or ability to play with toys or interact with people or other animals.

Changes in resting/sleeping patterns

We tend to accept that older dogs will rest and sleep more during the day than younger, more active dogs. However, it can be extremely problematic if an older dog starts to become wakeful and restless at night, particularly if this results in them waking the human members of the family, for example, by wandering around the house, scratching at doors, whining or barking. Sleep deprivation can be extremely detrimental, both for an older dog and also for their owners. Poor sleep is associated with a reduction in both cognitive and physical abilities as well as numerous adverse health-related effects. Sleep deprivation reduces the immune response, increasing susceptibility to illnesses and infections. It is also associated with increased pain sensation and increased risks of developing obesity and cardiovascular disease.[10]

There are several reasons why elderly dogs might become restless at night. In people, ageing is associated with changes in sleep patterns, including sleeping less deeply and waking more often at night. This appears to be influenced by both neurological and hormonal changes affecting the 'body clock' responsible for circadian rhythms such as the sleep–wake cycle. Recent studies suggest that dogs also experience similar changes as they grow older.[3]

Sensory decline may also contribute to disrupted sleep patterns in older animals. The sleep–wake cycle is partly regulated by exposure to light. In people, vision loss has been shown to affect the sleep–wake cycle,[11] which might also apply to dogs although this has not been studied directly. Sensory decline, particularly hearing loss, is a risk factor for development of dementia in people and could potentially contribute to the development of cognitive dysfunction in dogs (see below). In addition, sensory decline may contribute to reduced daytime activity, which can also increase the likelihood that a dog will be awake and restless at night (see below).

Particularly badly disrupted sleep patterns are seen in people with severe cognitive decline or dementia, and this also applies to dogs with CCD.[3] Waking at night is the most commonly reported clinical sign in dogs with cognitive dysfunction, and as poor sleep can adversely affect cognitive function this can become a vicious circle.[10] In addition to the underlying pathology specifically affecting their sleep–wake cycle, dogs with cognitive dysfunction may also be more restless or become distressed at night due to experiencing disorientation and/or anxiety when they wake in the night.

Another common reason for older dogs becoming restless and waking at night is discomfort. Dogs with joint disease such as osteoarthritis or other musculoskeletal problems may not be able to rest comfortably for very long, or at all. They may also struggle to access previously preferred sleeping places such as chairs or sofas. Pain from other sources, such as abdominal or dental pain may also prevent dogs from sleeping comfortably. Again, this can become an escalating problem because sleep deprivation is associated with increased pain perception.[5,10]

Another potential source of discomfort may be the ambient temperature of the sleeping area. Owing to changes in their physiology and body composition, older dogs are less able to regulate their body temperatures than younger dogs and they might become cold at night, particularly in winter if their sleeping area is unheated overnight.

Dogs that do not get sufficient physical or mental stimulation during the daytime may also be more wakeful at night, just because they are not tired. This is most likely to happen with dogs that tend to sleep for much of the day. While the main reason for this may be changes to the sleep–wake cycle as outlined above, it may be exacerbated by owners not spending sufficient time interacting with their elderly dogs during the day.

Changes in social interactions with people and other animals

It is not unusual for dogs to show changes in how they interact with other family members, both human and animal, as they get older. Some dogs become more needy of attention from their owners as they get older. They may start to follow their owners around constantly at home and, if not given attention, they may show attention-seeking behaviours such as barking, whining or pawing. These dogs may also become distressed when they are separated from their owners, for example, when owners go out or at night. This increased need for attention may occur because the dog is experiencing anxiety and needing more reassurance from their owners. Increasing anxiety is fairly common in older dogs, for a number of reasons (see emotional changes below). However, increased attention-seeking behaviours may also be seen in dogs that are not anxious, because the dog has learned that performing these behaviours 'works' to get attention from their owners.

Some dogs will tend to interact less with their owners, and possibly also other pets in the home, as they get older. They may no longer approach owners to request to be stroked or bring a toy, asking for a game. If the relationship between the dog and owners has previously relied on the dog initiating most of the social interactions, there may be a large reduction in the number of interactions that occur. This can be upsetting for owners, especially when a formerly very affectionate dog appears to have become rather aloof.

Even dogs that generally enjoy social interactions with their owners or other animals may become less tolerant of certain interactions as they get older. This might apply to certain types of interactions (for example, being approached while they are eating or resting), or when being handled in particular ways (for example, having their feet dried or being picked up). Or there may be particular times when they are less tolerant of interaction than others. These dogs may try and avoid interactions by moving away from the person or dog, or they may show behaviours such as growling, snapping, snarling or biting in order to try and prevent or stop the interaction.

There are several reasons why an older dog's desire to interact or tolerance of social interaction might reduce.

- Any medical problem that causes a dog to feel unwell or uncomfortable may reduce their desire to interact with people or other dogs generally or they may find certain types of interaction unpleasant or uncomfortable.
- Sensory decline, particularly hearing or vision loss, can reduce a dog's ability to notice and respond appropriately to normal social cues from people or other animals. This may result in them not initiating or joining in with social interactions at all, or if they are unable to respond appropriately to another dog's social cues this may result in tension between dogs and potentially aggression. In addition, dogs with hearing or visual loss may not be aware of a person or another dog approaching until they are very close, which can result in them being startled, and potentially showing aggressive behaviours such as snarling and snapping.
- CCD can be associated with reduced ability to recognise familiar individuals and/or recognise and respond to normal social cues and other subtle communication signals.[4] This can lead to difficulties in communication both with owners and other animals. As with sensory loss, this can result in tension and sometimes aggression, and some animals may withdraw from social interaction altogether. In addition, changes in the sleep–wake cycle in dogs with cognitive dysfunction can result in dogs being sleepier in the daytime, when their owners are most likely to want to interact with them.
- Ageing is associated with an increased susceptibility to negative emotional responses including anxiety and irritability. Both can contribute to a reduced tolerance of social interactions with both people and other dogs, and irritability will increase the likelihood of a dog responding aggressively during social interactions.

Changes in memory and learning including loss of previously learned behaviours

Just as people tend to become more forgetful as they get older, dogs also experience changes in their ability to learn and remember things as they age. CCD can be associated with a whole host of learning and memory-related problems.

- **Difficulty in learning new behaviours**, due to reduced ability to focus and concentrate as well as difficulty learning and remembering new associations.
- **Forgetting/loss of previously well-learned behaviours**. This may include cued behaviours such as 'sit', 'leave' or recall. However, it may also include behaviours that have been strongly learned and become habitual since puppyhood such as:
  - **house-training** due to a dog having difficulty remembering where they would normally go to the toilet and how to get there, or how to indicate to owners that they need to go outside. Some dogs may become confused at doors, and try to get through the hinge side of the door rather than the opening side (Figure 6.2). This is one

reason why a previously well house-trained dog might start to have toileting accidents indoors although there are others (see below)

- **behaviours that involve self-control** such as not jumping up to grab food from counter-tops, or from someone's hand and so on.

Owners that are not aware that their older dog is developing cognitive dysfunction may assume they are being naughty if they stop responding to behaviour cues or start stealing food or toileting in the house.

- **Spatial disorientation**: animals may be unable to recognise familiar places or remember how to navigate between them. This can result in animals becoming

Figure 6.2: Rufus 'stuck' on the wrong side of the door. Photo: © Stephanie Hedges.

Figure 6.3: Rufus stuck behind an obstacle. Photo: © Stephanie Hedges.

Another potential cause of poor responsiveness to behavioural cues is sensory decline, particularly hearing or visual loss. Dogs are often quite good at compensating for gradual deterioration in one of their senses through utilising their remaining senses, and owners may not realise initially that their dog is unable to see or hear particular cues and assume that they are just being naughty.

Changes in eating, drinking and toileting habits

As already mentioned, toileting problems are not uncommon in dogs with cognitive dysfunction. However, there are many other medical conditions that can alter toileting behaviour and increase the likelihood of a dog having toileting accidents in the home.

confused or appearing to be lost in familiar places such as in different rooms in the house or the garden. They may also get stuck behind furniture or in a corner of a room because they are unable to navigate their way around obstacles (Figure 6.3). Dogs may also have difficulty locating important resources including food, water, resting places and toileting locations, which can result in stress, indoor toileting as outlined above, and potentially also health-related issues including dehydration.

- **Temporal disorientation**: dogs with cognitive dysfunction may forget that something has just happened. They may ask for their dinner, and then appear to forget that they have eaten and ask again (some may argue that this is not uncommon even in dogs with no obvious signs of cognitive decline). Or they may ask to be let outside to go to the toilet, then come back indoors and immediately ask to be let outside again.

- Conditions that reduce a dog's mobility can increase the risk of them having toileting accidents indoors, either by making it difficult for them to get to a more appropriate toileting area in time, or by making it difficult or uncomfortable for them to squat for long enough to fully empty their bladder or bowels during one toilet trip.
- Conditions that increase a dog's thirst and/or urine output, such as chronic kidney disease, diabetes mellitus or hyperadrenocorticism, will increase how often they need to urinate. This will increase the chances of them needing to urinate at unusual times such as when left alone for a period of time or overnight. If their owners are not aware of this the dog may urinate indoors, or wake their owners at night asking to be let out. The same applies to conditions that increase faecal frequency and/or cause diarrhoea, such as digestive problems or inflammatory bowel disease.

- Some medical conditions, for example, some digestive problems, hyperadrenocorticism and diabetes mellitus can be associated with an increased appetit and can increase the risk of resource guarding problems where a dog may show aggressive behaviours to people or other dogs that approach while they are eating.

Emotional changes

Ageing in both people and dogs is often associated with increased susceptibility to stress and negative emotional states. In people, these include depression, increased anxiety and irritability associated with reduced tolerance or frustration. We do not tend to diagnose clinical depression in dogs, although some older dogs do appear to show signs associated with low mood and a reduced interest in the world around them. However, we do recognise an increased incidence of both anxiety-related behaviour problems and increased irritability in older dogs. These emotional changes are likely to be due partly to the effects of brain ageing and increasing cognitive decline. However, many medical problems are also associated with an increased risk of emotional-related problems.

Pain is often associated with anxiety: painful animals will be stressed, and they also tend to anticipate situations that might cause them discomfort. Pain can also exacerbate other types of fear and anxiety-related behaviour problems, such as noise fears.[12] Like us, painful animals can also be irritable: less tolerant of interactions with people and other animals, and more likely to show aggressive behaviours to prevent or stop an unwanted interaction. See Chapter 8 for more detail regarding pain and behaviour.

Cognitive decline and dysfunction tend to reduce an animal's ability to cope with or adapt to changes in their routine or environment, increasing the likelihood of them becoming fearful or anxious. Animals may develop specific anxiety-related problems such as separation anxiety, noise-related fears or generalised anxiety[6,13] or pre-existing fear and anxiety-related problems may worsen.

Increased incidence of abnormal behaviours

Some older dogs with cognitive dysfunction will show behaviours that can be classed as abnormal. These may be incomplete sequences of normal behaviours, for example, asking for food but not wanting to eat when food is presented, or asking to be let outside but appearing confused once the door is opened. These incomplete behavioural sequences may be repeated over and over again, and animals with cognitive dysfunction may also show other repetitive behaviours, such as apparently aimless wandering/pacing, repetitive licking or vocalisation, such as continual barking.

Animals may also show repetitive behaviours for other reasons. Animals that are painful or distressed, for example because they are anxious or frustrated, may show repetitive behaviours such as licking, circling, barking or pacing because performing these behaviours reduces stress and helps them to feel better. Some dogs may also learn that performing a particular behaviour over and over again is a good way to get attention from their owners. If so, they may continue to do this as an attention-seeking behaviour.

How to be the best possible owner for your elderly dog

There is plenty that we as owners can do to help elderly dogs continue to live their best lives, and I have outlined some thoughts and suggestions below. I have also discussed some of the more difficult aspects of caring for an

Table 6.1 Summary of the common types of behaviour changes seen in elderly dogs and their potential underlying medical and behavioural causes.

Behaviour change	Potential underlying medical and behavioural causes
Changes in mobility including: • difficulty standing up from laying down, potentially also difficulty making other position changes (e.g. sitting to standing, standing to sitting) • hesitancy or reluctance to jump up onto or down off things (e.g. getting into or out of the car, onto or off furniture, going up or down steps or stairs).	• Conditions affecting the musculoskeletal system and causing discomfort (e.g. joint disease or weakness such as muscle wasting). • Sensory decline, particularly visual loss, may reduce ability to judge distances accurately. • Age-related changes in proprioceptive ability reducing balance and agility.
Changes in desire or ability to exercise or play including: • less keen to go for walks or to chase a ball • unable to walk as far or as fast as they used to • reduced interest in particular types of toys.	• Conditions affecting energy availability/ causing rapid tiring (e.g. obesity, diabetes, hypothyroidism). • Conditions affecting the musculoskeletal system and causing discomfort (e.g. joint disease or weakness such as muscle wasting). • Painful conditions (e.g. dental pain). • Sensory decline (e.g. reduced visual or olfactory ability may reduce dog's ability to locate a toy, hearing loss may reduce interest in squeaky toys for example).
Changes in interactions with owners and other pets including: • increased attention seeking • reduced social interaction • irritability/aggressive behaviour.	• Conditions causing increased irritability including pain, inflammation, cognitive dysfunction, other central nervous system (CNS) pathology. • Conditions causing increased fear or anxiety including pain, sensory decline, endocrine diseases and cognitive dysfunction. • Reduced ability to recognise and respond appropriately to social signals from humans or other animals: cognitive dysfunction, sensory decline (especially visual or olfactory loss). • Normal learning (e.g. inadvertent reinforcement of attention-seeking behaviours by owners, learned fear-responses associated with interactions with people/other animals).

Table 6.1 (continued)

Behaviour change	Potential underlying medical and behavioural causes
Development or increase in anxiety, fearfulness or phobia including: • separation anxiety • noise-related fears • generalised anxiety • situation-specific fears e.g. fear of walking on particular surfaces, going outside • difficulty coping with changes in routine and environment.	• Painful conditions (e.g. osteoarthritis, dental disease). • Sensory decline especially hearing or vision loss. • Endocrine diseases that affect cognitive function and the stress response including hypothyroidism and hyperadrenocorticism. • Cognitive dysfunction and other CNS pathology. • Normal learning – development of fear-responses to specific stimuli because of classical conditioning.
House-soiling: passing urine and/or faeces in the house.	• Conditions reducing mobility/ability to reach appropriate toileting areas including painful conditions, musculoskeletal disorders and neurological disorders. • Learned negative associations with a particular toilet area: more common in animals that are fearful/anxious and can also occur secondary to conditions causing pain when toileting including osteoarthritis and colitis. • Conditions causing increased urine or faecal output or incontinence including digestive disorders, endocrine diseases, urinary tract disorders, and neurological problems. • Conditions reducing ability to locate or recognise appropriate toilet area (e.g. sensory decline (especially visual or olfactory loss), cognitive dysfunction. • Normal learning: development of location or substrate aversions or preferences.
Excessive vocalisation: • louder than normal • repetitive vocalisation • vocalisation at night.	• Sensory decline, especially hearing loss. • Cognitive dysfunction and other CNS pathology. • Separation anxiety (see above). • Normal learning: inadvertent reinforcement of attention-seeking behaviour by owners.

Table 6.1 (continued)

Behaviour change	Potential underlying medical and behavioural causes
Spatial or temporal disorientation: • appearing to become lost in familiar surroundings • getting stuck in corners/behind furniture • looking at the hinge side of the door when asking to be let out • appearing to forget having just been fed/let outside.	• Cognitive dysfunction and other CNS pathology. • Sensory decline, especially if fairly acute.
Repetitive behaviours including: • aimless wandering/pacing • repetitive licking • digging • circling • vocalisation.	• Conditions causing discomfort (e.g. osteoarthritis, dental disease, abdominal pain). • Conditions causing increased fearfulness/anxiety (see above). • Cognitive dysfunction or other CNS pathology. • Displacement behaviours in response to frustration. • Normal learning: inadvertent reinforcement by attention from owners.
Restlessness/waking at night	• Conditions causing discomfort (e.g. osteoarthritis, dental disease, abdominal pain and dog may become cold if ambient temperature is too low overnight). • Conditions increasing need to eliminate at night (e.g. endocrine disease, digestive disorders, urinary tract disorders). • Conditions affecting sleep-wake cycle and depth of sleep including sensory decline, cognitive dysfunction or other CNS pathology. • Conditions causing increased anxiety especially when separated from owners (see above). • Sleeping more during the day due to general lack of mental stimulation or physical exercise. • Normal learning: inadvertent reinforcement by attention from owners; waking in response to noises/other environmental stimuli occurring at night.

elderly dog, including making decisions about end-of-life care.

Always keep behaviour in mind

As already mentioned, it is important to monitor a dog's behaviour carefully as they get older, because changes in their behaviour may be the first indication that they are starting to struggle. The sooner the behaviour changes are recognised, the quicker action can be taken to identify any underlying health problems and/or make changes to the dog's environment or routine to help them cope better.

Ben's owners, concerned about the changes in his behaviour, made an appointment to see their vet. Based on the behavioural signs Ben was showing and a thorough clinical examination, the vet suspected that Ben was developing osteoarthritis secondary to hip dysplasia. This is a developmental abnormality where the hip joints do not form correctly, resulting in them being unstable.[14] This was confirmed by taking radiographs, which showed quite severe arthritic changes in both of Ben's hips.

Osteoarthritis is a painful condition where joints become inflamed, and over time extra bone can form inside the joint causing restricted movement. Dogs with osteoarthritis will tend to avoid doing activities that cause discomfort, and Ben's owners realised that all the recent changes in his behaviour were likely to be due to him avoiding situations that caused his hips to be painful. Once the underlying cause of Ben's behaviour changes was identified it was possible to make a plan to help Ben feel more comfortable, and also to try and reduce the rate at which his osteoarthritis would continue to deteriorate in the longer term.

Ben's vet started him on a course of pain-relieving medication straight away. Within a few days of starting this his owners noticed a significant improvement in Ben's mobility and activity levels. They also felt he seemed happier than before.

The vet also advised that Ben would benefit from losing some weight, as being overweight was likely to be exacerbating both the stress on his joints and his discomfort. Ben's owners were advised to reduce the total amount of food that Ben was fed daily, and to weigh this out carefully. Feeding some of his food in a variety of activity feeders or scattered on the floor would provide him with both mental stimulation and some physical exercise as long as he was comfortable with this. They were also advised to attend a regular weight clinic at the surgery to help monitor his progress.

Ben's owners were told that it was important to keep Ben active, both to help with his weight loss and also to improve his mobility through increasing his muscle strength and flexibility generally. Regular walks would be good for him, and the owners were advised to very gradually increase the distance they walked, and then to include gradual slopes and eventually some jogging/running into his walks. Rather than throwing the ball for him to chase on walks, Ben's owners were advised to hide it and encourage him to search for it using his nose instead, as this would have less impact on his joints than running, turning and stopping suddenly. The vet also offered to refer Ben to see a veterinary physiotherapist, who could advise on specific exercises to increase the strength and flexibility in Ben's hind legs, although Ben's owners did not take this up at this time. Hydrotherapy can also be very good for dogs with joint problems, and as Ben enjoyed swimming in the local river this was encouraged as long as the weather was warm, and the bank shallow.

The vet also advised Ben's owners to make some changes to help improve his mobility at home. Most importantly they were advised to put a strip of non-slip matting or carpet across the kitchen floor, so Ben could cross the kitchen to access his food, water and the back garden without any fear of slipping. The owners did this and immediately noticed that Ben no longer hesitated before entering the kitchen or crossing the kitchen floor. This should also help reduce the rate at which his osteoarthritis deteriorates in future.

Ben's owners were also advised to introduce a ramp to enable him to get into the back of the car without having to jump. However, the owners found, inadvertently, that Ben appeared quite happy to get into and out of their car through one of the rear passenger doors, and to sit on the back seat while they were driving. They therefore put a blanket on the back seat, and used a car harness to secure him here, rather than putting him into the boot. They also bought Ben a new bed, that was made of memory foam to support him comfortably, and large enough for him to lie out flat if he wished.

Thanks to these changes, Ben soon returned to being the happy, active dog he had always been. After a few weeks his pain relief medication was stopped and Ben seemed to be fine. However, his owners are aware that, even though they will continue to monitor both his weight and the type of activities he does carefully, he may well become uncomfortable again in future. They now know the types of changes in Ben's behaviour that might indicate he is starting to become uncomfortable, and the importance of taking him back to see their vet if they see these. Ben may well need more courses of pain relief in future, and as he gets older he may eventually need to be on pain relief permanently. However, for now Ben's owners are happy to have their bouncy Golden Retriever back.

Regular veterinary checks are essential for older dogs

As there are so many medical conditions that can potentially affect an older dog's behaviour it is essential not to ignore any behaviour changes or assume that they are 'just' due to ageing. Instead, it is important to arrange a veterinary check as soon as possible. The sooner a medical problem is diagnosed, the better the prognosis for treatment is likely to be. Even if an older dog is diagnosed with a chronic health problem that cannot be fully cured, such as osteoarthritis or diabetes mellitus, for example, these can generally be managed to ensure the dog stays as well and as comfortable as possible for as long as possible.

Remember that you are your dog's advocate with the vet. It is important to mention any particular signs or symptoms you might be concerned about, such as appetite loss or incontinence, as these may not be obvious to the vet on clinical examination. If these symptoms are not improving with treatment make sure to let your vet know, so they can investigate further and/or try something different.

Many health problems common in older dogs such as osteoarthritis can be associated with chronic or long-term pain. It is particularly important to identify and treat pain because this is extremely detrimental to a dog's welfare (see Chapter 8). Weight management is also important for arthritic dogs, and your veterinary practice will be able to help you with this. A great resource for owners of dogs with arthritis is canine arthritis management (CAM),[15] a group that provides support and lots of information about helping dogs with arthritis.

There are several supplements and medications available to support dogs with cognitive dysfunction and other ageing-related changes. Dogs with severe anxiety-related problems may also benefit from medication in addition to other stress-reducing strategies. It is always important to discuss these options with your vet, who will be able to advise you on what would be most suitable for your dog.

Even if an older dog is not showing any obvious changes in their behaviour, it is important that they receive regular health checks, annually or even biannually as they become more senior, as this may help identify problems in the earlier stages when they can be managed or treated most successfully. In addition to a thorough clinical examination there are specific screening tests for several health problems (for example, blood tests to check for kidney and liver disease, diabetes mellitus and thyroid disease). There are also special screening tests available for CCD, which may be offered by your veterinary practice, or if not, there are some available online (see the Resources section) although it is important to share the results with your vets. Many veterinary practices run special wellness clinics for older dogs, and it is well worth taking advantage of these if you can. Always mention any changes you have noticed in your older dog's behaviour to your vet, even if you are not sure how relevant they may be to their general health.

Figure 6.4: A large memory foam bed is supportive and allows an elderly dog to lie flat if they wish. Photo: © Rosie Bescoby.

Ensuring older dogs have good quality rest and sleep

As already mentioned, good quality rest and sleep are essential for the welfare of all dogs, and because there are a several reasons why older dogs might struggle with this we need to do our best to maximise their chances of having good quality rest and sleep.

Ideally, older dogs should have access to a choice of comfy beds in different locations around the home. Ageing is associated with several changes including skin thinning and fat loss, which means that older dogs are at risk of developing pressure sores if they sit or lie on hard surfaces for any length of time. It is important to provide beds that are well-padded and supportive (for example, made from memory foam), to minimise the risk of them developing pressure sores. It is also important to check an older dog for pressure sores regularly: these are most common over prominent bony areas including the elbows and hip bones. If found it is important to seek help from your vet as they can be painful and can easily become infected.

In addition to being comfortable and supportive, it is important that beds are easy for your dog to get into and out of, and large enough for them to lie out flat if they wish (Figure 6.4). Some dogs prefer beds with raised sides as this may help them feel more snug and secure, but these should ideally also be large enough to allow the dog to lay flat if they wish. If your dog appears to prefer curling up in a smaller bed, they should also have access to a comfy flat bed in case they want to stretch out. For older dogs with incontinence problems, having a waterproof layer under a removable, washable cover can protect the bed from too much damage.

A recent study demonstrated that giving pain relief to dogs with osteoarthritis significantly improved the amount and quality of their sleep.[5] Dogs with medical conditions that are likely to be associated with chronic pain should therefore be receiving adequate pain relief, not just to improve their comfort and mobility in the daytime but also to improve the quality of their sleep.

Older dogs are not as good at regulating their body temperatures and so they can easily become cold. Their sleeping area should be kept warm especially overnight in

Figure 6.5: Elderly dog wearing a warm fleece and Help 'Em Up harness. Photo: © Daniel Thompson.

Improving accessibility and mobility generally, both inside and outside the home

Ageing-related changes can affect an older dog's mobility and their ability to locate and access important resources in the home. Owners can make changes to help older dogs move around and access important resources more easily, and some of these changes, such as non-slip mats, can be beneficial for dogs with no obvious problems with their mobility as they may reduce the risk of problems developing in future. Because older dogs are less good at coping with or adapting to changes it is important to introduce any new items or pieces of equipment very gradually, and to make sure your dog is completely comfortable with wearing or using them.

Improving accessibility and mobility inside the home

the winter – electrically heated beds or heating pads inside their normal bed may be welcomed. For the same reason older dogs may need to wear a fleece or coat outside the home, especially when it is cold and wet, and if it is particularly cold they may benefit from wearing a comfy fleece coat indoors as well (Figure 6.5).

Keeping older dogs more active, both mentally and physically during the daytime can also help to ensure they are more likely to sleep at night (see below). In addition, increasing exposure to daylight and reducing exposure to bright artificial light in the evening helps people sleep better at night and may also help dogs.[2]

For dogs that become anxious at night it is worth experimenting to see if they feel less anxious with a night light left on, and/or an Adaptil™ diffuser plugged in close to their bed. They may also settle better if they have items containing their owner's scent, such as an old T-shirt, in their bed to snuggle up to.

- **Non-slip matting or carpet** in locations of important resources and on the walkways between important areas can improve accessibility for elderly animals with mobility problems. Julie Bedford, clinical animal behaviourist and owner of Sally, a 17-year-old Border Collie, advocates the use of a non-slip vet-bed. It is washable, which not only makes it easy to deal with toileting accidents but also, if the non-slip bits become less effective because they are clogged with hair or dust, washing can restore them.
- **Steps** may enable older dogs to continue to access preferred resting and sleeping places such as chairs, sofas or people's beds. The steps need to be shallow enough for the dog to navigate them comfortably (Figure 6.6).
- **Specially designed harnesses** such as the Help 'Em Up Harness™ can be very helpful for supporting dogs with mobility problems both inside the home and outside, for

Figure 6.6: Steps can help elderly dogs to continue to access favourite resting places – Jimmy on the settee. Photo: © Caroline Warnes.

example to assist them when standing up from lying down and to help them access their toilet areas.

Tanya Jeffery, a clinical animal behaviourist, has a very large Italian Spinone called Teo who is currently 10½-years old, and who has some mobility problems due to a degenerative neurological problem. She uses a harness to help support him. She says 'The best harness I have found for a large dog is the 'Help 'Em Up' harness. It fits very well and has a number of different lead points. It also has two handle points, one on the shoulder area and the other over the hind legs so that you can support your dog's weaknesses safely' (Figure 6.7).

Figure 6.7: Teo wearing a Help 'Em Up harness. Photo: © Tanya Jeffery.

Improving mobility outside the home

- Wearing a specially designed **harness** (see Figure 6.7). The harness can be used to help dogs get into and out of a car, as well as to support them while they are walking.
- **Non-slip ramps** can help dogs navigate steep steps outside the home, for example to access the garden, and also potentially to get into and out of cars. However, if a dog has never used a ramp before they will need to be introduced to using one very gradually, first by encouraging them to walk along it while it is laid flat on the floor, then walking up and down when one end is raised very slightly, for example on a small brick, then gradually increasing the slope until it reaches the angle needed to get into the car. Some dogs do not feel safe walking up or down a steep slope and if this is the case it would be better to lift them into the back of the car, possibly using a harness.
- **Protective boots and/or splints** can assist dogs that tend to drag their feet on the ground when they walk due to general weakness and/or neurological problems. They can help prevent skin damage and sores. It is very important to gradually accustom a dog to wearing boots or splints, to ensure they are correctly fitted, and that the dog is completely comfortable wearing them before using them on walks.
- **Specially designed carts** to support dogs with weakness of the back end, enabling them to be more mobile and potentially to continue to go for walks. As above it is important to accustom the dog to using the cart very gradually before using it for longer periods of time.
- **Dog buggy or stroller**, such as an adapted child's buggy that can be used to transport older dogs on longer walks, can work well for dogs that still enjoy going out but can no longer walk long distances. Again, it is important to accustom dogs to getting into and riding in the buggy very gradually. It may also be necessary to plan your route to avoid very bumpy surfaces, and to be very careful when going up and down kerbs and steps, to make sure your dog does not get jolted, which may be scary and potentially painful for them.

Improving access to food and water

- It may help to provide several water bowls around the house to ensure an older dog does not have to travel far to have a drink. This is particularly important for dogs with mobility problems, sensory decline or cognitive dysfunction who might struggle to locate and/or access the water bowl and those who have medical conditions that increase their need to drink water.
- Raising food and water bowls off the ground a little, for example by standing them on bricks or blocks of wood or using a proper bowl stand, may help dogs with joint and spinal problems to eat and drink more comfortably.
- Non-slip matting underfoot in the area of the food and water bowls will also help prevent dogs slipping while they are eating or drinking.
- It may be necessary to feed an older dog separately from other dogs in the household, particularly if they tend to eat more slowly or have different food. This will reduce the risk of them feeling tense or stressed in case another dog tries to push in to take their food.
- Older dogs may start to snatch food out of people's hands, even if they have always taken food gently previously, and this can sometimes result in them biting people's

hands. This may be due to ageing-related effects on sensory perception and fine movement control, loss of behavioural inhibition associated with cognitive decline and/or factors that increase appetite. If your elderly dog starts to do this it is important not to tell them off, but perhaps switch to offering food and treats in a bowl or on the floor rather than from your hand.

Helping dogs access toileting areas

- Dogs with mobility problems may take longer to get to their normal toilet area. Owners may need to encourage them to go outside more frequently to increase the chances of them reaching the right location before they need to pass urine or faeces. Depending on the severity of the mobility problem owners may need to assist their dog to stand up and also to get to the toilet area, for example using a harness. They may also need to support their dog gently while they squat to toilet. Some older dogs do not have sufficient strength or balance to remain still as they toilet and will find it easier to empty their bladder and bowels as they walk along, so owners will need to be prepared to move along with them.

- If a dog's normal toileting area is particularly difficult to reach (for example, because it is a long way from the house or accessed by steep steps) it may be necessary to teach the dog to use a toileting area closer to the house, or even provide a toileting area indoors (for example, by placing absorbent puppy pads in a large shallow tray or in a particular corner of the room).

- Dogs that can no longer squat properly to empty their bladder and bowels may get urine and faeces stuck on the hair around their rear ends and their back legs. This is a particular problem with dogs that have longer hair, and it may help to trim their 'trousers' regularly to prevent this. It may also be necessary to wash your dog's back end regularly if they do get soiled with urine or faeces and to monitor them carefully for any signs of skin soreness.

- Dogs with cognitive dysfunction may no longer indicate to their owners when they need to toilet, so again owners may need to remember to take them out to their toilet area regularly.

- If older dogs have not already learned to toilet on cue it would be a good idea to teach this, as the cue can then be used to prompt them to go to the toilet if necessary. The best way to start, just like with puppies, is to wait until your dog squats and starts to pass urine or faeces, then say your cue word, praise gently as they toilet, then reward them well as soon as they have finished passing urine or faeces. After a few repetitions, when your dog has learned the association between the cue and the act of toileting, it may be possible to use the cue as a prompt for them to go to the toilet. This is particularly helpful for dogs with cognitive dysfunction who may forget that they need to toilet but can also help dogs that are being asked to toilet in new locations for whatever reason. Another thing that can help to prompt a dog to toilet in a new location is the smell of their previously voided urine or faeces. This can be achieved by soaking up some of the dog's urine on some paper towel or picking up a small amount of their faeces and putting these in the new toileting location. If the new location already smells like their toilet area, they are more likely to use it.

The role of social and environmental interactions and mental stimulation in maintaining quality of life in older dogs

Why social interactions and mental stimulation are important factors in maintaining a good quality of life in dogs

Social relationships, with both people and other dogs, and mental stimulation through interactions with the environment are important factors in enhancing quality of life in dogs.[16] Quality of life can be regarded as a balance between the presence of positive (pleasant) feelings and experiences such as wellness, a sense of control over their environment and interactions, positive social interactions, mental stimulation, enjoyable activities such as eating, and the absence of negative (unpleasant) feelings and experiences (for example, pain and disease, stress associated with negative emotions such as anxiety and frustration, boredom[16]).

Ensuring a good quality of life throughout an animal's lifetime may have significant longer-term benefits. In humans, cognitive reserve, or the brain's ability to function adequately despite increasing amounts of damage, appears to be influenced by the amount of mental and physical activity and positive social interaction

Quality of life balance

Positive feelings e.g.	Negative feelings e.g.
• Happiness	• Fear
• Play	• Pain
• Social Companionship	• Boredom
• Mental stimulation	• Loneliness
• Physical touch	• Frustration
• A sense of control	• Hunger, thirst

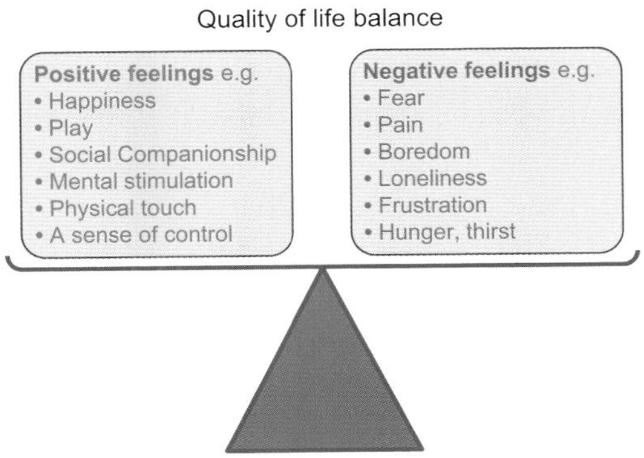

Figure 6.8: Balance model of quality of life. Modified from McMillan.[16]

people engage in throughout their lifetimes.[17] It is therefore likely that encouraging dogs to be active both mentally and physically, including encouraging positive social interactions with people and other animals throughout their lifetimes, as well as keeping them healthy and minimising stress may help reduce the rate of cognitive decline and likelihood of developing cognitive dysfunction.

As dogs get older, ageing-related changes and illness can push the balance more towards the negative side. As well as trying to minimise negative experiences for an older dog it is important to focus on increasing positive feelings through ensuring they have plenty of opportunities to engage in enjoyable experiences. However, it is also important to be aware that the types of social interactions and activities a dog finds enjoyable may change as they become older.

Tamsin Durston, clinical animal behaviourist and veterinary nurse, writes:

For me, what is most important for our older friends is quality of life. My feeling is that they deserve to enjoy their lives as much as possible, and we owe it to them to make sure they lead enriched, fulfilled lives in which all their needs are met. But we need to recognise that their needs will change as they grow older, and so we need to adapt to the way we live with them and the things we expect them to do and enjoy even ... as these might change ...

My Lelki always loved really long rambles out with me all over the UK, but also all sorts of training activities (nose work and agility and just 'fun stuff', trying a bit of everything) allowing her to use her brain and body. I listened to her, so she knew that she could say at any point 'Nah, I don't fancy this today' and I would say 'that's okay then, we won't do it, we'll do something different'. Lelki's hindlegs became weaker as she reached her 14th year, so we reduced our walks and I started to drive her to places where she could potter about gently at her own pace and didn't need to walk there and back too – so optimising her enjoyment.

As Tamsin says so beautifully, it is important to be prepared to adjust how we interact with our dogs as they get older, and particularly to listen to what our dog tells us they do and do not want to do. Their preferences may change permanently or may vary from one day to another and we need to notice and accommodate this.

We may need to be prepared to change how we interact with our dogs as they get older

Owners that have always enjoyed long walks or other activities such as running with their dog may find it quite frustrating if their older dog does not want to go for walks at all or cannot walk as far or as fast as they used to. I know from experience how hard it can be not to try to hurry an older dog as they stop to sniff yet again but if this is their main source of enjoyment on a walk it is so important to allow them plenty of time to do this. It can also be difficult to meet the needs of all dogs in a home if some are younger, fitter and need a longer walk.

It may be necessary to do a shorter walk with an older dog, then go for a run or take other dogs for a longer walk later. If an older dog does not cope well with being left alone at home, there are other options including driving somewhere and parking the car so that the older dog can rest in the back of the car after a short walk while you take the other dogs for a longer walk. Of course, only do this if the weather is such that the car is unlikely to overheat, and only in places where your dog can be safely left

Figure 6.9: Kali at the beach. Photo: © Tamsin Durston.

in the car. Another good option can be to use a buggy, which allows an older dog to accompany you and other dogs on a walk without having to walk the whole way (Figure 6.9).

Owners may also have to adjust how they interact with their older dog at other times. Dogs that have previously enjoyed snuggling up to their owners on the sofa or sleeping on the owner's bed may no longer be able to access these locations easily if they have mobility problems. If so you may need to put steps in strategic places to continue to allow your dog access to the furniture where you usually sit, or you may need to be prepared to spend time sitting with your dog in locations that are more comfortable for them, such as on the floor.

Dogs with cognitive dysfunction may no longer seek out or initiate interactions with their owners and may spend a lot of the day asleep. If so, you may need to be prepared to initiate all or most interactions with your dog, and encourage them to be more active during the day. However, it is important to do this carefully to avoid startling your dog or causing distress.

Dogs with sensory decline such as visual loss or hearing loss may no longer be able to see or hear their owners, which can make communication difficult. For dogs with hearing loss but not vision loss it may be necessary to use hand signals and gestures rather than spoken cues, while for dogs with visual loss but not hearing loss it will be necessary to use verbal cues. For dogs with both hearing and vision loss, gentle touches on their shoulder area can be used to tell them that you are there and to guide them in different directions.

Dogs with sensory deficits may be startled if they are approached suddenly, and they may snap if startled. For dogs that can still hear it is sensible to get into the habit of speaking to them before approaching or touching them. However, for dogs with hearing loss, particularly if they also have poor vision, it may be necessary to touch them gently to let them know you are there. If so, it is important to accustom your dog to being touched like this, by doing it when they are aware of you initially and checking they are comfortable with this, before trying it when they are not aware of you approaching. It may also be necessary to keep older dogs with sensory decline or cognitive dysfunction on a lead or a line attached to a harness when they are outside the home, to ensure they do not get lost.

You may also need to change how you handle your older dog. Things like drying their paws after a walk can become more difficult, particularly for a dog with osteoarthritis or other musculoskeletal problems. Lifting one paw to dry it can cause the dog to over-balance and could potentially cause discomfort as their weight is shifted onto the other limbs. With my dog Jimmy, who has some mild osteoarthritis in his elbow joints, we have a routine so he knows which order his paws will be dried in, and he is able to prepare for this by shifting his weight, ready for when the next paw is lifted. For dogs that find it difficult to balance on three legs it may help to have someone gently support the dog while the other person lifts and dries their paws or teach the dog to lie down while their paws are dried. Alternatively, invest in some good dirt-trapper mats that brush mud off the paws as your dog walks over them.

Grooming can also be a bit more difficult. Ageing is often associated with changes including muscle wasting, loss of subcutaneous fat, thinning and reduced elasticity of the skin. This means the skin is more delicate and bones are often more prominent. It is important to be gentle when brushing older dogs and it may also be necessary to switch to using a softer bristle brush or a rubber grooming brush.

The importance of focusing on activities your elderly dog enjoys

It is important to be aware of any changes in the activities your dog particularly enjoys and make adjustments for these. For example, play should be an enjoyable activity that improves a dog's quality of life. However, older dogs with mobility problems or sensory decline may start to find particular games with particular toys more difficult. Chasing a ball or playing tug may be uncomfortable for dogs with joint problems. It may be possible to adapt these games so that older dogs can still enjoy them, for example by not throwing the ball so far or focusing on searching for the ball rather than chasing it, or by playing tug very gently so as not to jar their neck or joints.

Owners of dogs with sensory decline may also need to make adjustments to the types of toys and games they play with them. Dogs with vision loss may struggle to chase a thrown ball but may be able to use their nose to search for it on the ground. They may also enjoy games that involve searching for food or other smelly items. Dogs with hearing loss may no longer show interest in squeaky toys but may be interested in moving toys or scent games.

Because many older dogs appear to enjoy sniffing, they tend to enjoy scent-related activities. These are low-impact activities so can be beneficial for dogs with mobility issues, as long as they can move around and lower their head comfortably to sniff, and also for dogs with cognitive dysfunction as well as those with sensory decline. This could include simple search games for food, searching for other scented articles, or tracking (as described in Chapter 4).

Other enrichment activities such as activity feeding or offering items to lick and chew can also be enjoyable for older dogs as long as the activity feeders or other items are chosen to suit the individual dog. For example, some older dogs will struggle with activity feeders or activities that require them to spend a long time standing up or moving around such as treat balls, and will find it easier to use activity feeders that stay in one place or that they can interact with while lying down such as Lickimats™ or chew items such as Kongs™. Some dogs have preferences for types of activity such as licking, chewing or searching, and it is important to ensure you are offering your dog the sorts of activities that they enjoy. Some dogs also like novelty, and will enjoy a range of different activities, while others prefer familiarity and would prefer to stick to one or two activities. It is also important to ensure activity feeders do not cause frustration for example because it is too difficult to get food out. Ideally activity feeders should be used in addition to, or to only replace part of, the dog's normal food ration, as we do not want older dogs feeling they have to use them in order to not go hungry.

Walks may also need to be different. One of the last senses to deteriorate in older dogs is olfaction, and older dogs will often get a lot of enjoyment out of sniffing. They will also be less able to walk far or quickly so the slow activities discussed in Chapter 4 would be appropriate.

Fun, reward-based training can also provide mental stimulation as long as a dog does not have severe cognitive dysfunction. This can also help in retraining any lost previously learned behaviours such as toileting outside/in a particular location. Using a marker to indicate when a behaviour will be rewarded may make learning easier. This could be a clicker or a word for dogs that can hear, or possibly a light flash or hand signal for dogs with hearing loss. Other simple behaviours such as targeting (touching a hand or object with the nose or paw) are fairly easy for dogs to learn and can be a fun and enjoyable way to interact with your older dog.

Helping older dogs with severe cognitive dysfunction and anxiety-related problems

While most older dogs will benefit from mental stimulation and a degree of novelty, dogs with severe cognitive dysfunction, and those that are generally anxious, are likely to find changes to their routine and environment very stressful. It may be necessary to minimise changes to their routines and environment as much as possible. Adaptil™ products and familiar-smelling items may help to maintain a sense of familiarity and security when unavoidable changes happen such as when going to the vets or having to travel to another places. Dogs that are highly anxious may also benefit from anxiety-reducing supplements or medication, and it is worth discussing this option with your vet.

Managing relationships with other dogs in the home

Obviously, there will be huge individual differences in the quality of the relationships between dogs sharing a home, and also in how these relationships might change as one or more of the dogs become older. It is important to ensure the needs of all dogs in the home are met, which may involve making various adaptations to their routines, activities and also to their environment.

Dogs that have always got on well often continue to do so as one or both get older, but sometimes relationships can become strained, particularly if an older dog becomes more irritable or less tolerant of another dog approaching or interacting with them (for example, because they are painful, have sensory decline or are developing cognitive dysfunction). This can be a particular problem if the other dog is younger and particularly boisterous. Another potential source of tension can be an older dog with cognitive dysfunction or sensory decline starting to behave in a way that other dogs in the home might regard as inappropriate (for example, by appearing not to respect their personal space or not responding appropriately to social signals such as posturing or growling). Other dogs can also find it very stressful if an older dog performs repetitive behaviours such as continual pacing or barking. It may be necessary to use barriers to separate an older dog from the other dogs in the home at particular times, such as when they are eating and resting, or even permanently if there is a lot of tension between them.

It is very tempting to consider getting a puppy or another younger dog as a dog gets older. However, introducing a new dog into the household may be extremely stressful for an older dog with severe medical problems such cognitive dysfunction or sensory decline or for a dog that has struggled to live with other dogs previously. It would be best not do this and wait until the older dog is no longer with you. However, some elderly dogs can benefit from the introduction of a younger dog into the household, especially if they have good social skills and the introduction is performed very carefully.[18] The opportunity to mentor and

interact with a younger dog can be very beneficial for an older dog, as Pat Tagg outlines below, as long as owners are prepared to manage them carefully and to ensure the needs of both dogs are met. Julie Bedford recently fostered a bitch and her litter of eight pups. She had intended to keep them completely separated from Sally, her 17-year-old Border Collie bitch. However, Sally had other ideas, and insisted on spending time with the pups, behaving like the perfect grandmother (Figure 6.10).

Giving dogs some control over their environment and social interactions

As mentioned above, having a degree of control over their environment and social interactions is an important aspect of improving an animal's quality of life.[1] We can give older dogs some choice in both how they interact with their environment (for example, by providing several beds in different locations around the home), and

Figure 6.10: Sally aged 17 years, with young foster pup. Photo: (c) Julie Bedford.

also in the activities we do with them and the way we interact with them. As Tamsin says above, it is important to allow our dogs to say 'no' if they do not want to do something. This involves learning and consistently responding to your dog's subtle communication signals that indicate they are not happy to engage in an activity or a particular social interaction, which may include hesitation to approach, or any of the lower-level signs on the Canine Ladder of Aggression[19] (see Chapter 5).

An insight into maintaining quality of life in working dogs as they get older

Pat Tagg is a clinical animal behaviourist and sheep farmer. She manages her flock of Polled Dorset sheep using working German Shepherd Dogs in the transhumance style of the hiking shepherds of Europe, which respects the natural ethology of both the sheep and the dogs. She also runs courses involving tracking, searching and traditional herding activities. Pat has some fascinating insights into how older working dogs can be supported so they can continue to do the work they love into their old age, and how relationships between younger and older dogs can play an important part in this. These have a lot of relevance for maintaining a good quality of life in our pet dogs as they become older, through continuing to provide opportunities for mental and physical exercise and social interaction, in ways that are suited to the individual dog and taking into account any health problems they might have.

Pat recognises that farm dogs tend to live very different lives to most pet dogs. Free-ranging farm dogs generally live in highly enriched environments, and young dogs have quite a lot of freedom to explore and learn about the environment for themselves, with minimal direct control from people. As their work with livestock involves performing tasks that are a natural part of their ethology human input is generally focused on shaping and facilitating their natural behaviours rather than controlling them. This mainly self-directed learning results in dogs with high levels of physical and mental resilience and the ability to think and respond independently when needed while working. However, before reaching this stage young dogs are at risk of experiencing both physical injury (for example, from falling off a haystack or tractor wheel arch) and mental distress. Adolescent dogs often experience frustration when they reach the stage where they are physically ready to work but their mental development is not yet sufficient to allow them to deal with the psychological pressures of working with livestock. In both these situations having an older dog as a mentor can be extremely beneficial: the older dog can support an immature dog both physically and mentally while they are learning how to control their behaviour, interact safely with the environment and also to work and interact with livestock.

Mentoring a younger dog can also be highly beneficial for the older working dog. A partnership between an older and younger dog can provide social support for both dogs and also enables the older dog to continue to work with livestock even as they become slower and potentially more infirm, because the younger dog will be faster and more agile. Pat has had several generations of dogs that have first been mentored by older dogs and then gone on to mentor younger dogs themselves (Figure 6.11).

Pat feels strongly that retirement without the opportunity to continue to work can be seriously detrimental to the welfare of an older dog, and that this should not be necessary if sufficient care is taken to support them both physically and mentally. She says 'Developing frameworks to keep older working dogs at

Figure 6.11: A partnership between an older and younger dog can provide social support for both dogs Krusty and Lara. Photo: (c) Pat Tagg.

work and consequently alive, vibrant, valued and healthy is not in my view difficult. I do not believe that a diagnosis of disease should automatically consign an old dog to retirement. That is the time to step up, work with the vet, conduct a risk assessment for enhancing quality of life and for recognising when enough is enough. It should be possible to ensure older dogs have a retirement worthy of the expansive experience gained over a working career, with comfort adjustments made to support a retired athlete's body. Protecting the mental health of the old farm dog is relatively easy, passing them a new charge and providing increased support for their bodies should suffice.'

Pat's elderly working German Shepherd dog Krusty was diagnosed with Degenerative Myelopathy when he was 10-years old. Pat outlines how she helped him to continue to do the activities he had always enjoyed, including working with sheep, travelling in the van to explore new places and tracking.

'We continued to work together, walking for miles every day. The hope being that muscle memory would keep him walking for a long time after his nervous system failed. This proved to be the case, Krusty was almost 14-years old when he died at home with the help of his vet. In the years after diagnosis, we implemented a framework of action to keep Krusty at work. In addition to the walking, aided in the late stages by various bits of supportive and protective equipment, we made an agreement to continue to travel to new places just as we always had. We surmounted the issues of getting into and out of a vehicle without causing pain or distress by making a serious commitment to start getting ready to go in plenty of time and to make more time. No short temper, no rushing, no exclusion of anyone. We'd been a team for years, age would not change that as far as we were concerned. We packed the van with a memory foam bed so that we could sit comfortably in green spaces wherever we stopped, and our exploration adventures continued until 48 hours before Krusty left us.

His formal tracking was enabled by laying a track to a post, and on the post I fixed a ladle into which I dropped some food. Using a sling to support his back end I followed where Krusty led: he was definitely still in charge of tracking. He sniffed his way towards the post, the ladle helped him by negating the need to drop his head to the floor which might have left him unbalanced. Where there's a will, there's a way. I wouldn't swap those memories from his later years for all the tea in China.

Coming to terms with the fact that your dog is getting older

Most people would agree that it is a great privilege to care for a dog throughout their lifetime, including into and through their old age. However, just as with elderly relatives, this is not always easy. There will be times when caring for an elderly dog can be difficult, frustrating or deeply upsetting, and it is important to realise that it is OK to feel like this.

As Tanya Jeffery, clinical animal behaviourist writes:

When you realise your dog is getting elderly this can be difficult to accept. This realisation may be because your dog's exercise tolerance and general mobility changes or due to an ongoing illness that affects your dog's ability to do what they once did with ease.

You may experience an element of sadness/bereavement due to the fact that you are no longer able to walk for miles, do certain sports or just be as active with your dog anymore. This may also relate to the more social aspects of dog ownership in that friends with younger dogs may be still able to do the activities you once enjoyed with your dog.

Sometimes facing the fact that your canine friend is getting older may also bring to the fore the distressing fact that one day they will not be here, as their elderly presence makes this issue even more real, and possibly upsetting. You may have to make adaptations to your daily routine, house layout, bedding and many other things due to living with an elderly dog.

Although this realisation and acceptance may be painful at times there are many things that can make the journey easier for you and your dog.

Julie Bedford, clinical animal behaviourist also writes 'Do not grieve for your elderly dog before they go ... enjoy each moment with them. Accept that they need you and enjoy spending time with them.' This is very wise advice. As far as we know, our dogs do not think about the future, they are only aware of what is happening now, and they will not understand if we are sad about something that has not happened yet. The best thing we can do is to spend as much time with our elderly dogs as possible and focus on and enjoy doing the things that they also enjoy.

Knowing when it is the right time to say goodbye

One of the hardest things for any dog owner is losing them at the end of their lives. And with the option of euthanasia available to us, in many cases we also have the huge responsibility of having to decide when is the right time to say goodbye. It is very rare indeed for dogs to die quietly in their sleep, however much we might wish this to happen. However, deciding on the right time to end their lives is never easy, and different people will make different decisions based on their own feelings, experiences and perception of their dog's well-being. There is always a balance between wanting longevity and maintaining quality of life. It is natural to want our dogs to stay with us for as long as possible, but it is also important to consider their quality of life as they become older and more infirm, and this is a time when it is particularly important to keep behaviour in mind.

Quality of life has been defined as 'the total well-being of an individual animal that considers the physical, social and emotional aspects of life'.[20] While some owners will be confident that they can accurately assess their dog's quality of life as they become older and frailer, others may find it is not always easy to be totally objective about this. There may also be disagreement between family members about their dog's quality of life.

Various end-of-life quality of life assessment tools are available (see Flavell[21] for a review of three of these). These have been primarily designed for use by veterinary staff, in discussion with owners, when assessing the needs of older dogs for hospice and end-of-life care. They incorporate various behavioural measures including mobility, appetite, thirst and keenness to engage in play and social interactions. They can certainly help to provide an objective

assessment of the quality of an animal's physical health although they are less good at recognising social and psychological aspects of well-being.[21] Therefore, they should always be used to support rather than to replace an owner's own assessment of and feelings about their dog's current quality of life.

Personally, I have always felt that quality of life is more important than longevity for my elderly dogs, and although I am not sure who first said this, I strongly agree with the dictum 'better a week too early than a day too late' when deciding when to put an elderly animal to sleep. Because my husband and I are both veterinary surgeons we have always had the luxury of choosing when, where and how to do this. We have always put our animals to sleep at home, so they have been in their familiar surroundings, surrounded by their familiar people at the end of their lives. I am aware that not everyone will be able to do exactly this, but in many cases, it should be possible to plan when and how your dog will end their life. This can help ensure the end is as good and stress free as possible, for you and also for your dog.

Tamsin Durston writes about how she planned the end-of-life for her elderly dog Lelki:

Lelki's immediate happiness was always our absolute priority – she had given us so much joy throughout her life. So when we felt her legs were deteriorating to the point where discomfort outbalanced the pleasure in life, we made a decision to say goodbye and actually set a date – I wanted to put her to sleep (I was so fortunate to be able to do this myself, it was a privilege and honour) before this decision was taken out of our hands – while she was comfortable. Setting a date might seem very macabre, but for us it meant we knew what was happening, we felt in control of her happiness, we could take the time off to dedicate to being with her, and could avoid her experiencing any sudden, traumatic event such as falling over dangerously or becoming stuck anywhere, and distressed/panicking. We were also able to ensure her last days were absolutely full of joy – she was totally spoilt, got to eat steak, cake, do everything 'norty', we would go lie on a blanket in all our favourite places so she could potter about, sniff or enjoy a food-releasing toy – whatever she wanted. So we felt it was perfect … we gave her the last gift we could and she had a really 'good' goodbye.

I would strongly recommend that all owners of elderly dogs discuss the options available and their preferences for ending their dog's life with their veterinary practice well before the time when this decision needs to be made. Obviously different people will have different preferences for where and how they would want this to be managed and this may also be influenced by the temperament of the individual dog. In most cases having the vet come to your home to put your dog to sleep is likely to be much less stressful for them than taking them to the veterinary surgery and planning ahead will increase the chances that your vet will be able to arrange this. If your dog is likely to be worried about people coming to the house or being handled it is also sensible to discuss options for sedation beforehand. It can also help to understand what the process of euthanasia will entail, so you know exactly what to expect. Your vet, or one of the veterinary nurses in the practice, should be able to talk you through this, and the Animal Welfare Foundation has also produced an excellent guide to the process of euthanasia called Saying Goodbye (see the Resources section). It is also sensible to think about what you would like to happen to your dog's body afterwards, for example whether you

would like them to be individually cremated or not, as it can be very difficult to make this sort of decision at the time.

There is often a dilemma about whether or not to allow other pets to witness an elderly dog being put to sleep, especially if this happens at home. I am not sure that there is a right or wrong way to manage this, and in the end, it will come down to what feels right for you and for your other animals. Personally, we have tended to shut our other pets (dogs and cats) out of the room just before we put the older dog to sleep. Once the process is over, we have allowed the other animals to come back into the room, and to approach and sniff the body if they wish. Some animals appear curious and want to approach and sniff while others seem wary or do not seem to want to approach. After this, we shut them out again, and give them something to keep them occupied while we move the body.

Unfortunately, despite the best of intentions, things do not always go to plan. There may be situations where a dog's health or quality of life deteriorate far quicker than expected, and we are forced to make decisions very quickly, so the end of their life is not quite as we planned. Sometimes a decision regarding euthanasia has to be made when a dog is under anaesthetic, if an exploratory operation reveals an inoperable condition for example, when their owner has not had an opportunity to say a proper goodbye. Although this can be extremely distressing, it is important to try not to be too hard on yourself if things do not go to plan and accept that you have done the best that you could for your dog.

While losing a dog at the end of their life is sadly an inevitable part of being a dog owner, it can be a truly devastating experience. Specialist pet bereavement support is offered by several organisations, including the Blue Cross (see the Resources section), and some veterinary practices also offer this service.

Dealing with the grief of other pets

On top of dealing with your own grief associated with losing an older dog, it can be extremely difficult to deal with other animals that also appear to be experiencing grief. This is most likely to happen when a dog has been particularly close to the elderly dog, and possibly reliant on them for social support. Dogs are also likely to pick up on, and respond to, our own distress. It may help both us and our other animals if we can keep to a reasonably normal routine and include as many fun activities as we can over the next few weeks. I have always left the deceased elderly dog's beds and toys around the home for several weeks afterwards, both to avoid any more sudden changes for the remaining dogs and also so that they can still smell the dog that has gone, although their scent will fade gradually. My experience is that this seems to help them accept gradually that the other dog has gone and is not coming back. If dogs seem to be struggling to cope with the loss of the other dog they may benefit from some additional behavioural and possibly psychopharmacological support, and it would be sensible to discuss this with your vet.

Conclusion

The process and effects of ageing in dogs can be very variable, and although there are likely to be some common issues there is no 'one-size-fits-all' set of recommendations that will suit all elderly dogs and their owners. Instead, it is important to recognise that each dog is an individual: their needs as they get older may differ from those of other older dogs, and any changes you make to try and meet these needs must be tailored to them.

In my view, the most important things to remember as an owner of an older dog are as follows.

- Always keep behaviour in mind: changes in an older dog's behaviour can be an indication of changing physical and mental needs and may also be an early indication that they are developing a health problem.
- Ensure your older dog has regular vet checks, particularly if they are starting to show behavioural or physical changes. Many health problems can be successfully treated, or if not managed, to ensure your older dog has the best possible quality of life for as long as possible.
- Above all, make sure to spend, and enjoy, the time you have with your dog as they get older. As they get older and their needs change, be prepared to make changes to how you interact with them and the activities you do with them. Try not to regret the things that you can no longer do with your older dog or focus too much on the future without them. Instead, enjoy spending time with them in the here and now.
- As your dog becomes older and increasingly frail, try to plan ahead to increase the chances that the end of their life can be managed in the way that is most acceptable to you, and that fully respects your dog's quality of life.

Resources

All the major dog welfare charities and other organisations provide advice on living with and caring for elderly dogs including:

- RSPCA: https://www.rspca.org.uk/adviceandwelfare/pets/dogs/health/seniordogs
- Blue Cross: https://www.bluecross.org.uk/pet-advice/caring-for-older-dogs
- Dogs Trust: https://www.dogstrust.org.uk/help-advice/getting-or-buying-a-dog/rehoming-and-looking-after-an-older-dog

Pet end-of-life information and bereavement support:

- Blue Cross bereavement support service: https://www.bluecross.org.uk/about-pbss
- Animal Welfare Foundation: information about euthanasia: Saying Goodbye: https://www.animalwelfarefoundation.org.uk/animal-welfare-advice/petcare-advice/#saying-goodbye
- RSPCA: https://www.rspca.org.uk/adviceandwelfare/pets/bereavement

Information and support for owners of dogs with arthritis:

- Canine Arthritis Management: https://caninearthritis.co.uk/
- WSAVA Dog Body Condition Score: https://wsava.org/wp-content/uploads/2020/01/Body-Condition-Score-Dog.pdf

Cognitive dysfunction assessment tools:

- Canine cognitive dysfunction questionnaire: https://petsci.co.uk/canine-cognitive-dysfunction-questionnaire/
- Purina cognitive dysfunction evaluation tool: https://www.purinainstitute.com/sites/g/files/auxxlc381/files/2018–08/DISHAA.pdf

Ongoing epidemiological studies that will help us understand more about ageing in dogs:

- Dog Aging Project: https://dogagingproject.org/
- Generation Pup: https://generationpup.ac.uk/

Figure 6.12: Pebbles, Saluki × Greyhound age 14. Photo: © Suzanne Rogers.

References

1. Wallis, L.J., Szabó, D., Erdélyi-Belle, B. and Kubinyi, E. (2018) Demographic change across the lifespan of pet dogs and their impact on health status. *Frontiers in Veterinary Science* 5, 200.

2. Rajapaksha, E. (2018) Special considerations for diagnosing behavior problems in older pets. *Veterinary Clinics of North America: Small Animal Practice* 48, 443–456.
3. Bódizs, R., Kis, A., Gácsi, M. and Topál, J. (2020) Sleep in the dog: comparative, behavioral and translational relevance. *Current Opinion in Behavioral Sciences* 33, 25–33.
4. Cory, J. (2013) Identification and management of cognitive decline in companion animals and the comparisons with Alzheimer disease: a review. *Journal of Veterinary Behavior* 8, 291–301.
5. Gruen, M.E., Samson, D.R. and Lascelles, B.D.X. (2019) Functional linear modeling of activity data shows analgesic-mediated improved sleep in dogs with spontaneous osteoarthritis pain. *Scientific Reports* 9, 14192.
6. Landsberg, G.M., Nichol, J. and Araújo, J.A. (2012) Cognitive dysfunction syndrome: a disease of canine and feline brain aging. *Veterinary Clinics of North America: Small Animals* 42, 749–768.
7. Salvin, H.E., McGreevy, P.D., Sachdev, P.S. and Valenzuela, M.J. (2010) Under diagnosis of canine cognitive dysfunction: a cross-sectional survey of older companion dogs. *The Veterinary Journal* 184, 277–281.

8. Notari, L., Burman, O. and Mills, D. (2015) Behavioural changes in dogs treated with corticosteroids. *Physiology & Behavior* 151(60), 9–16.

9. Speakman, J.R., van Acker, A. and Harper, E.J. (2003) Age-related changes in the metabolism and body composition of three dog breeds and their relationship to life expectancy. *Aging Cell* 2(5), 265–275.

10. Mondino, A., Delucchi, L., Moeser, A., Cerdá-González, S. and Vanini, G. (2021) Sleep disorders in dogs: a pathophysiological and clinical review. *Topics in Companion Animal Medicine* 43, 100516.

11. Zizi, F., Jean-Louis, G., Magai, C., Greenidge, K.C., Wolintz, A.H. and Heath-Phillip, O. (2002) Sleep complaints and visual impairment among older Americans: a community-based study. The journals of gerontology. *Series A, Biological Sciences and Medical Science* 57(10), M691–694.

12. Lopes Fagundes, A.L., Hewison, L., McPeake, K.J., Zulch, H. and Mills, D.S. (2018) Noise sensitivities in dogs: an exploration of signs in dogs with and without musculoskeletal pain using qualitative content analysis. *Frontiers in Veterinary Science* 5, 17.

13. Blackwell, E., Bradshaw, J. and Casey, R. (2013) Fear responses to noises in domestic dogs: Prevalence, risk factors and co-occurrence with other fear related behaviour. *Applied Animal Behaviour Science* 145, 15–25.

14. Corral, C. (2018) Canine hip dysplasia: aetiology and treatment. *The Veterinary Nurse* 9(5), 246–250.

15. Canine Arthritis Management (CAM) (n.d.) https://caninearthritis.co.uk/.

16. McMillan, F.D. (2003) Maximising quality of life in ill animals. *Journal American Animal Hospital Association* 39(3), 227–235.

17. Stern, Y. (2006) Cognitive reserve and Alzheimer disease. *Alzheimer Disease and Associated Disorders* 20(3 Suppl 2), S69–74.

18. Landsberg, G.M., Hunthausen W. and Ackerman, L. (2013) *Behavior Problems of the Dog and Cat*, 3rd edn. Saunders, Philadelphia, PA.

19. Shepherd, K. (2009) Behavioural medicine as an integral part of veterinary practice. In: Horwitz, D.F. and Mills, D.S. (eds) *BSAVA Manual of Canine and Feline Behavioural Medicine*, 2nd edn, BSAVA, Quedgeley, pp. 10–23.

20. Bishop, G., Cooney, K., Cox, S., Downing, R., Mitchener, K., Shanan, A., Soares, N., Stevens, B. and Wynn T. (2016) 2016 AAHA/IAAHPC end-of-life care guidelines. *Journal of the American Animal Hospital Association* 52(6), 341–356.

21. Flavell, S. (2019) The use of quality of life scales for hospice and end-of-life patients. *The Veterinary Nurse* 10(10), 533–537.

Chapter 7

Rehabilitation and rescue

Steve Goward

Before we begin, I would like us to consider the words that head this chapter, 'Rehabilitation and rescue'.

Rehabilitation: Why would we need to rehabilitate a dog? What has happened in their life that now requires an intervention in the way they behave in our world?

Rescue: Where have we rescued them from? Do all dogs that come into the care of an animal welfare organisation need rescuing? Why do we need to rescue dogs? These are some of the questions that we need to reflect upon in order to improve welfare in our animal loving society.

I will use the phrase 'rehoming centre' to mean rescue centre, shelter or kennels as this is the term used where I work at Dogs Trust. Dogs come into rehoming centres for many reasons.[1] In this chapter, we will follow a dog's journey from an animal welfare rehoming centre to their new home. My intention is to explore the processes that are in place to help our dogs overcome the past experiences that have led to their arrival at a rehoming centre. I will share my own thoughts, as well as those of my colleagues and mentors, on how we support staff, volunteers, adopters, and of course the dogs themselves, on their journey.

What do we mean when we say, 'rehabilitate?'

To rehabilitate someone who has been ill or in prison, means to help them live a normal life again through training and therapy. If someone has been rehabilitated, they begin to be considered acceptable again after a period during which they have been rejected or severely criticised. Synonyms include: reintegrate, retrain, restore to health, readapt.

If we take the phrase, 'to live a normal life again,' we must understand what a normal life is. We have to have standards to aspire to and universal ethics that help us agree on the best approach to the work we do. Our aim is to enhance the lives of the dogs we work with. To do this we must first understand their needs and how they communicate their emotions. Only then, will we better understand the effect we have on them.

The intake of dogs into rescue centres varies greatly across organisations. Although my thoughts are primarily based on the work I do with rehoming centres in the UK, I have also collaborated with international organisations as part of Dogs Trust Worldwide.

Let us consider why dogs need rescuing and the implications past experiences can have on the potential need for rehabilitation. If a dog has gone through a period of poor living conditions, abuse, neglect or some form of trauma, then it would be fair to say they needed to be rescued from that situation. It is likely that these dogs would then need additional intervention. However, not all dogs entering rehoming centres have previous negative life experiences. Despite this, they may still require some rehabilitation. Just because a dog has no previous reported behavioural problems, does not mean they will slip back easily into a home without some form of behavioural support. What if a dog, that had lived previously on a farm, roaming freely off-lead, was now required to walk obediently on a lead, greeting others appropriately? What would that dog do when his choices had been taken away? Alternatively, consider the dog who had attended work with his previous owners only to find himself facing a new life with a family who required him to remain home alone. Research tells us that many dogs are surrendered into animal welfare charities for behaviour reasons.[1] Although there may be many factors influencing the relinquishment of dogs into rehoming centres, behaviour is commonly cited, along with moving to a new house and personal circumstances. I would suggest that having to move home or changes in personal circumstances that may lead to a dog being surrendered, are likely to impact on the dog's behaviour. Such changes might even have set in motion behaviour changes seen in the dog leading to the owner's decision to relinquish the dog; for example, if the dog was suddenly being left for longer hours or given less exercise or interaction. Some of these issues may appear minor to those of us working and caring for dogs within rehoming centres. However, the ultimate test is whether the dog can be rehomed with the confidence that they will not be returned to us.

So, the journey begins …

When a dog enters our care for the first time, we are often unaware of the life that he/she has led and the learning that has occurred previously. If we are fortunate, we may have the opportunity to speak to the current owners and gather information through questions or the use of a handover form. Having detailed information about the dog's behaviour in the current home can be extremely valuable to rehoming centres. However, it is not always straightforward to accurately gather the important information.[2] Handing a dog over to a rehoming centre is often a highly emotional experience and it can be difficult to question owners on their dog's behaviour. Therefore, it is vital that those tasked with collecting or receiving dogs from owners are appropriately trained. They must gather the most essential information that will help the organisation identify the dog's needs and where any rehabilitation may be required. This should include positive areas of the dog's behaviour as well as the areas of concern. If a written form is used, it is recommended that the information is filled out ahead of the dog being surrendered rather than at the time. This allows time during the handover for discussion and expansion should there be the need for further clarification. For example, if a question on aggression evokes a response from the owner, then it is essential that this is explored further, and we gain a better understanding of these aggressive situations. With this information, we are better placed to keep both our staff and volunteers safe. It can also help to reduce situations where the dog may experience a negative emotional state that could lead to reduced welfare and possibly a recurrence of aggressive behaviour.

The first days and weeks in the kennel environment can be incredibly difficult for many dogs.[3] For those that have not experienced this situation before, it is far removed from the comfy sofa and quiet sleeping quarters of their previous home. Although it is often essential to get some basic protocols, such as veterinary checks, vaccinations and microchipping, completed, we should be mindful of the impact arriving in kennels has on a dog's ability to cope. Once the dog is in our care, the observations and recording of behaviours should begin.[4] If we have an appropriately detailed record of a dog's time with us, we are better positioned to act early should behaviour modification be required.[5]

There is much discussion in the behaviour world around assessments. It is difficult to predict which behaviours might be seen in a home, based on behaviours exhibited in a rehoming centre.[6] Although making predictions may be challenging and a home is clearly a very different environment to the rehoming centre, there is still the need to keep these records. Recording behaviours seen in centres helps us to maintain safety and welfare, while building a picture of each individual dog that enters our care.

Some dogs will require more support than others. Once it has been established that a dog needs a behaviour modification plan (BMP), it is down to the teams working with them to address the behaviours of concern. When looking at developing a BMP, the aim is, of course, to create a *happier* dog. With the list of areas to consider in Box 7.1, we can ensure we adopt an ethical and welfare focused approach to behaviour modification.

Box 7.1 HAPPIER dogs

- **H**ealth – good veterinary support.
- **A**ssessment – set protocols to help identify behaviours and preferences.
- **P**lanning – using our knowledge from the assessment and of our environment to plan the BMP.
- **P**rognosis (expectation setting) – help assess timescales and minimum achievement prior to rehoming.
- **I**nvesting in emotional change (creating resilience) – creating a base for future training.
- **E**nvironment – understanding the pros and cons of the kennel environment.
- **R**ecord keeping – tracking progress or lack of progress.

The terms training and behaviour mean different things to different people. I use the following example to help teams understand the differences and how they generally go hand in hand when working to successfully rehome our dogs. A training plan teaches a new behaviour; for example, teaching a dog to go to bed when cued, 'Go to bed'. A BMP may involve teaching a new behaviour, but that new behaviour will replace a (usually unwanted) existing behaviour; for example, teaching a dog to go to their bed when you approach the kennel, instead of barking and rushing at the door.

Veterinary involvement in any behaviour case is vital to ensure we are not dealing with a dog in pain or discomfort. If we see a sudden change in behaviour, we must ensure that there is not a medical reason for the change. It can be incredibly difficult to modify behaviour that is rooted in pain or discomfort.[7] In my experience, this is especially the case when we are dealing with aggression towards other dogs or handling by unknown people.

When we humans struggle with pain, we are able to verbally communicate this to others and hopefully find a way to alleviate it. Toothache, earache or even a simple headache can dramatically change our tolerance to situations. Some dogs can be hard to read when it comes to pain[8] and good observations and record keeping is essential. This is why it is vitally important to have a good relationship with the vet team and to develop best practice in the observation and recording of potential health concerns in the kennel environment.

Moose

Let us consider a case that entered one of our rehoming centres recently and follow the stages of the journey to finding a new home. Moose arrived in our care at the age of 12-months old. A big handsome Rottweiler cross, he had previously been handed to another animal charity by his owners. This meant that we had some historical background, but the information had not been collected by our team. Moose had no medical concerns and was healthy and pain free. The previous charity's staff had assessed him and described him as 'OTT' (over the top) with dogs. During his initial days in our care, Moose was an immediate hit with the carers working with him. There were so many great elements to his personality. He was playful, interested in food and trainable. His strength on the lead, however, did pose an immediate concern and a potential risk to staff. As per the usual assessment protocol, Moose was introduced to other dogs and was found to be bouncy and overexcitable. Again, it was recorded that he was OTT. His assessment stated that care would be needed when selecting which dogs he was introduced to.

Observations of Moose were recorded on his initial 7-day assessment. These assess daily activities that occur naturally in the rehoming centres such as: feeding, daily handling and exercise. He also underwent our more structured 'character assessment' where there is a more hands-on approach to finding out about each dog. At this point concerns were beginning to be raised about Moose. To record these, staff used escalation records (Figure 7.1), which are used to report behaviour changes to the centre training team. This team are then able to recommend appropriate actions to take. The early reporting of behaviour change is key to successful BMPs. If the behaviour is still in the trial and error stage of learning, that is, the dog is still trying to figure out what works for them, we are better placed to intervene and provide a solution that works for the dog and the handlers, than if the behaviour has become automatic.

One-off assessments are problematic, as much of what is seen on a given day will depend on the dog's recent experiences. For example, a dog that has been to see the vet or has experienced a difficult meet and greet with another dog, could be assessed as avoidant or anxious. If this was the only time the dog was assessed during their stay with us, then this would potentially be an inaccurate assessment of that dog in general. Ongoing assessments are required to build up a picture of the dog and how they interact with the environment they are in. If one-off assessments are conducted they should be reviewed on a regular basis and updated as the dog's behaviour develops.

In Moose's case, the staff began to report his reactivity to other dogs as they passed his kennel. His response was above and beyond what might be considered typical for many dogs. Moose was also beginning to react to the sight of other dogs out on a walk, rearing onto his hind legs, pulling and vocalising. In a matter of days, this escalated to reacting to just the sound of other dogs barking.

Record of Dog Behaviour Escalation		
Date:	**Member of Staff Reporting:**	
Dog name:	**Breed/Colour:**	**Dos's Assessment Grade:**

Near Miss (Defined as an incident that unless avoiding action was taken, would have led to a more serious incident occurring): Y / N

Incident Description, Give as much detail as possible regarding context:

Environmental Factors, consider time of day, other activities occurring, trigger stacking effect:

Action Taken:

Staff Member involved:
Reported to:
Further Action Required Y/N:

Figure 7.1: Escalation record form.

Feedback from those who spend the most time with our dogs is invaluable. The better we know our dogs, the easier it is to provide the things they value or reduce exposure to things that worry them. Consider something you really enjoy, a favourite pastry or a smile from a loved one perhaps. Now with that in mind, imagine how much better you would feel if you received that just a little more often and how willing you would be to do something to receive it. The way we identify the most valuable rewards (also known as reinforcers) is to preference test the dogs we work with. This in itself can be hugely rewarding to many dogs – it can act as a form of enrichment as we go through the process of finding out what they like most.[9] If it is noted that they enjoy toys, working out which types are favourites and how they are played with can be useful for creating training plans. The same applies for food. It may be that we need higher value rewards for certain exercises as distractions around rehoming centres can challenge even the most food loving dog. I encourage our teams to rate the individual dog's reinforcers from 1 to 5 and to use the least valuable reward possible, while still getting a positive reaction. There is then the possibility to increase the value should the dog begin to find sessions harder as they move through their BMP.

Time in kennels

Rehoming centres vary greatly and there are many factors that might impact on a dog's behaviour and stress levels while they are with us.[10] By observing and recording the interactions of our dogs with both people and other dogs, we can build a picture of their likes and dislikes. This gives us information to help us match dogs to potential adopters, create bespoke BMPs and track if known behaviours are improving or worsening in their new environment.

As with every element talked about in this chapter, the importance of training for those involved in the dog's journey is key to raising our standard of care. By developing the skills of those who handle the dogs daily, we improve our ability to educate others, rehabilitate the dogs and raise welfare standards. In my opinion, the greater the understanding of those that handle the dogs daily, the greater the impact we can have on the dogs in our care. This investment in people is often a challenge due to factors common across rehoming centres and organisations. It usually boils down to time and money; both of which are often in short supply. When it is difficult to source good up-to-date information due to the expanse of resources and the myriad of opinions out there, it can be very difficult to prioritise staff training. I recommend having an induction process for all new staff that maps out all the areas that should be covered by their mentors and other specific roles within the staffing structure. This document should detail the topics that need to be covered and the resources that are available to support the learner. If each new kennel staff member has a mentor to guide and support them during their first months, we are more able to achieve consistency and best practice. This investment in staff aims to maintain standards of care and ensures good working practices are followed by all who handle the dogs.

Management of behaviour

When we have a dog showing undesirable behaviours, it is important to intervene as soon as possible. This reduces the practising of the behaviour, reduces risk, impacts on the dog's emotional state and enhances welfare. In the early stages, different ways of managing behaviour are often used to lower risk and reduce the practising of the behaviour. This may be through the use of equipment or certain protocols in the day-to-day activities of a rehoming centre.

The introduction of equipment can vary from dog to dog. Some are very accepting of equipment, whereas others require more time and a structured plan. The introduction of equipment in a positive way adds to the dog's understanding of what training is all about with us. Each time we have a positive interaction with our dogs, there is an investment in relationship. In turn, there is an increase in trust and how the dog views our interactions. This may seem like time wasted if you have a dog that has a more pressing behaviour needing modification. However, the more we can do to create the positive bias to our interactions, the more likely we will achieve success when we get to the trickier behaviours. I always encourage our staff to work on the basics of name recognition, recall, loose lead walking and settle behaviours. Each of these can be done as part of the daily activities in any rehoming centre. Every time we reinforce any of these desirable behaviours, they will strengthen.[11] On a daily basis, if we ensure we reinforce attention to their name, when they walk on a loose lead, and when they approach us, we are likely to see changes in their behaviour even before we begin the main BMP.

Back to our case study, Moose. The training team recommended that he be introduced to, and walked on, a harness. Moose's reactivity, combined with his strength, made him a risky dog for staff to walk around site. It was assessed that it would be safer to walk him on two leads with two handlers until further training had taken place.

Emotions and motivation

The centre training team began the process of establishing what might be motivating Moose's behaviour. He had no medical concerns, something we will always try to ensure is not a contributing factor with any behaviour case. Moose had not been walking with any other dogs since his character assessment. This was in part due to his strength and in part due to the lack of 'robust' dogs who would tolerate his OTT style of interaction. Often sociable and resilient dogs are used in the BMP of a dog that is showing undesirable behaviours around other dogs. These 'stooge' dogs are usually well known for their positive interactions with other dogs in the rehoming centre. It is important to consider the welfare of the stooge dogs that might be part of any BMP for other dogs with behaviour concerns. For dogs that have an aggressive response to other dogs it is even more important that we ensure the welfare of the stooge dog is not compromised.

When Moose was introduced to other dogs again, we observed the interaction and compared it with his earlier mixing and home history. We hypothesised that Moose was frustrated when he was stopped from greeting another dog due to a barrier (for example, a lead, bars of his kennel, compound fences).

With any undesirable behaviour we observe, it is important to try to understand the motivation and the emotion behind the behaviour. With this information, we are better placed to have a positive impact on the individual's welfare and can create a welfare-friendly BMP. We must be mindful of the emotions and motivations for behaviours when we make decisions about what we will teach our dogs. If you have a frustrated dog wanting to greet other dogs and you attempt to teach a static behaviour such as sitting, you may find that the dog struggles. Particularly, if the interaction with the other dog is far more rewarding than any piece of food or toy you could offer.

Dogs that feel anxious, fearful or frustrated are likely to be experiencing reduced welfare compared with those dogs that are not experiencing these negative emotions.[12] Our aim is to minimise negative states and promote positive states for all dogs in our care. The ability to achieve this will of course vary greatly depending on their experiences and health status.

Setting up for success

When we think about teaching our kids, colleagues or volunteers, we think about the environment and how we can get the best from them. We want them to take on information, retain it and look forward to coming back for more. This might involve minimising distractions, creating a safe and comfortable learning space, keeping them hydrated and with enough fuel to be alert but not so much as to have them sleepy. We would aim for the content to be interesting, fun and presented in a way that means something to them. We would try to ensure they had slept well and that they were free from pain or discomfort. This should be no different when we think about teaching our dogs.

Dogs enter our care from varied circumstances and some of these dogs may require rehabilitation. The approach we take must take into account the potential negative experiences they may have had to endure in their past. Before we begin training, we must establish if we have got the basics sorted. There are several things that impact on our ability to learn; feeling safe and having quality sleep top the list. Other maintenance behaviours are eating, drinking and toileting.[13] If we look at these vital behaviours more carefully and provide optimum opportunities for these maintenance behaviours to be performed well, then we are setting ourselves, as well as the dogs, up for success. For dogs that are house trained it may be difficult for them to toilet in the kennel so identifying these dogs and getting them out first and last can help. Simple changes to how dogs are fed, where the water bowl is kept and the type of bed the dog has access to, can make all the difference.

Feeding in a way that promotes a sense of safety is important. If the rehoming centre house dogs in pairs, it is essential to ensure these dogs are not worried about the other dog around the resources that are important to them. Having a water bowl at each end or, depending on kennel design, indoors and outdoors, can provide dogs with choices. Having bedding choices can also be beneficial for paired dogs that might have different needs. Dogs that are fed either side of a door or hatch can become anxious about not knowing when the door or hatch will be opened. By feeding further apart or even by taking one dog out to be fed in another area can be beneficial. These daily processes are usually put in place to speed up the job from the staff's perspective but do not always take into account the negative effect it could have on certain dogs. For example, often, water bowls are kept at the front of the kennel, so it is easy for the carers to fill them up. However, if the dog is worried about approaching the front of the kennel due to the passing by of people or other dogs, then they may not get the water they need. For some dogs, the addition of a crate or a piece of furniture that allows them to feel safe behind (on top or inside of) can improve sleep and rest. These small considerations can add up to some big improvements in the success of rehabilitation within a rehoming centre environment. Therefore, before you begin your BMP, think about the individual dog's maintenance behaviours and whether there is anything you can do to improve their emotions around these vital activities and their ability to achieve these as well as possible.

Planning and carrying out a BMP

In the assessment phase, we aim to find out as much as possible about the dog and about the behaviour. In the planning phase we use this information to help us decide on the best way forward with that particular dog.

The assessment and planning phases are an investment in your BMP. Without them, you are likely to be focused purely on the problem behaviour and are more likely to work solely on a training plan with a focus on stopping that undesirable behaviour occurring. In my experience, this is where people can become frustrated. It is easy to be swayed into using more aversive techniques to stop behaviour rather than understanding why the behaviour is occurring and addressing that. Some common terms used in BMPs are given in Box 7.2.

Moose's loose lead training followed a standardised plan familiar to the staff and used at many of our rehoming centres. We have developed a series of standardised training plans for our staff to use to help gain consistency of approach, as our dogs will have several handlers in any given week. With standardised training plans for the basics, we are better placed to achieve consistency and be able to track their progress accurately. Obviously, each dog is different and there may need to be some alterations to the plans, but the tracking of their progress generally remains consistent. For some dogs, this work might need to be done indoors or in a location that has fewer distractions and at a time with less traffic moving around the centre. Even when we are working on the basics, we need to be mindful of how we can set up for success. We all know there are times when a dog is more or less likely to respond to our requests. Therefore, knowing when and where to train, as well as knowing what each dog finds reinforcing, is key to successful training in the rehoming centre environment.

Merely managing, rather than modifying behaviour, can potentially put staff, volunteers and prospective adopters at risk. Behaviour develops over time. From a dog's perspective, if a behaviour is successful, they will repeat it. Behaviours that are not successful are usually lost or changed in an attempt by the dog to find a solution to their needs.[14] In our case with Moose, his need to interact with other dogs motivated his challenging behaviours. He would pull, jump and vocalise in an attempt to get to the other dogs. Owing to his size, this behaviour while walking made it difficult for staff to control him. These behaviours were likely to have been successful in the past and therefore were being repeated. When we stop these behaviours being successful by managing the exposure and having two handlers to hold him back, then his behaviour may well change as he tries a new tactic to achieve his goal.

The potential for redirection with frustrated dogs is seen in rehoming centres as the nature of the day-to-day activities may not fulfil the individual dog's needs. Redirection is where a dog might grab an alternative, more accessible, target if the intended target is out of reach or unattainable. An example of this would be a dog that wants to get to another dog but is unable to achieve his goal and the frustration may result in him grabbing the lead or even the handler. In my experience, this often occurs in young dogs that have a strong desire to interact with either people or other dogs. Due to time constraints and protocols around mixing of dogs, they can be left frustrated and develop coping strategies to deal with this frustration.

Dogs that rag the lead or grab hold of handlers' coats or body parts, may well be redirecting their frustration at not being able to get to, or away from, a particular stimulus. The ragging and grabbing behaviours are very difficult to ignore and therefore often end up getting a response from the handler, which may reinforce the behaviour being displayed at the time. Ragging and grabbing is unlikely to have been the first versions of frustration behaviour, but might be the first that have been acted upon by the handler. Therefore, from the dog's perspective, it is a success. This is why it is crucial to report and record new behaviours or escalations of behaviour while working with dogs in our care.

As with Moose, his behaviours of jumping and vocalising can be seen as attempts to deal with his frustration around other dogs. If this motivation for his behaviour is not considered within his BMP, we are likely to experience either greater intensity of these behaviours or a change to something harder for his handlers to ignore. With regards to ignoring unwanted behaviours, I do have concerns about having a general rule around ignoring undesirable behaviours for the very reason just described. In my experience, this is where some behaviours escalate to a more problematic (from the human perspective) behaviour, requiring a greater level of intervention. This is why we really need to understand the motivation and emotion behind the behaviours we are dealing with when working with behaviour cases both in the rehoming centre and in the home environment.

Ensuring that everyone who handles the dogs understands how behaviour develops, sets us up for early intervention. It is immensely important that we recognise behaviours that indicate a negative emotional state as early intervention in these cases will impact on both the dog's welfare, and potential successful rehoming. A plan for staff development is crucial. Dog handlers must have up-to-date knowledge and strategies to deal with common behavioural concerns. Staff and volunteer knowledge and understanding is a vital part of the holistic approach to dog welfare in the rehoming centre environment.

If we think about dogs that are fearful of other dogs and exhibit similar behaviours to Moose (jumping, lunging and barking towards the other dog) then by knowing what the emotion and motivation is, we can ensure that the correct BMP is put in place. Moose wanted to decrease his distance to other dogs and was frustrated when he could not. For dogs that are fearful and want to increase their distance to the other dog they too can feel frustration at not being able to achieve this. The way we would assess the differences between those that want to interact and those that are fearful and therefore want to avoid the interaction, we will generally rely on the dog's body language and choices of behaviour in the presence of the other dog. Again, training for all those involved in the handling of dogs is needed to ensure we are confident of the underlying emotion and in turn create the most appropriate BMP for each dog. We would generally employ a systematic desensitisation and counter conditioning programme for these dogs. Our aim would be to ensure we expose them to another dog at the appropriate level for the individual dog. We then look to change their emotional state in

another dog's presence. We have focused here on the dog-to-dog issues that are a common concern for owners and rehoming centres alike. This is also the approach we generally take when trying to address most behaviour concerns with the dogs in our care.

Earlier I talked about the importance of creating a **HAPPIER** dog (Box 7.1). Understanding the dog's health status, likes and dislikes and planning our approach to a behaviour challenge, helps us set up for success. It is vital to track what is working, and what is not, so we are able to set our prognosis and rehome with confidence. Our dog handlers have such an influence on what and how our dogs learn. If they have the knowledge to identify areas of concern and we put in place ways of working that promote good welfare, we will hope to see fewer severe cases develop in our centres. Added positive effects are increased staff safety, consistent working practices and confidence in rehoming dogs with known behavioural concerns.

Box 7.2 Examples of common terms used in treatment of dogs with known behavioural concerns

Behaviour Modification Plan/Programme (BMP): a plan that sets out the process to modify a behaviour.

Positive reinforcement: the addition of something the dog likes which may increase the likelihood of the behaviour being repeated.

Threshold: this will vary from dog to dog and essentially means the point where the dog is no longer able to cope with the intensity or distance of the stimulus. Our aim is to maintain the dogs we work with under threshold, so we do not see the undesirable response to a given stimulus.

Punishment: this can sometimes be complicated when using the learning theory terminology. For further information about learning theory revisit Chapter 3. In its simplest form, punishment is the addition of something unpleasant in an attempt to stop the current behaviour; punishment reduces the likelihood of the behaviour occurring again. Not all dogs will find the same things punishing. For some, a raised voice towards them can be scary and stop them in their tracks so it is therefore punishing; others might simply ignore the raised voice. The important message here is we all know how it feels to be punished and use of punishment would go against what we are trying to achieve while building trust and relationships with the dogs that we care for.

Marker: something that indicates to the dog that he will get the reward. This might be a word like 'good' or 'yes' or it could be a clicker or visual signal like a thumbs up when working with deaf dogs. A marker needs to be introduced through a pairing of the marker with a reinforcer, such as a tasty treat. This needs to be done repeatedly and in different contexts, until the dog knows when he/she hears the word, clicker or sees the visual marker that the treat is on its way.

Cue: something that indicates to the dog that they should perform a certain behaviour. Examples include the word 'sit' or a hand signal that cues the behaviour such as a lowering of a flattened hand to mean down. Cues need to be taught and paired with the behaviour through a series of training sessions until the dog understands the cue in a variety of contexts. I often ask staff what cues their dog knows and then get them to show me with their hands behind their back. It is amazing how many dogs will sit ten times out of ten when the handler raises their hand as they say the cue 'sit' but how few will sit without the raised hand and only the word 'sit'. It is important that this information is shared with new adopters who might be tempted to add physical pressure to the dog's rear end if the sit cue is not followed by the dog.

Systematic desensitisation: 'Exposing pets repeatedly to stimuli that caused fear, anxiety or aggression in sufficiently small doses so as not to cause the response. The stimuli are then gradually increased at increments that do not lead to a recurrence of the response. The stimuli are repeated so many times with no effect that they become inconsequential.'[15]

Counter conditioning: There are two types of counter conditioning.

- Respondent counter conditioning – a stimulus that previously evoked a negative response now evokes a positive response. We are changing an emotional reaction and thus the observable behaviour.
- Operant counter conditioning – a stimulus that evoked an 'unwanted' response now evokes a 'wanted' response. We may or may not be changing emotion but are definitely changing behaviour.

Learning theory is a huge topic and not one we have time to delve into in this chapter but one that is vital for all those working with dogs in any setting. Tamsin Durston talks more about learning theory in Chapter 3 and has some wonderful insights and explanations on this topic. For success to be achieved in the rehoming centre environment a structured staff training and development process should be in place to support those that are working so hard to improve the lives of the dogs in their care. Without access to up-to-date information and resources it is common to turn to the internet or other media outlets for information. Unfortunately, this does not always deliver the most appropriate or up-to-date information available and can lead to confusion or even increase risks to those working with the dogs.

Moose's BMP

In addition to the loose lead walking, a bespoke plan was put in place for Moose and his response to other dogs. We introduced a 'Go play' cue for times he was able to interact with other dogs and regular canine interaction was a must for his routine. This meant that he was positively reinforced by getting to interact with another dog on the 'Go play' cue. A 'Not today' cue was then introduced for times he was not able to greet a dog while out on a walk. This cue was introduced away from other dogs, under threshold, at the distance he could remain engaged with his handler. The positive reinforcement used for this behaviour was scattered treats on the floor. Gradually, this was developed to moving away from the dog and then having treats scattered on the floor to find. This increased predictability for Moose as his handlers increased communication about when he was and was not going to socialise. For the times he could not greet another dog, he was given access to this 'find it' game, which helped to keep his arousal levels low. The find it game was also used when he heard dogs while out on a walk. The cue 'Not today' indicated to Moose to look to the handler as treats were about to be scattered in the opposite direction to the other dog. Using these planned strategies, we have counter conditioned his behaviour by reducing his frustration levels and maintaining his positive outlook when seeing other dogs. If we had elected to use punishment to reduce his jumping and vocalisation, we could run the risk of changing his positive associations with dogs to one of anxiety or fear. As we have said before, we are intending to have a positive impact on our dog's welfare with any training we do with them. The use of punishment and aversive techniques may seem a quicker route to achieve the humans desired outcome. However, there is often a cost to the relationship and future willingness to work with the person who uses punishment to reduce behaviours.

The team continued to manage him around the kennels and simply shut him in the back when his neighbours went in and out instead of trying to modify his behaviour in this context. Knowing where the difficult areas are within the environment you are working can be helpful to avoid situations where proximity to other dogs is an issue. Sometimes it may be possible to move kennels to a quieter block or one with easier exits to reduce arousal levels and trigger stacking effects.

Trigger stacking

I would like to talk a little about trigger stacking as this is something that can have a real impact on our BMPs. You may have heard the saying, 'The straw that broke the camel's back' and I am sure most of us have experienced days where nothing seems to go right for us and at some point, we just snap! Often the thing we snap at, is something that on its own, and under ordinary circumstances, would seem insignificant. On some days, there may have been several events that have occurred within the day, reducing our ability to cope and pushing us over the edge. This can also happen with dogs and is something we should all be mindful of in the rehoming centre environment.

Sometimes, similarly to Moose's BMP, we just need to say, 'Not today'. If the dog we are working with has had a really tough morning due to a tricky dog meet or a trip to the vet, then it may be better not to engage with the BMP or at least lower the criteria. The example of the vet visit is a common concern for rehoming centre staff and adopters alike. In the 2019 (Figure 7.2) study[16] it shows how the cumulative effect of potential stressors involved in

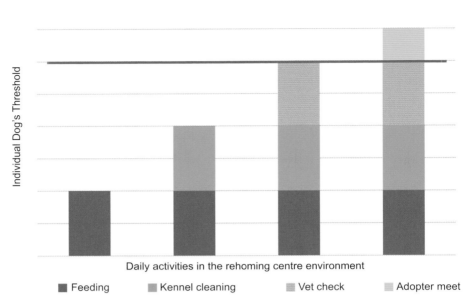

Figure 7.2: The trigger stacking effect.

a veterinary visit may lead to distress. Each event has a level of stress associated with it when it occurs individually (for example, car rides may be less stressful than being handled by veterinary staff) but stack up to result in distress when they occur within a short space of time.

Figure 7.2 displays the trigger stacking effect and how events in the dog's daily life can cumulate to reduce the ability to cope on a given day. Note that in the first column there is only one event that the dog finds stressful or exciting and is therefore able to cope and recover. The subsequent columns have events that occur within a time frame that reduces the dog's ability to cope with the stressful 'triggers'. There are many factors that need to be considered when looking at the trigger stacking effect. This diagram is a very simplified expression of how the build-up of triggers can lead to a reaction from a dog once over their threshold. Each dog's threshold will be different based on their history, previous learning and their individual character. If the triggers are experienced far enough apart the effect may be reduced as the dog may have had time to recover from the previous triggers. The triggers will be individual to each dog and will need to be identified during the assessment of each dog. The triggers do not have to be fear inducing but could increase arousal levels through excitement or frustration.

An awareness of all dogs in our rehoming centres is not an easy thing to achieve; there are usually high numbers of dogs and low numbers of staff and knowing each one's emotional state is a tall order. I often hear people say that their dog is, 'a bit off today', or 'not his usual jolly self'. What I would encourage anyone, whether in the rehoming centre or at home with their own dogs, is to listen to that gut feeling and pay attention to it. It could be the difference between the dog having an incident free day or a reaction caused by the culmination of small events.

Environmental trigger stacking factors

For dogs that are affected by noise, movement, things that create arousal, an increase in anxiety or fear response, it can be a real challenge to keep them under threshold. There has been interesting research carried out by Fagundes et al.,[17] on the potential connection between noise sensitivity and pain. They found that in clinical cases where pain was identified, there was, 'widespread associated generalisation to the environment and avoidance of other dogs'. These cases responded well once the presence of pain was identified and treated.

As always, the initial discussions when working with a behaviour case should be about the health status of the individual. Our aim is to set up every interaction to be as successful as possible. I know this is not always possible due to the rehoming centre design and generally how busy a rehoming centre can be. However, if we take into account all the known triggers that we have identified during our assessment period and have mitigated them during our planning of the BMP, then we have at least reduced the potential instances of trigger stacking on a daily basis.

Noise in kennels is a common issue for most organisations and knowing when these are at their best and their worst can help us identify when and where to work with these dogs. For those of you that work in kennels on a daily basis, you may well have become habituated to the noise and it is worth assessing your own environment using a simple decibel app on your phone. Try it in different locations and at various points in the day as it can help to remind you just how loud it can get. When we plan our BMPs we should have in mind all the things that may contribute to the trigger stacking effect. We can then put things in place to reduce the occurrences or intensity of these events. This may be walking at specific times, feeding in an alternative way or using barriers or screens to reduce visual triggers in the environment.

The use of barriers can help when getting dogs in and out of kennels to reduce the risk of redirection and reduce the need to shut dogs away when getting neighbours out (see Figure 7.3).

Setting prognoses

Our ultimate goal is to find these dogs their forever homes and to create space for the next dog that needs our help. 'So, when will they be ready?', 'Isn't it just better to get them out quickly?' and 'Won't much of the behaviour improve in the home?' are all questions I have heard many times and there is no single answer. Each dog's progress will need to be assessed and decisions made based on that individual's assessments. Depending on the behaviour you

Figure 7.3: The use of barriers in a Dogs Trust kennels.

are trying to modify, it may be preferable to temporarily foster the dog to reduce certain behaviours only seen in kennels; for others it may be advisable to stay within our care for longer to maintain consistency and ensure safety. The length of time it may take us to achieve the confidence to rehome an individual dog will vary greatly depending on many factors. There should be minimum requirements set out to ensure adopter safety and dog welfare is maintained. This should include the ability to safely treat them with any veterinary needs and any day-to-day health care requirements such as grooming and exercise.

If we choose to rehome the dog with an ongoing BMP in place, then we should aim to give support in the new home as much as possible. This will reduce risk to the dog and to others, and ensure the dog's welfare is not compromised. Prognosis setting is incredibly difficult, which is why it is vital to have good records. It is then easier to plot a dog's progress, or lack of progress, within their BMP. If we have been attempting to modify a behaviour for weeks or even months with little improvement, then we may need to look at altering the BMP, considering alternative environmental choices or possibly the use of behaviour medication to assist in our approach.

For those dogs that are improving, there should be clear goals that must be reached before adoption becomes a possibility, so that we can plot the improvements and have a clearer timescale in mind. However, we should remain mindful that sometimes the final goals that we want to achieve can be the hardest. The final part of the prognosis setting is all about the expectations of our adopters. If we tell our adopters that the dog will get better once he/she is away from the kennels and in fact, he/she gets worse, then we have set off on the wrong foot and the risk of return is much higher.

Having videos to show adopters of their chosen dog's journey through the BMP can be a great way of setting expectations. They can then see just how far their dog has come while you have been working with them and why it is so important that they continue the good work started at the rehoming centre. It is also important to fully explore their hopes for their chosen dog and to establish realistic goals with a timeframe that is appropriate for the individual dog.

When we think of Moose, with his excitement and strong reaction to other dogs, we could expect that, with a continuation of his training, the opportunity to play regularly with appropriate dogs and his young age, his prognosis was very favourable. However, if we are dealing with an older dog that was fearful of other dogs, poorly socialised when young so has been practising his behaviour for a long time, we might be cautious about how sociable he might become in the future. For such a dog, we would aim to improve their confidence at a certain distance and reduce their reactions to dogs approaching but not expect that they would be fully comfortable off-lead with other dogs in the park. Predicting what a dog will achieve on their BMP is difficult. I hope that we can get to the place where the dog is fully comfortable off-lead in the park, but we will only know this over time. We must have high expectations but not so high that we inadvertently set the dog and new owner up for failure. If the adopter's vision of life with their new pet is not in some part met, the potential for return to kennel is greatly increased.

Matching dogs to families

When there is interest from a prospective adopter, we will of course consider whether the environment and the family's circumstances are a good match for the individual dog. The dog's assessment can help us with the matching process and if there seems to be a good match, the meet and greet will go ahead. Staff need training and have a good understanding in the practice of introducing dogs to potential adopters. As with our BMPs, we want to set things up for success, which means we need to know as much as possible about the dog we are introducing to the family. When we share any training the dog has had or a particular game they love to play, we are creating an opportunity to talk to the family about the dog's needs. We can explain the training we have done and the value of providing certain opportunities that are important to the dog. It is also a time to discuss areas to avoid or work on more slowly should they have behaviours under rehabilitation. Research indicates that simply engaging the dog in a playful act or even just settling near to the potential owner, the chances of adoption proceeding improves compared with those dogs that remain uninterested or avoidant of the adopter.[18]

Moose had interest from a couple who had seen him on our website. They had no other dogs but lived some distance from the rehoming centre. They completed a 'home finder questionnaire' and were contacted by a member of staff involved in his training. Initially, videos of Moose were sent to the couple for them to see him and consider if he was right for them. They included videos of Moose reacting while on-lead as well as his current training progress. These videos had been filmed as part of the record keeping for his BMP. It is important to note here that we should not put a dog in a situation to deliberately create a reaction/response in order to film them. However, as the footage was available, it was sent in advance to give the couple the ability to visualise what was described.

This is incredibly important when rehoming a dog who has demonstrated behaviour that could cause a problem for future owners. When they had seen the footage, they were still keen to meet him and travelled to the centre to do so.

They initially met Moose at the centre with his handler. After this, they went for an off-site walk in a country area with a member of the centre training team. This allowed the couple to spend time with him in natural surroundings and allowed them to practise some of his training when they met dogs. Having adopters practise the BMP themselves is a vital part of the process. Reading a BMP alone is not as effective as experiencing one through observation and first-hand practical experience. Most people need to physically do the training themselves and are then more confident to continue it in future. It also helps to build the relationship with the trainer as they receive help and feedback on the day. This opportunity to share information with potential adopters is in my opinion the best chance we have to support them and prepare them for the continuation of the training that is likely to be required. Getting compliance from potential adopters is not always easy and there is a skill that often needs to be learned. No matter how good the dog trainer is, if they cannot get the important information across to the adopters, then they are unlikely to be able to continue the BMP progress needed for a successful adoption.

Supporting dogs in homes

Earlier I mentioned that research has shown a proportion of dogs are relinquished to rehoming centres due to behavioural concerns. In another piece of research, it was stated that two-thirds of dogs rehomed had some behavioural concerns.[19] Interestingly, of those dogs returned to the rehoming centre, 87% had what was described by the adopters as 'undesirable behaviours'.

We need to be aware that 'undesirable behaviour' is a very general phrase. A behaviour that one person finds undesirable may be of no concern to another person. The research was limited to one animal rescue shelter and reported low incidents of aggression. I am not saying that the proportion of dogs adopted from rehoming centres with behavioural concerns is high across the board. However, it should not come as a shock that dogs that have undergone a difficult period and end up in a rehoming centre, may have developed some behaviours that need support.

The research backs up that the work we do while we care for dogs is only part of the story; to be considered a successful adoption, the dog needs to stay in the home. There are of course always situations that change and reporting of behavioural concerns from adopters varies hugely. A more recent study[20] suggests that approximately 15% of dogs adopted in the UK, USA and Italy are returned to the rehoming centre after adoption. What appears to be consistent in the literature is the need for further development of strategies to reduce relinquishment in the first place and to reduce return to kennel rates due to behavioural reasons.

Once we have put time and effort into preparing these dogs to go to a new life with their family, we need to be prepared that there might be further hurdles to overcome. For many of these dogs, it is unlikely that the behaviour will simply go away. Wherever we can, we should aim to support the new adopters with their dog. This support can take many forms and each organisation should have resources they can share with their adopters. Although not all organisations will be able to produce all the

resources, there should be no problem with pointing potential adopters to information on other welfare organisations websites. The goal is to support dogs and their families to achieve a successful adoption. Having good resources available for adopters to access is important to enable them to prepare for their new arrival. Providing various forms of information can support them in the transition from kennels to the home and should reduce some of the trigger stacking situations we talked about earlier. With an understanding of how their new dog shows they are struggling (having been shown by rehoming centre staff) new owners are much better prepared to intercept before things go wrong.

It is vitally important to follow up on the progress of dogs that had BMPs when they were in the rehoming centre. There are many ways to keep in touch with adopters and the use of Zoom, WhatsApp or a simple phone call can make all the difference to an adopter who is struggling. Through contact we can see where things are going well or when extra support and guidance might be needed.

Moose and his family had no further issues with other dogs. They continued his training as demonstrated and were able to introduce him successfully to some new doggy friends. They sang his praises on walks as he was now able to have positive interactions with other dogs.

Celebrating success

Within the animal welfare industry, we are often faced with difficult circumstances and tough decisions to make. Day-to-day activities in rehoming centres involve hard work in often difficult environments. Although some people might come into the industry with a picture in their mind of how it will be, they soon come to realise it is not all cuddling puppies and walking dogs on a lovely spring morning. Do not get me wrong, there are times when this is a part of the job. I spent the first half of my 20 years with Dogs Trust doing this on a regular basis, which is one of the reasons I have enjoyed my work so much. We all find different things in our work satisfying. However, for those of us that work in an organisation that rehomes animals there is no better feeling than finding the right home and being confident that they will live a full and happy life with their new family. For all those working with dogs that have behaviour concerns to overcome, the investment of your knowledge, experience and passion is time well spent and should be celebrated by you and your organisation.

It can sometimes seem like a never-ending cycle of animals that need our help. Sadly, until we address the issues around poor breeding and responsible ownership, and promote positive training and rearing of puppies, our job will still be needed. Fortunately, we are very lucky to have adopters that go the extra mile and volunteers that support us in all areas of the work that we do. We should work together with those amazing adopters that take on the baton and continue the work with their new family members, often for months or even years in some cases. When I, after almost 10 years, moved from the rehoming centre where my animal welfare journey began (you might call me a long-term resident of the kennels), the staff and volunteers made me a photo board of some of the dogs I had been lucky enough to work with and learn from. To this day, I am thankful to have been part of their journey wherever their path led. Take time to celebrate each other's success and remember to thank each other for the amazing work you do.

Figure 7.4 illustrates the elements we have discussed in this chapter which will hopefully serve as a reminder to all those that work with dogs in rehoming centres and those that adopt them that the process is not always smooth, but it should be rewarding and with a positive goal in mind.

Conclusion

Through this chapter I have talked about a dog's journey through a rehoming centre to a forever home. Although Moose's case was not a complicated one, and one that had a successful outcome for him and his new family, I hope it has helped to highlight the need for good behaviour knowledge across the spectrum of those involved in his journey. In my experience, these lower-level cases are just on a path like all of us. Where we end up depends on what we experience, the support we get and the choices we make. For our dogs, we have a responsibility to support them along the way and give them opportunities to make the right decisions. We should base our approach to this on good science and good ethics. I firmly believe that we can influence and direct a dog's potential, but to do so we all need to be better prepared and understand the species we are living with.

I chose Moose to be the featured case study with the help of a very experienced and respected colleague Heather Wren. She is part of our Canine Behaviour and Research team at Dogs Trust and has worked with all our rehoming centres to share her knowledge and experience in the topic of training and behaviour. I chose Moose partly because this type of behaviour around other dogs is a common one in the rehoming centre setting, but also to highlight the importance of early intervention when dealing with behaviour issues. We could have ignored his OTT behaviour or have chosen an alternative approach to stop or supress his responses to seeing other

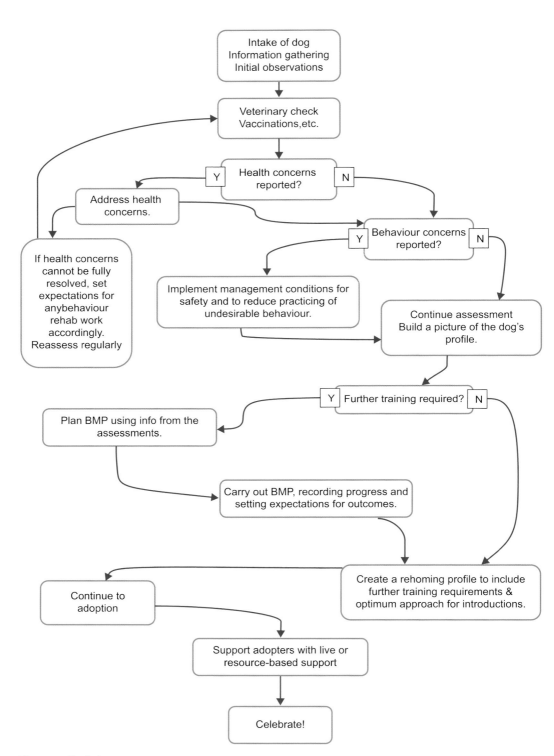

Figure 7.4: The dog's journey.

dogs. We might well have been able to rehome him, but I would not have had the same confidence in his future if we had sent him on his path ill-equipped to deal with his emotional responses.

My thanks go to Heather for her contribution to this chapter and for her amazing work alongside our incredible team at Dogs Trust and of course the countless people involved across all the animal welfare organisations doing their very best for the animals in their care. My passion is providing the opportunity for people to learn about how we can raise our standards within the rehoming centre environment, to develop our ways of working to enhance the dog's journey and to share that with as many people as possible. I believe having development opportunities for our staff and volunteers is the way to achieve this. I encourage all organisations, big or small, to look at ways to ensure all those that handle dogs on a regular basis have the information they need to support the dogs in their care and set them on that path to their successful and positive new life ahead.

References

1. Patronek, G.J., Glickman, L.T., Beck, A.M., McCabe, G.P. and Ecker, C. (1996) Risk factors for relinquishment of dogs to an animal shelter. *Journal of the American Veterinary Medical Association* 209, 572–581.
2. Stephen, J. and Ledger, R. (2007) Relinquishing dog owners' ability to predict behavioral problems in shelter dogs post adoption. *Applied Animal Behaviour Science* 107, 88–99.
3. Stephen, J. and Ledger, R. (2006) A longitudinal evaluation of urinary cortisol in kennelled dogs, *Canis familiaris*. *Physiology & Behaviour* 87(5), 911–916.
4. Griffin, B. (2009) Wellness. In: Miller, L. and Hurley, K.F. (eds) *Infectious Disease Management in Animal Shelters*. Ames, IA: Blackwell, pp. 17–38.
5. Overall, K.L. (1997) Recognising and managing problem behavior in breeding catteries. In: August, J.R. (ed.) *Consultations in Feline Internal Medicine, Current Therapy 3*. WB Saunders, Philadelphia, PA.
6. Christensen, E., Scarlett, J., Campagna, M. and Houpt, K.A. (2007) Aggressive behavior in adopted dogs that passed a temperament test. *Applied Animal Behaviour Science* 106, 85–95.
7. Hansen, B.D. (2003) Assessment of pain in dogs: veterinary clinical studies. *ILAR Journal* 44(3), 197–205.
8. Pelaez, M.J., Poncet, C., Dupre, G. and Bouvy, B., (2009) Description of owner's pain assessment in 137 dogs treated with carprofen following orthopaedic and soft tissue surgery. *Wiener Tierärztliche Monatsschrift* 96(1/2), 12–18.
9. Dawkins, M.S. (2003) Behaviour as a tool in the assessment of animal welfare. *Zoology (Jena)* 106(4), 383–387.
10. Beerda B., Schilder, M.B.H., van Hooff, Jan.A.R.A.M. and de Vries, H.W. (1997) Manifestations of chronic and acute stress in dogs. *Applied Animal Behaviour Science* 52(3–4), 307–319.
11. Burch, M.R. and Bailey, J.S. (1999) *How Dogs Learn*. Wiley, New York.
12. Désiré, L., Boissy, A. and Veissier,I. (2002) Emotions in farm animals: a new approach to animal welfare in applied ethology. *Behavioural Processes* 60(2), 165–180.
13. Stamp Dawkins, M. (1988) Behavioural deprivation: a central problem in animal welfare. *Applied Animal Behaviour Science* 20(3–4), 209–225.
14. Thorndike, E.L. (1927) The law of effect. *The American Journal of Psychology* 39, 212–222.
15. Landsberg, G.M., Hunthausen, W. and Ackerman, L. (1997) *Handbook of Behaviour Problems of the Dog and Cat*. Elsevier, Amsterdam.
16. Edwards, P.T., Smith, B.P., McArthur, M.L. and Hazel, S.J. (2019) Fearful Fido: investigating dog experience in the veterinary context in an effort to reduce distress. *Applied Animal Behaviour Science* 213, 14–25.
17. Fagundes, A.L.L., Hewison, L., McPeake, K.J., Zulch, H. and Mills, D.S. (2018) Noise sensitivities in dogs: an exploration of signs in dogs with and without musculoskeletal pain using qualitative content analysis. *Frontiers in Veterinary Science* 5, 17.
18. Protopopova, A., David, C. and Wynne, L. (2014) Adopter-dog interactions at the shelter: behavioral and contextual predictors of adoption. *Applied Animal Behaviour Science* 157, 109–116.

19. Wells, D.L. and Hepper, P.G. (2000) Prevalence of behaviour problems reported by owners of dogs purchased from an animal rescue shelter. *Applied Animal Behaviour Science*, 69, 55–65.

20. Protopopova, A. and Gunter, L.M. (2017) Adoption and relinquishment interventions at the animal shelter: a review. *Animal Welfare* 26, 35–48.

Chapter 8

Vets

Amber Batson

A dog's behaviour will be affected by diseases including those causing pain, and certain behaviours may even lead to the development of disease. Appreciation of the links between behaviour and disease, as well as the impact of medications and neutering on behaviour can be essential in providing the best health care and welfare opportunities for our pet dogs. The veterinary environment in which assessment of these life-affecting events will take place can be stressful for owner and dog, and taking steps to minimise stress in these circumstances plays an invaluable role in being able to make the right decisions and diagnoses as well as fostering optimal client–vet–pet relationships.

A dog called Jungo

Consider 'Jungo' an 18-month-old neutered male Labrador cross breed living with his owners and their two children (10- and 7-years old) in a typical semidetached house in south England.

Jungo's owners contacted a vet behaviourist as since around one year of age Jungo has shown reactivity (predominantly barking, occasionally growling) towards unfamiliar people. The problem significantly worsened when he went to the vets a few months ago for his first annual vaccination.

Since going to the vets that day (where he was considered to be healthy) he has increased his intensity of growling at unknown people, sometimes even lunging towards them, and has shown some growling towards his family members. A few weeks after his vaccination, when it was obvious the problems had worsened, the owners took him to see a local dog trainer. For the last 2 months they have worked on the issue, mostly in training sessions at the dog school, giving him treats for staying calm at a distance with a variety of different people and plans at home for him only to be given treats when he offers calm behaviours, such as sitting or lying down. The trainer advised increasing Jungo's daily exercise, including faster exercises such as ball chasing, to help ensure he was mentally and physically tired enough.

The trainer had advised that Jungo must only be given toys, chews or playful interactions when the adults in the house were fully present to supervise, and to ensure Jungo was given plenty of time in his crate in the kitchen so he felt safe and undisturbed by the children in the house.

The vet behaviourist was contacted because the problems had not improved and the trainer wondered if Jungo may need behavioural medications, although the owners are thinking about rehoming him.

During the vet behaviour consultation, it was discovered that Jungo howls and barks excessively when left alone in the daytime (both owners work several hours five days a week, and both children are at school) and has done this since around eight months of age. He also barks a lot at any loud noises such as the neighbours slamming their front door, cars backfiring or fireworks. Jungo has had to visit the vets on two separate occasions for swallowing inedible items in the house, once some cushion stuffing and the other time a sock. He has been chewing and swallowing clothing materials regularly since a young age, which the owners felt was a very 'Labrador' behaviour and they were not concerned because on all the other occasions he had pooped out the material.

By investigating and understanding what the likely motivations for these behaviours are and the ways disease affects behaviour, we should be able to help Jungo and his family.

Disease and behaviour: a two-way street

There are multiple ways in which disease processes in the body can contribute to or even be the sole cause of behaviour problems. This chapter will consider some examples of this but to cover all diseases is outside its scope.

Behaviour and gut health

Perhaps one of the main diseases that may affect behaviour are those which affect gut health. We are now starting to really appreciate that the gut (stomach and intestine) plays an essential role in overall health and behaviour via its constant communication to the brain. The gut is comprised of several relevant components, perhaps most noticeably a large population of living organisms that it houses. These organisms, predominantly bacteria but also including viruses, protozoa and fungi, form a community that, along with providing nutrients to the host via their role in metabolising food stuffs, also modify the immune system, neutralise infiltration from gut pathogens (unwanted bad guys) and produce and balance a large number of chemicals that impact on brain function.

Communications occur between the gut and other body systems and one of those continuous 'chats' is referred to as the gut–brain axis (GBA). The gut microbiota can produce and use up a variety of chemicals such as serotonin, gamma butyric acid and dopamine that are well known to underpin the activity of the brain (when these chemicals are involved in brain communication, we refer to them as neurotransmitters). Studies into how the GBA influences dog behaviour have only recently begun, but include research that suggests they may influence the tendency of an individual to develop aggressive actions or for the individual to develop fear issues including phobias.[1,2]

Chronic skin inflammatory disorders such as atopic dermatitis and psoriasis in humans are now being linked to abnormalities in the gut microbiota (intestinal dysbiosis) perhaps because the microbiota plays a large role in production of inflammatory agents (for example, cytokines) and has actions helping skin (epithelial) cells to modify into their different roles. We are finding that we may need to talk about the gut–skin–brain axis, after all, skin disease is also linked to behavioural change and intestinal dysbiosis, another emerging area of veterinary medicine.[3,4]

Analysis of Jungo's behaviour, by descriptions from the owner of his body language and actions, as well as some video footage they brought to the consultation, revealed fear of approach and proximity by unfamiliar people. Fear-based behaviours may have intestinal dysbiosis as a contributing factor. Jungo also shows pica, the repeated ingestion of non-food items or those with no appreciable nutritive value. Pica as a behaviour may be of psychological origin or the result of medical issues.[5] Pica has been linked to early weaning, dietary type, frequent experience of stressors, administration of certain medicines (particularly those increasing hunger or altering the gut microbiota), digestive abnormalities such as exocrine pancreatic insufficiency, malabsorption disorders, gastritis or gastric ulceration and other sources of chronic pain. It would be important in a case like this to consider gut health as a possible contributing factor and have that assessed and potentially treated. Other medical issues that commonly contribute to undesired behaviours are those causing pain.

Pain and behaviour

In 2020, Professor Daniel Mills and his co-authors suggested that as many as 80% of the behaviour cases they see as vet behaviourists may have had pain as a contributing factor.[6] In that paper, they discuss how musculoskeletal pain (for example, that present in the hips, stifles, back or neck) appears to be the most common site of pain contributing to behavioural problems including noise sensitivities, aggressiveness or self-defensiveness and some abnormal behaviours such as excessive licking of surfaces, tail chasing and pica.

Why is it that pain causes the development of behaviour problems? There are several reasons due to changes in the body that occur when a tissue is injured, and inflammatory chemicals are being produced. Think of yourself if you have ever hurt a part of your body such as your back or your neck – you do not want others to touch you, or even approach you, as you do not want them to worsen your pain. One of the first behaviours we often see in the painful animal is increased self-defence. There are four main behaviour categories we use when trying to self-defend.

- **Flight** – we try to move or even run away from the potential threat.
- **Fiddle about** – we use language to communicate, please do not come close, I do not mean any harm to you, please do not harm me. Canines clearly cannot speak to us through verbal language to tell us of their intentions, however, they can use their body language. We call those body movements aimed at defusing a potential threat 'appeasements'.
- **Freeze** – we go very still in the hope that the threat will move away.
- **Fight** – the use of aggression with the intention of moving the threat away from us.

The type of behaviour seen may vary depending on the context of the potential threat, particularly perhaps whether the source is a social one (approach by unfamiliar person) or a non-social one (sudden loud noise), and who is doing the approaching – the animal themself, or the potential threat. Studies have suggested that social potential threats are more likely to include the fiddle about category of actions alongside the other categories, whereas non-social potential threats have limited fiddle about actions but a higher number of flight or freeze attempts.[7–9]

When a dog is in pain somewhere in their body, we are more likely to see one or more of these self-defence behaviours than we usually see in that individual. The owner may or may not notice the dog attempting to increase the distance between themselves and stimuli that for various reasons may increase the likelihood that they will experience more pain; or attempting to avoid those stimuli all together (for example, people attempting to touch them, approach by other dogs and chewing when dental pain is present). As a result, escalation of distance-increasing behaviours such as growling or snapping towards a stimulus may appear sudden where the owner had not noticed that the dog was previously using a different strategy such as freezing, or certain appeasements such as lip licking and head turning. Such escalation might also occur when the dog is in a situation where previously they were able to avoid approach by a possible threat such as when they were off-lead at the dog park, but now that option is not possible, such as being approached by that stimulus while on a short lead attached to the dog's collar.

Acute versus chronic pain

Pain can be acute, meaning that it has only been present in the individual as a new experience for a short time or chronic, where pain has been present for a prolonged period. Behavioural changes that have been identified in the dog as occurring around the onset of a new pain (for example, in the case of acute injury and/ or surgical procedures) may include: vocalisations, restlessness, aggression, specific 'pressure releasing' postures (such as the 'prayer' posture, seen where there is pain at the front of the abdomen causing the dog to rest weight on the forelimbs on the ground and lift hindquarters up into the air), self-mutilation (such as chewing their skin near the site of the pain) and anorexia. Reduction of behaviours such as self-grooming, play, exploration and withdrawal behaviours such as apathy can also occur as a result of new pain.

We normally define chronic pain as having been present for several weeks or longer, and that the pain experience may be associated with the production of long-term stress chemicals such as cortisol. We will be looking at the effects of stress chemicals on behaviour shortly, but simply for now, chronic stress alongside chronic pain (particularly repetitive stress) creates a frequently maladaptive cycle in which the perception of the pain worsens, creating a range of side effects. Such side effects include the experience of 'wind up' – in this situation the stress chemicals switch on, or further 'sensitise' the tissues, receptors and nerves responsible for detecting and messaging potential tissue damage to the brain. This means that any potential pain in the body is detected even faster and is experienced in a greater intensity. This is true of both the original site of the pain but also in subsequent parts of the body that the individual has pain in, even if unrelated to the original area.

Chronic pain sufferers often also demonstrate allodynia – feeling pain in experiences that would not normally cause pain, such as being touched gently on their skin, or stress induced hyperalgesia (SIH) where more pain is felt than would be expected for a stimulus known to cause some pain or discomfort. The differences between chronic pain in the musculoskeletal system compared with chronic pain in internal organs (visceral) and how this may impact on overall pain sensitivities still appears to be under some debate although it has been recognised that abdominal (predominantly intestinal) pain can result in lowered pain thresholds in humans, and in Mills et al. 2020, they reported a case where hip pain appeared to be the main driver of the development and maintenance of pica, predominantly in that case, stone swallowing.[6]

Recognition and diagnosis of pain can be a complicated area so it is important if we as owner or professional are suspicious that pain could be a component of a behavioural problem, that a thorough history-taking and clinical examination is undertaken to rule in or out a wide variety of possible bodily systems.

For example, it may be difficult for the owner to notice if a dog is avoiding chewing on one side of the mouth more than the other even when considerable dental disease is found on examination. In 2020, Rusbridge described how some brachycephalic dogs may suffer from chronic pain as part of Chiari malformation (CM) – a developmental condition where there is overcrowding of the brain and upper spinal cord. 25% of dogs diagnosed with CM showed aversion to having the ears, head or neck touched.[10] Diagnosing soft tissue pain such as that in ligaments, tendons or even fascia (the connective tissue that lies under the skin) currently remains a significant challenge.

Interview with Sarah Bignell-Howse

Sarah Bignell-Howse (BVetMed, MRCVS) qualified from the Royal Veterinary College in 2000 and has subsequently undertaken additional training to help manage chronic pain in animals. In 2018, she opened the Metta Pet Clinic[11] so that she could dedicate more time to supporting patients experiencing chronic pain.

A change in behaviour may be one of the first indications that a dog is in pain. Do you think you have seen or heard of that commonly in your career as a vet?

I qualified as a vet back in 2000, and at that time the link between behaviour change and pain was less established so it was not commonly talked about. Thankfully, developments in understanding chronic pain have moved on a great deal and with this a deeper appreciation of the relationship between pain and behaviour has evolved so now it is much more common for vets to be aware and discuss this.

It is imperative that we really listen to what people are saying about their dogs as these changes are so insidious. It is important as veterinary professionals that we ask the right questions to tease this information out.

An obvious limp, or reluctance to move may be a clear indication to an owner that their dog is in pain. What other behaviours do you find as indicators of possible pain in your work?

Perhaps one of the most common signs is where the dog has become a little more withdrawn than they used to be. Also increases in sensitivity to noises is very common, as is a change in how or where they like to be touched. Slight hesitations in getting in and out of the car, preferring to walk on certain surfaces or changing where they choose to sleep can all indicate pain. Sudden jumping up when laying down or asleep and repeated licking of certain areas of the body are also important for us to notice. As a vet, asking about changes in the dog's routine, their tolerance to noise or interactions with other dogs, humans and other animals in the household can help us identify that the dog may be in pain.

The joints and bones of a dog are common sites of pain. What other parts of the dog are you finding pain in when you assess the dog for possible problems?

It is very common to find pain in the muscles, soft tissues and fascia well away from the original/suspected area of pain. This is often due to the dog having to change the way they move and stand to relieve the initial source of discomfort. Over time, the areas that are compensating become overworked and sore. However, before I even lay hands on my patients, I spend a lot of time observing how they stand, move, sit and lie down. This can give a great deal of information regarding areas of soreness. It is then a case of a very gentle assessment because signs such as allodynia (where normal touch is perceived as painful) might only be picked up by a slow and gentle touch. I then move on to examining the muscles and soft tissues noting discomfort but also note changes in temperature, pliability, muscle tone and volume.

If a dog is diagnosed with an injury or disease that is causing ongoing pain, what do you recommend the owner and their vet consider as part of a pain management strategy?

A multimodal, multidisciplinary approach is the key strategy to get the dog as comfortable as possible for as long as possible. From a vet's perspective this includes identifying the type of pain as well as the source(s) so that a suitable plan of treatment can be tailored to the individual dog. Addressing the dog's environment and lifestyle is critical. Each dog will face unique challenges in their homes that need to be identified and solutions created to make life easier, more comfortable and reduce further injury. Ensuring that all aspects of the pain picture are addressed by combining any medicines or supplements with adjunctive therapies such as physiotherapy, laser therapy, acupuncture and hydrotherapy is important as are regular veterinary re-examinations to monitor response to treatment.

Social interactions and pain

There has been increasing attention to the possible role of social interactions on the perception of an individual's pain. In his edited collection, Dr Franklin McMillan refers to our developing knowledge of how social pain; pain felt when socially isolated or socially rejected, activates the same pathways in the brain that are triggered during a physical pain experience.[12]

Dogs are highly social animals as has been described elsewhere in this book. Being left alone for any period of time, particularly when it is not the dog choosing to go off to undertake activities on their own (such as explore or scavenge) but instead they are behind a barrier (for example, within a crate, pen or behind a door) when the figure they are bonded to leaves, may be a significantly negative experience for many dogs. It remains a possibility that social isolation/social rejection by human caregivers, may exacerbate existing pain, alongside causing a stress response in the dog, and even causing a psychological pain experience in the healthy dog.

In Jungo's case, it was recognised that he howls and barks excessively when left alone in the daytime and has done this since around 8 months of age. Separation related problems such as excessive barking are moderately common in the pet dog and are recognised as having several potential underlying motivations that stem from being socially isolated or left by an individual (normally a human) they are bonded to (attachment figure).

De Assis and colleagues[13] were the first to attempt to find patterns within the behaviours shown by dogs with separation issues in order to help establish various underlying motivations and their findings included that frustration, fear and increased reactivity (for example, barking at loud noises) when alone may contribute to these separation problem behaviours.

Jungo is demonstrating behaviours when left alone suggestive of a distressed state. Multiple studies have shown how stress hormones, particularly cortisol, may become elevated when a dog is left by the person they are bonded to, and/or when left alone. More recent research (in other mammalian species) has also shown how social stress (being exposed to social instabilities

Behaviour is of course affected by many variables. The difficulty will always remain how much one variable, such as removal of reproductive hormones, may influence behavioural change in one individual more than in another. However, what would remain of great importance is to consider each dog–owner unit as an individual case with discussion about the medical and behavioural pros and cons of neutering based on factors such as dog age, temperament, breed, behavioural history and owner's requirements or concerns, allowing for informed decision making.

Let us return to Jungo. Neutered around 10 months of age and then developing a tendency towards reactivity to unfamiliar people. Could this be the result of loss of testosterone as previously described? He certainly fits in to the age category in which post-castration development of aggression towards unfamiliar people was most commonly reported. Could a learning experience during the clinical procedure of neutering result in this behaviour change rather than it solely being the response to hormonal loss?

Figure 8.1: Having fun at the vets. Photo: © Natalie Light.

Visiting the vet clinic

It is reported that as many as 78.5% of dogs visiting the vet clinic may exhibit signs of fear.[21] The previous vet experience may have a significant impact on a current attendance, even if the current visit appears relatively neutral.[21] From an evolutionary perspective, holding onto and prioritising memories of potentially or actually threatening or harmful events is a sensible strategy. Linking these experiences to potential predictors that trigger the recall of the event, would mean that you can identify potential threat before it occurs, offering a better opportunity for avoidance.

Interestingly, nearly 40% of dog owners report that their dog 'hates' the vet.[22] A trigger for Jungo's deterioration in behaviour towards unfamiliar people was a recent trip to the vet's for annual check-up and vaccinations. Even if the owner and/or vet felt that the experience, including the injection, was 'neutral' for Jungo, it is possible that this triggered the memory from a previous negative experience, such as the vet visit when he was neutered.

Elsewhere in this book we have considered learning types, including single trial learning that may result in classical conditioning. Where this type of learning occurs, we have an association between something the dog is born knowing about that triggers unconscious, reflex processes in the body that often result in an involuntary behaviour. Dogs are born knowing about pain, and this triggers reflexes of attempts at avoidance and/or self-defence such as growling, stiffening or biting. Being restrained is also likely to be something a dog is born knowing about that induces fear responses and again, attempts at avoidance or self-defence.

If unfamiliar people were a neutral experience for Jungo when he was dropped off at the vets on the day of his castration, restraint by one of these unfamiliar people, particularly when paired with the pain of an injection into his muscle (a common part of premedication given before an anaesthetic) or placement of an intravenous cannula prior to the procedure, could result in this single trial, classical conditioning. Restraint after the procedure on the day to remove the cannula, or to assess/clean his painful wound, along with restraint to examine the wound on subsequent check-ups, could further strengthen that association. Learning theory alone may be enough to explain why some dogs develop well-established behavioural responses to stimuli such as approach by the vet, or approach/proximity of unfamiliar people. While we might hope that this response is specific to unfamiliar people in the context of the vets, several factors might result in the 'generalisation' of this behaviour response to other situations – previous under socialisation to people so that actually Jungo already had some nervousness of strangers prior to the castration, a few negative experiences away from the vets with unfamiliar people before or after the castration or of course perhaps the loss of testosterone itself has reduced his 'confidence' making it more likely for his brain to generalise fear responses. There is increasing evidence that the adolescent period, particularly the early adolescent period may see an increase in fear responses in mammals, it is recognised that stress responses are handled differently by the adolescent brain, and Jungo may have been in the adolescent phase at time of castration, or possibly still in that phase at the time of vaccination.

What can we do? We probably cannot return the testosterone to his body (topically absorbed ... safe for use on dogs) although in a recent publication, Brent and colleagues do present a case in which subcutaneous daily injections of testosterone were given to a neutered dog to apparently improve medical issues as well as having some effect on undesired behaviours. More research on this topic is clearly needed.[23] Melatonin has received some recent attention for its possible benefits on reducing fear responses that have occurred as the result of castration.[24] A multisystem, brain and body approach is probably most beneficial – a variety of studies have shown enrichment and puzzle solving to have fear-reducing effects, so stress reduction, positive 'oxytocin' boosting experiences, activities to engage body and brain as well as considering positive reinforcement training, along with certain fear-reducing medicines (see further in this chapter) may all be part of the attempted solution, and these activities and trainings have been covered elsewhere in this book.

Stress, behaviour and disease

Stress is a normal physiological process to help an animal adapt to changes in the immediate environment. Acute stress occurs within seconds of a potentially exciting or threatening stimulus that requires action from the body. Acute stress is accompanied by internal release of chemicals such as noradrenalin, adrenalin and osteocalcin, that help prepare the body for faster activity as well as an increase in sympathetic nervous system activity: the flight or fight system. These two internal mechanisms increase the individual's speed of reactivity, increase blood flow to muscles to help them move the body faster, increase heart rate, blood pressure and breathing rate as well as decreasing pain perception.

The body is unable to sustain such intense changes for more than several minutes, so the mammalian body developed a second system – the chronic stress pathway, which starts to take over the maintenance of increased activity when it is necessary for a longer period of time.

Think about it like this, a dog sees and hears a group of unknown dogs moving towards her in a tense, reactive manner. In less than seconds, the dog has tensed her muscles, raised her heart rate and blood pressure, started to breath faster and has now turned and begins to move quickly away from the group. This is acute stress in action. However, she trots quickly away, it becomes apparent that this group means business, after a few minutes, the dog notices the group is not slowing down, the chase is continuing. The unknown dogs are persistent. Minutes come and go, and the chase goes on. The dog's heart is beating fast, her blood pressure is high, lactic acid has built up in her muscles. She needs a new strategy. She needs a slightly longer-term plan. This is chronic stress. By now her hypothalamus and pituitary gland deep in her brain tissue are releasing chemicals to switch on the adrenal cortex (the outside part of the gland) to release glucocorticoids, the main one of which is cortisol. Cortisol has several functions in the body but in essence it provides a way of the dog finding alternative energy sources in her body to keep going, this includes switching off 'energy rich projects' such as building new white blood cells, producing and maintaining a healthy reproductive tract to get pregnant, as well as projects such as growing new thick and healthy hairs. Cortisol also communicates to the brain: do not feel sleepy right now, sleep is not a good option. Mammals evolved a chronic stress pathway to keep them going at times of prolonged activity including flight or fight. However, ultimately

there is a natural end. Either the group of dogs will tire and give up, or they will catch up with this individual and she may be attacked or she may use something like a freeze, fight or series of fiddle about behaviours to offset their behaviour. Whichever outcome occurs this time, her chronic stress pathway can switch off again, normally within a maximum of a few hours, and the body can return to a normal resting state.

Chronic stress is not inherently bad, it is there to help us physically manage to deal with a range of situations. However, in a domestic environment it is often not possible for the outcome to come to natural conclusion within several minutes or even an hour or two.

Jungo watches as his family all leave the house in the morning. He is a social animal, needing the safety and security of his group. But he is left alone. He tries to follow them by jumping up at the front door they left through, jumping at the windows to see if he can spot them. Jungo is in an acute stress state. He paces, whines, howls, and barks, but they do not return.

His body switches to the chronic stress pathway so he can maintain his attempts. He continues to bark and howl. He continues to pace around the hallway. His brain and body signal that he is getting too hot, he is panting, partly to lower his body temperature. He lies down on the cool kitchen floor, staring towards the front door then hears a loud noise outside, he startles and starts barking again. This inactivity interspersed with reactions to outside noises continues.

After 4 hours, one of Jungo's owners return. Jungo bounces around frantically in a ritualised greeting. He picks up one of the children's sports socks that are lying on the ground. The owner panics that he might swallow them so grabs them from him and scolds him, sending him into his crate.

In a domestic environment, dogs may find that they are unable to escape from frustrations, unable to avoid potential threats, they cannot undertake actions that make them feel safe, they sometimes learn no one listens to their important communications. They did not evolve for chronic stress to keep going for hour after hour, maybe day after day, sometimes week after week or longer. This is when the chronic stress chemicals such as cortisol become a problem for the body.

In human medicine, there is a specific area of interest known as psychoneuroimmunology. It is a scientific study of how the brain interacts with the nervous system and the immune system. Investigating the effects of long-term chronic stress is a large part of the research in this medical field. Behaviour and disease are even more intimately entwined than how disease causes behavioural change, because behaviours, or at least perhaps the inability to perform certain species' specific behaviours, can actually lead to, or certainly contribute to disease. Sleep is very much an example of the links between normative brain/body function and behaviour.

Both a reduction in species appropriate sleep amount and quality, or a total deprivation of sleep for a period of time, have been shown to have significant effects on tendencies towards specific diseases via the impact on the immune system: elevations of various proinflammatory agents, suppression of immune cells (though the changes in immune response vary according to the duration of sleep reduction/loss), as well as having an effect on the activity of the stress pathways (predominantly sleep loss is associated with an increase in stress chemicals) and on behaviour and cognition (increased reactivity and decreased learning capacities as some examples).

Dogs have been shown to need somewhere between 10.5 and 14 hours sleep over a 24 hour period. They are polyphasic sleepers taking their sleep in 1–3 hour patches, often with the longest sleep period in the middle of the night. Research has shown that the majority of pet dogs prefer to sleep in social contact with a familiar dog or person, and that they like choices with regards to ground versus slight elevation in bed position, comfortable surfaces and the ability to move freely to help with any temperature regulation. The lack of these options, along with certain diseases including sleep apnoea, REM sleep disorder and pain or significant itchiness in the body may result in reduced sleep amounts or quality.

Supporting the dog for the veterinary procedure

While the underlying intentions towards the dog are positive, preventative and curative health procedures, as far as the dog is concerned, a trip to the vets itself is not exactly a positive experience. Arriving at a practice, being in close proximity to strangers who want to touch you, restrain you, poke you – sometimes with instruments, and often inject you, is not exactly a great day out. If we are lucky, it is a fairly neutral experience and you might enjoy a small treat at the end of it. For many dogs it is a considerable negative experience with one study showing that fewer than half of all the dogs entered the practice calmly, 13% had to be dragged or carried in, and more than three-quarters of dogs being overtly fearful during examination.[21] More than half of dogs visiting the vets experience elevated stress levels when asked to get onto the weigh scales. It is recognised that the owner's concern about the stress a dog experiences at the vets can be a cause of owners delaying or even refusing to seek veterinary attention for their pet.

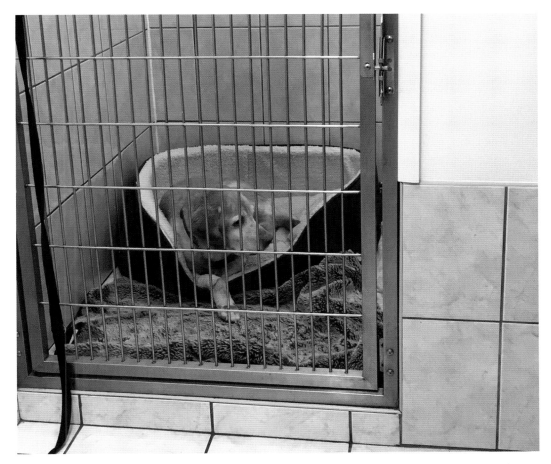

Figure 8.2: When dogs have to stay overnight at the vets, depending on the situation, they might be able to use their own bedding. Photo: © Rosie Bescoby.

First experiences really matter, and attention has been brought to the idea that the first 'medical' handlings of a puppy may significantly influence their lifelong tendencies both in the veterinary context but also potentially in other non-veterinary situations. In a preliminary study, it was shown that puppies who were fearful at their first veterinary visit (2–4 months of age) were fearful in the same context as young adults.[25]

There has been significant attention over the past few years on recognising negative emotional states in dogs attending veterinary clinics and how various environmental changes and handling techniques may reduce the negative experience, often referred to as the 'fear free' approach. Reducing negative emotional states and reducing stress in the canine patient confers several benefits including: prevention of fear/stress worsening the presenting symptom (for example, illness or injury); consideration of trigger stacking; increasing the risk of reactive (including aggressive) behaviour on handling; limiting the effect of stress on any samples being taken; limiting the effect of stress on any medications (for example, sedation) that may need to be given; improving perception of vet visit by owner leading to increased likelihood of owner returning in the future and improving vet–client–pet relationship ultimately affecting client compliance and treatment success.

A helpful beginning to a 'fearLess' at the vets approach would be the individual animal being better prepared before arrival. Educating dog owners in habituation programmes for the sights, smells, sounds and feels of the vets before they first bring their puppy to a clinic gives the best opportunity for the first vet experiences to be more positive. Depending on the country in which the dog is living, there may be legal requirements for the pup to have already had veterinary procedures (for example, placement of a microchip before the owner even collects the pup from the breeders). Using gentle, minimal restraint handling along with using positive distraction (for example, licking tasty paste off a clean surface such as rubber toy, or searching for a tasty treat held firmly between the breeder's fingers) is essential to avoid that first vet experience resulting in potential 'single trial' fear/pain learning.

In human paediatric medicine, the use of topical anaesthetic cream has been considered for use when infants need to undergo venupuncture, and overall the findings suggest there may be a small amount of benefit but in many cases, not as effective as distraction with sugar water or breastfeeding. In rabbits, the use of topical anaesthetic cream has been shown to significantly reduce the pain response to ear tattooing. However, to date, there have been no published reports about the safety or effectiveness of using topical anaesthetic creams in puppies prior to injections such as vaccines or microchipping. Based on human paediatric research, it would remain a concern that it is the proximity and restraint by unfamiliar people that elicits the greater stress response rather than the pain of the needle itself, so concentrating on gentle handling and positive distraction probably remain the most effective methods of minimising distress. The use of topical anaesthetic cream in adult dogs may be safer (in human infants concerns have been raised with the use of lidocaine induced methemoglobinemia, but we have no data on this in dog neonates) and more behaviourally effective (adult dogs may be less fearful of stranger proximity and/or restraint than puppies, or at least have developed alternative coping strategies) and has been shown to reduce the behavioural response to intravenous cannula placement if the cream was applied 60 minutes before the cannulation.

Fast exercise has been shown to increase cortisol levels that may remain elevated for at least one hour in the dog, although other chemical changes that might influence behaviour such as catecholamines, nerve growth factor, lactate levels and changes in blood and tissue glucose levels, will also occur. Given that elevations of adrenalin, noradrenalin and cortisol and any decrease in body/brain glucose will impact on the behavioural responses of an animal subjected to additional stressors at that time, namely potentially faster physical reactions and less consciously inhibited responses, it would be recommended that dogs attending the vets are not subjected to faster exercise within preceding hours of an intended vet visit where possible. Many owners may have the idea that recent exercise will 'tire' the dog and make them less likely to offer undesirable behaviours at the vet clinic, whereas an understanding of exercise physiology suggests that in fact, the opposite may be true. In comparison, calm, exploratory exercise with opportunities for sniffing, may result in physiological changes that promote relaxed, desirable behaviours.

Studies show that dogs are particularly perceptive and responsive to their owner or handler's emotional states. If the person who will be attending the clinic with the dog can aim to keep themselves calm and relaxed before and during the appointment, this may be particularly beneficial. Ideas could include booking appointments so as to have enough time not to be rushing to arrive on time, waiting with the dog in the car until the vet is ready for the appointment so as to avoid any stress to themselves or the dog about how the dog behaves in the waiting area, listening to a favourite audio-story or music during the wait and to be aware that it is OK to stroke the dog if the dog is comfortable with this, as a way of reassuring the dog and calming themselves.

Research has shown that, in general, dogs show less stress at the vets if they remain in the proximity of the owner. There may be a tendency for some practitioners to feel the dog shows more undesired attempts at escape in the presence of the owner so they recommend examinations or procedures away from them. Work published in 2020 showed that dogs whose owners sat next to them in a chair during the vet examination (dogs were examined on non-slip matting on the floor) showed a reduced number of stress measurements compared with dogs whose owners were not in the room for the same examination.[26] Given the response to an owner's emotional state and behaviours, it is possible that some dogs may be more stressed during examination if the owner themselves is particularly distressed. Human studies have shown people are more relaxed (activation of the parasympathetic nervous system) when sat compared with standing, and even when the chair allows for neck support compared to a chair, that does not. Listening to classical music has also be shown to reduce stress in people and dogs, including dogs during veterinary examination, so the social effect of having quiet music playing during the examination may be dually beneficial. There are several ways that vet clinics may be able to help the owner, and therefore in turn, the dog, remain calmer during examinations.

Riemer[27] produced an excellent publication detailing a variety of ways in which dogs attending vet clinics can have their potential stress reduced or mitigated, therefore this section will defer to that detail. In short, a summary of considerations includes the following.

- Avoiding immediate greeting by staff on arrival at the practice.
- Allowing the dog time to sniff and explore the clinic on arrival and the examination area before any staff intervention occurs.
- Promoting limited numbers of animals in the waiting area by: keeping clients and patients in their cars where possible before the actual appointment; developing 'sniff' zones outside the waiting area for those without transportation; communicating the value of limited animals in the waiting area including appointment time reminders; advising clients if clinics are running late; providing screens within the seating area to minimise exposure to other animals where remaining outside the practice is unavoidable; and for owners to bring a towel or blanket of the dogs for them to rest on during any waiting period.
- Use of non-slip flooring and use of cleaning products that can remove stress pheromones from paw secretions without the use of strong fragranced odours.
- Placement of weigh scales away from corners and allowing dogs the time to walk on and off by themselves.
- Training of staff to recognise body language, vocalisations and behaviours of stress in the dog and providing them with strategies to use when they notice these of significant presence and/or escalating in a given individual. (The use of 'stress scoring'; for example, 0 – dog positive and calm, 5 – dog highly distressed, may be

beneficial to help staff make alternative plans for certain dogs within one visit, as well as helping the vet and client to discuss options to reduce future stress in dogs with repeatedly high scores.)

- Education of vet and nursing staff to use minimal restraint handling (including the use of the floor for many examinations and procedures in the dog [see Figure 8.3]) and to respond to fear or stress increasing signs during examination.

- Positive distraction during parts of the examination or procedure (see overshadowing section below).

- Use of fear-reducing medicines in patients known to have strong reactions in the clinic, or to be used in patients developing such associations where it is important to stop examinations or procedures and make plans to re-attempt on a different occasion where possible, rather than risk the development of traumatic conditioned

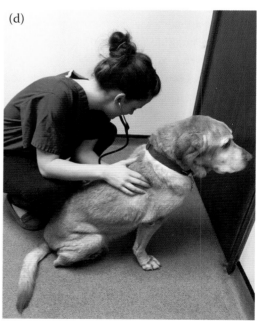

Figure 8.3a–d: Veterinary assessment of a dog using a comfortable surface on the floor. Photo: (a,b) © Sarah Bignell-Howse; (c) © Natalie Light; (d) © Rosie Bescoby.

responses as the result of continuing in the moment with a highly stressed individual (see section of anti-anxiety medications).

- Administering pre-medications (ideally with anti-anxiety components) to dogs in the presence of the owner and allowing time for their effect before moving the dog away from the owner into the hospital for a procedure. Where this is not possible, considering the use of fear-reducing medicines given at home before the trip to the vets for a procedure involving a hospital stay.
- Minimising hospital stays and maintaining low-stress handling for the duration.
- The use of minimised pain procedures (for example, local anaesthetic creams or skin blocks, selecting smallest needle gauge size, use of pre- as well as post-procedure pain relief).
- Consideration of behaviourally mindful postoperative wound management such as using body suits, or padded collars rather than plastic Elizabethan collars where possible and providing enrichment ideas for postoperative confinement or lead exercise (see Activities section). (See Figure 8.4 for pictures of alternatives to Elizabethan collars.)

Use of positive distraction to facilitate lower stress handling and procedures (overshadowing)

When we present the brain with two or more stimuli simultaneously, we have the possibility of 'overshadowing'. If the brain recognises one stimulus as of far greater value than another, the brain may prioritise all/or the majority, of its attention to that stimulus. Such stimuli can be a negative ('I must pay attention to this potentially life-threatening sound/sight/feel'), or

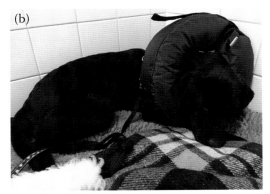

Figure 8.4: Alternatives to Elizabethan collars to prevent dogs from licking or chewing their wounds. (a) Coat. Photo: © Ruth Moots. (b) Inflatable collar. Photo: © Tamsin Durston.

positive ('I must pay attention to this potentially amazing life-affecting sight/smell/taste').

Overshadowing does not have to involve stimuli that are polar opposites in terms of being amazing or being unpleasant. It just means one stimulus is more 'valuable' to that individual. For example, when dogs are restrained for an injection such as a subcutaneous vaccination, it is fairly common for the vet to pick up and pinch a piece of skin on the neck scruff. If for an individual, the way this is done induces discomfort or fear, and that is more 'valuable' to the dog than the needle going through their skin, then this is also overshadowing – they are both unpleasant experiences, but the skin hold is more 'valuable' than the needle and the dog may well not have even noticed the needle going in.

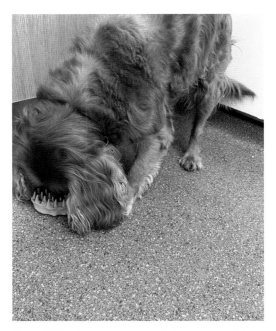

Figure 8.5: For dogs who are nervous in the veterinary clinic environment distraction can help. Photo: © Amber Batson.

In training terminology, we normally refer to this 'value' as 'salience' – we would say the skin hold is more salient than the needle placement for this individual. The author of course acknowledges that skin lifting can be a neutral event for many dogs that just facilitates effective subcutaneous needle placement, it is more the amount of skin and intensity of 'hold' that can affect the dog's perception of restraint or discomfort.

In some circumstances, a veterinary professional might decide to place a muzzle on a dog as experience reveals that many dogs go quiet once the muzzle has been fitted. Muzzles can of course be invaluable tools to keep people who are working near a dog's face, or who are working with a dog with known aggression, safe. However, it is important that we recognise the majority of dogs have not had previous positive associations made with muzzle placement – therefore this is not a positive form of distraction to the dog but most likely a negative one. A study looking at muzzle use in the dog

highlighted how the muzzle might restrict the dog during social interactions and explorative behaviours as well as limiting communication, for example, physically restricting or blocking facial expressions/movements.[28] The same study saw owners describing behaviour responses to the dog wearing a muzzle as resulting in 'calm' behaviour, which may indicate acceptance of the muzzle, or may also have been indicative of a fear induced freeze, yet on first application, more than 65% of owners reported the dog trying to pull the muzzle of with their paws or by face rubbing, moving slowly/backwards (15.4%), panting (13.1%), lying down (10.5%), and growling (0.5%), among others.

It is important that we distinguish between occasions where the muzzle is necessary for human safety during an essential procedure (perhaps to administer intravenous sedation to a dog requiring emergency surgery) and its use to potentially induce a freeze response to carry out a non-urgent task. In their recent paper, Reimer and colleagues[27] state 'Muzzles must not be abused to manhandle a resisting dog, and to carry out a procedure despite the dog's struggling. In such cases, other measures, such as short-term sedation, pre-visit medication, and in the longer-term behavioural training must be used.'

If we use fear-inducing stimuli to overshadow other fear inducing or pain causing stimuli, then the vet still remains the reliable predictor of scary, potentially painful things. Overshadowing can be achieved using things the dog finds particularly pleasant rather than relying on things the dog particularly dislikes. Examples can be, knowing that a dog has a particularly itchy spot on their rump that they really enjoy having scratched, and then the handler scratching that itchy spot well at the same time as the vet gently inserts a needle for vaccination. Many dogs are keen on trying to get tasty food (providing stress levels have been kept low prior to reaching the examination room, and that the owner brings with them one of the dog's favourite foods) – the key when using food to overshadow is to ensure the food remains their entire focus, so the handler should hide the food in their hand, or possibly smeared across a toy (such as inside a Kong™ or Lickimat™) and have the dog search for the food, starting immediately prior to the vet carrying out the procedure.

Used well, overshadowing can be a highly effective tool to prevent stress pathways being triggered, to help keep the dog physically still and calm for certain procedures – particularly those involving needles, and for preventing the dog from learning negative associations about the vet.

Overshadowing has its main limitations when: we need to do a procedure that may well be followed by administering medicines or tests, where an empty stomach is preferable (although the times when this is essential for anaesthesia or sedation may be significantly lower than commonly perceived, see Westlund[29] for a review of food use in clinical practice), the dog's fear of the vet or procedure is too salient so that any other stimuli are too minor in comparison including tasty food, or when the procedure is going to take a long time such as an operation under local anaesthesia or a diagnostic imaging procedure.

Overshadowing can be a useful tool to maintain positive associations with the vets after positive initial experiences or after a retraining programme.

Teaching the old dog new tricks – can we retrain dogs to think differently about vets?

Counter conditioning normally refers to a 'retraining' programme used when an animal has developed a conditioned fear response to a stimulus so that the sight or sound or smell of the stimulus immediately elicits switching on of the stress pathways and a fear behavioural response.

This type of learning has been described in the chapter covering training and previously in this chapter with regards to neutering. One of the important things to remember when attempting to counter condition is that the presentation of the conditioned stimulus immediately triggers the unwanted internal chemicals/reflexes. This means when we start a counter conditioning programme, we have to be clear about exactly what stimuli and how they are presented specifically, affects that individual dog (for example, proximity to the dog, different smells and intensities, in which environments/contexts). It can then be helpful to break down the stimulus into more 'unrecognisable' pieces: for example, we might start with the smell of a mild antiseptic on a cloth in the owner's garden: rather than a strong antiseptic smell being on clothes worn by a human being in the vet clinic, and pair the dog sniffing the scent with something positive, for example, a food treat.

The positive element is key as we are intending to replace the reflex feelings of fear with reflex feelings of pleasure – this is why the training is referred to as 'counter' literally meaning 'opposite' conditioning. Once we have introduced the dog to the stimulus broken down into smaller pieces, we start pairing the pieces back together again (for example, smell of antiseptic on a towel), present at the same time as a person resting their hand on the back of the dog's neck (a common site for injections) with receiving a food treat. We might then add in the person wearing a stethoscope around their neck, while in the presence of antiseptic smell and touching the dog, and then practice this in different locations – owner's garden, a friend's kitchen, outside the vet clinic and so on before ultimately doing this inside the vet practice itself. Note the author prefers to avoid this type of retraining within the core of the dog's own home as to avoid any negative associations if the training is not going as well as intended, in what should be perceived as their 'safe' space.

In 2019, a study[30] showed that a 4-week retraining programme undertaken by owners with their dogs who had been identified as already fearful at the vets, was not particularly effective at reducing their fear at the vets. One of the main issues affecting this type of retraining programme with dogs is that the context of the vets – a specific building, that smells a specific way (medical scents, stress pheromones of other animals, potentially the smell of infectious agents such as bacteria and yeasts) where touch by unfamiliar people wearing uniform is going to occur, is a huge and obvious predictor of the experience they will undergo. Any counter conditioning programmes need to take this context into consideration and once there is evidence a dog is learning about a variety of the vet stimuli at home, such as showing calm, positive body language in the presence of non-vet unfamiliar people, being gently touched on a variety of body parts, being touched by instruments such as the stethoscope, being in the presence of antiseptic smells, this must be replicated within rooms of the clinic as well. Supervision during this type of training, either potentially in person by a behaviourist, or perhaps more practically by the behaviourist viewing video footage of the training, should help to ensure the owner is able to make the new association with 'dog experiencing vet stimulus' followed by 'receipt of pleasurable reward, for example, tasty treat' so that we are sure the owner has not rushed the training, misunderstood elements of body language or accidentally overshadowed with the presence of tasty food.

Counter conditioning has the potential to be extremely effective, however, it remains that the brain has two sets of memories about the stimulus: the original memory that the stimulus (for example, vet examination) was scary, and now a second memory that vet examination can be pleasurable. On a given day, arrival at the vets has the potential now to elicit one of two different memories.

It can be difficult to maintain the easiest memory for the dog to choose as the positive one, when attending the vets is potentially a scary, pain inducing experience. It is essential to remember that counter conditioning will be rapidly unlearned if the vet becomes the predictor of bad things again.

One of the ways to avoid losing the positive associations once we have counter conditioned a dog to the vet, is to use 'overshadowing' for future vet experiences, as well as practising some of the counter conditioning programme in between 'real' vet visits.

Pharmaceutically influenced behaviour

Some procedures require sedation or anaesthesia, either due to the invasive nature of the procedure or requirement for absolute stillness, or because the individual patient is too physically reactive to carry out a particular task without significant risk of injury (for example, nail clipping or blood sampling).

It is important to remember that sedation does not result in loss of consciousness. The phrase 'chemical restraint' is the most accurate as it gives the appropriate description of an animal that is less able to move as the result of the drug administration. Animals that have been sedated are still conscious and may be aware of stimuli and events in their surroundings and what they are directly experiencing. This is particularly important to remember when painful procedures are being undertaken such as minor surgeries including wound stitch ups, or torn nail removals, as the dog may well be able to feel the pain but not necessarily able to physically do anything about it.

Sedation drugs can be combined with pain relievers, some of which, such as opioids (morphine like medications), may have some mild sedating properties of their own. This is beneficial to the dog undergoing a painful or uncomfortable procedure, and may reduce the overall perception of pain intensity, but does not necessarily remove all of the pain experience. The use of local anaesthetics to totally numb tissues and cause 100% blocking of pain recognition should be considered in as many sedated procedures as possible.

As the sedated dog is still conscious and can experience fear and pain but is often less physically equipped to do anything about it, chemical restraint should be considered as a possible act of 'flooding'. It is essential for the welfare of the dog and for future learning that gentle and respectful handling occurs during chemical restraint and is combined as above, with the use of the most effective pain reduction where pain is a possibility. Some sedation drugs have an anxiety-reducing effect in the body and these sedatives should be used in preference to those without that known property where possible.

Some individuals who have known fear responses once at the veterinary clinic, may benefit from the use of fear-reducing (anxiolytic) medicines prior to clinic attendance. Table 8.1 presents a summary of some of the most commonly used medicines to reduce fear in dogs before a veterinary clinic visit. This is not meant to be a complete list as the variety of anxiolytics and also potential combinations, is wide ranging and outside the scope of this chapter.

The Chill Protocol has been used by the Cummings School of Veterinary Medicine at Tufts University, USA, for several years. It combines three different pharmaceuticals given before the trip to the vets, to reduce fear responses including defensive aggression, in dogs. The reported protocol states:

1. Gabapentin (20–25 mg/kg PO) should be administered the evening before the scheduled appointment.
2. A combination of gabapentin (20–25 mg/kg PO) and melatonin (small dogs, 0.5–1 mg PO; medium dogs, 1–3 mg PO; large dogs, 5 mg PO) should be administered at least 1 to 2 hours before the scheduled appointment.
3. Acepromazine (0.025–0.05 mg/kg oral trans-mucosal) should be administered 30 minutes before the scheduled appointment.

Home administration of medications for disease treatment

Owners administering medicines to their dogs at home can be a considerable source of stress to both owner and dog. Dogs are typically good at taking a variety of tablets if the tablet is wrapped well inside a 'sticky' treat such as meat paste, pate or soft cheese. There will be individuals who remain suspicious of any oral medication or dogs who will not eat certain medicines due to obnoxious smell or taste. Teaching dogs to take oral medications before they need to, can be hugely beneficial and the author often recommends that owners create a 'treat time' context from as early as 4 or 5 months of age whereby they find the dogs preferred wet treat (something that is damp but can be rolled into a sticky pea or slightly larger, dependent on dog size ball). Twice a week, the owner should bring out a wipe-clean place mat and lay it on the floor in a different location to normal feeding, and then put one or two of the treat balls on the mat. Hopefully, the dog eats both treats quickly and then the

Table 8.1 A summary of some of the most commonly used medicines to reduce fear in dogs before a veterinary clinic visit.

Medicine	Dose rate	Recommended time and method of administration (CA: clinic attendance)	Main limitations	Reference for use in dogs	Reference for use in other species
Benzodiazepines: Diazepam	0.5–2 mg/kg	Oral 1–3 hours before CA.	Paradoxical excitement reported in up to 30% of individuals. Sedation. Ataxia. Hunger.	Herron et al. (2008)[32]	
Alprazolam	0.02–0.1 mg/kg	Oral 45–60 minutes before CA.	Paradoxical excitement less commonly reported. See in the text regarding 'disinhibition' of behaviours including aggression.		
Gabapentin	10–30 mg/kg	Oral 1–3 hours before CA.	May cause ataxia in some individuals.		Van Haaften et al. (2017)[33]
Imepitoin	20 mg/kg	Oral 2 hours before CA.	May cause ataxia and increased appetite.	Engel et al. (2018)[34]	
Dexmedetomidine	125–250 ug/m^2	Careful application to mucosal surface, e.g. gum. 30–60 minutes before CA.		Hauser et al. (2020)[35]	
Trazodone	3–10 mg/kg	Oral 1 hour before CA.	Can result in moderate sedation, limiting ability to appreciate if truly anxiolytic.	Gilbert-Gregory et al. (2016)[36]	

owner can remove the mat, clean it, and store it away out of sight until the next 'treat time'. Once the dog is good at spotting the mat going down and keen to quickly eat both treats, the owner can reduce the activity to once weekly. It is a good idea to only use this type of food treat for this activity to avoid the dog tiring of the taste over time. Alternatively, the owner can teach the dog to catch and swallow the treats once they have laid the mat down as a treat time signal. Should medicines need to be given to the dog, the owner can then place the mat on the ground, give one treat as normal, give a second treat containing the medicine, and then give a third treat without medicine, before removing the mat as normal.

Administering medicines such as drops to the ears and eyes can be a more offensive experience for the dog particularly if we are attempting to give those medicines at times when the tissues we are treating are painful. Owners should be advised to make sure the dog has received any pain reducing medicines at least one hour before applying topical treatments if this is relevant. It is then ideal to call the dog into a room and close the door, before going to a cupboard or fridge to get out the medicine; it would appear far more stressful and detrimental to the owner–pet relationship if the owner has to chase the dog around the home before applying any medicines. Where possible, owners should have been demonstrated gentle handling techniques to apply the medicines and change any dressings and should use positive overshadowing such as a toy smeared with a favourite paste, or a second person with tasty treats in hand, to distract the dog while undertaking the procedure. Most dogs will become familiar with the context of entering a set room, or the owner going to a particular cupboard to get what they need, by standard associative learning, and this may incite a fear response. In the author's opinion,

it is better that this happens, and the administration of the medicine is predictable for the dog, rather than the dog feeling ambushed at any time. Where the procedure is too difficult or fear inducing to the dog, for the owner to carry out without detriment to their relationship with their pet, alternative plans need consideration. This may include taking the dog to a friend or neighbour's house for someone else to administer the medicine, receiving home visits from a pet professional (use a room for treatment that the dog does not spend much time in to avoid negative associations with their 'safe' space), taking the dog to the vet clinic for the procedure or alternative treatment type (for example, once weekly ear gel applied at the vet clinic, rather than twice daily drops at home).

Finishing on a positive note after medicine application or dressing changes, should be a focus, so the author recommends the owner has something calm but highly enjoyable for the dog to do immediately after treatment such as a small edible chew, Lickimat™ from the freezer (Figure 8.6), frozen stuffed food toy, or a non-edible scent game or grooming session, depending on the dog's preference. Spending 5–10 minutes bonding time with the dog after medicine administration should help increase their oxytocin levels, decrease any stress chemistry and re-establish the positive bond between owner and dog.

Prescribing cage rest with behaviour in mind

A variety of different activities that can be undertaken with dogs have been considered in Chapter 4. This is a short summary of some basic points to consider when a period of confinement is considered necessary as part of veterinary treatment/surgical recovery.

Figure 8.6: Enjoying a Lickimat™. Photo: © Boo Blackhurst.

Enough space to comfortably lie and achieve quality sleep

With dogs taking around 12 hours sleep in every 24 hours, meeting this essential need during periods of confinement must be considered. Crates may be considered when marked restrictions in movements are deemed necessary, but it is important to ensure the dog is able to move around without getting limbs trapped in bedding, and has enough comfortable space to stand up, stretch out, and lie in a flat lateral recumbency manner to facilitate both slow wave and rapid eye movement sleep patterns. Dogs show a strong preference for sleeping in social proximity, so the owner making temporary adjustments to their own sleeping arrangements if the dog and crate cannot be carried upstairs, could be a consideration. Many recovery plans do not require such extreme physical restriction, in which case a barrier used to create a pen within a room that allows a choice of sleeping areas and allows a little more free movement may be appropriate.

Consideration of the temperature within the confined area is important, as is the availability of water without it hindering the dog's movement or lying within the space.

Minimising rebound effects

When certain behaviours are restricted or fully prevented for a period of time, we often see them performed with greater intensity and longer duration for a while as the dog's brain and body attempts to play 'catch up'. Confined dogs often show a strong desire to pull on the lead, bounce around, jump up and down when brought out of confinement and that can be detrimental to the recovery phase.

One option is to use 'stations' between the confined area and the place that we need to take the dog to (for example, garden for toileting). We can place plates, placemats, towels, boxes a few metres apart from outside the confined area and out to the garden, with a few around the garden space too, and place treats or smear pastes (liver paste, reduced salt marmite, yoghurt and so on) on the station or on a toy placed on the station, for the dog to walk from one place to another. This can encourage the dog to exit the confined space with their head down, following their nose and reduce the tendency for them to be looking up at the owner which increases 'jumping' tendencies.

Another option for some owners may be able to ask the dog to 'pause' after a few steps and reward them with a treat placed on the ground or the owner coming down to dog level to massage or groom them for a few moments before walking on a little further.

If the walk to outside is particularly risky at a stage in recovery, then the use of indoor litter trays may be necessary for a short period of time.

Meeting more needs while in the confined area, or perhaps with the dog on-lead exploring enrichment in a small room in the house, may reduce rebound tendencies too.

- **Meet social needs**. Ideas include: owner sitting in the pen with the dog for grooming, massage, stroking, rest periods. The owner could read or listen to music with the dog. Bringing the scent of familiar people or dogs into the confined area, for example, worn T-shirt, other dogs' beddings. Maybe if the dog is part of a multi-dog household, they can spend some chewing time together in a slightly larger pen if appropriate.
- **Food enrichment**. Ideas include: edible chews. Filling hollow rubber toys with wet/moist food and giving these frozen to the dog. Smearing tasty pastes or moist food on to mats designed for dogs to lick. Stuffing cardboard tubes with paper or cloth and hiding treats in the centre. The use of specific puzzle toys for dogs. Confinement has the potential to increase frustration in the dog so doing food enrichment after the dog has recently eaten, rather than when the dog is hungry is the author's preference.
- **Non-food scent enrichment.** Ideas include: borrowing some toys from friends or neighbours' dogs so the confined dog has the opportunity to investigate something novel and something with other dogs' scent on. Collecting twigs, leaves, pieces of plants from outside the home for the dog to investigate. Collecting feathers, coat brushings, bedding from other pets and placing inside old tights and hanging up for the dog to sniff.
- **Auditory enrichment.** Ideas include playing a variety of different outdoor sounds such as rainfall, bird song, other animal noises for short periods of time. Playing different genres of music at different times.

A multimodal approach to the dog with behaviour and medical problems

Let us return to Jungo. What did I do to help him with his unfamiliar people reactivity, separation anxiety, noise reactivity and swallowing undigestible items?

Jungo was assessed by me at a neutral environment (village hall) in which some basic non-food enrichment had been placed for him to investigate. Observations of his movement and behaviours raised questions about possible pain in his hind legs. Full history-taking found that he was passing soft faeces several times a week and had been for several months – the owners had understandably considered this to be fairly normal in a dog that had a tendency to eat a variety of edible and inedible objects. A full behavioural history was taken.

Jungo was referred back to his vets and following a single dose of dexmedetomidine oral gel for its anti-anxiety properties given at home, he had a topical local anaesthetic cream administered to a foreleg after clipping of the hair outside in the car park, then had an intravenous cannula placed 45 minutes later in the presence of his owner. He was then admitted into the clinic for a clinical examination then a general anaesthetic to allow for a blood sample and hip radiographs to be taken. He was found to have mild hip dysplasia changes, with normal blood test results and evidence of Giardia infection on faecal samples. His vets dispensed a course of fenbendazole treatment for the Giardia and started him on nonsteroidal anti-inflammatory medicine for suspected hip pain, along with a joint supplement.

Behaviourally, his exercise regime was changed to incorporate less fast exercise, with lots of opportunities for sniffing and exploring, along with an introduction to hydrotherapy to help build up the muscles around his hips (see chapter on non-vet professionals). He underwent a period of visiting the owner's parents each day rather than being left by himself and began counter conditioning programmes to loud noises, being left by himself and towards being in proximity of unfamiliar people, approximately 1 month after starting on the pain relief for his hips.

Within 3 months of initial vet behaviour consultation, he had shown no further episodes of pica, was making good progress at being left for a few hours a day by himself at home and showed limited reactions to close proximity of strangers. He no longer had reactions to loud noises and his faecal consistency was considered normal. His longer-term plan is to remain on joint supplements for his hip dysplasia, continue with hydrotherapy and appropriate exercise plans to slow down progression of degenerative joint disease, and to work towards a counter conditioning programme to examinations at the vets. In the meantime, the use of anti-anxiety medicines before vet clinic attendance and/or the use of food treats to overshadow examinations has been successful in reducing his fears at the vets.

Conclusion

There are many ways in which disease can affect behaviour and how behaviour can affect disease. Veterinary examinations and procedures for both diagnostic and treatment purposes as well as prophylactic interventions, have the potential to affect both the short-term and the long-term behaviour of the dog.

Keeping behaviour in mind when a dog is attending a veterinary clinic, using fear and therefore stress-reducing approaches to both the environment and in any handling of the dog are paramount in maintaining a positive vet–dog–client relationship. Considering the relationship between the gut–brain–skin among other elements of a multisystem 'whole dog' approach to medicine and behaviour will make vet professionals more effective in overall health and welfare treatments.

Awareness of how medicines, both psychopharmaceuticals and conventional systemic medicines for example, steroids, non-steroidals, oral antibiotics, nutraceuticals, inhalational agents, may impact on behaviour is outside the scope of this chapter but warrants consideration.

Behavioural problems are a common cause of relinquishment of ownership in dogs, alongside a common reason for the animal's euthanasia, delving deeper into the possible pain and disease components of these problems is a key element in improving canine welfare.

References

1. Kirchoff, N.S., Udell, M.A. and Sharpton, T.J. (2019) The gut microbiome correlates with conspecific aggression in a small population of rescued dogs (Canis familiaris). PeerJ 7, p. e6103.
2. Mondo, E., Barone, M., Soverini, M., D'Amico, F., Cocchi, M., Petrulli, C., Mattioli, M., Marliani, G., Candela, M. and Accorsi, P.A. (2020) Gut microbiome structure and adrenocortical activity in dogs with aggressive and phobic behavioral disorders. Heliyon 6(1), p. e03311.
3. Craig, J.M. (2016) Atopic dermatitis and the intestinal microbiota in humans and dogs. Veterinary Medicine and Science 2(2), 95–105.
4. Harvey, N.D., Craigon, P.J., Shaw, S.C., Blott, S.C. and England, G.C. (2019) Behavioural differences in dogs with atopic dermatitis suggest stress could be a significant problem associated with chronic pruritus. Animals 9(10), 813.

5. Masson, S., Guitaut, N., Medam, T. and Béata, C. (2021) Link between foreign body ingestion and behavioural disorder in dogs. *Journal of Veterinary Behavior* 45, 25–32.

6. Mills, D.S., Demontigny-Bédard, I., Gruen, M., Klinck, M.P., McPeake, K.J., Barcelos, A.M., Hewison, L., Van Haevermaet, H., Denenberg, S., Hauser, H. and Koch, C. (2020) Pain and problem behavior in cats and dogs. *Animals* 10(2), 318.

7. Gähwiler, S., Bremhorst, A., Tóth, K. and Riemer, S. (2020) Fear expressions of dogs during New Year fireworks: a video analysis. *Scientific Reports* 10(1), 1–10.

8. Stellato, A.C., Flint, H.E., Widowski, T.M., Serpell, J.A. and Niel, L. (2017) Assessment of fear-related behaviours displayed by companion dogs (*Canis familiaris*) in response to social and non-social stimuli. *Applied Animal Behaviour Science* 188, 84–90.

9. Mariti, C., Falaschi, C., Zilocchi, M., Fatjó, J., Sighieri, C., Ogi, A. and Gazzano, A. (2017) Analysis of the intraspecific visual communication in the domestic dog (*Canis familiaris*): a pilot study on the case of calming signals. *Journal of Veterinary Behavior* 18, 49–55.

10. Rusbridge, C. (2020) New considerations about Chiari-like malformation, syringomyelia and their management. *In Practice* 42(5), 252–267.

11. The Metta Pet Clinic (n.d.) www.mettapetclinic.co.uk.

12. McMillan, F.D. (2019) Mental health and well-being benefits of personal control in animals. In: McMillan, F.D. (ed.) *Mental Health and Well-Being in Animals*, 2nd edn. CABI, Wallingford, pp. 67–81.

13. De Assis, L.S., Matos, R., Pike, T.W., Burman, O.H. and Mills, D.S. (2020) Developing diagnostic frameworks in veterinary behavioral medicine: disambiguating separation related problems in dogs. *Frontiers in Veterinary Science* 6, 499.

14. Fatjó, J. and Bowen, J. (2020) Making the case for multi-axis assessment of behavioural problems. *Animals* 10(3), 383.

15. Packer, R.M. and Volk, H.A. (2015) Epilepsy beyond seizures: a review of the impact of epilepsy and its comorbidities on health-related quality of life in dogs. *Veterinary Record* 177(12), 306–315.

16. Kutzler, M.A. (2020) Possible relationship between long-term adverse health effects of gonad-removing surgical sterilisation and luteinising hormone in dogs. *Animals* 10(4), 599.

17. Kutzler, M.A., (2020) Gonad-sparing surgical sterilisation in dogs. *Frontiers in Veterinary Science* 7, 42.

18. Roulaux, P.E., van Herwijnen, I.R. and Beerda, B. (2020) Self-reports of Dutch dog owners on received professional advice, their opinions on castration and behavioural reasons for castrating male dogs. *Public Library of Science ONE* 15(6), p. e0234917.

19. Farhoody, P., Mallawaarachchi, I., Tarwater, P.M., Serpell, J.A., Duffy, D.L. and Zink, C. (2018) Aggression toward familiar people, strangers, and conspecifics in gonadectomised and intact dogs. *Frontiers in Veterinary Science* 5, 18.

20. McGreevy, P.D., Wilson, B., Starling, M.J. and Serpell, J.A. (2018) Behavioural risks in male dogs with minimal lifetime exposure to gonadal hormones may complicate population-control benefits of desexing. *Public Library of Science ONE* 13(5), p. e0196284.

21. Root, A.L., Parkin, T.D., Hutchison, P., Warnes, C. and Yam, P.S. (2018) Canine pseudopregnancy: an evaluation of prevalence and current treatment protocols in the UK. *BMC Veterinary Research* 14(1), 1–12.

22. Döring, D., Roscher, A., Scheipl, F., Küchenhoff, H. and Erhard, M.H. (2009) Fear-related behaviour of dogs in veterinary practice. *The Veterinary Journal* 182(1), 38–43.

23. Brent, L., Lissner, E.A. and Kutzler, M.A. (2021) Restoration of reproductive hormone concentrations in a male neutered dog improves health: a case study. *Topics in Companion Animal Medicine* 45, p.100565.

24. Salavati, S., Mogheiseh, A., Nazifi, S., Tabrizi, A.S., Taheri, P. and Koohi, F. (2018) Changes in sexual hormones, serotonin, and cortisol concentrations following oral administration of melatonin in castrated and intact dogs. *Journal of Veterinary Behavior* 27, 27–34.

25. Volk, J.O., Felsted, K.E., Thomas, G.J. and Siren, C.W. (2011) Executive summary of the Bayer veterinary care usage study. *Journal of the American Veterinary Medical Association* 238(10), 1275–1282.

26. Godbout, M. and Frank, D. (2011) Persistence of puppy behaviors and signs of anxiety during adulthood. *Journal of Veterinary Behavior: Clinical Applications and Research* 1(6), 92.

27. Stellato, A.C., Dewey, C.E., Widowski, T.M. and Niel, L. (2020) Evaluation of associations between owner presence and indicators of fear in dogs during routine veterinary examinations. *Journal of the American Veterinary Medical Association* 257(10), 1031–1040.

28. Riemer, S., Heritier, C., Windschnurer, I., Pratsch, L., Arhant, C. and Affenzeller, N. (2021) A review

on mitigating fear and aggression in dogs and cats in a veterinary setting. *Animals* 11(1), 158.

29. Arhant, C., Schmied-Wagner, C., Aigner, U. and Affenzeller, N. (2021) Owner reports on the use of muzzles and their effects on dogs: an online survey. *Journal of Veterinary Behavior* 41, 73–81.

30. Westlund, K. (2015) To feed or not to feed: counterconditioning in the veterinary clinic. *Journal of Veterinary Behavior* 10(5), 433–437.

31. Stellato, A., Jajou, S., Dewey, C.E., Widowski, T.M. and Niel, L. (2019) Effect of a standardised four-week desensitisation and counter conditioning training program on pre-existing veterinary fear in companion dogs. *Animals* 9(10), 767.

32. Herron, M.E., Shofer, F.S. and Reisner, I.R. (2008) Retrospective evaluation of the effects of diazepam in dogs with anxiety-related behavior problems. *Journal of the American Veterinary Medical Association* 233(9), 1420–1424.

33. Van Haaften, K.A., Forsythe, L.R.E., Stelow, E.A. and Bain, M.J. (2017) Effects of a single pre-appointment dose of gabapentin on signs of stress in cats during transportation and veterinary examination. *Journal of the American Veterinary Medical Association* 251(10), 1175–1181.

34. Engel, O., Masic, A., Landsberg, G., Brooks, M., Mills, D.S. and Rundfeldt, C. (2018) Imepitoin shows benzodiazepine-like effects in models of anxiety. *Frontiers in Pharmacology* 9, 1225.

35. Hauser, H., Campbell, S., Korpivaara, M., Stefanovski, D., Quinlan, M. and Siracusa, C. (2020) In-hospital administration of dexmedetomidine oromucosal gel for stress reduction in dogs during veterinary visits: a randomised, double-blinded, placebo-controlled study. *Journal of Veterinary Behavior* 39, 77–85.

36. Gilbert-Gregory, S.E., Stull, J.W., Rice, M.R. and Herron, M.E. (2016) Effects of trazodone on behavioral signs of stress in hospitalised dogs. *Journal of the American Veterinary Medical Association* 249(11), 1281–1291.

Chapter 9

Non-veterinary professionals

Kirsty Grant and Amber Batson

There are many individuals who help dog owners with different aspects of caring for and managing their dogs. If all interactions between these pet professionals and our pet dogs are done with behaviour in mind, we can provide a more effective service for the owner, ensure a positive experience for the dog, and benefit the animal professional's business too.

In this chapter, we consider encounters with professionals that dogs are likely to meet from their point of view. We then explore how those encounters could take place with canine behaviour in mind.

What is a pet professional?

There are so many people who come into contact with our dogs in their role as a pet professional including those who help with day-to-day elements of dog ownership, such as groomers, walkers, sitters and trainers. There are also professionals who we turn to when things go wrong, such as vets, vet nurses, behaviourists, canine physiotherapists, hydrotherapy pool staff and people offering a multitude of different complementary and alternative therapies. Elsewhere in this book trainers, behaviourists and the veterinary profession have been considered, this chapter explores how other services provided to dog owners can be given with behaviour in mind. We particularly focus on dog groomers.

There are a wide range of complementary and alternative therapies being made available to dog owners for their pets. Some are evidence-based with a strong scientific foundation, and others are not. To offer some therapies and services people have to pass a qualification and register with a regulating body, but to offer others they do not. Some professions have 'protected titles' – titles that under a country's law can only be used by an individual who has passed recognised qualifications in that field of study and/or is registered with a particular professional body, such as a veterinary surgeon. However, many professionals who work with dogs do not have such protected titles, and in the UK these include people who refer to themselves as animal or veterinary physiotherapists, behaviourists, massage therapists, aromatherapists and groomers to provide some examples. This means that anyone can call themselves these titles without necessarily having any qualifications. It is useful for dog owners to be aware of this and to check the qualifications, experience and any professional registrations before seeking treatment for their dog. In short, if as dog owners we need a service or other professional help and want to ensure our dog has as good an experience as possible, we should start with taking care to research what type of professional would be best and if the approach or therapy is well accepted as being successful in what we are seeking it to do.

First impressions

There are several elements of a dog professional interacting with someone's pet dog that are the same regardless of the professional context.

Let us start with how the professional initially meets the dog. First impressions last, we say and that is certainly true. Single trial learning (learning takes place in a single pairing between a response and a stimulus) is a common way of learning, and 'what we learn first, we learn best'. Getting a new relationship between a professional and a pet dog off to the right start is essential for a positive long-term relationship and an effective service regardless of the reason for the interaction.

Smell first

As explored elsewhere in this book, dogs experience their world predominantly through their sense of smell. Meeting a new individual by becoming familiar with their scent first can be a useful method of reducing stress at an initial 'in person' meeting. If the professional can provide the dog owner with an item of clothing that has been worn for at least a few hours, a pair of socks, a T-shirt perhaps, then this can be placed in a sealed Ziplock type bag and given to the owner. The owner can then remove the item from the bag at home and place it on the floor in a room where the dog spends some time but that is not their core resting or eating place. The dog should be allowed to explore the item all by themselves, rather than be lured towards it for treats or

have the item moved towards them. Owners will often find the dog is keen to have a good sniff for several seconds or longer (see Figure 9.1). It is worth leaving the item in the same place for a few hours if that is safe, so that the dog has the opportunity to return for further investigations should they want to. After that, if the owner returns the item to the Ziplock bag, they can represent the item the following day in the same way. If the professional was able to offer two or more items, such as a pair of socks, then one 'fresher' scent can be reserved for another introduction a few days after the first.

Getting closer

Dogs often show discomfort with people moving into their personal space, so the common approach of offering a hand towards a dog for them to sniff may be less than ideal for many dogs. Allowing the dog to move towards the person and sniff them first, while the person looks away, is likely to make a more positive greeting. If the new person gives the dog a treat (that the owner knows the dog likes) once the dog has approached and sniffed them and before the dog shows any signs of anxiety, it is more effective than waiting until the dog shows signs of becoming nervous.

Reacting appropriately

Multiple studies have shown that responding to increasingly negative body language is an important part of stress reduction. Education of therapists in the recognition of increasing negative emotions and accompanying physiological stress (see Chapter 8 for further detail on the process of stress in the dog's body and brain) would be highly beneficial. As would the understanding that many behaviours offered by a dog at times of stress are not voluntary,

Figure 9.1: Dogs exploring material that smells of the professional they will soon meet. Photo: © Kirsty Grant.

George and Mildred

George and Mildred were two 5-year-old Labrador crosses that had lived with their owners since they were 9-week-old puppies. At short notice, the owners had to go away overseas for a month so needed a house and dog sitter. They were recommended a professional sitter by a friend who happened to be available for the required dates, but she lived the other side of the country so meeting in person before they left was not an option. The house sitter sent two pairs of worn socks all in separate Ziplock bags via first class post to the owners who introduced one sock each day to the dogs by placing it on the floor in their dining room. The dogs spent many minutes sniffing the first sock and slightly less time with each new sock introduced afterwards. A few days later the house sitter arrived, the day before the owners had to leave. They met outside the house on part of a walk close to the dogs' home, where the sitter joined them walking back to the house. As she got close to the dogs, George was very keen to approach her and he sniffed her for a few seconds and then wandered back to his owners, a few minutes later Mildred did the same. The owners and sitter both remarked how it was as though the dogs had always known her, and a peaceful positive month for the dogs followed.

but rather involuntary, probably unconscious reflexes of self-defence driven by the brain.

Unfortunately, there has been a long-held opinion by some professionals that undesired behaviours, such as pulling away from touch, growling or even biting, will be reinforced and therefore more likely to occur again, if they are 'rewarded' by removal of the touch or proximity, or giving a treat at that time. However, this view is finally being shown not to be true in recent studies.[1,2]

Many behaviours are driven by the emotional state of the brain in that moment and as such are not necessarily voluntary, conscious actions. Negative experiences, such as increasing fear or pain, will make it more likely for a dog to show further fear and stress behaviours. Ignoring canine body language and behaviours associated with negative emotions, such as the head turn, panting, and lip licking, and continuing to touch or stay close to the dog, which is causing those negative emotions, will result in increased negative emotions and an escalation of stress and its behavioural outcome. Different dogs exhibit different behavioural strategies as avoidance techniques: as negative emotions escalate some will offer increasing amounts of appeasing body language and behaviours, some will show a prolonged freeze response (stay very still and rigid for several seconds or minutes), and some will offer defensive or even offensive aggression (see Kendal Shepherd's Canine Ladder of Aggression, Figure 5.4). Noticing early signs of negative emotions and stopping the activity or moving slightly away from the dog, allowing them to move freely and to decrease their negative emotional state will prevent escalation and improve the experience the dog is having. Representing the stimulus (for example, hand pressure, a brush or clippers) in smaller incremental steps such as lighter touch on part of the dog's body that you know they do not respond to in a negative way, or that they find a positive experience, can then be done before moving gradually back towards the part that the dog reacted negatively to being touched. If this is done while asking the owner to offer small pieces of food and calm verbal reassurance, it can be very effective at maintaining a reduced-stress state in the dog.

In some circumstances, perhaps due to the necessity of imminent treatment, this will not be enough to prevent negative emotion and therefore undesired behaviour escalation. Making decisions about how essential certain procedures are, is an invaluable part of promoting positive experiences in the dog receiving treatment; behaviourally minded professionals will recognise this but not all professionals are behaviourally minded, hence the need for owners to be confident at recognising when their dogs are anxious and knowing what to do about it. In some circumstances, it might be necessary to forego certain treatment elements in favour of maintaining a positive relationship with the dog for a future treatment. The saying 'Quit while you are ahead' is relevant. Alternatively, the use of positive overshadowing as described in the vet chapter might be worth considering – this needs to be applied before the dog reaches a more persistent negative state. In some situations, anti-anxiety medications prescribed by the vet and given before treatment may also be worth considering (see Chapter 8). In some cases, treatment under sedation where that medication includes anti-anxiety properties may be the best course of action.

The impact of 'trigger stacking' has been considered in other parts of this book so is not repeated here. However, therapists should advise the owners of their patients to aim for low-stress, calm behavioural activities in the hours before the treatment to minimise the risk of negative experiences and emotions stacking up before the visit.

Let us consider Bella, an 18-month-old cockerpoo living with an active working family with school-aged children. The family had all participated in daily brushing, with the mum taking most of this responsibility including foot washing after walks. Following the advice of their breeder, Bella first visited a pet grooming salon at 6 months of age where she had a 'puppy groom'. This was a 2 hour visit where she was bathed and dried, she also had some trimming done around her eyes, feet and anogenital regions. On collection, 'Mum' was told that Bella was not very happy about having her face and feet being handled so they must practice more at home and 'be firm'. On subsequent visits, Mum noticed that Bella was becoming increasingly unwilling to enter the salon, this then became acute when she was 12-months old after her coat had become matted, which required it to be clipped to a very short length. The dog groomer explained that Bella had been muzzled in order to groom her legs and had growled and tried to bite during the drying process. After this visit the owner had to carry her from the car to get her into the salon. The mum was advised that a groomer who worked on a 1-2-1 basis might be better for Bella. Since she was around 8-months old, Bella had been walked by a dog walker five days a week and while the walker had always reported Bella to be particularly 'barky' towards certain other dogs walked at the same time, she recently had reported that Bella had become snappy and 'grumpy' with many more dogs, including those she had previously seemed OK with. The dog walker felt that Bella was throwing her weight around as she was becoming an adult. This meant she could no longer be included in group walks and would not be able to use the day care, which she visited when the families had longer workdays and after-school commitments.

Groomers

Put into human terms, the grooming process falls somewhere between the hairdresser, the doctor and the dentist – it may feel very invasive, there is a lot of physical closeness and handling involved, and there may be some discomfort or even pain. Many groomers spend thousands of pounds and invest months or years of hard work in training and refining their skills, but dog behaviour, communication and needs are not covered in depth in any of the accredited courses and so this understanding varies according to individual groomer's personal interest and experience.

For a lot of dogs, being groomed is an essential part of their care. Many breeds have been bred to have coats that are not self-sustaining and with the recent increase in cross breeding dogs with opposing coat types, many have developed coats that require high levels of maintenance, far more than the parent breeds they came from. In a short to medium coat of straight hair, the shed hair easily passes out from the coat either when the dog rolls and rubs against surfaces, or when they scratch, and it also just falls out especially during any seasonal shed. Most curly coated breeds, however, do not have a seasonal shed, instead the hair continually grows in a consistent way and requires clipping or trimming. Dogs like Bella usually have some aspects of both parent breeds and so commonly have a continuously growing curling coat that also produces a seasonal shed. In this type of coat, the hair is easily trapped and requires careful manual removal. When this does not happen, it becomes entwined with the other shed hairs and the growing new hair causing the hair to become matted.

Matting constitutes a serious risk to health and welfare. It is uncomfortable, it impedes the dog's movement and causes pain to the skin when it is moved. It constricts the blood vessels restricting capillary function, particularly in the extremities. Severe matting can cause 'flesh death' in ears, toes and tail. The area between the toes and pads can become hard with mud, grit and matted hair, causing changes to the gait while also increasing the risk of fungal and bacterial infections. Matted hair can conceal injuries, infections and foreign bodies. It prevents the normal function of the coat, and traps damp, heat, spores and parasites within. Matting around the anogenital area can become soaked and embedded with faeces and urine leading to infection and even flystrike.

For those owners who are able to do the job at home, there is no shortage of availability of grooming equipment and short courses. There are multiple benefits to this as it allows the grooming process to be split into shorter and more frequent sessions than would be realistically possible within a professional relationship. In taking this active role, the owner also invests time in the daily body checks, which identify changes and injuries quickly. This frequent attention ensures that common issues such as overgrown nails, matted hair, parasites, crusted eyes and dirty/matted anus and genitalia regions, do not get time to develop. However, work and time commitments mean that many people struggle to meet all their dog's grooming needs so finding the right professional to become another member of the dog's healthcare team is an important decision. For average coats, (short to medium coats, shedding but minimal trimming) visits are recommended every 8–12 weeks and for more high maintenance coats (curled, long, combination coats, clipping/trimming always required) then 4–8 weeks depending on additional attention from the owner is needed. For a cockerpoo like Bella that would amount to well over 100 visits over an average lifespan. Even for the first visit and for puppy visits it is common practice for owner/guardians to drop dogs off, leave and then collect once the grooming process is finished. Being left alone with the groomer is not a legal or an insurance requirement, and it can create a situation in which the dog is potentially emotionally vulnerable.

When we think about grooming it can be helpful to look at the different elements that are involved, which can contribute stress. This gives us the opportunity to consider how we can remove elements or at least reduce their impact. Table 9.1 shows elements of the grooming experience that might be negative for the dog and potential solutions to mitigate the risk.

Oral examination and/or dental treatments

A full examination inside a dog's mouth is made to diagnose any disease process and therefore this should be done by a veterinary surgeon. Increasing numbers of groomers are offering teeth cleaning that is more than just the use of toothbrush with toothpaste, but in fact utilises equipment such as ultrasonic brushes, designed to remove plaque (a sticky microbial film) and tartar (a mineralised plaque resulting in a hard residue). Thorough examinations of all surfaces of all teeth is extremely difficult in the conscious patient and can cause a significant level of fear. Using noise-making equipment to press on the teeth, rub along the gums, being adjacent to the tongue is highly likely to induce a fear response in most dogs. The Royal College of Veterinary Surgeons (RCVS) produced a statement regarding 'anaesthesia free dental procedures in cats

Table 9.1 Potentially negative elements of grooming and solutions.

Potentially negative element of the grooming process	Solutions
Being left by their caregiver: This is usually done with minimal or no preparation, even for a puppy's first visit or for a first visit to a new groomer. Studies have shown that dogs exhibited an elevated stress response during routine veterinary examinations if their caregivers did not remain present. Although this hasn't been applied to a grooming context, enough similarities exist to suggest a parallel.[3]	• Owners should stay for the grooming session. • If planning to leave the dog with the groomer, non-grooming familiarisation should be done. • Employ groomers who can come to the clients' home.
The presence of unfamiliar dogs: Multi-dog salons will typically either use a rolling schedule for arrival or intake all the session's dogs at the same time. The dogs, who are unlikely to be familiar with each other, are often crated or tethered in close proximity, which does not allow them to use body language signals and give each other space to lower the risk of anxiety and aggression.	• Visual barriers and space between individual dogs if waiting can be incorporated into the design of the premises. • 1-2-1 grooming. • Create calm areas for waiting. • Provide a piece of the dog's own bedding in their resting area, which will smell familiar to them. • Provide something simple for the dog to chew or lick away from direct proximity of others.
Scent: There are multiple reasons why the grooming parlour is an area of potential stress for dogs. Dogs have a delicate and sensitive olfactory system that can identify dilutions 1 part per trillion and potentially even in excess of that.[4] The raised temperature and humidity created by bathing and drying will increase odour volatility of chemical products and detergents, many of which are highly perfumed to appeal to human preferences and to create scent that will linger for days or weeks. In addition, all dogs and people will be generating odour, whether this is pheromones giving deliberate information or the constant chemical changes in the body particularly while anxious or excited.	• Ventilation – use fresh air flow rather than scented products to cover any 'bad' smells. • Use unscented or neutral products both in the environment and on the dog's body. • Ensure a calm environment both for dogs and people. Avoid stress caused by time pressures, overbooking, missing breaks and pain (feeling hungry, thirsty, needing the loo).
Being picked up/lifted: Even when being lifted in a way that does not put undue pressure on the body or cause discomfort, being picked up removes the dog's autonomy and can impact on their ability to feel secure. Being picked up usually involves the human first bending over them and enclosing with their arms. In unpublished work, this has been shown to elevate the dog's heart rate even when done by a familiar contact.[5]	• Use ramps or steps for the dog to walk onto the table or into the bath. • Practice putting the dog's front paws up on the raised area so the dog is able to control when the lifting process happens.

Table 9.1 (continued)

Potentially negative element of the grooming process	Solutions
Restraints: The majority of groomers use some means of restraint whilst grooming. Straps around the dog's neck and abdomen that fix to overhead bars on the table are an industry standard. Some have adaptions that further reduce movement and wide straps that increase the amount of support that can be applied underneath the dog to the extent that a small dog can be suspended with their feet off the ground. Dividers prevent the dog from moving away from the groomer. Muzzles worn for part or all of the session are used for protection from bites. Restraint is often taught as necessary for safety (of dog and groomer) but it is clear that being restrained during intimidating, scary or uncomfortable procedures has a detrimental effect on an individual's sense of safety. There can be pressure to 'get the groom done', sometimes with costs. A team approach between the caregiver and all the professionals who are part of the dog's life, enables alternative ways for necessary procedures to be carried out while minimising the trauma caused. Grooming could be completed while at the vets under sedation, clipping the coat off and cutting nails, allowing a few months in which to work through a behaviour modification program to alter the emotional response to grooming. This approach requires the vet, trainer/behaviourist, groomer and owner to all be active parts of the process. Local professional networks are key to improving welfare standards. Improved knowledge of body language and communication.	• Respect the dog's body autonomy. • Use a Y-fronted harness if a restraint must be used, such as with a higher table position for small dogs or a high sided bath. Avoid any pressure to the neck area and the abdomen. • Allow sufficient time for rest breaks when the dog requires them through the session to minimise the elevation of stress levels. • Set the table at a lower level so the dog can safely step or jump down to the floor. • Provide a clear route on and off the table for the dog. • Groomer to sit while in close proximity, this lowers the body position and prevents looming over the dog. • Coordinate with other professionals to find solutions. • Manage human expectations: a relaxed dog is more important than an aesthetically pleasing groom.
Unstable/slippery surface: The dogs often have to stand on tables that raise and lower to 90–150 cm off the ground commonly by the means of either foot pumped hydraulics or by an electric motor, and in baths whilst water and slippery products are poured over. If the dog's body is relaxed, there is usually sufficient grip on the hard rubber matting to prevent slipping. However, if a dog is fearful and clenches their feet trying to feel more secure, they risk losing their footing leading to the risk of falling and more anxiety.	• Keep the table as low as possible or groom on the ground. • Add softer matting, such as non-slip mats, yoga mats or towels, which enable the dog's nails to grip. • Ensure the surface the dog is being asked to stand on is secure and does not wobble.

the owner, where the therapist is ground based so as not to be leaning over the dog would be most ideal for the majority.

Where it is necessary for the dog to be stationary or even moderately stationary for elements of the treatment, it may be helpful to prepare the dog for this by creating some positive, calm experiences in the presence of a chosen signal such as a yoga mat, or clearly patterned beach towel, that can be laid on the floor as a signal that a physically still experience is about to occur. Studies have shown that dogs pay more attention to visual signals than auditory ones, and perhaps even greater attention to scents. Putting a scent on the mat or towel (such as a few drops of vanilla essence or a few drops of rose water) may help them associate the signal more clearly with the ensuing experience. Note the authors do not recommend the use of essential oils for this as they produce a strong odour that may be overwhelming to the sensitive dog nose, this will be covered later in this chapter with respect to inhalation and ingestion-based therapies. The signal should only be brought out at times when the dog is already calm, to be quietly laid down in a calm room, and then if the owner sits next to or on the signal itself, to spend time stroking, gently massaging, grooming the dog while talking in a relaxed, reassuring tone to the dog for a period of minutes. If the dog shows no interest in being calm with the owner at that time, then the signal gets put away and brought back out at a more appropriate time. If the dog falls asleep during the session, then the owner can wait until the dog gets up from rest by themselves or can quietly move away from the dog and observe when the dog is ready to get up, then remove the signal at that time. If the dog remains awake for several minutes of positive interaction, the owner can use a phrase such as 'we're done' and then casually get up themselves, remove the signal and

then go with the dog to find something more active but still positive and calm for the dog to do, such as an edible chew toy or frozen food toy, or some smells to find in a toy box or garden.

The signal should not remain on the floor or anywhere detectable by the dog outside of these calm, positive intervals. Research has shown calm, positive social interactions such as these can be associated with the release of the positive social hormone oxytocin, as well as reductions in stress chemistry and improved heart rate variability (a measure of reduced stress).

The owner can then get the signal out at home, once the therapist has arrived, been introduced and is settling ready for treatment if the dog's treatment is at home, or take with them in a bag, and lay on the floor in the clinic's treatment room, once the dog has arrived, settled and had opportunity to explore the room. Practising calm, positive sessions with the signal at home, should continue perhaps a couple of times a week between physical treatments to 'recharge' its value.

The previous recommendations in this chapter remain important during treatments including: recognition of body language so if the dog becomes anxious, fearful or frustrated the therapist can respond to this by giving the dog a short break and resuming with something the dog is known to find positive; the use of reassuring chat with the owner; treats given to the dog by the owner or therapist from time to time as appropriate; and ending on a positive note with the dog receiving some treats from the therapist and time to explore the room freely.

If the dog is more tense during treatments than would be ideal, allowing the dog time with the owner in the treatment room for reassurance, stroking, treat finding and maybe some gentle play, can be useful as a desensitisation/

trigger reducing procedure before the client and dog leave.

Hydrotherapy

Hydrotherapy is a subcategory of physiotherapy and therefore many elements of the behavioural considerations already discussed, will be relevant. Therapeutic benefits potentially come from the warm water itself, and other benefits include increased cardiovascular activity, strengthened various muscle groups, increased range of motion of certain joints and weight loss from exercise.

Partially or fully immersing a dog in water can be quite scary for them, with one study showing one-third of dogs at one hydrotherapy centre exhibiting likely fear responses at their first swim.[8] Even a dog who will enter water and swim by themselves in natural waters, such as lakes, may appear fearful at a hydrotherapy centre and there can be several reasons for this. First, in the grooming section we discussed the sensitivity of odour detection by the dog. For hygiene reasons, as in human swimming pools, chlorine is often used, predominantly as an antibacterial and antiviral agent. Some centres are now using bromine instead, also an effective antimicrobial. There are some practical differences between chlorine and bromine, including bromine remaining active in the water after interacting with organisms (whereas chlorine becomes inactivated) as well as their effectiveness at different temperatures and when exposed to sunlight. They also differ in cost. Bromine is reportedly less tissue irritant than chlorine so may have positive behavioural effects, however it has a significant odour similar to that of chlorine.

The smell of the centre on arrival may be a deterring, offensive odour to the dog. Allowing time for the dog to relax outside and inside the building would be ideal prior to swimming. Eating treats before swimming is not recommended as the physical exertion of swimming diverts blood flow from the stomach and intestines to the muscles. Eating before such exertion has the potential to cause stomach pain and increase the risk of nausea or vomiting. However, licking small amounts of tasty paste from a dog toy or from a tube, significantly reduces the amount of food consumed so this can be used to offer rewards to dogs while they are settling before entering the pool.

Nganvongpanit and Yano described how swimming in chlorinated pools can lead to a variety of medical concerns including dry hair/skin, skin abrasions, eye inflammation and ear infections.[8] No such studies have yet been reported on the use of bromine in the water. In the UK, the Canine Hydrotherapy Association provides inspections for centres with one of their goals to help minimise these side effects. Rinsing the pool water off the dog after swimming is therefore common, and many therapists may consider the use of shampoo, as in the above section on grooming. The ability of a shampoo, compared with a water rinse, to remove the odour of chlorine from the hair is debatable. In human research, the use of shampoos that contain chlorine binding agents is considered necessary to effectively remove the molecules of chlorine from hair. For behaviourally mindful washing and drying, see the previous section on grooming.

Studies have shown that swimming is a physically demanding activity for the dog, even those that are used to the activity and are physically fit. Swimming has been shown to significantly increase heart rates and production of lactic acid; a by-product of anaerobic (more intense) exercise. Owing to the muscular exertion creating energy, heat rises within the body and dogs are limited in the ways that they can reduce that heat. Nganvongpanit and colleagues showed that swimming at lower temperatures (for example, 25°C) resulted in heat loss from the dog into the water, whereas swimming at 33°C and 37°C, resulted in significant temperature increase as the dog was not able to lose heat into the water.[9] When a dog's temperature is high and when lactic acid is building in the blood stream, the dog will increase the breathing rate, often to include panting with shallow breaths to allow for heat exchange via the airways and to expel more carbon dioxide, which assists breakdown of lactic acid. Cortisol (the main chronic stress hormone) levels also rise during swimming. Swimming is a physical and psychological stressor, given that energy is required for the muscular activity but also remaining buoyant to avoid drowning, and the necessity to work hard to address any rising temperature levels are a priority for the brain and body.

Solutions

As with many other therapy types, being in the presence of a calm, reassuring owner is likely to offset some of the negative emotions felt during the swim. The presence of a therapist in the water with the dog to reassure them, assist with any buoyancy or swimming technique issues, and to monitor the intensity of exertion is highly beneficial.

Regular breaks to allow the dog to put their paws on an in-water surface gives opportunity for temperature and lactic acid reduction, as well as giving them a break from any psychological stressors that are present during the swim.

Some dogs 'panic' or 'excitedly' swim and this increased physical exertion will significantly increase their internal temperature. Keeping swim periods shorter, allowing more frequent, longer breaks as well as considering a slightly lower water temperature (28°C rather

than 31°C) may be appropriate. However, some dogs 'freeze' in the water, offering limited physical exertion out of fear, or due to a medical condition such as paralysis, and the lower water temperatures might be less ideal in these cases.

As with any exercise, warming up and cooling down periods are essential to limit soft tissue strains and to provide adaptive phases for the cardiorespiratory (and arguably, digestive) systems. With the obvious exception of paralysed patients, dogs should be provided with a calm, non-slip surface after the swim to undertake some gentle ambulatory exercise before a car journey home. The inclusion of an enriched environment that the dog can move around in while heart rate, lactic acid levels, temperature etc reduce after the swim and allows some gentle muscle stretching, and calm positive time with the owner, could be considered.

Many hydrotherapy centres now offer water treadmills as part of their service (Figure 9.2). The medical pros and cons of treadmill over 'free' swimming are outside the scope of this book, however, treadmills do offer the benefit of the dog being able to be more in control of their movements, particularly when not accomplished swimmers. Familiarisation of the dog with the ramp and the treadmill, by walking up and through a few times, before the doors are closed and water is slowly added, may suit more anxious dogs. It is also often easier for the owner to lean over the front of the treadmill and reassure or offer rewards to the dog than in free swimming.

In a 2012 publication,[10] vet behaviour scientist Paul McGreevy wrote 'In general, we train dogs with negative reinforcement (NR), positive reinforcement, and punishment. Applying physical pressure-release (NR) and providing reinforcers only when a desired behavior is performed (positive reinforcement) are seldom reported in the canine intraspecific ethogram, so it seems that we generally train dogs with

Figure 9.2: A dog on a water treadmill, the owner is present too. Photo: © Amber Batson.

modalities that have minimal inherent relevance to their social learning ... This may be a significant failing on our part.' For these 'hands-on' therapies and treatments, we should consider the valuable role that observational or social learning can play. Being present while another calm and relaxed dog participates in the activity can offer the opportunity to learn in a more meaningful and species appropriate way. The new dog experiences the sights, sounds and smells of the activity while observing that the familiar dog is taking part willingly and receiving attention and contact. If it is not possible or suitable for another dog to be present, a human may be able to demonstrate taking part in the activity.

Non-physical therapies: senses other than touch

Mostly non-physical therapies include inhalational and ingested treatments. These include pheromone treatments, zoopharmagonosy,

aromatherapy, herbal medicine/phytotherapy and homeopathy including flower essence remedies.

Interview with Karen Webb Dip.IAZ
www.letyouranimallead.co.uk

Some treatment types available for dogs include the inhalation or ingestion of certain 'naturally' occurring compounds, as a zoopharmacognosy therapist, what do you feel is important for dog owners to consider about this process?

The safety and well-being of the dog is paramount and should not be approached without knowledge and understanding of the 'naturally' occurring compounds and the process involved. Zoopharmacognosy is the practice of offering a choice of remedies to the dog for self-selection. Remedies contain the same or similar constituents to those found in the dog's natural environment and include essential oils, absolutes, herbal powders, fixed and macerated oils, algae, vitamins and minerals.

Essential oils are highly volatile medicinal chemicals. A cocktail of chemical constituents and they are potent. They can have a profound influence on emotional, physical and behavioural issues. They must be treated with caution, their constituents understood and their use respected. They must never be forced on a dog. The chosen route of administration might be via the olfactory system (smelling or sniffing including activation of the vomeronasal organ) or orally (ingestion or sublingually or via the buccal membranes). Essential oils can also be topically applied. It is essential that the route of administration is chosen by the dog, not the therapist.

When therapists are considering exposing dogs to various compounds, such as essential oils, distillations or entire plant elements, how would you recommend the behaviour of the dog is considered?

The dog must always be free to walk away from any exposure to essential oils, aromatic waters or hydrosols (distillations) or entire plant elements. They must never be restrained, and no remedy should be forced on the dog in any way whether via the olfactory system, ingestion or being applied topically.

Because of the dog's amazing sense of smell the aromatic molecules from a bottle of essential oil will be smelt by the dog as soon as you start to remove the cap from the bottle. It is important that the essential oils are opened at a safe distance from your dog and not in close proximity to their nose. This allows the dog to come towards the essential oils if they choose to do so. The dog may choose to walk away. It is important that both the therapist and the owner do not dictate through any commands or

signals how they should behave, nor encourage them to come to the essential oil. The dog must be free to choose. Applying a remedy topically should never be done without the consent of the dog. Offering, applying or forcing an essential oil on a dog when it is not needed is unsafe and can be detrimental to the dog.

How does an education in dog body language and behaviour assist you in your treatment of an individual?

To have the knowledge and understanding that enables interpretation of the signals being given by the dog, in order to offer any treatment safely and successfully is crucial. It is also essential that the therapist is aware of their own body postures and movements when interacting with dogs. When offering essential oils, you must be able to determine what is a positive or negative response from the dog. Appreciating the subtle signs the dog may give also requires good observational skills, you are looking at the whole dog not just one part.

A dog's movements or body language signals can indicate their interest in an aroma but signals such as licking their lips with ears drawn back, a slight or distinct head turn, blinking or change in breathing might communicate their dislike. The importance of knowledge and understanding is an absolute requirement for the safety and well-being of the dog.

We have previously identified in this chapter how sensitive the canine nose is to odour. Great care should be paid when introducing pheromones or products like essential oils into the dog's environment. Care should be taken when introducing any inhalational product into the dog's environment, considering whether the dog truly has the ability to move away; an example would be to not apply an inhalational to the bedding of dogs in travel crates, or directly next to sleeping areas such as pens/kennels or crates where the dog has no option to move away. Ensuring the dog has another suitable resting area (warm, familiar, comfortable etc) away from the product creates choice.

The application of odorous products with potential pharmaceutical properties, onto the dog's body or hair coat remains controversial until further safety and behavioural studies are completed.

Dog walkers and pet sitters

Like Bella's family, many dog guardians opt to use dog walkers, playgroups or day care facilities to provide exercise and company for their dogs during working hours or as support during busy times. With good knowledge and management these visits can create a positive social network, positive experiences and enrichment and also enable the family to better balance their needs. However, there are many areas for concern and potential problems.

Dog walking is a largely unregulated profession and there are no recognised routes for qualification. Most companies and individuals will be able to provide a DBS (disclosure and barring service) check and it is common to also have a current animal first aid certificate from a recognised provider together with public liability insurance. The standard financial model of these businesses incentivise dog walkers towards group walks as the fee per dog is typically around £15 for an hour's exercise so when factoring in travel time and overheads it is difficult to meet a minimum wage without catering for multiple dogs. There are differing local authority restrictions on the number of dogs per human guardian while in public spaces.

Dog walkers typically collect the dog from their home while owners are absent and transport them to an area for a period of exercise before returning them home, these journeys can be either solo or with other dogs. Dog walkers might also offer drop-in visits where they visit the house for an agreed length of time during the day and include play, enrichment, grooming or just being company for the dog.

Building a relaxed and calm association with the dog walker entering the home is important for the dog's comfort and the overall safety of all parties. As discussed in the previous section, dogs can often feel conflicted or anxious about having someone enter their home and this may be even more likely while their usual caregivers are not present. To prepare the dog for having a dog walker arriving when the owners are absent, scent introductions can be done as described earlier in this chapter, and then the homeowner and walker can come in together followed by calming activity and relaxation, gradually building a delay between the walker and owner entering until the dog walker enters much in advance of the owner. This would be a way of gently preparing the dog for the walker to arrive on their own, while the dog is alone.

We must also consider how the dogs are transported to the exercise area and consider if this is appropriate for the individual dog. Most commonly this will be in a car or van; stacks of fixed crates are common as well as larger crates, which can house multiple dogs. The noise, presence and odour of other dogs in such close quarters, particularly while confined has the potential to be a significant stressor affecting the level of arousal both during the exercise period and after the dog is returned home. Keeping the social groups familiar and using scent introductions for any new individuals can help – see earlier in this chapter for human scent introduction and then consider using this method for the scent of other dogs too, such as allowing access to bedding another dog has rested on, or a cloth that has been wiped gently on an individual.

Behaviourally minded dog walkers limit the numbers of dogs transported at the same time, have as large as possible distances between dogs and barriers between them, and provide calm activities during and after transport such as sniffing around for some treats, licking or a small edible chew. The dog walker's choice of location and activity will have a huge impact on the dog's emotional and physical well-being as a group or as individuals. Exploring new safe environments with novel stimuli will be enriching to many dogs and a useful part of their socialisation and life experience. Ideally dog walkers will know to avoid sustained fast play and repetitive high-impact activities whether on or off-lead and instead be encouraging sniffing and exploring. Dogs tend to be attracted towards objects in the environment and so if walking in a field where there are not many physical objects, we would expect more frequent bouts of fast movement and for the dogs to be more focused on anything within that area, which would include other animals. Walks in environments such as woodland, however, can increase the number of objects of interest to check out (for example, trees, often with signs from other dogs left on them) and decrease the distance between them. This encourages a slower pace with more exploration closer resembling the activity patterns we see in many free-ranging dog populations.

If group play or running will be taking place, warm-up and cool-down periods should be included; such periods do not have to be 'hands on' but engaging in five minutes of slow gentle movement including bending, stretching and flexing (for example, in searching for treats placed around a log) before going into a large open area can help reduce the risk of physical injuries and foster a healthy emotional state during and after walks.

What happens when the dog is returned back to an empty home also needs consideration. For example, dogs might be crated or returned to an area in the house, they might need to be washed or dried before being left, the walker might need to provide fresh water or food/chews, the dog might not be comfortable being left again – all of which could be done with behaviour in mind or not. These factors all impact on the dog's ability to relax and sleep following their walk.

Day care premises are regulated under the Animal Welfare Regulations 2018 in the UK. This care is usually provided on a half-day or full-day basis and involves multiple dogs. The best day care providers have a high ratio of staff to dogs, it is vital that the staff's primary role is to be present and interacting in a positive caregiving way with the dogs.

Arriving at and departing day care providers are points of potential difficulty. How the dogs join or leave a larger group of dogs even when they are familiar to each other is an important consideration. There are several ways to ease this process. If it is a new introduction, the dogs' scent can be exchanged by allowing the new dog to sniff and mark around an area that the others can then investigate followed by visual meetings such as parallel walking on a loose lead or walking at safe distance (the minimum distance that all dogs are able to still engage in calm behaviours). Next, an individual meeting is needed to allow dogs to engage in species appropriate communication including: approaching on a curve, pausing to turn away, sniffing the ground, peeing and so on followed by introducing a second dog before merging the groups once relaxed and calm. A period of calming activity can be helpful after greetings take place, such as sniffing, licking or chewing.

As in the previous section, the range of activities chosen by the day care provider ideally will mimic what has been observed in free-ranging dog societies, such as exploring novel stimuli, sniffing, climbing or watching; this encourages curiosity and mental engagement while minimising anaerobic activity and high arousal. Day carers can provide scented articles of interest that change every few days, they can regularly rotate toys and objects, play soft ambient music and natural sounds. They can provide objects for proprioceptive stimulation such as different surfaces to step on and dig at, platforms, slopes and corners to negotiate or things of visual interest that have elements of movement.

Rest and sleep are critical parts of successful day care as dogs require multiple sleep periods through the day and night in order to maintain a healthy brain and healthy bodily functions. Offering a wide choice and multiple locations of resting areas, including elevated areas, a choice of surfaces, temperatures and aspects will help dogs to be able to take the sleep they need. A structured approach to the day is a useful way to achieve this; by following the main activities with opportunities to chew or have a filled toy such as a Toppl® or Kong™, the day care can increase the probability of periods of calm rest and sleep.

Dog walkers and day care staff need an excellent standard of education in dog communication and behaviour, both for the day-to-day care and management but also, as we see in Bella's situation, to avoid misinterpretation of responses, which can contribute to a delay in the investigation, diagnosis and treatment of injuries and can lead to incorrect labelling of behavioural problems.

Dog walking fields and enrichment centres

The opportunity to exercise and spend time with a dog, off-lead, without the possible interruption from other people, other dogs or traffic can be a benefit in behaviour modification programmes, in training without distraction and just an opportunity for relaxing, social exploration and play, away from the owner's own home.

There is no doubt that one of the main reasons owners choose to use a private dog walking field is to avoid stimuli that are known triggers or antecedents for undesirable behaviours in their dog.

Our young female Bella has started to show the undesirable behaviours of snapping and growling at other dogs approaching her when out on walks. The motivation for these behaviours needs consideration and would need assessing by a professional. Issues could include pain in her body (as was diagnosed in her case), fear from previous negative experiences, fear from under socialisation at a younger age, hormonal changes related to reproductive cycling or a physiological phantom pregnancy (see Chapter 8), fear from an inability to use avoidance behaviours if on a short leash and so on. While the underlying motivations are considered and addressed, avoiding approach by other dogs to prevent further negative experiences, and avoiding inducing stress responses to prevent Bella from practising the undesired behaviours will be helpful to future behaviour modification. The use of local private dog walking fields can be part of this, along with contacting friends, neighbours or family that may allow Bella to use their private gardens for exploration and exercise. Choosing different times of day, quiet public locations, will make this practical and affordable.

When considering what type of field to use, or when setting up a private field as a business,

Dog Walking Fields online directory was set up by yourself in 2014. Can you explain how it came about?

I set up my own field in Chertsey, Surrey in 2012 (Field of Freedom) having spent many years discussing the idea with my great friend Celia Felstead. We wanted to find a field to rent to give our own dogs a safe space to move freely around off-lead, without the worry of meeting any other dogs and thought that other dog owners may be interested in this opportunity as well.

I wanted to find out if there were any similar fields, or public enclosed fields, where I could take my dogs, to run off-lead safely in other parts of the country. So, 2 years later, I asked the question on social media and invited people to share the locations of anywhere they knew, so others could also benefit. Many people said of my field, 'Oh I wish there was somewhere like this near me!' This was how the Dog Walking Fields directory began in 2014.

I began to contact owners of privately owned facilities to ask if they would like to have the location of their fields published. I became overwhelmed with the response and sharing locations on a county-by-county basis was not enough, we needed a directory. I was joined by Jo, a volunteer who created a database and a pin map and then in 2016, Samantha Bailey joined, built and hosted a basic website and this grew into the website directory and searchable map we have now.

We maintain the ethos of sharing knowledge and keeping the resource freely accessible to all. Each field has a free listing on the website and anyone searching can look them up on by area. Fields are advertised on all the social media platforms.

What do you feel are the benefits of a field that a person can have sole use of, while walking their dog?

There are many.

- Reduction in stress and anxiety for owner and dog. They can relax with no need to scan the horizon for approaching dogs/people if their dog is reactive.
- A safe, uninterrupted place to train off-lead and practice recall, or meet up for a 1-2-1 session with a behaviourist or trainer.
- Local rescue centres use the fields to give their dogs a break from the stress of kennels.
- Newly acquired foster or rescue dogs can be assessed in an open environment and safely introduced to the family and/or their existing dog on neutral territory. Many overseas rescue dogs seem to have a need to escape from enclosures when they first arrive, especially if they have been free-ranging street dogs or confined in a shelter.
- The fields provide somewhere all the family can visit together and enjoy peaceful time with the dog. They can be really helpful for families with young children where walking the dog in a public place with children can be overwhelming.
- Disabled, elderly, arthritic dogs, or those on restricted exercise (if they have had surgery, for example) such as post-surgery, can amble around without fear of getting lost, or being injured by more exuberant dogs.

- Danger of livestock chasing is removed.
- Owners of dogs who are on the Index of Exempted Dogs (Dangerous Dogs Act) who must keep their dogs muzzled and on a lead in public can allow them to run freely without, as it is private land (the suitability of doing this can vary from field to field and is affected by an individual field's insurance so business and dog owners should check with their insurance company).

How popular are the fields?

The fields are extremely popular – it is not unusual for fields to be booked weeks in advance and many people visit at least once a week. There has been an average of 100 new listings on our website per year. Currently [12/03/21], there are 630 UK wide. There is a huge demand and with increasing dog ownership throughout the Covid-19 pandemic, it would seem likely demand will continue to rise.

Dogs with reactivity issues to people or other dogs seem to make up a large percentage of the reason why people choose to use the fields. This gives people the opportunity to relax on their walk, but also importantly the opportunity to avoid further negative encounters (such as 'friendly' dogs running at them on public walks) while working with a professional to resolve the problem. Property development also creates a concentration of people and dogs with less space to walk.

Some public areas in England and Wales are covered by Public Spaces Protection Orders (PSPOs) – previously called Dog Control Orders (DCOs). These restrict where and how many dogs can be exercised off-lead. Off-lead exercise is being squeezed into smaller areas.

Is there much variety in what an individual field may offer?

Yes, they are all different. Some are flat with no obstacles. Some have agility equipment, or natural obstacles to climb, jump over and sniff. Some have indoor and outdoor enrichment areas, sensory gardens, woodland, long grass, short grass, lakes, streams, paddling pools, sandpits for digging, some even have mini self-service cafes, dog wash/bathing sections and picnic areas. Most have seating, shelter and toilets for humans. Water, poo bins and bags are usually provided. There might be parking for several cars or there may be none. Some have high fencing (6+ feet) and some have lower fencing, some are less than 1 acre and some are larger than 15 acres.

If someone was thinking of opening a field like this as a business, what advice would you give them?

Read the FAQs on our website and join our networking group on Facebook for advice from others who have been through the process. It is still a fairly new and niche business and we are all learning as we go along. Planning permission will probably be required (for a change of use and/or to run a business from the site) and they will need public liability insurance.

Work in harmony with any other similar business in your area, do not try to compete, or copy them, nobody likes that, rather try to provide something different. Dog owners like to have a choice of venue, it is a day out for some, more than just exercising the dog. Variety is key. There is no governing body or trade association, you have to follow your own code of practice, and make your own decisions, although we are a supportive community.

some useful behaviour considerations would include the following.

- The security and height of the fencing.
- Whether booking management is set up in such a way as to avoid the sights and sounds of other dogs or people arriving? Many, but not all, fields provide a gap between one person's session finishing and the next person's starting so that no other people or dogs are in sight when loading and unloading your dog. Field users should be respectful of other people's sessions and have a plan about where to wait away from the field should they arrive early, and to set an alarm or 'clock watch' to ensure they do not overrun in the use of their slot. Remember people use the fields for different reasons, many field users are working hard to resolve issues with their pets and appreciate the space these fields offer to help achieve that.
- Consider the space and facilities you would like. Some businesses offer enrichment areas such as paths through longer grass, tunnels, platforms, different paths and ponds. Many dogs benefit from enriched spaces but open areas may be helpful to others.
- Repetitive activities, such as repeated ball throwing and chasing, have been associated with the development of joint disease, particularly hip and elbow arthritis.[11] Sliding and stopping or repeated jumping activities probably have a great impact on joint loading to influence degenerative joint change. For both medical and behavioural benefits, interspersing faster activities with slower ones is probably most beneficial.
- Choosing a field that offers a mix of activities or taking items with you (such as using it as an opportunity for a 'backpack' walk concept courtesy of Steve Mann, IMDT) are worth considering.

Final thoughts

In conclusion, there are many ways in which dog professionals can run their businesses with canine behaviour in mind and in doing so improve the service provided and its value to the dog and owner. Further education in understanding and responding to canine body language and actions is invaluable in improving the relationship between professional and pet dog. The value of careful introductions also, cannot be underestimated. There are huge benefits in creating a support 'village' for dog owners in both the physical and emotional elements of providing care. Dog professionals are the key to this.

We hope this chapter has provided some simple practical ideas to benefit both the dogs and the professionals.

References

1. Reid, P.J. (2019) Treatment of emotional distress and disorders – nonpharmacologic methods. In: McMillan, F.D. (ed.) *Mental Health and Well-being in Animals*. CABI, Wallingford, pp. 345–363.
2. Riemer, S., Heritier, C., Windschnurer, I., Pratsch, L., Arhant, C. and Affenzeller, N. (2021) A review on mitigating fear and aggression in dogs and cats in a veterinary setting. *Animals* 11(1), 158.
3. Stellato, A.C., Dewey, C.E., Widowski, T.M. and Niel, L. (2020) Evaluation of associations between owner presence and indicators of fear in dogs during routine veterinary examinations. *Journal of the American Veterinary Medical Association* 257(10), 1031–1040.
4. Angle, C. et al. (2016) Canine detection of the volatilome: a review of implications for pathogen and disease detection. *Frontiers in Veterinary Science* 3(47).
5. The Dog Pulse Project (n.d.) http://www.dogpulse.org (accessed 30 May 2021).
6. RCVS (2014) A statement on anaesthesia free dental procedures for cats and dogs. www.rcvs.org.uk/document-library/a-statement-on-an

aesthesia-free-dental-procedures-for-cats-dogs (accessed 13 April 2021).

7. Bragg, R.F., Bennett, J.S., Cummings, A. and Quimby, J.M. (2015) Evaluation of the effects of hospital visit stress on physiologic variables in dogs. *Journal of the American Veterinary Medical Association* 246(2), 212–215.

8. Nganvongpanit, K. and Yano, T. (2012) Side effects in 412 dogs from swimming in a chlorinated swimming pool. *The Thai Journal of Veterinary Medicine* 42(3), 281.

9. Nganvongpanit, K., Boonchai, T. and Taothong, O. (2014) Physiological effects of water temperatures in swimming toy breed dogs. *Kafkas Univ Vet Fak Deg*, 20, 177–183.

10. McGreevy, P.D., Starling, M., Branson, N.J., Cobb, M.L. and Calnon, D. (2012) An overview of the dog–human dyad and ethograms within it. *Journal of Veterinary Behavior* 7(2), 103–117.

11. Anderson, K.L., Zulch, H., O'Neill, D.G., Meeson, R.L. and Collins, L.M. (2020) Risk factors for canine osteoarthritis and its predisposing arthropathies: a systematic review. *Frontiers in Veterinary Science* 7, 220.

Chapter 10

Assistance dogs

Nina Bondarenko

Since I began training assistance dogs during the late 1970s in Australia, the practice of utilising dogs to help people live better lives has grown exponentially throughout the world. Now, assistance dogs are commonly seen in public – helping people with mobility, alerting hearing-impaired people to sounds, and now alerting and supporting people in medical emergencies. Articles in the press and on digital media are constantly citing the value of these dogs for the help they give to people in ways that cannot be replicated by equipment. Many studies have concluded that dogs are invaluable for the mental and emotional benefits they offer people, whether assisting someone in daily life or visiting care facilities and hospitals as therapy dogs. In fact, the key justification for using dogs to assist people has been the many ways in which assistance and therapy dogs can improve a person's quality of life.

Having run many residential training courses for placing assistance dogs with their human partners, I know very well the unique ways that dogs can do what no machine or piece of equipment could. Dogs 'live in the present' and this can really help a person who is living with a long-term debilitating illness or condition. Dogs are thrilled to wake up in the morning and greet each day with enthusiasm and a wagging tail! If you are used to thinking about how difficult your life is now and how it will only get worse, not better, a dog's attitude can be very comforting. Many of my clients have described how they stop thinking about their condition and focus on working with and managing their canine partner and this helps to lift depression and keeps them focused on immediate tasks, rather than dwelling on the past or worrying about the future. Also, because people need to use non-habitual actions in order to train and exercise their dogs, their health and fitness frequently improves, so that they then feel more positive about life. When you are playing with the dog you frequently twist and turn and move and use muscles that you do not normally use. And because you are playing with the dog, you are enthusiastic and relaxed and enjoying it. It is not forced exercise or fitness training for you – just an enjoyable activity that you can share with your dog.

When I was first training these dogs, I had no idea about their inventiveness and cleverness but also I had totally underappreciated the wide range of ways in which they can help people emotionally as well as physically. Studies talk about how assistance dogs get people with disabilities out into the street and out into the community, and how people will now come up to them to talk to them about their dog; they then get to know their neighbours and develop an enriched social group and social community. It also breaks down the barriers for people who might be frightened of talking to someone with a disability. While this social interaction might be true of anybody who owns a dog, nevertheless the hidden benefits of the emotional responsiveness and interactivity of dogs

The dog who changed his owner's mind

I remember on one course, a client with multiple sclerosis had come to me on the first night after the day's training and announced that he was giving up and going home. When I asked him why, he said that he had been watching the videos of the training and he was painfully reminded of how disabled he now was. He said he was shocked and despairing as he watched himself struggling to do things during the day. Because he lived alone and had a very restricted routine, he was not confronted by the weakening of his condition. I tried to chat to him and encourage him to stay on longer and just give it a go but he was very upset and he really wanted to go home.

The next morning, he came in with a big grin on his face. I said to him 'You look like you are prepared to stay here on the course. What happened?' He laughed and he said 'that dog of mine is such a clown – he has made me laugh all night! He has picked up his bowl and put it on his head. He has dragged his bed over and put it next to me and then climbed underneath it! He has skipped around the room pulled faces and tossed me his toys for me to play with him – I haven't laughed so much for ages. I couldn't possibly part with this dog now!'

with their owners are far more remarkable. It is only recently, however, that some new studies have focused on the impact that this work has on the dogs themselves, and questions have started to be asked about the welfare of assistance dogs. This has led to questions about training methods and assumptions about how and why dogs should help people.

In this chapter, I share my experiences of decades of work in this field with many case studies described throughout.

Training assistance dogs

It was at one of the early Assistance Dogs International (ADI) conferences[1] that I saw fully trained and certified assistance dogs (referred to as 'Service Dogs' in the USA) wearing electric shock collars and/or choker chains or prong collars. This was startling and completely unexpected for me because I had set up the training programme for all puppies, dogs and people at Canine Partners (UK) (called Assistance Dogs for Disabled People at that time) based on errorless learning principles, positive reinforcement and training with behaviour in mind. All our puppies worked eagerly and never needed to be forced to comply or obey. In fact, many people at the time commented on how 'happy' our dogs appeared to be while working.

At the conference, I met various attendees with their service dogs and I asked them why they needed an electric collar. They explained that the dogs would frequently disobey without it, and that the dogs typically needed to go back to the training facility for 'refresher courses'. Several of the attendees had conditions such as cerebral palsy, which causes muscle tremors and coordination difficulties – electric and prong collars require precise timing in order to deliver the desired information to the dog about his/her behaviour so I was especially concerned about the mental welfare of the dogs in this situation.

I discussed this with several service dog users, and they all stated the same thing – 'A dog must obey on the first command.' When I asked them why, they would typically respond either that a dog is dog and must obey the pack leader or that a human life depended upon it. I questioned if it was ethical to put the responsibility of a human life on a non-verbal animal of a different species in order to justify the use of punitive equipment and aversive methods. Especially since dogs were considered to be the mental and emotional equivalent of a three-year-old child. But they just reiterated the point that dogs must 'serve people'.

Benny

On my return to the UK, I did a home visit and check-up on one of our recently placed dogs. Benny was a young Golden Retriever partnered with Eric who used a power wheelchair with neck and wrist support. He always kept his mobile phone on his tray so that he could call his emergency contact if necessary. The day before I visited, he had been working at his computer and Benny was lying outside in the sun chewing a bone Eric had just given him. Suddenly Eric's arm went into spasm and knocked his phone onto the floor. Eric was about to call Benny to pick it up but he could see the dog was having a lovely time in the garden. So, Eric decided to wait a while and let the dog relax before interrupting him. Suddenly Benny appeared beside his chair, and gently put the bone onto his lap. The dog then reached down, picked up the phone and replaced it onto Eric's desk. Then he picked up the bone from Eric's lap and trotted outside again! Eric was in tears while using the phone to call me – telling me how grateful he was and how in awe of this little dog he felt. No commands were given but Benny was highly motivated to be of assistance thanks to the positive training he had received, and therefore the work itself had become reinforcing to him. He does it because he enjoys it and the intensity of the emotional response from Eric is better than any treat.

This is why I was so baffled at the thought of dogs refusing to assist and especially with the idea that they needed to constantly return to the training centre to be 'reminded' how to obey. All our puppies, like Benny, had been taught to bring dropped items and we randomly phased out verbal cues during the training. This helped the puppies to see the dropped item as

Figure 10.1(a–c): Dogs can learn to help with the washing. Photos: © Dawn Rayment.

the cue. But Benny took it a step further – he was relaxing in the sun chewing on a new bone when he heard the phone drop in the house, and yet he was still very willing to stop what he was doing and voluntarily find the phone and return it to Eric. And I delighted in the way he handed over the bone to Eric for safe keeping while he fulfilled his mission.

This willing response in situations that were never encountered by the dogs in training was typical of the dogs we trained using positive reinforcement methods. The dogs were not slaves or 'tools' to be used by the person but were willing partners – hence the name of the charity Canine Partners. Through the training they learned component behaviours, such as holding something, or tugging something or using their nose or paws to press or pull something. Then they were given little puzzles to solve such as 'how to open the washing machine door' or 'unzip a jacket'. The dogs could develop their own strategy for doing every task so that, when faced with something unexpected or completely unfamiliar they could be confident to try different approaches until the goal was achieved. So long as the human partner was able to reciprocate with appropriate feedback and praise, the dogs would strive to be successful.

Ajax

In fact, on one occasion I received a phone call from another of our partnerships. In this case, Steve had the deteriorating condition of multiple sclerosis, which impacted on all aspects of his mobility and dexterity. He was always dropping things because the signals from hand to brain were being impaired so his dog, Ajax, frequently had to pick up the same item several times in a row before Steve could keep hold of it. (I was always amazed at the fact that our dogs would willingly do this because it could be considered technically 'punishing' to ask

the dog to repeat a task that they had already completed correctly.) On this particular occasion, Steve had lost most of his hand control and was simply unable to get hold of the mobile that Ajax was handing to him. Bear in mind that to carry out the task, Ajax had to find the dropped item, pick it up, place his forelegs on Steve's knees, and reach forward with his head to find Steve's hands in order to place the item into them.

This was repeated four or five times and Steve became very distressed. He believed that if he could no longer take the dropped items, then he would not be eligible to keep his beloved dog. Meanwhile Ajax was standing up, forefeet on Steve's lap, patiently holding the phone. Suddenly the dog cocked his head, stared at Steve's face and then carefully leaned forward and pushed the mobile into Steve's mouth! By taking the weight of the phone in his mouth, Steve was able to hold onto his mobile long enough to be able to manoeuvre it into his hands and hold it. He burst into tears of delight and relief and promptly phoned me to tell me the extraordinary story. After this, Ajax always placed the phone in Steve's mouth unless he held out his hands first. On 'good days' Steve had enough control over his hands to take the phone but on days when he was struggling, the dog just adapted unhesitatingly. The interesting aspect about all this is that, from a trainer's point of view, I would have presumed initially that Steve was correct in his assumption that we could no longer justify leaving the dog with him if he could not take hold of items that the dog handed him! I could not have imagined what else we could teach the dog to do instead of placing the items in Steve's hands – Ajax showed more creative imagination than me.

We had developed training exercises to teach the dogs to always 'find the hands'. This was in the event that the dog was placed with people whose hands might not be in their laps. For example, thalidomide survivors might have their hand coming directly out of their shoulder, and some people have paralysed hands or arms that tend to be in a position such as under their heart. We had never thought of how a dog might help someone who did not have the strength or control in their hands to keep hold of the wallet, purse, phone, or remote control. More importantly, had we taught the dogs to just obey without question, it would have been impossible for Ajax to try something different. It was because Ajax was taught to be flexible and creative during training that he was able to figure out a solution to the changing circumstances and to find a different way of fulfilling the retrieve exercise. In order to do this the dog had to visualise the aim and the ultimate objective for the retrieval exercise. The ultimate aim is for the person to hold the object and keep it – the dog has to understand that it is not enough just to put an item on the person's lap or their hand. Ajax understood that Steve needed to take hold of the phone and keep hold of it, before the task could be considered complete.

Where and when do dogs acquire such understanding?

If we cannot visualise a potential situation, then as trainers we cannot train for it. When I first started training dogs to assist disabled people, I tried to find out from them all the different situations that they might encounter so that we could prepare the dogs appropriately. But just as they cannot imagine all the different scenarios, neither could we. So as soon as we encountered a new situation, we would start training the dogs appropriately. The dogs were the same – they would encounter something unexpected or new, and modify

their behaviour accordingly; relying on feedback from their owners to inform them of the correctness or otherwise of their choices.

A significant part of the training on the residential course for the disabled people who were learning to work with their trained assistance dogs, was how to reward and reinforce all desirable behaviours. The residents on the course were taught to use whatever rewards worked best for their particular dog and were then taught gradations or levels of reinforcement and were trained how and when to use a specific reward and at what level. Level 1 was the minimum pressure, food reward, sound or movement and Level 10 was the most exuberant, full-on enthusiastic intensity of praise or touch, or most delicious high-value food. For example, to use touch as a reward they were taught to touch very lightly with the fingertips if possible or hand if lacking finger dexterity. Or to touch with a gentle stroking motion. Or to touch with a 'pat, pat, pat' motion. Or to do long stroking, slightly pressing, rubs. Or to pet vigorously on the back and over the hind quarters. Tellington Touch or TTouch was taught to those whose hands were sufficiently mobile to be able to carry out the actions of at least the basic circles so they could reward their dogs specifically and appropriately. (Pronounced [TEE-touch], the Tellington TTouch Method is a training system that uses bodywork and non-habitual movement to influence behaviour and health.)

Food rewards were also taught in the same way. Low-value food such as the normal kibble was used to randomly reinforce a routine behaviour, such as to sit or 'go to your mat'. Very high-value novel food items were used during teaching sessions for new or challenging behaviours or to reward the dog for responding well under distractions. Clients were taught to use different types of food rewards as well as other rewards in the most appropriate way for their own particular dog. One of the criteria for accepting an applicant onto the course was that they needed to demonstrate that they were able to positively reinforce and reward a dog consistently.

Clients are also taught what not to use as rewards. For example, many people are inclined to grab a dog and hold them around the neck to hug them. Although some dogs can tolerate and even enjoy this, many dogs find it very stressful and show avoidance behaviour. This of course can be very detrimental to the relationship and can mean that the dog starts to avoid the person and hang back away from them. We help people to practice ways to demonstrate their love and gratitude that are suited to their particular dog. Our training programme was focused on teaching clients to understand how dogs learn and how they perceive the world, so that they could support their dog as much as possible.

The dog training literature is still full of references to the idea that a dog must be trained to obey without question or resistance, especially in the field of assistance and therapy dogs because people living with disability are vulnerable. The reasoning is that the dogs must comply reliably and unquestioningly because the person's safety and well-being is the dog's responsibility. But from where did this idea of dog's obedience to humans come? Early dog training literature came predominantly from police and military trainers such as Konrad Most,[2] William Koehler[3] and others and from sheepdog trainers who needed the dogs to chase sheep but not bite or kill them and selectively bred dogs that would be compliant in this way. However, people are increasingly questioning and challenging this idea that dogs can and should be forced to comply and to obey without question and the last two decades have seen a significant increase in the popularity of reward-based methods of training and in people seeking relationships with dogs that reflect a changing societal attitude towards understanding their behaviour. The use of aversive dog training methods and equipment is being closely examined and we can no longer rely upon an individual's opinion or belief system. Instead, we need to access the latest research into behaviour, positive reinforcement and behaviour modification systems based upon the LIMA protocol[4] (LIMA stands for least intrusive minimally aversive) 'a set of humane and effective tactics likely to succeed in achieving a training or behaviour change objective'. The work done by Dr Susan Friedman (BehaviorWorks. org) based upon applied behaviour analysis (ABA) and ethical standards has now become the framework within which many trainers and behaviourists and assistance and therapy dog trainers now operate. This is very encouraging for the future of assistance dog training throughout the world.

Back-chaining

A key process used to train assistance dogs is back-chaining and/or 'component behaviours' and we should mention it here. Back-chaining is a process by which a dog is taught the final step of a sequence (or chain) of behaviours first, and then preceding steps are added until all the steps that lead up to the final step in the sequence have been learned. For example, to teach a dog to push the footplates down on a wheelchair, we might start with the footplate almost down but not quite. All the dog must do is to paw at the plate and it will lock into position – in other words the final step of the sequence of pushing a footplate down. The dog is immediately successful and is rewarded for this action. Then the plate might be elevated another few inches and the dog is reinforced for pushing the plate down till it locks or clicks. When the dog is fluently pushing the plate down from halfway, we will

Figure 10.2: Dogs can learn to pick up litter, carry it and put it in a bin through back-chaining. Photo: © Natalie Light.

to use their nose to push rather than paws to pull. Target training in puppy class will have taught each dog to use a nose to push or press, so that makes it more likely that the dog will use this action as a default but, if necessary, we could give a target cue for the dog to push the footplate forward until it cannot go any further. If we just left it up to the dog to try to work out what was required, the dog would be likely to pull down on the footplate, since that action and behaviour had been reinforced many times previously during the training to push the footplate down.

By standing the dog, we change the 'picture of the problem' for the dog and make it highly likely that the dog will choose an appropriate action that we can reinforce. Once again, by back-chaining, we can gradually lower the footplate until the dog can crouch down and use their nose to nudge the footplate up enough to be pushed into the upright position. Also, this helps the dog to recognise the difference between pushing up and pulling down, simply by whether the dog is standing or sitting. This position can be an additional cue to the dog as to what might be expected in solving a problem.

Another example of back-chaining is teaching a dog to retrieve an item and place it in a person's hand. Most people begin by tossing a toy or ball and then calling the dog to them, hoping that the dog will bring the ball as it returns. However, this does not make clear to the dog that we require the item to be placed in a hand, or on a lap, on a table or counter or in a basket. It also relies upon the dog's individual interest in balls and toys and any inherent desire to bring an item to a person. Dogs might be highly inclined to bring back a ball to be thrown again but show very little interest in bringing a set of keys, a mobile phone or a remote control, for example. Rather than relying upon the dog's interest in playing with a ball, we

then lift up the plate to just above the dog's paws. The dog now has to pull at the plate in order to get it into position so that it can be pushed down. Once the dog understands the requirement to get the plate fully down, it can problem solve and work out the best way to get at the plate while it is upright. So, the action of pawing at a plate, pulling it outwards and then pushing it downwards until it locks into place is back-chained. This is a form of 'errorless learning'.

Component behaviours (in this case sitting and pawing at a footplate, pulling the footplate towards the dog, and then pressing down on the footplate) are used to achieve the one fluent action of putting down the footplates. When the dog needs to push the footplates up so that the person can exit the wheelchair, we would need to start at the opposite end of the sequence – in this case we would start with the dog standing and facing the footplates, not lying down or sitting since this would encourage the dog can back-chain a retrieve so that the dog is absolutely clear about the ultimate aim of the exercise – not to play with the item but to find a hand into which to place the item. The final step in a retrieve is that the dog places the item onto an outstretched palm. Later in training, this final step might be to place the item in or on a designated area or position, but that can be part of the generalisation training for the dog. So, to back-chain we would initially teach the dog to drop an item onto an outstretched flat palm. Once the dog is very clear that the aim is to get an item onto the palm to earn reinforcement, then the steps that lead up to that action will be quickly mastered.

The dog will have to learn to hold the item, to hold it while moving, to hold it while distracted or traversing an obstacle course, to hold it while the person's hand is shaking or twitching, and to hold it until the person gives the cue to drop it into the hand. Then the dog has to pick it up from the ground, from on a table or counter, from in a basket or other receptacle or from another person's hand. The key to the dog learning to add on these steps leading to the final action is that the dog knows the aim of the exercise – to get that item into a flat open palm. So, this more complex part of the training can usually proceed swiftly and the dog will gain in confidence and fluency.

And finally, we are now profoundly aware of the importance of giving an animal choice during training. This can be as subtle as pausing the moment that the dog hesitates and waiting to see if the dog will decide to continue with the training or not. If the dog effectively says 'no', then we stop and wait until the dog offers behaviour indicating that they now want to continue with the lesson. This is especially vital when teaching dogs to do things that may be uncomfortable, such as getting teeth cleaned or staying still while children rush around and shout loudly. By giving dogs a clear cue that means 'Do you wish to continue or not?', we can empower them to voluntarily offer behaviours that would be difficult or unethical to coerce.

Dogs need to feel safe in a training environment, and that includes knowing that the environment is predictable and that they have 'agency' within that environment. As someone who has a long-held anxiety while undergoing dental treatment, I can cope and continue with it so long as the dentist allows me a clear signal to stop whenever it gets too uncomfortable. Knowing I can stop it at any time, means that I am more relaxed and calmer and am able to go through treatments more easily and confidently. My anxiety regarding dentists arose from dental treatments as a child when I was forced to endure pain and discomfort without let up. Dogs are the same. Trainers sometimes force dogs to tolerate and accept handling or treatment, but the ethical and humane approach is to teach the dogs that they can offer the behaviour when they are ready and will not be forced to continue training if they are uncomfortable or unsure. This is truly modern enlightened training.

Guiding eyes

Guide dogs or Seeing Eye dogs were the first type of assistance dog and are the most widely recognised of all assistance dogs. People are in awe of the way these dogs lead the unsighted person through the activities of their daily life and they are the most commonly seen assistance dog.

Many people believe that the training involved in developing the skills needed for a dog to guide is the most advanced possible. And it was ground-breaking at the time it began. The history of the Seeing Eye began in Europe in the 1920s when Dorothy Harrison

Eustis moved to Vevey, Switzerland, from the United States to set up a breeding and training facility for German Shepherd dogs, some of which she trained as guide dogs. Different programmes training dogs to guide the blind were set up throughout the world, using a 'blueprint' training programme. And the main breed for the work changed from German Shepherds to include Labradors. However, more recently programmes are experimenting with a wide range of breeds and mixed breeds in order to better fulfil the needs of individual clients. More importantly, the training approach is changing from a standardised pattern used by most facilities to approaches that reflect a wider understanding and acceptance of canine behaviour and cognition as well as individual personalities.

For example, to teach dogs to avoid overhanging obstacles it was considered reasonable training practice for the trainer to deliberately crash into obstacles. The resulting noise and discomfort was considered to be effective feedback for the dog in order to ensure that the dog remained vigilant for any overhanging branches, signs or low doorways. One of the possible fallouts of such an approach is that a dog might become over-sensitised to the need for avoidance and become almost unable to walk down a busy street with overhead signs or scaffolding. When a sight or sound becomes a trigger for avoidance, this can lead to other similar sights or sounds also becoming triggers. This process could escalate to the point where the stress of such encounters would influence the dog to avoid going down the street at all, and therefore be ineffective as a guide dog.

No food or praise was used in training in most of the programmes that I visited throughout the world. I remember having discussions with other trainers many years ago and the argument against using food to reward dogs was that the dog should just 'obey' because many people interpreted the use of food for rewards

as 'bribery'. However, dogs do not naturally chase down criminals or assist disabled people or perform tricks and obedience routines. Many of the tasks that we require of dogs are not part of their normal behavioural repertoire. And so, the motivation to perform all of these different actions would certainly not be internally motivated or in other words something that the dog does because it is a normal and natural expression of canine behaviour. They always need some form of reinforcement for their behaviour; any behaviour that is reinforced will reoccur. Just as 'success is reinforcing' so failure can also be reinforcing. In other words, the more you fail at something the less you will try.

I had by chance seen a young guide dog working in a town where we regularly did training sessions with our assistance dogs. I followed the dog and owner down a complex street situation with twists and turns, building site scaffolding and crowded streets. The dog worked calmly and methodically, negotiating all the obstacles and challenges successfully and the owner remained silent throughout. Then it came to the odd little crossing point that bisected the shopping mall. This crossing point was a road on a curve. Traffic came around a blind corner to four sets of traffic lights. The pedestrian crossing point was very wide so there were two sets of pedestrian crossing buttons on each side of the road. The guide dog owner had several large bags of shopping over her arms. Her dog headed for the nearest buttons and waited for her to press them but she commanded the dog to go forward. The dog hesitated then angled closer to the buttons, but she could not reach them because her bags were in the way. She again commanded in a louder voice, and the dog was clearly stressed about what to do. I stepped closer and said 'Your dog is in front of the buttons' but she just snapped at me 'This is a working dog, don't interfere!' and even more sharply commanded the dog forward. The dog then turned and went sideways to the other set of buttons, but she still could not find them because of her bags. She angrily jerked the harness and shouted at the dog. Meanwhile traffic was coming and going in front of her. Finally, the dog hurried forward across the road (fortunately the car slowed down to let her cross) and guided her to the buttons on the other side of the road. She again shouted at the dog to go forward and they moved off into the next part of the shopping precinct.

What struck me was the fact that she had not said one encouraging or grateful word to the dog during the entire trip, even after the dog got her across that dangerous road. I discussed this later with our trainers. I marvelled at the wonderful work that the dog had done and the high level of training that was involved but remarked, 'I felt sorry for the dog because she should have been very grateful for being taken so safely through such a complex environment.' One of the new team members had previously worked for a guide dog training organisation and she said 'We never use food rewards or praise during training because it distracts the dogs.' At that point, I realised that I could never train dogs or any animals in that way. Even as a young girl I praised our family dog for things he did. When riding horses, I always wanted to stroke and praise them when they were taking me out into the bush, into the sea, across busy roads or indeed wherever I asked them to go. Praising an animal seems to me to be inherently part of the joy of living and working with them.

In one case in Italy, I was working as a consultant with a trainer who had initially worked with an Italian group that trained guide dogs using a great deal of coercion and punishment for 'mistakes'. She decided to set up her own assistance dog training centre based on her study of canine behaviour and positive reinforcement principles and was approached by a woman, Paula, who had previously owned two guide dogs trained using 'traditional methods'. This woman had heard of Daniela's training approach and was keen to have a dog trained in a positive way. Daniela had a young Labrador that was part-way through training so she thought it would be helpful to see how the dog worked with an experienced guide dog handler so she could make any improvements or adjustments in the dog's training. Paula took the handle and the young dog stepped out into the street smoothly. They negotiated obstacles and street crossings and were about to return to the trading centre when Daniela realised that Paula was crying softly. Alarmed, she stopped the dog and asked what was wrong. 'She feels so happy!' was the response from Paula. 'It is a joy to be with this dog. If only it had been like this with my other dogs! They always felt miserable and worried and I hated having to be constantly commanding them.' Daniela instantly knew that she had made the right choice to use positive reinforcement and behaviour shaping principles to teach the young dog how to guide.

I have talked to trainers of dogs used to guide people in different parts of the world, and the one thing they always remarked on was the problem they had with some dogs refusing to guide, or making major, sometimes dangerous, mistakes when guiding. And I remember inviting a guide dog owner with his dog to a bite prevention workshop for children that I was running for a local council. I asked him to demonstrate how his dog helped him to negotiate the room so that some of the young kids in the workshop could overcome any fear of or prejudice towards dogs and become interested in the human–animal bond. To my dismay, the dog took him around the room from rubbish bin to rubbish bin and scavenged for food. I had previously attended various lectures on the raising and training of Seeing Eye dogs and guide dogs in the USA in which they explained that they never use any food as a reward for desirable behaviour or correct responses and the rationale behind this approach was that they did not want the dogs 'distracted by food'. So, there was a dissonance between the aim and actual practice.

During this time, I was using food and other positively associated reinforcers during the training of our assistance dogs, and we did not really have clients calling us for help to stop their dogs' scavenging as they worked in streets and shops or in people's houses. So, I found this opposition to the use of rewards for an animal difficult to understand. However, the good news is that organisations such as Guide Dogs UK no longer work in these outdated ways and are developing training approaches and systems that give a young dog choice during training in order to build up self-confidence in decision making. Rob Ellis (Training and Behaviour Consultant at Guide Dogs UK) outlines the positive changes that are taking place at Guide Dogs UK:

> The key to success for any organisation is to develop a learning culture that adopts change. We are striving to achieve that in Guide Dogs UK. Not only do we want to keep up with the best external professional practice but also we want to share our knowledge with the International Guide Dog Schools and the wider pet community. In order to achieve this we have developed ongoing continuous professional development materials for our staff covering all aspects of training, behaviour and welfare. Our Standardised Training for Excellent Partnerships (STEP) programme consists of 37 different behaviours which are all taught utilising positive reinforcement.

This is an important point. In the 1960s, in Victoria, Australia, I visited the Lady Nell Seeing Eye School for training guide dogs. At that time, they were running an experiment using Dingos – Australian wild dogs – and were raising and training a couple to become guide dogs. They explained to me that this idea was based upon the sighting of an adult male Dingo leading his blind female mate to water. The thinking at the time was that the Dingo might have an inherent capacity to guide other Dingos when needed, so this ability could possibly be used for guiding people. However, the Dingo is a wild dog and not a domesticated pet, they are primitive in their responses and absolutely immediate and intense. As a member of the Dingo Study Foundation at the time, I had a Dingo puppy that had been born and raised from wild-caught parents in a home to the age of 10 weeks. Zula was an extraordinary creature but her natural, almost reflexive response to enclosure or confinement was to dig, burrow, climb, chew and scratch her way out. Any unexpected sound or sight triggered a flight response that was immediate and extreme – she would run and keep running until she found a hiding place. She was not a nervous or anxious dog, and in fact was very outgoing and interactive with people but her 'survival' response would take over. Clearly these qualities are diametrically opposed to those needed for a stable, steady and reliable guide dog. It is important that the selection and training of the dogs is optimised based upon the latest research and knowledge.

Rob continues:

> We ensure a dog centric approach to both training and well-being. We have adopted the hierarchy of behaviour change model created by Dr Susan Friedman and have embraced The Five Domains framework by David Mellor as a means of ensuring

that our dogs, in all roles and at all ages thrive both physically and mentally. When designing the training programme, we benefited from the shared knowledge and guidance of some expert external practitioners such as Michele Pouliot who has done so much good work for Guide Dogs worldwide and Chirag Patel who worked with us and continues to inspire so many of us. A really exciting advancement in our programme was the adoption and development of husbandry behaviours such as teaching a chin rest and the 'bucket game' devised by Chirag Patel.

To explain how the training approach has changed, Rob also talked about the 'avoidance' type of training that I had previously observed in different countries. 'Teaching a dog to stop when a car approaches has long been an important part of guide dog training. At Guide Dogs UK we don't teach or modify behaviours through punishment. Instead, we want the car to become a cue for a behaviour and an opportunity for the dog to gain reinforcement. We teach the dog that the car approaching within a certain distance cues the dog to stop. This is taught by precise marker training and positive reinforcement.'

So, as Rob has explained, this new improved training approach, utilising science and research into canine cognition and behaviour, has transformed the training of dogs that will be guiding people in the 21st century.

Sense or smell – the science behind seizure alert and medical alert dogs

It was during a 2 week residential training course to partner assistance dogs with disabled people, that one of our students suffered an epileptic seizure and was hospitalised. The dog (Poppy) that Lanie was in the process of learning to work with had put her paws onto the girl's lap and stared at her and whined. Moments later Lanie had her seizure. As she was being taken away to hospital, Poppy was frantically sniffing the area where the girl had collapsed. We just assumed that Poppy was investigating the odours from the medics who had been in the room.

Lanie came back the next day and rejoined Poppy on the course. A few days later, Poppy repeated her actions of standing with front paws on Lanie's lap and staring at her. Lanie, without thinking, called out to her carer who came running over just as Lanie started to go into a slight seizure. 'Poppy's telling me!' she said afterwards, 'Poppy is telling me before I seize.' After they were placed together as a team, Poppy continued to work as Lanie's assistance dog, helping her into her wheelchair and bringing and carrying items, opening doors and so on. But every now and then, even if she was upstairs on her bed, Poppy would suddenly come running down and stand up in front of Lanie and prevent her from moving forward. Soon Lanie was being given enough warning so that she could call her carer, get out of her wheelchair and lie down safely.

We taught Poppy to bring a blanket to put over Lanie, as well as to put the phone next to her head and lie down beside her. At the time, I was training other dogs by teaching them the tiny little actions that some family members had identified as precursor cues to the actual seizure – perhaps the person licked their lips several times or did some repetitive gesture with fingers or whatever. We would reward the dogs for every response or taking notice of a particular gesture or movement or sound. At first, we would exaggerate the gestures, noises or movements, but quickly the dogs refined their detection and begin to alert to less and less obvious cues. After that it was relatively easy for the dogs to transfer this response to their new owner. Once the dogs learned the cues that were specific to that person, they could quickly notice and alert the person. Interestingly, usually the dogs began alerting and responding much earlier than the physical cues that other family members had noticed. I wondered if it could possibly be odour-related, but I assumed that we had trained the dogs to notice any actions that were slightly 'off' or out of the ordinary, so they were back-chaining and adding even more cues to their repertoire. (Back-chaining is part of the reason that motivationally trained assistance and therapy dogs are so helpful – they can use what is known in computing terms as learning algorithms. Each time the dogs learn something specific, they add this to their repertoire of behavioural responses and incorporate it wherever applicable.)

Science is now following the possibility that odour is indeed the key factor, along with physical cues, in helping a dog to identify and action any warning signs of an impending seizure.[7] When I began working with diabetics whose blood sugar levels drop, they explained that they found it difficult to notice the lowering blood sugar level, with the risk that, if they did not quickly take something to bring the levels up, they could fall unconscious and might even go into a coma. As the condition is life-threatening, I was training the dogs to detect the difference between normal blood sugar and low blood sugar and then indicate this to the owner so that the owner could reward the dog. Then we trained the dog to find and bring to the owner whatever they needed to raise their blood sugar level, such as a fruit juice or sugar sweets – the dog was trained to detect, alert and respond, just as a paramedic might.

We would use breath, urine and sweat samples to ensure that the dog was exposed to the same smell within different contexts to identify the specific odour that was common to all samples. Since we as trainers cannot smell the difference, we needed to ensure that the dogs were exposed to enough different samples in order to work out what specific odour would be reinforced. In other words, we rely upon the dog working out what was required.

Some of my clients also reported that their family members had noticed very small changes in their behaviour just before a drop in blood sugar levels – for example, a slightly slowed down or slurred speech, or a hesitancy in movement in an otherwise brisk and active person. I was able to include these triggers/cues into the dog's training – by coupling the physiological cues with the target odour, I was able to train a dog to make an informed decision and respond appropriately. The physiological cues serve to reinforce the detection of the target odour and help the dog to avoid 'false positives' or false alarms. As it turns out, recent research has shown that dogs find it harder to discriminate between low blood sugar and normal blood sugar, than between high blood sugar levels and normal, so the addition of extra cues can assist the dog in carrying out this task in daily life. In fact, this is one reason why it is not so easy to train a dog that already lives in the household to alert and respond to low blood sugar levels. If a dog is exposed to the changes in the smell of the owner on a daily basis, without being given any feedback about them, the dog can learn to habituate to the changes and eventually to ignore them. The dog may have already noted the smell and reacted in some way, to which the owner has not responded. Or if the owner's family has chastised the dog for jumping up or barking or behaving in an agitated fashion, then the dog will also learn not to react to the odour change. It becomes quite a challenge to identify if the dog can detect the smell in the first place, and then establish if the dog is actively ignoring the scent or trying not to react to it.

The time-honoured way of training operational substance detection dogs (such as drug, biological substance, explosives, or mine detection, for example) was to use play as a reward for an indication. Trainers would select dogs that were highly active and very eager to chase a ball repeatedly and such dogs were frequently very possessive over the ball or toy reward. Trainers would then use a ball reward, that is, the chance to chase a ball, as the reinforcement for any correct indication behaviour. With this method or this approach, you need to always select highly active very energetic dogs that might be very possessive over items and might very intensely try to hang onto the ball. This is not a problem for trainers because they can just manage the dog and manage the 'ball drive' as they describe it, but this is not appropriate, suitable, or even possible in many cases for someone who is a diabetic or someone who suffers from seizures. They need a dog that is calm, quiet, attentive, and sensitive to their needs and their moods and able to quickly sense and respond to cues in a complex family environment. In addition, the people may not be physically adept at playing vigorously with an athletic lively and very intense dog.

By using the dog's food as a reinforcer for first noticing the target odour then indicating it and finally alerting the owner to target odour, training can proceed smoothly and calmly. Such training means that a wide variety of different breeds, types and personalities of dog can be used for this work as well as work in therapy and as assistance dogs. The final step in the sequence of identification, indication, and alert is the response of retrieving the appropriate sugar source to the person's hand, or wherever they can reach in any situation, whether it is inside the home or out in public. In fact,

we can now identify differences in scenting style and ability between individual dogs in any branch of detection work training. Dogs are now being trained throughout the world as medical detection dogs – alerting their owners for an increasing range of medical conditions that appear to have a unique odour.[8–10]

Therapy dogs

During 2010, SCAS (Society for Companion Animal Studies UK) was running a series of training courses for people wishing to use a dog or other animal in animal assisted therapy or animal assisted intervention activities. This course covered everything that was required for such work: from the legal aspect and health and safety regulations; to choice and selection of animals; to protocols for working with facilities and hospitals; and the care, welfare, husbandry and training of the animals as well as training the animal handlers. I was teaching all aspects of training, welfare and deployment of animals and I was discussing the signs of stress and discomfort compared to signals of excitement and arousal. During the sessions, I encountered trainers and handlers of therapy dogs that they were using as 'visiting dogs' in care facilities and hospitals who had never learned the differences that I was describing. There was lively discussion about the signs of stress as opposed to excitement. Many handlers of dogs that they use for therapy are convinced that their dogs 'love' the work and can hardly wait to get into the facilities to meet the client group – whether that be people with dementia, children and/or adults in hospitals before and after surgery, or in care and respite homes.

Dogs are social creatures and one of the aspects of dogs that make them such enduring companions is that they seem to 'love' to be with us, to be with people even if they have conspecifics (canine companions) as part of their social group. This characteristic helps many dogs with a suitably stable temperament and appropriate training to participate in therapy and visiting sessions proactively. Often an experienced dog will take the lead in selecting particular individuals with which he/she will interact. Even puppies will demonstrate an awareness of a higher need in an individual and will tend to stay with that person. One of our volunteer 'puppy parents' of our assistance dog puppies took her puppy to a hospice for the people to see or to toss a ball for and stroke, but the puppy ignored everyone in the room and headed directly to a man who was sitting in the corner alone. This puppy stared at the man and then gently placed a paw on his knee. The man was hunched over looking at the floor, but he looked up at the puppy and then smiled and stroked him on the head and started to talk to him. The staff were shocked and amazed because he had been there for several years and had not spoken to anyone. Needless to say, that puppy was invited back.

After the lectures on signs of stress and discomfort in therapy dogs, one handler decided to retire her dog from such work because she realised that her dog was displaying symptoms of stress and low-level pain. She later asked her vet for a thorough overall check-up of the muscular-skeletal system, and her dog was diagnosed with arthritis and a blood deficiency. The owner realised that she had been making her dog work with challenging children, while the dog was in some pain and distress. As the symptoms were similar to what you might expect from an ageing dog, they went unnoticed and ignored. This is not at all uncommon, unfortunately. I was lecturing at a conference for animal therapy and assisted intervention, and one organisation showed a video of their therapy Golden Retriever working with a large group of teenagers on the autism spectrum. The children were crowded around the dog, which had been commanded to lie down and stay. The children pushed each other, and the dog. They sometimes petted the dog gently and at other times they bumped the dog or stumbled over him. The dog showed low head carriage, flattened ears, pulled back mouth fissure, tucked tail, and other signs of stress and discomfort, such as a drawn face with skin tight over the head, as well as panting and increased respiration. Then the dog was commanded to stand up to accompany the children outside and the children were allowed to hold the dog's lead. I observed the dog lean forward and struggle to rise, and then take a minute or two to become steady on his feet but was being dragged forward as the children headed out the door. It was clear to me that the dog was in pain, showing a pronounced limp and stiffness over the hindquarters. I was trained as a judge of working dog breeds, so am very quick to notice impaired movement.

As it happened, the people who had shown the video were in attendance together with the dog from the session and I questioned them about the dog's hip status. They admitted that the dog had not been vet checked and that they were unaware of any problem with the dog except that he was very slow to get up or lie down, which they described as 'laziness'. We had a good discussion during the conference about the welfare of any dog that was being used for therapy in any way, and it became clear that very few people who were using dogs for animal assisted interventions had included health and veterinary checks. Some had taken the animal for a check-up so that they could get a vet signature on a document stating that the dog was therefore qualified as a therapy dog. But they had not thought to ask for a comprehensive health evaluation or indeed ensure that the dog's hips and joints were in good working order. On my recommendation, the Golden Retriever was X-rayed, found to have severe hip dysplasia, and was removed from the therapy dog programme.

Trainers are not usually vets. They learn how to train tasks but learning how to evaluate a dog's gait for anomalies that could indicate underlying problems is not part of their education. Learning how pain impacts on behaviour should be an integral part of the trainer training curriculum. Fortunately, there is now growing body of research into how pain affects an animal's responses and welfare, for example, Paul McGreevy is Professor of Animal Behaviour and Animal Welfare Sciences at University of Sydney's Faculty of Veterinary Science and has published many papers on how to assess the impact of pain on the behaviour of animals.

Being a therapy dog might seem to be a wonderful 'job' for dogs – these dogs are regularly taken to a facility where people are allowed to greet and stroke them, sometimes toss a ball for them or assist in husbandry activities such as brushing or putting on harnesses or leads. Conferences on animal assisted therapy are a great place to see videos of these dogs and other animals in action, and the 'feel-good' factor of dogs helping people in this way is a strong reinforcer for people to want to use their dogs as therapy or visiting dogs, as well as the more highly trained dogs that work in conjunction with individual occupational or physiotherapist programme for individuals.

I remember the IAHAIO (International Association of Human–Animal Interaction Organisations) 2007 Conference, held in Tokyo, Japan. The theme was 'People and Animals: Partnerships in Harmony' and among the oral presentations, workshops and poster sessions, the use of dogs and other animals within a therapeutic framework included children with autism, adolescent psychiatric patients, traumatised children living in a communal setting, relief of postoperative pain, brain injury rehabilitation, children's literacy and reading improvement, intensive care units, people with aged dementia, at-risk juveniles, psychiatric service dogs, hearing and guide dogs, advocate services for forensic interviews of abuse victims, and horse assisted activities for disabled children. Since that time, even more programmes and organisations have been created in many more countries throughout the world. Owing to the lack of regulation of these activities or an internationally accepted rule of law for the assessment, training, and deployment of dogs for animal assisted interventions and activities, questions will continue to be asked concerning the health, welfare, and well-being of the dogs. As an evaluator for the Delta Pet Partners Program in the USA, I found that several of the people who applied to have their dog certified as a therapy dog became extremely angry if the dog failed the assessment due to temperament or behaviour problems and they vigorously insisted that the dog was suitable. It struck me that they were not concerned so much for the welfare or well-being of the dog but for their own status as owners of a 'therapy dog'. If a dog is fearful of moving equipment, or sudden noises and movement, or slippery floors, then that dog will be highly stressed in a therapy or visiting dog environment. Yet the owners would argue that the dog was 'fine' and 'loved the work'.

One study considered the effect of therapy dogs on the staff in a paediatric hospital.[11] The authors found that facility dogs may be related to several benefits for healthcare professions in relation to work-related burnout, job perceptions, and mental health, but that they do not influence all components of these areas. It is interesting to see that in some cases the beneficiaries of the dogs are not the client group but the staff.

With the proliferation of assistance dog programmes in a relatively unregulated industry, the use of dogs for canine assisted interventions and activities can be a wonderful adjunct to the many treatment and rehabilitation projects but may also put many dogs at risk. It is very encouraging to see the development of ethics, and standards of practice from the pioneering work done by Assistance Dogs International to various organisations and councils throughout the world. In the UK, we developed a code of ethics as part of the course on animal assisted interventions run by SCAS.

More recent and rigorous research is starting to look at exactly what the specific benefits to patients or the client group are, and to question the impact of the use of therapy dogs in general. One study showed that dog therapy is effective in improving the emotions and behaviours of institutionalised patients with dementia.[12] However, serious questions are being asked and the answers are not what many owners of therapy dogs want to hear. For example, one study found no effects of therapy dog interactions on adolescent anxiety when compared with the presence of a stuffed dog toy (although perhaps this shows our love of dogs is so great that even a stuffed dog toy helps!).[13] Another study comparing anxiety of children in hospital assigned to a group for animal assisted interactions and one group doing puzzles, the former did not significantly reduce anxiety and pain, although further investigation was needed due to various experimental design factors.[14]

Final thoughts

As I wrote in a study unit on assistance dogs discussing the use of owner trained dogs for therapy visits:

There are drawbacks to this type of arrangement, however. There is no real control over people bringing untrained unprepared animals into facilities. Untrained improperly managed animals can pose a threat to residents and staff. To ensure the safety and well-being of patients and residents as well as the safety of their caregivers, therapy dogs must undergo assessments for health temperament and behaviour. Dogs need to be current with vaccinations against distemper, canine hepatitis, Leptospirosis, rabies and parvovirus. Any dog showing signs of illness such as vomiting, diarrhoea, skin infection or ear infection should not make therapy visits until cleared by veterinarian.[15]

That being said, it is encouraging to see the range of tasks and activities that involve dogs developing throughout the world. Dogs evolved alongside human beings and are integral to our modern lives in so many ways. Dogs come in all shapes, sizes, and personalities and there is the right dog for almost any job, provided that the training is reinforcement-based, and gives the dog choice.

Dogs live and work so closely with people and, being non-verbal, they have developed the ability to observe us in detail and notice the tiniest signals and cues, which help them decode what we intend and what we expect of them. The high level of cooperation of which they are capable and their interest in us as a species means that they can learn to work for us and with us, not as servants or slaves but as partners and friends, as long as trained in the right way and thought is given to letting them live their best dog lives too. We owe it to them to keep honing our training techniques and scientific understanding in order to honour their gift to us. We need to be a dog's best friend.

References and notes

1. ADI Assistance Dogs International (assistance-dogsinternation.org) is a worldwide coalition of non-profit programmes that train and place assistance dogs. Founded in 1986 from a group of seven small programmes, ADI has become the leading authority in the assistance dog industry. ADUK and ADEu, AD Australia are all members of ADI, and accredited assistance dogs are those that have been trained by accredited member organisations of ADI and the International Guide Dog Federation.

2. Most, K. (2001) *Training Dogs – a Manual*. Dogwise Publishing, Wenatchee, WA.

3. Koehler, W. (1962) *The Koehler Method of Dog Training: Certified Techniques by Movieland's Most Experienced Dog Trainer*. Hungry Minds Inc.

4. IAABC (n.d.) IAABC statement on LIMA. https://m.iaabc.org/about/lima/ (accessed 10 April 2021).

5. IAABC (n.d.) Hierarchy of procedures for humane and effective practice. https://m.iaabc.org/about/lima/hierarchy/ (accessed 10 April 2021).

6. Mellor, D.J. (2017) Operational details of the Five Domains Model and its key applications to the assessment and management of animal welfare. *Animals*, 7, 60.

7. Maa, E., Arnold, J., Ninedorf, K. and Olsen, H. (2021) Canine detection of volatile organic compounds unique to human epileptic seizure. *Epilepsy & Behavior* 115, 107690.

8. Amundsen, T., Sundstrøm, S., Buvik, T., Gederaas, O.A. and Haaverstad, R. (2014) Can dogs smell lung cancer? First study using exhaled breath and urine screening in unselected patients with suspected lung cancer. *Acta Oncologica* 53, 307–315.

9. Reeve, C., Wentzell, P., Wielens, B., Jones, C., Stehouwer, K. and Gadbois, S. (2018) Assessing individual performance and maintaining breath sample integrity in biomedical detection dogs. *Behavioural Processes* 155, 8–18.

10. Elliker, K.R., Sommerville, B.A., Broom, D.M., Neal, D.E., Armstrong, S. and Williams, H.C. (2014) Key considerations for the experimental training and evaluation of cancer odour detection dogs: lessons learned from a double-blind, controlled trial of prostate cancer detection. *BMC Urology* 14, 22.

11. Jensen, C.L., Bibbo, J., Rodriguez, K.E. and O'Haire, M.E. (2021) The effects of facility dogs on burnout, job-related well-being, and mental health in paediatric hospital professionals. *Journal of Clinical Nursing* 8 February.

12. Vegue Parra, E., Hernández Garre, J.M. and Echevarría Pérez, P. (2021) Benefits of dog-assisted therapy in patients with dementia residing in aged care centers in Spain. *International Journal of Environmental Research in Public Health* 18, 1471.

13. Megan, K., Mueller, E.C., Anderson, E.K. and Urry H.L. (2021) Null effects of therapy dog interaction on adolescent anxiety during a laboratory-based social evaluative stressor. *Anxiety, Stress & Coping* DOI: 10.1080/10615806.2021.1892084.

14. Barker, S.B., Knisely, J.S., Schubert, C.M., Green, J.D. and Ameringer, S. (2015) The effect of an animal-assisted intervention on anxiety and pain in hospitalised children. *Anthrozoös* 28(1), 101–112.

15. Bondarenko, N. 'Assistance Dogs' Study Unit 1 for Thomson Education Direct 39502200 (now Harcourt Direct).

Chapter 11

Human behaviour in mind

Suzanne Rogers and Jo White

Throughout this book we have considered what a behaviourally minded approach to caring for dogs might entail. What we have not yet considered, however, is how to make it a reality on a large scale – how to change the cultural practices that are harmful to dogs, into practices that ensure that dogs have a life worth living and are thriving in our care; and how to do this in a way that enables the people who love and 'use' dogs to be engaged. What we have not yet considered fully is a behaviourally minded way of changing *human* behaviour, and so we will turn our attention to this now.

Exploring change

Have you ever tried to change your behaviour? Most of us, at some time, have wanted to eat less, exercise more or stop smoking, for example. Did you have the knowledge needed to make the change? Did you know what to eat or how to exercise, for example? Did you have the motivation to change? Did you understand the benefits of making the change? Most of us know that if we maintain a healthy weight, we might avoid certain health issues. Did you make the change and maintain it? If so, was it easy? If not, then why not?

We know from campaigns such as the 'eat five portions of fruit or vegetables a day' that it is very easy for people to have a high awareness of the 'rule' but not to live by it. The five portions recommendation is thought to be very widely known, in 2018 a UK government health survey showed that only 28% of people eat that many portions.[1] We often understand the benefits of changing but despite having the desire, knowledge, and motivation, changing our behaviour is difficult.

Bailey and Charlie

Bailey was a very *very* large dog. He was morbidly obese and on the brink of being seized by an animal welfare organisation because his owner, Charlie, was unable to meet Bailey's needs regarding getting him back to a healthy weight, and neighbours had reported him multiple times due to concerns about the dog's welfare. Animal welfare officers and vet nurses had made several attempts to help but Bailey was not losing weight, Charlie seemed to be struggling to grasp the need for change and there was a real risk that Bailey would have to be taken away. We come back to Bailey and Charlie later in this chapter to find out how they got on.

Yet when it comes to animal welfare, we often assume that if we explain to people why change is needed, they will instantly change the way they behave towards and manage their animals.

The root cause of compromised welfare in dogs is human behaviour – what humans do, or do not do. When we ask dog owners to make changes to benefit their animal, we need to be aware of the gap between knowledge/awareness and behaviour. Frequently, professionals helping dog owners tend to focus on short-term services and providing recommendations of how owners should address the issue. However, there is a mountain of evidence-based information about what does, and does not, lead to behaviour change in humans – it is found within fields including the social sciences such as psychology, development approaches, behavioural change theories, counselling skills, social marketing and so much more (Figure 11.1). We recognise the need to apply what has been discovered from those fields to our work driving change for dogs and will outline some of the key concepts in this chapter.

Understand – Change – Impact

HBCA uses a three-phase approach (see Figure 11.2) to plan strategic campaigns, projects and other pieces of work that practically apply the science of human behaviour change.

- Understand – We use theories, models, and tools to make sure we truly understand the problem. This step is vital, otherwise we might plan an intervention based on assumptions, which might be inaccurate resulting in an ineffective plan and intervention. For example, before considering things we could do to change what people feed their dogs, or why they might buy puppies from unscrupulous breeders, we need to truly understand why they are doing those things in the first place, so that we can be confident that our planned activities will work.
- Change – We then use the understanding of the behaviours and wider context to

Figure 11.1: There are many fields of research and application that are relevant to human behaviour change science, some examples of which are included in this figure. © HBCA.

Stages of a project, campaign, or just a conversation

Figure 11.2: At HBCA we first understand the issue and behaviours, we can then plan interventions to change them, and finally we measure the impact of those changes. Throughout each stage a research and development approach is used to take into account learning and feedback. Figure © HBCA.

map the findings and design an intervention to deliver change. We use the science of human behaviour change to identify evidence-based interventions that best fit the issue we need to change, and again we consider the theories, models, and tools from a range of fields. For example, we can now consider what interventions might change what people feed their dogs or their decisions regarding purchasing puppies.

- Impact – Finally, we use behaviour science to consider the impact of the interventions on the target audience. It is important to identify and highlight successes, sharing and disseminating the results appropriately to have the maximum impact. For example, the indicators regarding people changing the way they feed their dogs might be decreased incidences of tooth decay reported by vets. Indicators regarding people buying puppies from unscrupulous breeders might be a

change in policy regarding breeders and reduced numbers of dogs being bred in such contexts.

Throughout this process, we use a research and development approach of establishing a baseline, then piloting and evaluating our activities so that we can develop them as we go. We are mindful that our aim is sustainable behaviour change, not transient temporary changes, so we are sure to monitor relapses or 'tailing off' in the adoption of the desired behaviours and change our approach accordingly. We will come back to this framework later.

The four principles of human behaviour change

HBCA has summarised the output of the huge body of work exploring human behaviour into four principles: change is a process;

understanding psychology is key in driving change; the environment influences change; and change must be 'owned'.

Principle 1: change is a process

The process of behaviour change has been studied from various different angles and there are many useful theories and models to explore. One approach we use a lot at HBCA is the 'Theory of Change', which considers what is needed for change by starting with the goal and identifying the precursors of each milestone – working backwards. It is a process often used in project planning and can also be done retrospectively to understand how change happened. For example, developing a theory of change to address the issue of the incidence of obesity in pet dogs would first describe the goal (dogs are a healthy weight) and work backwards from the goal. So for dogs to be a healthy weight people need to be feeding them appropriate diets, for that to happen people need to be able to access appropriate diets from their local shop, for that to happen people need to know what diet to buy, for that to happen there needs to be a change of diets available so that unhealthy diets are not so readily available and people need to know what a healthy diet consists of, for that to happen …. You can see how a lot of information can be mapped out this way as different threads of requirements are explored (for example, other threads could be that for dogs to be a healthy weight people need to be exercising them in accordance with their needs and diet, or to be able to recognise what a healthy weight looks like and so on). This approach is becoming increasingly used in strategic planning of animal welfare projects but can be a useful tool in many other contexts, including for behaviourists to take clients through the steps of change needed to reach their goals.

The 'Transtheoretical model of change'[2,3] outlines stages of change in individuals through five stages (pre-contemplation, contemplation, preparation, action and maintenance). Let us consider an example of an owner who has a brachycephalic breed of dog and is considering getting a second dog. In pre-contemplation they would be unaware of the issues these breeds face and be considering buying a new brachy pup. In contemplation, some of the welfare issues might be 'coming onto their radar' and they have developed some awareness of the issues. In preparation, they might be seeking further information regarding breeds and preparing to buy a non-brachy breed of pup, then in the action stage, buying a non-brachy breed. The maintenance phase would be still not buying a brachy pup even if considering purchasing a third dog, and continuing to understand the issues these breeds face. At any point there might be a relapse – for example, the owner might buy a brachy breed if someone they know breeds such dogs and offers them one, or they might relapse when in preparation stage by browsing brachy breeders on the internet.

The key message is that change is a process, it is not instant, and we need to understand where people are along that process to be able to support them in moving to the next stage. For example, if a vet has a client who does not truly appreciate the need to regularly give their dog opportunity to exercise and is not considering doing so, if we suggest ways the change can be maintained (for example, suggesting nice places to exercise) we are not likely to be successful. In this situation the client might require further motivation or information before they consider preparing for the change and doing the new behaviour of exercising their dog. This concept of change as a process is not only useful for people working with individual clients such as vets and behaviourists but also for anyone who might want to influence someone else's behaviour.

Sometimes it is important to remember bridges. When we want to change human behaviour, it is often tempting to provide the solution (the other side of the bridge) and explain why it is so important to get there for the well-being of animals and for ourselves. Getting to a target weight is a good example, we often explain why being a healthy weight is good for animals and humans. We seek to motivate the person to want to be there and help them to see what it would be like once they are there. However, if we forget to show them the bridge, how to get there from where they are now, and that it is safe to cross, they will stay in the security of where they are now. Using the target healthy weight example, 'how to get there' might include weighing the daily food allowance, regularly weighing the dog, walking the dog for at least 30 minutes a day, adding structured bursts of activity such as two 5 minute games of fetch a day, and so on.

Alongside the need to change behaviour is the important element of embedding the new behaviour, so that the person does not return to their previous ways. Research into the formation of habits suggest that it presents a powerful tool in creating positive behaviours, together with understanding and addressing negative ones. This is particularly relevant for activities undertaken routinely, which is pertinent for those engaged in looking after animals. Whether it is feeding or health care, habit formation could be the key to delivering sustained positive management changes.[4]

Fogg[5] suggests that rather than approaching a big change in one step, breaking it down into smaller component parts and working to form many 'tiny habits' can be successfully used to create, alter, or maintain a behaviour, without the need for increased levels of motivation and willpower. Fogg utilises the principle of linking new behaviours to current habits that are part of an existing routine, this increases the chance of the behaviour being performed and ultimately becoming a habitual behaviour. For example, to encourage dog owners to clean their pet's teeth, we could work with them to identify a behaviour they do weekly, such as the weekly grocery shop, and 'tie it' to the behaviour of cleaning teeth (for example, 'After putting all the groceries away, I will brush my dog's teeth'). In practice, as behaviourists, vets, and fellow dog owners we need to support people through the process of creating good habits. Most of us know the importance of 'shaping' behaviours we are training our dogs to do in small steps, we need to use the same approach to shape our own behaviour and to develop habits that will benefit our animals.

Another useful model and tool in understanding behaviour and driving change is the COM-B model and behaviour change wheel,[6] which bring together theory-based tools developed in behavioural science, to understand and change behaviour. The first steps are especially useful in practice with dog owners to consider the problem, defining the target behaviour, identify what needs to change and how to bring about that change, and we have applied this framework of thinking both to better understand the dog's behaviour from the dog's point of view, and also the owner's target behaviour.

Principle 2: understanding psychology is key in driving change

This principle explores how the mind impacts on behaviour and includes areas such as how much change is someone's autonomous decision and how much is as a result of influence by others; how the mind works in processing new information; what factors affect our motivation for change; how barriers for change are often very deep-seated beliefs and values and how to best address this, and much more.

Understanding the motivation for change and how new behaviours are discarded or maintained is necessary in planning effective projects or driving change (for example, understanding why some people use aversive training techniques and others do not). An understanding of the relationship between behaviour change of individuals and how that translates to increasing the dissemination of information and change throughout a community is vital in planning and adapting projects that rely on the spread of best practices.

We would like to introduce four key concepts in this section: confirmation bias; confrontational versus empathetic communication; transactional analysis; and the righting reflex. **Confirmation bias** is the phrase used to describe the understanding that we are more likely to take on information that fits with what we already know and believe than information that challenges us. If we believe that dogs thrive when confined for 12 hours a day in a crate, then we are more likely to notice 'messages' that back up that view (for example, messages from the marketing departments of products related to keeping dogs in crates, such as those offering specific bedding or covers for the crate) and we are less likely to notice messages suggesting that dogs do not like to be confined. To counter this effect, we can focus on common values: if we create dialogue focused on the similarities between us and our 'target' by focusing on the values we share (for example, a love of dogs and a desire to solve the problem), we have a good foundation for more in-depth exploration of our differences. We can see an example of this when we revisit Bailey and Charlie at the end of this chapter.

In terms of the psychology of communication, studies in the field of motivational interviewing (a counselling approach that is aimed at eliciting behavioural change) show that **confrontation** in a conversation is a robust predictor for failure of the client to change, whereas **empathetic communication** is a strong predictor of change. The challenge for behaviour professionals working with clients is the need to impart an understanding that the client's behaviour is having a negative effect on the dog without a confrontational element and sadly few behaviourists, vets and other professionals are trained in such counselling skills.

Transactional analysis is an accessible model that is useful in tracking your counselling performance during interactions with clients or indeed other dog owners. It is based on the premise that we all can be communicating from one of three 'states' – the parent, adult or child. In the parent state we might overly impart information, in a way that is perhaps a little condescending or top-down. This might create feelings in the other person causing them to react from a 'child state' – the person might feel inferior, disempowered and might experience some negative feelings associated with school and education. The 'adult state' is where we are operating with logic, reason and level-headedness at the forefront. In any interaction each person can be in any of the three states, but the aim is to maintain adult-to-adult communication in a consultation setting. In practice, if we feel that we are teaching too much, or that we are ourselves being nudged into our child state by someone, and can recognise it, we can consciously get back to adult state, for the most effective communication. This model can be helpful to have in mind whether we are working in a professional capacity with clients, or in situations when we interact with other dog owners. For example, sometimes conversations with other dog owners we meet when our dogs interact with other dogs can be challenging or potentially sensitive (for example, if we want to help our dog out of a situation when they are being intimidated by another dog but the other dog's owner does not recognise the body language signals we see).

The **righting reflex** is another motivational interviewing term that describes the human desire to provide solutions for others. However, when we make suggestions and provide ideas, counter-intuitively it is likely to have the opposite of the intended effect – when faced with one side of an argument we are likely to bring up the other side, so you might generate more ideas against your solutions than you do in support of them. Example conversation topics where this might be an issue could include tail docking, different training methods, keeping dogs outside, crating for long periods of time, leaving dogs alone at night who are upset by being separated from you and so on. Also, by giving the client an opportunity to practice vocalising reasons why not to change, for example, you enable those ideas to become more strongly held, or more embedded. Providing solutions can therefore disempower your client when you are aiming for the opposite outcome. Instead of providing solutions we must develop skills that help people to come up with their own solutions and ideas, where we are the facilitators.

A model that illustrates the psychology of change in a nutshell is the 'elephant and rider' model coined by the Heath brothers.[7] Imagine a rider on an elephant (which is not condoned as elephants are wild animals and the process of training them to accept riders is never kind); see Figure 11.3. The rider represents the rational, logical side of how we make decisions, and the elephant represents the emotional side of our decision making. The elephant is much larger than the rider, just as our emotions have a much larger role in our decision making than we might appreciate. Therefore, to motivate, inspire people and change behaviour we need to reach the emotional side of our audience. In practice, this might mean framing our 'messages' in terms of how the dog feels, what makes dogs happy and so on rather than using potentially colder, more rational language, such as focusing on health benefits. This reiterates the

Figure 11.3: The elephant and rider analogy illustrates the role of emotions in our behaviour as well as our rational side. Picture drawn by Kirstin Calvin.

importance of truly considering how we communicate with clients and not just the content of our message.

Behaviourists, vets and trainers are working as teachers, educators, facilitators, counsellors, persuaders and much more, but are often not trained in those skills. To change the world for dogs we need to develop those skills and value their importance just as much as we value our other professional knowledge and expertise.

Principle 3: the environment influences change

Continuing with the elephant and rider analogy – a person riding an elephant without a clear path to follow will just be meandering through a forest. The third element needed for change is a clear path; in real terms this could mean having a strategy or the right environment in terms of education or legislation – if we are not acting with a supportive legislative background (although the Animal Welfare Act 2006 covers a lot of ground in the UK), we will be more limited than if we were. An example of how the physical environment can change behaviour is how changing the design of a rescue centre can be used to influence changes in both canine and human behaviour; changing what the dogs can see/hear is likely to influence their behaviour and changing some behind the scenes elements of the environment can encourage changes in human caretaking behaviours, such as enabling a focus on providing enrichment.

The environment is a significant factor maintaining some of the negative practice in the dog sector. Sometimes the culture surrounding how dogs are trained, disempowers individual owners, and create an environment that is not conducive to change. Routines become embedded and behaviour is often not at the heart of decisions.

Education also falls under this principle as it is another way of providing the 'path' in our elephant and rider analogy. Any discussion considering the reasons behind animal welfare issues will identify a lack of education as one of the root causes, yet education so often is not given the attention it deserves. At HBCA we are passionate about education for children, as it presents the opportunity to proactively and sustainably address the need for positive human behaviour development and change as a preventative measure for avoiding animal suffering. If we can instil compassionate behaviours in children, we will reduce the need to re-educate adults. As the future generation, children drive cultural change-they are the key to sustainable change.

The element of 'culture' and learned behaviours is hugely significant in the dog world. Indeed, those of us who have been involved with dogs for most of our lives have so much received wisdom that sometimes it takes a non-doggy friend to question what we are doing for us to even notice our embedded beliefs and behaviours. Culture and learned behaviour is no excuse for cruelty, however, and culture and knowledge can change, sometimes very quickly.

Principle 4: change must be 'owned'

There is a saying 'Tell me and I forget, show me and I remember, involve me and I truly understand', which perfectly illustrates this principle of change. People need to truly appreciate the relevance of the desired behaviour change to them for change to happen. If we understand that people learn and change if they are not just told what to do through resources or typical top-down educational outreach, not just shown what to do through demonstration, but are truly involved in the process of change, we can facilitate that change (for example, in encouraging people to finish courses of antibiotics for their dogs). This process involves enabling people and communities to explore issues and come up with solutions themselves rather than 'train them' to implement a preconceived solution.

People only change if they believe they can; this is the essence of self-efficacy theories. Self-efficacy can be thought of as a task-specific version of self-esteem. Individuals are more likely to engage in activities for which they have high self-efficacy and less likely to engage in those they do not. In practical terms this again highlights the need for us to provide a safe space for owners to try out new behaviours, under our guidance, and not just tell them what to do and then leave them to try it alone. A good example for this is when owners need to give dogs medicine – we are sure many readers will have experienced thinking your dog has swallowed a pill only for it to be spat out several minutes later! Vets can make giving pills to dogs look very easy and the veterinary profession is increasingly recognising the importance of not just showing owners how to give pills but giving them the opportunity to practice doing so in the consultation to develop the owner's self-efficacy before they continue to administer the course of treatment at home.

The concept of positive deviance also comes under this principle – positive deviance is an approach based on the observation that even though most individuals or groups in a community usually have access to the same resources or face similar challenges, some find better solutions than others. Usually considered to be a community-driven approach, it enables people to discover these successful behaviours in their communities and develop a plan of action of dissemination. This is where breed specific or interest-specific social media groups can sometimes be useful – sometimes good

practices emerge on such support groups that can rapidly gain traction through the power of social media not only by highlighting the 'good' but also by making such behaviours normal for that community. However, we can also apply positive deviance to our work with owners and even ourselves. If we look for the good things, the good behaviours, the small successes, highlight them and build on them we can drive change.

These principles are only the tip of the iceberg that is the vast amount of research exploring the fascinating field of human behaviour change. Concepts do not always neatly fit into one principle or another but reflect our current framing of the concepts that underpin what is included in the study of human behaviour change, there are many alternative ways they could be categorised.

Problem solving with behaviour in mind

Although this book is authored by fantastic behaviourists, we have not yet considered the work behaviourists do in detail so let us explore how having canine and human behaviour in mind is used by an animal behaviour consultant. When people encounter problems with their dogs, they tend to go through a range of responses – some immediately call the vet as they suspect, or want to rule out, pain as a reason for the behaviour. Others might change the dog's diet or start adding a supplement to their feed; others might turn to a specific training method or activity, or turn to a herbalist or aromatherapist, some might wait and see if the behaviour gets worse or disappears without any intervention and so on. With so many professionals in the animal behaviour industry, and so much information easily accessible online, there is no shortage of people to turn to – and this brings both positive and negative effects for dogs. In terms of the process of change, if the goal is to change the dog's behaviour, when an owner has recognised that they need help with their dog, they move through the stages of pre-contemplation and contemplation as they decide to engage some help. However, they might fall back through those stages due to peer pressure from people they know. As a behaviourist it is useful to fully understand the person's motivation for calling you so you can start to explore their values, which is a key part of building rapport with clients and the empathic conversation needed for change.

As described in Chapter 8, a high percentage of behaviour problems are rooted in present or past pain. When pain is addressed or ruled out as a cause sometimes the unwanted behaviour goes away, but sometimes the dog needs help to re-learn. Many trainers and owners turn to 'methods' of training for the answer. As we saw in Chapter 3, some seemingly kind approaches are not so kind when we consider learning theory. In addition, although training might help in some situations it often does not address the cause of a problem, but rather attempts to address the symptom. For example, let us consider a dog who is biting people when they touch his/her collar. The owner first rules out pain, by having the dog checked by a vet, and then turns to a trainer for help. The trainer, depending on what method they advocate, might suggest several courses of action. One trainer might suggest training the dog to be OK with people touching his/her collar. Another trainer might suggest using a clicker to establish a positive association with the collar being touched. A herbalist might suggest a calming supplement. All these approaches might be effective to a greater or lesser degree. However, the one thing they have in common is applying a tool to tackle how the problem manifests, not the cause of the problem. Only looking

at a problem through a restricted lens might overlook important issues and could make the problem worse or put dog and owner in a dangerous situation. Communication is key. The owner might well have turned to solutions you do not think are appropriate and how to navigate this requires skills following human behaviour change principles.

By addressing the root cause of the issue, and any limiting beliefs or embedded behaviours on the human side, we can be sure to solve the problem effectively and safely and ensure that we will not just get another symptom emerging as the problem is being tackled. Also, it would not be ethical to train a dog to put up with pain or fear (even if you use reward-based training) without tackling that underlying pain or fear; and it would not be ethical to focus on training the dog if the rest of their life is so 'unhappy' due to their needs not being met, that they are not in a position to learn. Many trainers, physiotherapists, nutritionists and other professionals would consider the management/whole picture, but these are few and far between. This book has explored what a 'behaviourally minded' approach across the dog world would be like, and in this chapter we have started to explore the importance of the owner's behaviour so that we can ensure the necessary changes are made.

Finding the cause – the process

In a consultation, or sometimes through a pre-consultation survey, the behaviourist first takes a full history – they will ask lots of questions and some might seem irrelevant at the time, but the behaviourist will be building up a picture of the owners and dog – their partnership, the owner's experience, attitudes and aspirations, the dog's background and previous experience that might be relevant to consider later, the management regime, what has been done to solve the problem so far, any welfare issues that need to be discussed, anything that highlights the need to involve another professional such as a vet or nutritionist. The behaviourist will consider all twenty-four hours in the dog's day, to determine how well their needs are met and make suggestions where changes would help. Behaviourists go through all the possible reasons for the development of the problem behaviour and suggest approaches to solve it. There are five main elements to this process.

1. Considering whether the behaviour is normal for dogs, normal but out of context, or abnormal. Many behaviours are normal for dogs but are unwanted. It is important to understand which category the behaviour falls into before considering how to modify, provide an alternative outlet, or prevent it, and behaviourists use their extensive knowledge of canine behaviour to understand the problem.
2. What learning is involved? As was introduced in Chapter 3, there are many different ways that dogs learn and behaviourists have a full understanding of this, which is important when considering how to train them to do something different. If a behaviour has become automatic (classically conditioned), then it will need to be tackled in a different way if the dog is still learning about an object or experience. If the animal has developed a phobia of something, it is different to if the dog is anxious about something.
3. An understanding of physiology is important. In Chapter 8, we learned about the physiology of stress and the impact on behaviour. Another example is that the chemicals involved in the biology of aggression mean that movement can make it worse, thus it is important to do slow or stationary work with dogs with aggressive tendencies. There is certain physiology associated with stereotypical or other abnormal behaviours that can make these behaviours addictive and some sexual behaviours have physiological aspects that must be considered in order to provide an appropriate plan of action.
4. Welfare – behaviourists care about the animal and human, and safety and welfare is of paramount importance. If a dog is suffering through management or training regimes, the behaviourist will work with the owner to address this as a priority.
5. Owner–dog relationship – behaviourists also have counselling skills as often part of the problem lies with the owner's perception of the problem, confidence in themselves, own fears and concerns and expectations.

The behaviourist will then provide his/her thoughts on the main elements of the problem and start to talk through the approaches to solve it. There is likely to also be an element of observing the dog, assessing the environment, and perhaps on training or handling, although this is often in a later session depending on the problem. The behaviourist will work with the owner to put together a plan or programme – it is no use imposing a plan on an owner when they do not have the time or inclination to carry out the recommendations. This is likely to involve management changes, handling, and training practice, and of course input from vets or other professionals as appropriate. However, crucial to all those things the behaviourist will apply the principles of human behaviour change to every stage and every interaction with the dog owner to drive change and embed new behaviours.

Consultations are not like they are sometimes depicted on television – with an aggressive dog, for example, the behaviourist is unlikely to suggest that the dog is put in the situation where they will show that behaviour as this would not be safe; it is also unnecessary.

Considering wider change

Often behaviourists, vets or other professionals working with dogs observe situations where canine welfare is compromised and want to do something about it, whether with an individual owner or at the community or even policy level. So how can we help more dogs, not just the ones we come across in our day-to-day professional lives? There are many groups of people planning and implementing campaigns and actions on the basis of what 'feels' right to do, and what should make a difference, but how could this be done in a more strategic way?

To consider this further we can return to the 'understand – change – impact' framework to approaching projects described above.

Understand

A useful tool in the 'understand' phase is the problem/solution tree. A problem statement is developed (tree trunk) and then the associated causes (roots) and effects (branches) are identified. The root causes are explored by sequentially seeking the 'causes of causes', and the effects are extrapolated to provide an understanding of what will happen if nothing changes. Next, the problem is 'flipped' to the future where there is no problem (for example, the problem could be 'The frequency of obesity in the pet dog population is increasing', which becomes 'The frequency of obesity in the pet dog population is decreasing'). This is called the 'solution tree', or sometimes the 'objective tree'. The causes are 'flipped' to become results (for example, if a cause is that people do not recognise obesity in dogs, the 'flipped' result

would be that they can recognise obesity; if a cause is that people feed too many treats to their dog, the flipped result might be that dogs are fed according to their calorific requirements), and then activities that lead to the result can be listed (for example, tools to help people recognise healthy weights of dogs or healthy portion sizes for their pet). The effects are 'flipped' to impacts (for example, obesity in dogs results in a myriad of physical issues, as well as mental issues when they become unable to do some natural behaviours, which results in obesity becoming normalised, which results in the maintenance of the situation – when 'flipped' this means that the impact of dogs having a healthy weight is that incidences of issues caused by obesity decrease, healthy weight animals becomes normalised and so on). SMART (Specific, Measurable, Achievable, Realistic, Timed) indicators can be created for each impact, ensuring that the ability to measure impact is considered from early on in the design process. This process provides a broad picture of the sorts of thing that could be done, and how success could be measured. Figure 11.4 illustrates the basic process.

The value of undertaking a problem–solution tree to understand an issue is that it is simple and easy to do, it enables collaboration by different relevant parties, and provides a 'blue-sky' brainstorming environment and approach. In addition, it also starts to highlight people's assumptions about a problem, which can then be explored to see if they are supported by evidence. If there is a research gap where work is needed, or indeed if there is evidence that suggests the assumption is incorrect, research can be undertaken. It is premature to focus too much on the solutions identified as a more in-depth analysis of the behaviour involved is needed. However, the process of creating a problem/solution tree

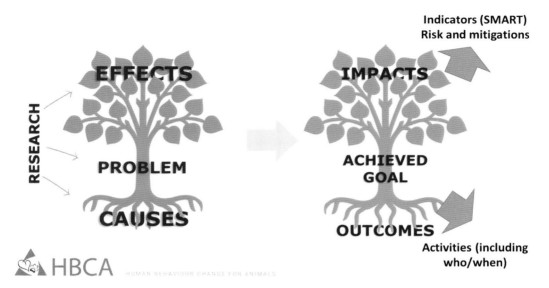

Figure 11.4: The problem–solution tree is a useful tool to ensure we understand problems and to plan appropriate solutions. Figure © HBCA.

acts as a useful 'vision board', an inspirational insight into possible solutions in a wide context. In our experience, this exercise is also beneficial at nurturing motivation in a team.

Change

There are many different types of possible interventions to change behaviour, each has advantages and disadvantages and must be considered on a case-by-case basis and in the wider context. In this section we will list some typical ways we can drive change and discuss each briefly.

Legislation and enforcement

A common reaction to address a welfare issue is to attempt to ban the practice that caused it, however, perhaps the most significant issue in terms of legislation is enforcement. In most countries, there is some legislation to protect animals, but it is often subjective, under resourced and without test cases and common usage prosecution is unlikely to take place. In cases where the instinctive reaction is to get a 'ban', it would be pertinent to fully consider all the legislation currently in place, and research what entity is responsible for enforcement, what warnings systems are in place, and previous records of prosecutions using that legislation, before deciding on the most appropriate strategy. Perhaps an awareness and education campaign regarding existing legislation might be a better approach or perhaps enforcers need training in how to recognise compromised welfare and so on. Developing animal-protection legislation is a valid approach and can indicate progression towards a more compassionate society. For legislation to be effective, the resources must be available for enforcement and the societal background must be conducive to compliance with the proposed legislation.

Regulation and control

Regulation schemes can help to bring different service providers, boarding kennels for example, up to certain standards, reward compliance, enforce rules, and therefore drive incremental progress. Membership schemes, where membership is dependent on meeting certain standards and is subject to renewal every 12 months, can also help to inspire members to improve standards, create a cohesive community of service providers or owners, and be financially self-sustainable. However, the main concern is that by introducing minimum standards through registration schemes, the minimum then becomes the 'goal' and progress can stagnate. Also, if the scheme does not include the majority of service providers, there might not be much incentive for people to join in. We can dream about a 'behaviour friendly breeders' network that genuinely meets the needs of dogs, but despite some efforts in this area, we think we have some way to go before behaviour is truly in mind.

Membership schemes utilise some key principles of the science of human behaviour change. For example, by 'labelling' themselves as members of a scheme that stands for high welfare standards, people are then more likely to act in accordance with that label. For example, if one of the criteria for membership of an ethical training or behaviour organisation is that certain principles have to be obeyed, then through being 'labelled' as a member, people are more likely to continue those behaviours of a good trainer/behaviourist with which they now identify.

Social norms are also relevant here – norms are the rules of behaviour that are considered acceptable in a group or society. People who do not follow these norms might be shunned by other members of the community or suffer another consequence. Norms can change – for example, being part of a membership scheme could become a norm, which would provide motivation to be part of it and therefore welfare-friendly management.

One of the key elements to successful regulation and membership schemes is that they are created with input from the community itself – the scheme will then be locally relevant and there will be more 'buy in' to the standards set than if a scheme was imposed by authorities or outsiders. Another key element needed for success is good management of the logistics – inspections, membership databases and so on – which can be a significant drain on limited resources.

Incentive-based schemes

Incentives can be positive or negative: charging fines for breaching certain standards is an example of negative incentives, giving rewards for exceeding standards is an example of positive incentives. In the context of dogs in competition settings, negative incentive schemes are common in the form of inspections, or disqualification but, in our opinion, behavioural welfare concerns are not often taken into account with any real meaning. Inspection systems (for example, inspections of boarding kennels) can be run by authorities: at regular intervals, for example, inspections of boarding kennels or veterinary checks at dog shows. The fines can be used to fund the Inspectors, rendering schemes financially sustainable. The challenges associated with such schemes are usually based in the lack of involvement of the owners – the top-down inspection approach can generate negative feelings towards the authorities, and the owners are less likely to be enthused to make changes or to strive to meet higher standards than the ones required to pass an inspection.

Community engagement

Interventions that focus on empowering the community to drive change from within, perhaps through education, skills development and so on, can help to address key welfare concerns and it is in this area that the author's key interest lies. A community could be defined geographically, or interest based (for example, dog owners in a village in Spain, or an international online community of people interested in a certain breed of dog). However, there are certain factors that must be properly considered for community engagement to be successful. For example, if the community does not perceive that change is needed, there is unlikely to be any enthusiasm to work towards such changes imposed by an external organisation. Likewise, providing education might not address welfare concerns if lack of knowledge was not the barrier to good practices. Usually there is an element of knowledge needed, but the issue of access to resources is much more of a barrier to the desired behaviour.

Community-based interventions can struggle to become sustainable as the intervening organisation often lack the funds and ability to support communities through change, help them address challenges encountered along the way, and address in the wider context. Even when change does happen, practices sometimes revert after the intervening organisation leave (remember the transtheoretical model of change introduced earlier – behaviours can slip back at any point along the change process).

Successful approaches truly involve the community in exploring the current situation, the challenges they face, and then when planning solutions takes place it is undertaken by the community, for the community. This approach can lead to sustained change as the communities take responsibility for the welfare of the animals in their care and generate strategies for solving issues that arise.

On a good day we are optimistic that the community of dog lovers can change, so that dogs are not negatively affected by people wanting to own them. However, on a bad day, the embedded psychology and culture of the

way we keep and use dogs seems insurmountable. The source of genuine optimism is that the community of people who do recognise the effect humans have on dogs is growing, rapidly.

Alternative technologies and livelihoods

Interventions that attempt to reduce or stop the use of animals by introducing alternative technologies illustrate another approach. For example, technologies to help blind people are developing rapidly and might decrease the reliance on assistance dogs, and the developments in technology of special effects might decrease the involvement of dogs in film sets and similar situations that might compromise their welfare.

Encouraging a business that uses dogs in a way that compromises their welfare to give up their business or to significantly change the way they do things, is likely to pose challenges. For some service providers, their activities are more than a livelihood, but part of their identity and others have deeply embedded views on the use of dogs. Well-run programmes encouraging such changes are fully participatory and explore the person's inspirations and aspirations before considering the changes needed to make the business dog-friendly, or to identify locally available livelihood options, and eventually supporting the person in the adoption of a new livelihood until they are established.

Raising awareness

A typical approach is to raise awareness of a welfare issue to drive change, and this can be successful if that awareness leads to behaviour change. 'Stick throwing' is an example – the information that throwing sticks or stones can cause significant injuries to dogs seems to have been enough for many people to throw other objects for their dogs instead of sticks. For many owners, awareness that this approach is available was enough to cause them to adopt the system. However, for other issues this approach will not be successful; the reasons depend on the issue, but one example is that if owners feel an awareness campaign is criticising their way of caring or training their dogs, the outcome might be that the criticised behaviours become even more firmly embedded. Raising awareness can be successful when the unwanted practice is already recognised as something that should be reduced – in these cases drawing attention to the practice could be beneficial and lead to sustained change.

Education and training

It is very easy to believe that if we provide information, that people will change their behaviour accordingly. However, as mentioned at the beginning of this chapter, a lack of knowledge is not usually the only barrier and therefore interventions that focus on education and training can be less impactful than we might hope. Where lack of knowledge or skill is identified as a need, it is important to ensure that the training or education is provided in a way that is based on sound human behaviour change principles to maximise the impact and it should be done in conjunction with other tools.

In summary, to plan an effective campaign or to drive change requires first that the situation is well researched. Only when we understand the true causes of the issues, the wider context, the stakeholders involved, and the factors responsible for maintaining the behaviour, can we plan how to change it.

Impact

If you drive a car, you do not have to understand everything about how the car works to be able to successfully reach your destination. You just need indicators or signs that tell you that everything is OK and to keep going, or when something requires your attention, and when you should stop. In cars, these signs tend to be in the form of lights and gauges on your dashboard – and someone else has decided how to work out what we really need to know.

Whether we are changing our behaviour to benefit our own dogs, or working with clients, we need to develop our own 'dashboards' so that we do not have to continually look at everything that is happening but can quickly and simply detect if something requires our attention, or indeed if things are going wrong. More than that, we also need to know when things are going right. So, what is on your dashboard? What indicators are there? Who is involved in keeping an eye on them and so on. There are many guides to how to write good indicators, the simplest tool being the SMART method, which states that indicators should be Specific, Measurable, Achievable, Realistic and Time-Bound (although there are other similar versions). This dashboard analysis could be applied to our training goals, or if we work professionally with clients, we could monitor how well our prognoses match the outcomes of our cases, the quality of rapport we have with clients, and so on.

Bailey and Charlie

At this beginning of this chapter, we left Bailey and Charlie struggling, but 2 years later so much had changed, and Bailey was svelte. Charlie had totally changed his understanding regarding what a healthy dog looks like and had implemented several changes that resulted in Bailey's new shape. Why did he change?

In the first consultation it was very clear that Charlie had very strong opinions regarding Bailey being an appropriate weight and having a 'normal' level of activity. Those opinions were not founded in the evidence base regarding animal health, ethology and so on. During the history-taking stage we not only had to be careful not to condone what he was describing or be seen to agree with his reasoning but also it was important to give him the time to explain his perspective. Through the use of reflective questioning, we gained a clear understanding of the issues and also identified some of Charlie's core values and the belief frameworks he was operating under. This enabled us to explain and summarise the situation using language that matched his values, minimising the risk of confrontation yet staying true to what we needed to explore.

We explored how to assess weight in dogs by thinking about what Bailey's dress size would be if he was a human — not just Large (L) but XXXL (triple extra-large!) and we drew pictures of what dogs should look like from above (not circular, but with a 'waist'). We mapped out all the things they did in a day to identify where changes could be made and learned that Charlie spent a lot of time on the toilet (that is another story) and that this was also when he tended to feed Bailey lots of treats. We used this 'hook' of habitual time on the toilet to change the behaviour of giving treats to using a feeding enrichment device to make the food last longer while still meeting the need of giving Bailey something he enjoys. We also introduced more movement as the toilet was at the end of a corridor, perfect for a game of fetch. We did practice this behaviour during the visit to develop self-efficacy — with trousers firmly in place. We put together a plan of action and with veterinary support too, the weight gradually came off.

Concluding thoughts

This chapter has outlined some of the ways that behaviourally minded approaches could improve the lives of dogs throughout our society. It has introduced the subject of human behaviour change, as a multidisciplinary approach to driving change and improving the lives of animals.

The whole book has provided an insight into the concept that having 'behaviour in mind' can help incrementally improve the lives of dogs whatever they are 'used' for, and is optimistic that if this way of thinking were to be adopted then many people would reconsider what we expect of our dogs in the first place.

References

1. NHS Digital Services (2020) Health Survey for England 2018. Available at: https://digital.nhs. uk/data-and-information/publications/statistical/health-survey-for-england/2018/final-page-copy-2 (accessed 28 August 2020).

2. Prochaska, J.O. and DiClemente, C.C. (1983) Stages and processes of self-change of smoking: toward an integrative model of change. *Journal of Consulting and Clinical Psychology* 51, 390–395.

3. Prochaska, J.O., DiClemente, C.C. and Norcross, J.C. (1992) In search of how people change: applications to addictive behavior. *American Psychologist* 47, 1102–1114.

4. White, J. and Sims, R. (2021) Improving equine welfare through human habit formation. *Animals* 11, https://doi.org/10.3390/ani11082156.

5. Fogg, B.J. (2012) BJ Fogg: health & habits [Video file]. TED Fremont. Available at: https://www.youtube.com/watch?v=AdKUJxjn-R8&sns=em (accessed 28 September 2017).

6. Michie, S., Atkins, L. and West, R. (2014) *The Behaviour Change Wheel*. Silverback Publishing, Sutton.

7. Heath, C. and Heath, D. (2010) *Switch: How to Change Things When Change Is Hard*. Random House, New York.

Chapter 12

Other topics

Suzanne Rogers

When deciding what to focus on in this book there were many topics that did not quite make it and during the process of putting the book together, even more emerged. A series of books could be written on how to embed approaches that truly take dog behaviour into account and each chapter in this book could have been a book itself. This chapter provides a brief summary of some of the topics that have not been covered and includes information from interviews with people who are doing fantastic things in their fields of expertise.

Behaviour in mind: the family dog

Before I had a child, I could not imagine that my relationship with my dog might change. Having worked with rescues and seeing how many dogs end up in rescue centres as family groups expand or change, I would often 'joke' that if I were to have a baby and there was a problem with the dog and the child, the child would be the one to be rehomed.

How totally naïve I was … Along came my daughter, Summer, in spring (!) 2012 and things did change. We had two large lurchers at the time, Woody and Pebbles and the first thing I struggled with was being pregnant and doing the basics in dog care – I had a very difficult painful pregnancy and walking them around the field felt like an insurmountable challenge some days. Once she was born it turned out that carrying a baby on the outside was much easier than on the inside and walks resumed. The greatest challenge was the use of space in our tiny cottage. Life seemed to be a logic puzzle (remember the puzzle of how you get a fox, a

chicken and something else across a river in a boat where you cannot take everyone at once and only certain combinations can be left?) and I must have opened and shut the baby gates a zillion times a day (later they became futile as the dogs decided they were agility equipment rather than barriers). Keeping a baby and two dogs all happy in a relatively small space was not easy.

As Summer grew older the dogs saw the huge benefits of having a child in the house – they quickly discovered the best place to be was underneath the high chair where food was magically likely to drop on your head and they became very useful at tidying up mess. But they were unsure of her tendency to emit lots of noise and fall over – keeping everyone safe was a full-time job.

A few years on and we adopted a second child (because I seemed to lack the biology that helps mothers forget the pain of childbirth and there are children in the care system). By then Woody had sadly died and Pebbles was getting older; I recognised that having a 2.5 year old in the house would not necessarily be easy for

Figure 12.1: Summer and Pebbles. Photo: © Suzanne Rogers.

her. It actually worked out well as Pebbles was at the age where she mostly wanted somewhere warm to lie down and food pots to clean, more than bouncing time, so the new human in the family was not a huge challenge for her.

There is so much I learned about having babies, children and dogs, some of it the hard way. Here are a few key things.

- **Baby wearing** – if you carry your baby in your arms you have to do everything one handed and even that is a challenge. The use of slings and baby carriers frees you up to be able to not just go for dog walks with the baby but also do things in the house. Embracing baby wearing really worked for me and took away some of the element of 'need to get up to do a quick chore but then I have to move the baby, move the dog, get everyone the right side of doors and so I might as well stay sitting a bit more'.
- **Treat logs** (Figure 12.2) – Walking with toddlers and young children is totally different to walking pre-children. Children bimble along, play with sticks in puddles, sit down and refuse to go anywhere (until you do something creative like get them to pretend a stick is a broomstick), jump off every log you come across and so on, you do not get very far. For many dogs this results in 'Come on, what are you doing?' messages. Taking small treats to hide in logs and pastes to squeeze onto them was a really good tool for getting the dog to cope with the walking with children experience.
- **Having people around** – I was so surprised at the number of children, and parents, who are genuinely nervous around dogs. It is vital that when people visit with the aim of letting the children play while you get a cup of tea and the chance to talk to an adult (never works out quite that way) your dog can cope with being perhaps shut in a different room with enrichment rather than joining in and potentially resulting in a situation

Figure 12.2: Pebbles finding the small bits of treats I have hidden in and around the log whilst the children play. Photo: © Suzanne Rogers.

that reinforces the guests' nervousness around dogs.

- **Involving children with enrichment** – About the age that children stop dropping so much food at mealtimes they are about the right age to become more closely involved with providing enrichment for your dog. Summer used to love being given a small cup of dog food kibble and putting it out in a big heart shape on the floor, then letting Pebbles in and watching her find all the bits. She also loved dragging a smelly chew all around the house and leaving it at the end of the route then following Pebbles as she followed the trail. When she was able

to draw and write she would design new trails, keeping her busy for ages!

I am especially interested in the expectations we have of pet dogs, especially family dogs. We expect them to be very turn off- and on-able – to fit into our daily lives and live by our (often arbitrary) rules. We expect so much of them while often treating them in ways that compromises their welfare. For example, not meeting their eating ethogram needs, expecting them to cope with many people in the house but also to be left alone, expecting them not to use our soft raised surfaces such as sofas and beds as their beds and so on. The way dogs adapt to living in our busy worlds is remarkable but sometimes sharing our lives with dogs is not a smooth journey.

Justine Williams recognised that people often need support when including a dog in their family and founded Our Family Dog. Just as people attend National Childbirth Trust (NCT) classes to prepare for their babies, she runs the equivalent to prepare for puppies, and shares information and top tips. Justine explains, 'Our Family Dog aims to address the mismatch between the expectations and reality of dog ownership by preparing people for and supporting them with dog ownership. The difficulty is that people often do little or no research prior to getting a dog – there's a general sense of 'how hard can a puppy be?' – which makes early intervention challenging. With this in mind, our resources predominantly target owners in the early weeks with their new puppy. This is when the challenges of puppy parenting are felt most and the need for help is at its greatest. Our model combines expert advice with peer support, both to offer reassurance and support to new puppy owners when they are feeling overwhelmed and anxious, and professional and credible guidance to cut through the conflicting and often inaccurate advice online.'

Justine provides an example, 'Kelly sought advice from Our Family Dog about what to do about her 9 week old puppy, Coco, a cockapoo, who kept crying at night. She had been told in another online forum to ignore the crying, but she did not feel this was the right thing to do. Our resources helped Kelly to better understand the care needs of puppies and resulted in her moving Coco into her bedroom temporarily, which in turn meant Kelly could respond to Coco's needs when she stirred at night and settle her back to sleep again. The outcome was a less anxious puppy and less anxious owner.'

Behaviour in mind: boarding kennels and doggy day care

Many people need to go to work, on holiday or have other circumstances when they need someone to look after their dog short-term. Although covered briefly in Chapter 9, I had the privilege of interviewing Laura Stone who runs Amity Pet Care in Redhill, Surrey, and wanted to include her perspective here. Laura first explained how she works with potential new clients.

Before any new dog steps foot on our premises, we request new clients to complete extensive information about their dog's health and behaviour background including how they feel their dog interacts with others and much more. We meet new dogs at their own property, and while it is not always realistic to judge a dog's behaviour during this initial meet, as they are often excited to meet new people, it gives an opportunity to meet them in an environment they are familiar with as dogs may behave and interact differently in new places. We also start to assess how a dog will interact and respond to us, without adding other dogs into the mix. For new dogs, we invite their human to bring them for a garden visit at our premises, to allow the dog to explore before being introduced to other dogs, which can help them to settle, acclimatise, and reduce arousal levels for future visits. We are lucky enough to have a couple of day care dogs, whose owners are happy for us to use as 'stooge dogs', so we can bring a new dog in and have them in one section of our garden area, and have the stooge calmly in a separate section, so the new dog can see them from a safe distance, and we can assess how they react. We introduce new dogs to one or two dogs at a time, to ensure they will be able to interact in an appropriate, safe way, and all interactions are carefully supervised and monitored throughout.

Laura's interest in canine behaviour means that she can identify when dogs might struggle in a day care setting. She explains:

Many dog owners expect day care to help to 'socialise' their dog but if a dog shows any sign of being at all anxious around other dogs or behaves at all inappropriately, day care would not be an appropriate service option. Anxious dogs could easily be flooded or overwhelmed in a day care setting, which could lead to behavioural issues developing or worsening. Some dogs benefit more from just having a social small group dog walk to break up their day and providing them with a shorter session where they can interact with other appropriate dogs, whereas some dogs may just prefer a 1-2-1 walk and may not feel comfortable interacting with other dogs. It's so important to match each dog to the right service for them, and tailor it to meet their needs, not just the owner's.

Laura then describes how her business has behaviour in mind for the duration of the dog's stay.

It is vital that dogs attending day care are able to interact in an appropriate, safe, and balanced way, but also, that the attendants or carers closely monitor all play and interactions, and step in to pause if the play goes on for too long, gets to boisterous, or the play is not equal (for example, one dog is trying to move away but cannot, one is not comfortable with the interaction and

so on). It is important that attendants are very knowledgeable on dog body language, as signs that a dog is uncomfortable can be subtle. It's generally advisable to have dogs in smaller, carefully matched groups, with similar play styles.

Laura does not just focus on behaviour when the dogs are active.

Resting is another essential component of a dog's routine. Being deprived of adequate rest can increase the likelihood of illness, frustration, and lower tolerance, so we actively encourage the dogs in our care to have periods of rest, as being active for an entire day care day of around 5–10 hours would be counterproductive. We provide appropriate furniture and a calm environment – having smaller groups of dogs makes this fairly practical to achieve, whereas larger groups may be far trickier!

Finally, Laura described the enrichment Amity Pet Care provides.

Tunnels and safe climbing apparatus are great for outdoor or open place spaces, as well as being good for breaking up their space and sight-lines, rather than having one big open area. Feeding time is also a brilliant opportunity to add some enrichment with puzzles, stuffable toys, licking mats and so on, as appropriate for each individual dog.

There are many options for holiday care for dogs including home-from-home care where people take dogs in and treat them as if they were their own, house sitters that care for animals while staying in your house and boarding kennels. The best boarding kennels have many similarities with rescue kennels with behaviour in mind as described in Chapter 7 and would include: being designed so that animals are not separated from other dogs merely by metal fences but have areas they can go without having to be in such close proximity to dogs they do not know; having own bedding from home available during the stay at the kennels; ensuring they have enough time outside their pens to not need to soil the area they are confined in; being treated as individuals by staff (that is, getting attention if solicited and being left alone if not). When I was a teenager, I worked at a boarding kennels for several years and was given the freedom to really care for the dogs as individuals. I used to enjoy working out what each dog seemed to want – some just wanted to sit on me for a while, others to play, others to be talked to but not touched and so on. I wish more kennels would invest in teenagers in that way.

There are some situations where you will be able to take your dog on holiday with you. Examples of touches that have shown the holiday accommodation has canine behaviour in mind include: access to secure areas for exercise and where unexpected other dogs are unlikely to appear; a place to wash dirty paws (or the whole dog!) with towels available too; throws to put over the furniture (not just signs saying not to let the dog on furniture as if your dogs are used to being allowed on sofas at home, this will not work); welcome chews and treats; washable enrichment toys; dog-friendly hosts.

Behaviour in mind: behaviour modification

There are numerous books providing the detail regarding how to understand and address

Figure 12.3: Pebbles on holiday in Wales. Photo: © Suzanne Rogers.

behaviour problems in dogs and this is outside the remit of this book. One aspect I would like to draw attention to, however, is the emerging focus on trauma-informed approaches to behaviour modification. This approach assumes that an individual is more likely than not to have a history of trauma and so recognises the presence of trauma symptoms, acknowledges the role trauma may play in an individual's life, and takes this into account when creating the behaviour modification plan. Jessie Sams is an animal behaviourist with a specific interest in this area. She explains:

> Incorporating a trauma-informed approach into behaviour modification can better support caregivers to meet the emotional needs of their dog, which in turn enhances their relationship. This is especially true of rescue dogs and puppy farm survivors where the provision of education around the effects of stress, trauma and lack of socialisation and how to recognise these signs in their dog in order to increase their sense of safety. Supporting caregivers to implement predictable routines such as set feeding times, walks, rest and play in conjunction with learning how their dog chooses to interact with them can facilitate recovery. Over time the positive interaction and relationships can allow their dogs to begin to thrive.

My absolute favourite account of a trauma-informed approach to providing a home for a rescue dog is by Natalie Light (author of Chapter 1) who rehomed Drax, an Irish Wolfhound, and has kept a diary through Facebook posts to show his progress.[1]

Sometimes dogs are lucky enough to be fostered or even rehomed by animal behaviour professionals who recognise the importance of changing their own behaviour in the process of helping a dog change theirs. Behaviourist Susan Gammage describes how she worked with her latest foster dog.

Leo was found as a stray, a 2-year-old entire male, who had probably been used for breeding. When he was found he could not be touched and was a flight risk and a bite risk, not helped by having ear problems. After veterinary treatment and being neutered by South East Dog Rescue we took him on as a foster. Leo was very scared of people; he would not eat if there was a person in the same room and any movement would cause him to run and find a high place to hide. We changed our behaviour around Leo. For example, when feeding him we put his food on the ground and walked away until he had finished eating. When moving around near Leo we turned our backs towards him, we did not try to stroke him or attempt any counter conditioning or coaxing using food. Over time, Leo started to approach us but only from behind, nudging our legs. Slowly over the next six weeks he grew more relaxed around us but still not to the point where he would solicit attention. However, he would come and relax and sleep within a few feet of a person sitting down. Leo displayed two strategies when pressured into contact with people, he would either flee or freeze. Unfortunately freezing often looks like acceptance but as experienced foster carers we recognised Leo's subtle stress signals, yawning and lip licking. Ten weeks into fostering Leo and he is now soliciting attention when I am seated. The most important factor in helping Leo change his expectations around people is that we are aware of any subtle stress signals and changing our behaviour to enable him to adapt his behaviour to learn to trust that people will not put him in a position where he feels uncomfortable.'

Behaviour in mind: Dog population management

This section was based on an interview with Dr Elly Hiby (International Companion Animal Management Coalition [ICAM]).[2] She highlighted some examples of how the best dog population management programmes are run with behaviour in mind.

Well-managed mass vaccination campaigns

There are many aspects of the logistics of managing mass vaccination campaigns that can be done in a behaviour-minded way. For example, having someone supervise the line and making sure owners are giving each other's dogs some space can help make the experience as positive as possible for the dogs and their owners. The supervisor must be ready to pull the dogs out of the line if they appear fearful or aggressive and can take these dogs to a separate 'quiet' area where the dogs are vaccinated quickly and can then leave. If there is staff capacity then taking the time to do some desensitisation to vaccination handling while waiting in line and rewarding calm behaviour can help to reduce the chance of the dog having a negative experience, which in turn makes it more likely that the owners will seek preventative veterinary care in the future.

Compassionate catching and handling

Most dog population management programmes involve catching and handling

roaming dogs. The ICAM Dog Population Management guide[1] has a comprehensive section on humane handing. The guide considers each step within the handling process and explores how improvements to the dog's experience could be made. For example, catching a dog can be broken down into four steps, which can each be done with behaviour in mind:

Step 1: attracting the dogs attention
Step 2: initial approach
Step 3: gaining trust through first touch
Step 4: restraint through gently restricting their movement and lifting by fully supporting their body weight when carrying.

Shelters with behaviour in mind

Most countries rely on shelters as part of a comprehensive dog population management programme even though it could be argued that approaches that address the cause, rather than the symptom of dog population management issues, should be the focus on this work. Chapter 7 introduced some of the ways that rescue and rehoming centres can be managed with behaviour in mind.

Neutering with behaviour in mind

Some programmes seem to aim to neuter all the dogs they come across but neutering should be decided on the basis of an individual animal's welfare and behaviour, not only population level considerations. For example, male dogs that are already fearful might not be good candidates for castration as this is likely to reduce their confidence further, and may well have minimal impact on population size (unless they are the only male with access to an intact female).

Consideration of roaming dog social structures

It is still very uncommon for programmes to properly consider the implications of the social structures of roaming dogs when we sterilise all/some of a 'pack'. Although it is likely that there are not particularly stable packs, more of a melee, packs are likely to be even less stable after sterilisation. Elly says, 'I would like to test what happens if you only spay the females and do not bother with castration. The females are the limiting factor for population growth, so they are what really matters for managing populations. We need more research on this to find out, for example, if leaving the males intact helps maintain territories and the status quo with neighbouring dogs, or if castration takes everyone down a peg or two and they all become more tolerant?'

Careful consideration of policies

Although roaming has obvious risks to the dog themselves and other animals and people, it can be functional, rewarding (for example, if scavenging to meet nutritional demands) and provide a relatively high quality of life. Sometimes, in an attempt to control roaming dogs, confinement and leashing laws are brought in suddenly, which can have a negative effect on the dogs. Policy changes with behaviour in mind would include gradual introduction of new policies with preparation in place regarding education and awareness raising – for example, increased confinement requires habituation and provision of meeting behavioural needs in new ways for the dog, such as more regular walking and supervised off leash exercise.

Another area where policies are used in an attempt to manage roaming dog populations is in waste management – the idea is that if food waste was managed properly there would be fewer dogs. Elly says:

I don't think people should be trying to starve dogs to control population size. It's not always the case that dogs are reliant on waste for their nutrition, as many are owned roaming and the waste tends to be very low in nutritional value, really they are scavenging for 'fun'. But if it's high-value waste like offal from a slaughter-house, dogs might well be reliant on it and if you take that food source away with improved waste management, they will get hungry, defensively aggressive over what food there is and possibly predatory – that is, dangerous. When considering waste management changes, time needs to be taken to consider the implications on both dog welfare and behaviour first – you must check out whether dogs rely on that waste as their food source as opposed to scavenging for entertainment.

Finally, the ultimate aim of dog population management programmes is for every dog to have a caregiver, for their needs to be met and for the human and canine members of communities to exist in harmony with each other. In some Northern European countries, this has been achieved through widespread and strong responsible ownership behaviour, however in other countries (for example, the UK and USA), progress in population management has also involved high rates of sterilisation, leaving puppy 'production' mostly down to commercial breeders. This means that it will become increasingly rare for puppies to be acquired from the single litter of a friend's pet dog that grew up in the kitchen in exactly the sort of environment that they will spend the rest of their pet life in – that is, the perfect set-up for appropriate socialisation and habituation – and so the possible welfare and behaviour concerns might move towards the implications of commercial breeding, as indeed we are seeing as a result of puppy farms in the UK.

Behaviour in mind: welfare issues

There are many ways that dogs suffer due to human behaviours, some of which could be done with behaviour in mind, some that are intrinsically harmful and some that are controversial. For example, dogs are used in medical research laboratories and although some elements of experiments are intrinsically harmful there are improvements that could be made to the way the animals are managed and handled. At Human Behaviour Change for Animals (HBCA) we have worked a little in the research animal sector training staff in how to embed a culture of care into their work and implement the three Rs: reduction (reduce the number of animals used); replacement (avoid or replace the use of animals) and refinement (use methods that reduce animal suffering and improve welfare). It is outside the scope of this book to suggest ways that research labs could be run with behaviour in mind although there is a drive to improve welfare especially given the link between less-stressed animals and improved scientific results.

Another example of where improvements could be made is the use of dogs in film and television. Although animal welfare advisers are now present during filming, some of the requirements pose welfare concerns. With the amazing technology now available I would hope that the use of animals in film will decrease, although some technology still requires animals to track movements and so on before the special effects are added. Useful ways to keep behaviour in mind when filming include: to use reward-based training; ensure any equipment is appropriate, comfortable and has been introduced in a gradual way; ensure the dog has access to drinking water; regular breaks and so on.

There are other ways we use animals that pose significant welfare concerns that will not be covered here at all. These include working dogs such as police dogs and guard dogs, as well as more sinister uses for dogs such as dogs being farmed for meat, dog fighting and hunting with dogs.

Final words

The book has provided an insight into the concept that having 'behaviour in mind' can help incrementally improve the lives of dogs whatever they are 'used' for and is optimistic that if this way of thinking were to be adopted then many people would reconsider what we expect of our dogs in the first place.

References

1. Drax's Galactic Adventure (n.d.) https://www.face book.com/Draxthewolfhound.
2. International Companion Animal Management Coalition (n.d.) https://www.icam-coalition.org.

Index